THE NOBLE SAVAGE

THE NOBLE SAVAGE

A STUDY IN
ROMANTIC NATURALISM

BY

HOXIE NEALE FAIRCHILD

New York
COLUMBIA UNIVERSITY PRESS
1928

THE PLIMPTON PRESS, NORWOOD, MASS.

PRINTED IN THE UNITED STATES OF AMERICA

To

MY MOTHER AND MY WIFE

PREFACE

TEN years ago, as a student in Professor Wright's course in the Romantic Movement, I presented a "term paper" on the Noble Savage. That paper, with long interruptions due to the war and its consequences, has slowly expanded into a book. My original ambitions were both to give an exhaustive treatment of the savage in English romantic literature and to discuss the savage in relation to romantic naturalism. I soon found, however, that to realize both these aims in a single book would be the work of a lifetime some portion of which I had hoped to devote to other projects. Since the latter aim appeared to me the more interesting and the more important, I ended by studying romantic naturalism through the Noble Savage. Hence, though I trust I have provided enough objective facts to support my interpretation of the subject, I am far from claiming to have discovered every savage who appears in the literature of the English Romantic Movement. I have simply inspected with some care the works of admittedly important writers of the period, with a view to discovering what part the Noble Savage played in their thought. I reinforce this material with examples drawn from many minor writers, but with no pretense whatever to exhaustiveness.

When I began my task, the Noble Savage in French literature had already received the attention of Professor Gilbert Chinard, and to his *L'Exotisme Américain* and his *L'Amérique et le Rêve Exotique* the first chapter of this study owes much. The savage in English literature, however, was ten years ago an unexplored subject. But in 1925, when the first draft of this book had already been completed, Dr. Benjamin H. Bissell published his dissertation, *The American Indian in English Literature of the Eighteenth Century.* Since the two studies overlap, I must say a word as to the relation between them.

Dr. Bissell's book deals only with the American Indian, while I regard Negroes and South Sea Islanders as Noble Savages no less than the redskins. Though he makes a few excursions beyond his assigned boundaries, he limits his material to works published during the eighteenth century. Of my material, over half is drawn from the early nineteenth. Having limited his field more strictly than I, Dr. Bissell is able to treat it more intensively. He devotes much attention to historians and travelers, and to the appearances of actual Indians in England. To these divisions of the subject I make little more than incidental allusion. He is able, also, to examine very obscure writers, whereas my guiding question has been, " What attitude was taken toward the Noble Savage by writers of admitted significance in the Romantic Movement? " Dr. Bissell devotes some attention to American Literature, which I ignore entirely. His book, also, is more objective than mine. Though he does not, of course, refrain from interpretation of his facts, his prime aim has been to collect Indians. My chief purpose, on the other hand, has been to use the Noble Savage as a means of studying romantic naturalism. Hence, though the two studies overlap, they by no means coincide.

After reading Dr. Bissell's dissertation, I carefully revised my own treatment of the eighteenth century phase of the subject. Whenever I have found that he is merely traversing ground covered in my first draft, I have let my original observations stand, and have made no comparative comments unless the differences in interpretation seemed important or interesting. But whenever I make use of material which I owe to his industry, my indebtedness is acknowledged. A large number of his minuter points I have either ignored entirely as out of scale with my method of treatment, or have briefly referred to in summarizing passages. By these means I have saved my own work without doing injustice to his. In fairness to myself I may add that I have been so fortunate as to find several Indians who had escaped Dr. Bissell's attention.

The present book would have been even longer in the writing had it not been for the privilege of a year's uninterrupted work in England. To the donors of the William Bayard Cutting Travelling Fellowship, and to the officers of the University who enabled me to enjoy the benefits of that fellowship, heartfelt thanks are therefore due. The staffs of the libraries of Columbia University and of the British Museum have assisted me with their usual efficiency and courtesy. The criticisms of Professor Ashley H. Thorndike, of Professor Charles Sears Baldwin, and of Professor Ralph L. Rusk have been of great value. But to Professor Ernest Hunter Wright, who has guided my labors from their earliest stages to their present fruition, I wish to acknowledge a particular debt of gratitude.

In order to avoid swelling the dimensions of this already lengthy book to unreasonable proportions, I have omitted all but a few absolutely essential footnotes. Consistency in this matter has been difficult, but I hope the principles which have guided me will be evident to the reader. Apart from a few special cases, notes are used only when I wish to acknowledge indebtedness to other authorities, or when the text itself does not show what work I am citing. An appendix lists the authors, titles, and places and dates of publication of my sources.

H. N. F.

New York City, July, 1927

CONTENTS

THE NOBLE SAVAGE

CHAPTER I

THE SHAPING OF THE NOBLE SAVAGE
CONVENTION

UNLESS it is explained at the outset, the term "romantic naturalism" as it will be used in this study may be confusing to students of philosophy or of continental literature. It will be applied, not to philosophical materialism or to literary realism, but to that peculiar form of naturalism which arises from a desire to find the supernatural within the natural, or, in other words, to achieve an emotionally satisfying fusion of the real and the unreal, the obvious and the mysterious. Whatever our private definition of romanticism may be, there can be no doubt that one important aspect of the Romantic Movement is the return to nature. The wave of illusioned naturalism which begins to rise about the middle of the eighteenth century and which has given place to other forces by about 1830 includes not only the cult of scenery but the cult of the child, the peasant, and the savage. In many critical and historical studies, a relation between the Noble Savage and romantic naturalism has been assumed. To examine and explain that relation is the purpose of the present book.

In my opinion, the rather common restriction of the term "Noble Savage" to the American Indian has no logical basis. Negroes, South Sea Islanders and other sorts of savages are often regarded in precisely the same

light as the redman. To me, a Noble Savage is any free
and wild being who draws directly from nature virtues
which raise doubts as to the value of civilization. The
term may even be applied metaphorically to romantic
peasants and children when a comparison between their
innocent greatness and that of the savage illumines the
thought of the period.

But the Noble Savage as he appears in the Romantic
Movement cannot be understood without some knowledge
of his origins. This chapter, therefore, must provide the
necessary running start. Without tracing in detail the
early history of the literary-philosophical conception which
constitutes our subject, I wish to show how that conception
took form. The Noble Savage idea results from the fusion
of three elements: the observation of explorers; various
classical and medieval conventions; the deductions of philosophers and men of letters. It is the second of these
elements — the conventions which were given new life by
the explorers' narratives — that must first be examined.

The conception of a Golden Age is to the ancient world
as the Noble Savage idea to the modern world. Each represents a protest against the evil incidental to human progress; each looks yearningly back from the corruptions of
civilization to an imaginary primeval innocence. Just as
it takes an excessively rich diet to make one appreciate
bran, so it is in slightly over-ripe stages of culture, such as
the Augustan Age of Rome and the eighteenth century Enlightenment, that one yearns for simplicity. There is
a similarity between Rousseau's view of the state of nature
and Ovid's picture of the Golden Age. To Ovid, the Iron
Age represents what Rousseau calls " the moral effect of
the arts and sciences."

During the Middle Ages the notion of a Golden Age

was kept alive by such works as the *De Consolatione Philosophiae* and the *Romance of the Rose*. From this tradition, as interpreted by Mantuan and others, rises the Renaissance pastoral. But, as Mr. Greg reminds us, " Pastoral literature must not be confounded with that which has for its subjects the lives, the ideas, and the emotions of unsophisticated mankind, far from the centers of our complex civilization. The two may be in their origin related, and they occasionally, as it were, stretch out feelers towards one another, but the pastoral of tradition lies in its essence as far from the human document of humble life as from a scientific treatise on agriculture or a volume of pastoral theology." [1] Corydon and the Noble Savage are both connected with the Golden Age. The differences between them will appear more clearly as we go on. Suffice it to say that while the romanticist is likely to accept, in some form or another, the idea of a Golden Age, he is likely to reject the pastoral as a literary form by definition urban and insincere. He sees in the actual peasant or in the savage a truer picture of primitive virtue. Most writers of the Romantic Period who praise the peasant detest the pastoral. They find in the British rustic something much more like the natural man of their imagination than like the Corydon of the pseudo-classicists. When Wordsworth calls *Michael* " a pastoral," he is using the term almost polemically. " Here," he seems to say, " is the story of a *real* shepherd." The situation becomes more involved when the romanticist rescues the peasant from the hands of the pseudo-classicists and presents him to the world as a Noble Savage. What concerns us at this point is that the pastoral as an art-form has little to do with the origin of the Noble Savage, but that the Golden Age proper has a great deal to do with it.

[1] *Pastoral Poetry and Pastoral Drama*, p. 6.

Prior to the discovery of America, then, there existed a powerful literary tradition which was to add the authority of antiquity to the most enthusiastic reports of the explorers. It is pretty certain that but for this tradition the Noble Savage had never been born. At any rate, he would have lacked the *cachet* that was lent him by the comparison between his virtues and those of the primitives of mythology. Again and again we shall find Noble Savages likened to men of the Golden Age.

Whether the Greeks and Romans regarded as Noble Savages any of the barbarous peoples with whom they came in contact is a question beyond the scope of this study. One familiar instance of such an attitude, however, is provided by Tacitus.

" Rousseau," observes Morley, " wrote about the savage state in something of the same spirit in which Tacitus wrote the *Germania*." [2] The *Germania* is more than a bald description of Teutonic life: it is a contrast drawn with didactic intent. In the first century of the Christian era, the Roman Empire, outwardly at the height of its pride and magnificence, was beginning to decay at the core. In its outward wealth and inward poverty, it resembled the eighteenth century Enlightenment. Juvenal lashed this decadent age with stinging satire; Tacitus held before it the example of the simpler, more virile and more virtuous barbarians who were destined to cause its downfall.

Let us examine some of the characteristics ascribed to the Germani. They are, first of all, exceedingly brave and hardy. From the complex requirements of luxurious Roman life they are free. " The possession or use of silver and gold they do not greatly affect." Contrast with this happy condition the avarice of Rome.

The Germani are intensely democratic. " Thou shalt

[2] *Rousseau*, Vol. I, p. 178.

not know the lord from the slave." What do you say to that, haughty patricians? And what a difference between the open-hearted friendliness of the barbarian and the envious distrust of the Roman! " Greater hospitality and entertainment is nowhere more bountiful than there, it being a cursed deed to bar any man his house." Hospitality, we shall find, is a characteristic virtue of the Noble Savage.

" Matrimony is severely kept among them, the thing most commendable in all their manner of life. . . . They live therefore in most strict chastity, uncorrupted with the allurements of shows and spectacles, or provocations in banquetting. As well men as women are ignorant of the secrets of learning." The idea that sexual vice is the fruit of sophistication is expressed by Rousseau in his second discourse.

And unlike too many Roman ladies, German mothers perform their duties faithfully. " Every mother nurseth her own children with her own breasts, and sends them not to nurses or other women." Compare with this the early pages of *Émile*, where Rousseau insists that every mother should suckle her own child.

A witty French critic warns us that in research, unless we are very careful, we always find what we are seeking. Perhaps to call the Germani Noble Savages would be merely to furnish an illustration of this peril. But surely we do find in the *Germania* something closely akin to the idea we are studying. Tacitus pictures a noble and virtuous race living in a state of savage simplicity, and implies a contrast between the moral excellence of that race and the vices which were sapping the strength of the more complex and pretentious Roman civilization.

The *Germania* merits inclusion in our list of traditions because of its influence on later writers who dealt with savage life. Montaigne, who draws what is perhaps the first full-length picture of the Noble Savage, was a great admirer of the Roman. Rousseau also knew his Tacitus well. We shall find him using the *Germania* to bring home a point in his first discourse. Tacitus' remarks on Germanic poetry — too familiar to require quotation here — proved interesting to those romanticists who liked to imagine a connection between primitive song and primitive virtue; and in this way also the *Germania* powerfully helped to mold the conception of the Noble Savage.

Analogous to the conception of a Golden Age are the various classical and medieval legends concerning an island of peace and plenty hidden afar in the western seas. Atlantis, the Hesperides and Avalon are fundamentally the same place. Wits might call it the " land of cookery," but to most men of the Middle Ages it was the Land of the Blest. Indeed, this locality, originally pagan, became confused with the Earthly Paradise. In vain did the doctors insist that the Earthly Paradise was either an island off the east coast of Asia or a valley somewhere on the Asiatic continent. For the popular mind the Blessed Isles were Earthly Paradise enough, and all men knew that the Blessed Isles lay westward.

The learned and the popular, the Christian and the pagan, traditions were reconciled by the discovery of America. Did not the newly-discovered island or continent lie both eastward and westward? And did not the bounty and beauty of that land equal all that was ever said or sung of the Blessed Isles? " I am convinced," wrote Columbus, " that there is the terrestrial paradise."

The identification of the Caribbean islands with the Earthly Paradise naturally lent prestige to their inhabitants. There were, to be sure, certain doctrinal perplexities. Here were savages living, to all intents and purposes, in Eden, and yet necessarily in a state of sin. One could not, of course, be too literal in the matter. Perhaps it was because the savage had never heard of the curse of Adam that he was able to obtain food without the sweating enjoined upon the rest of mankind. But theology aside, it is certain that the Noble Savage owed much of his popularity to the fact that he lived, not merely in America, but in the Fortunate Isles.

To those who were willing to forget doctrinal perplexities, the savage state, with its unconsciousness of sin, irresistibly recalled the Garden of Eden. Eden, in fact, bears much the same relation to Christian mythology that the Golden Age bears to classical mythology. Origen compares the two states of innocence, and Dante is following a venerable tradition when he makes Matelda, the guardian of the Earthly Paradise, say to Dante, Virgil and Statius: "They who in olden times sang of the golden age and its happy state perchance dreamed in Parnassus of this place." In a period when pagan and Christian traditions were mingling, the savage luckily found his naked innocence supported both by Ovid and the Bible.

Francis Bacon's chief obstacle was to be the jealous monastic suspicion of free thought. "I hear the former sort say," he writes, "that knowledge is of those things which are to be accepted of with great limitation and caution; that the aspiring to overmuch knowledge was the original temptation and sin whereupon ensued the fall of man; that knowledge hath in it somewhat of the serpent, and therefore where it entereth into a man it makes him swell; ... that experience demonstrates how learned men have been arch-heretics, how learned times have been inclined to atheism, and how our contemplation of second causes doth derogate from our dependence upon God, who is the first cause." This pious spleen against intelligence tended to make men receptive to the Noble Savage idea.

Bacon here is tilting against the schoolmen, but much that he says would apply even more accurately to the softer, tenderer, more mystical strain in medieval religion. The gentle St. Francis, as is well known, distrusted books as sources of wordly pride. This feeling, combined with his sense of an intimate union with all natural things, anticipates the romantic attitude. The existence of hermit visionaries like Richard Rolle testifies to the primitivistic element in religious thought. These simple saints were trying to break through the hard scholastic shell to the naïve wonder of primitive Christianity. It would be absurd to say that they loved ignorance: they merely insisted that goodness was worth more to the soul than theological subtlety. But as the following chapters will show, it is not easy to maintain this standpoint without contrasting goodness with intelligence. The result of such a contrast is that the savage is admired not merely for what he is, but for what he is not.

In the Golden Age, the Blessed Isles, the *Germania* of Tacitus, the scholastic distrust of learning and the mystical aversion to sophistication, we discern tendencies which go toward building up the complex figure of the Noble Savage. These traditions were part of the intellectual baggage of the men of letters who read the explorers' narratives. We are now to listen to the voyagers themselves.

Columbus is the first of a long series of explorers to praise the good-will and generosity of the Indians. "Certainly, where they have confidence and forget their fears they are so open-hearted and liberal with all they possess that it is scarcely to be believed without seeing it." And

" it cannot be said that, because what they gave was worth little, therefore they gave liberally, because those who had pieces of gold gave as liberally as those who had a calabash of water; and it is easy to know when a thing is given with a hearty desire to give."

The explorer is everywhere anxious to assure the reader that the Indians are fit to receive the teachings of mother church. " They do not know any religion, and I believe they could easily be converted to Christianity, for they are very intelligent." — " They are a people guileless and unwarlike." — " These people are without any religion, not idolaters, but very gentle, not knowing what is evil, nor the sins of murder and theft." — " They are a loving people, without covetousness, and fit for anything. . . . They love their neighbours as themselves, and their speech is the sweetest and gentlest in the world, and always with a smile. . . . The king is a man of remarkable presence, and with a certain self-contained manner that is a pleasure to see." In short, " they are the best people in the world, and the gentlest."

The physical beauty of the Indians delights Columbus no less than their moral attractiveness. They are " all of good stature, a very handsome people. . . . Their eyes are very beautiful." At a certain island Columbus sends out an exploring party, and we are informed that " the Christians reported to the Admiral that this was a handsomer and finer people than any that had hitherto been met with. But the Admiral says that he does not see how they can be a finer people than the others, giving to understand that all those he had found in the other islands were very well conditioned. . . . They saw two girls whose skins were as white as any that could be seen in Spain."

There is a strong aesthetic element in the Noble Savage idea. Unfortunately, the virtues of the ugly are never so apparent as those of the beautiful. Hence men like Sir John Hawkins would sail to the Guinea Coast, cram their ships with ugly blackbirds to whom they never refer with the slightest sympathy, and then cross to the West Indies, selling the Negroes to the Spaniards and praising the virtues of the handsome Indians. Even Bishop Las Casas did not hesitate to advocate the importation of negro slaves to lighten the burden of his beloved Caribbeans. We shall see that the humanitarian current of the Romantic Movement caused the Negro to be included in the roll of Noble Savages alongside of the American Indian and the South Sea Islander. The Noble Savage is, however, originally a Carib, and in the early stages of his development owes much to his *beaux yeux*.

Elsewhere in the reports of Columbus are found other interesting facts. "They go naked, as I have said, without arms and without law." — "Many live in one house." — "I have not been able to discover whether they respect personal property, for it appeared to me things were common to all."

The narratives of Columbus illustrate the first step in the formation of the Noble Savage idea. The Caribs are represented as a virtuous and mild people, beautiful, and with a certain natural intelligence, living together in nakedness and innocence, sharing their property in common. But though Columbus is enthusiastic about the Indians, he does not compare them with the Europeans. For such a comparison a stimulus was soon provided by the brutality of the Spaniards. Humanitarianism is the motive back of the *Breuisima Relación de la Destruyción de las Indias* of Las Casas.

By 1539, when Las Casas' book appeared, Spanish gold-lust had made oppressed slaves of the free and amiable beings described by Columbus. "God," the Bishop exclaims, " made this numerous people very simple, without trickery or malice, most obedient and faithful to their natural lords, and to the Spaniards, whom they serve; most humble, most patient, very peaceful and manageable, without quarrels, strife, bitterness or hate, none desiring vengeance. They are also a very delicate and tender folk, of slender build, and cannot stand much work, and often die of whatever sicknesses they have; so that even our own princes and lords, cared for with all conveniences, luxuries and delights, are not more delicate than these people . . . who possess little, and who do not desire many worldly goods; nor are they proud, ambitious, or covetous. . . . They have a very clear and lively understanding, being docile and able to receive all good doctrine, quite fitted to understand our holy Catholic faith, and to be instructed in good and virtuous habits, having less hindrances in the way of doing this than any other people in the world. . . . Certainly these people would be the happiest in the world if only they knew God."

But the Spaniards have dealt with these poor souls most monstrously. " Among these tender lambs, so highly qualified and endowed by their Lord and Creator, the Spaniards have made entrance, like wolves, lions and tigers made cruel by long fasting, and have done nothing in those parts for forty years but cut them in pieces, slaughter them, torture them, afflict them, torment them and destroy them by strange sorts of cruelty never before seen or read or heard . . . so that of the three million and more souls who inhabited the Island of Hispaniola . . . there are now no more than two hundred natives of that land." The pleasant impression made upon the Indians by the comparative clemency of Columbus has been completely eradicated. " The Indians began to see that these men could not have come from heaven."

The Apostle to the Indians is terribly in earnest. He knows the Indians, and loves them as a father loves his children. He does not claim perfection for them, but he recognizes them as perfectible. He does not assert their superiority to the Spaniards, but his indignation against his countrymen contains the germs of such an assertion.

English views of savage life tend to be less highly colored and enthusiastic than those of the Spanish and French.[3] But though it seems probable that the Noble Savage is chiefly a product of Latin minds, Professor Chinard slightly underestimates the extent to which English explorers gave support to the cult of the Indian.

There are, for example, decidedly sympathetic passages in the *Voyage of Sir Francis Drake from New Spain to the North-west of California*.[4] This celebrated voyage was begun in 1577. The narrator reports that the savages — here natives of Brazil — go stark naked, but he does not philosophize upon this observation. The " naturals " seem to be a civil and gentle folk: " Our general went to prayer ... at which exercise they were attentive and seemed greatly to be affected with it." The savages, indeed, worship the whites as gods, at first making sacrifice to them by tearing their own flesh, and when this is frowned upon by the voyagers, bringing offerings of fruit. The savage king and his people crown Drake with flowers, " with one consent and with great reverence, joyfully singing a song." They wish the English to remain with them for ever. " Our departure seemed so grievous to them, that their joy was turned into sorrow." Incidents such as these are ready-made for literary treatment.

[3] For the very important observations of French explorers and missionaries, the reader should consult Chinard's *L'Exotisme Américain* and its sequel, *L'Amérique et le rêve exotique*.

[4] Hakluyt, *Principal Navigations*; Vol. IX, pp. 319-326.

Strenuous efforts were being made to " boom " Virginia as a field for colonization. This may partly account for the enthusiasm of Philip Amadas and Arthur Barlow in their *First Voyage Made to the Coast of Virginia*.[5] These gentlemen find the natives fearless and trustful. They are " a handsome and goodly people, and in their behavior as mannerly and civill as any in Europe." Later it is reported: " We found the people most gentle, loving and faithful, void of all guile and treason, and such as live after the maner of the golden age." This comparison with the Golden Age is particularly interesting. When men began to think of the American Indian in terms of traditional literary formulas, they were well on the way toward the formation of the Noble Savage idea.

A very influential account was doubtless Raleigh's *Discourse of the large, rich and beautiful Empire of Guiana*.[6] The portions of this account which are of interest to us deal with various tribes along the Orinoco River — a region which is the habitat of the Noble Savage at his noblest and most savage.

Raleigh's opinion of the natives is consistently favorable. Of one tribe he says, " These Tivitivas are a very goodly people and very valiant, and have the most manly speech and most deliberate that ever I heard, of what nation soever." This tribe relies for sustenance entirely on the bounty of nature. " They never eat of any thing that is set or sowen: and as at home they use neither planting nor other manurance, so when they come abroad, they refuse to feed of aught, but of that which nature without labour bringeth forth."

Raleigh agrees with many other voyagers in ascribing

[5] *Ibid.*, Vol. VIII, pp. 297-310.
[6] *Ibid.*, Vol. X, pp. 338-431.

rare physical beauty to the savages. Of a Cacique's wife he writes: " In all my life I have seldome seene a better favoured woman. She was of good stature, with blacke eyes, fat of body, of an excellent countenance, her hair almost as long as herself, tied up againe in prettie knots. . . . I have seene a lady in England as like to her, as but for the colour, I would have sworne might have been the same." Praise from Sir Hubert!

The following is a portion of an account of an interview with a venerable chief: " I asked what nations those were which inhabited on the farther side of those mountains. . . . He answered with a great sigh (as a man which had inward feeling of the losse of his countrie and libertie, especially for that his eldest son was slain in a battell on that side of the mountains, whom he most entirely loved) that hee remembered in his father's lifetime, etc., etc. . . . After hee had answered thus farre he desired leave to depart, saying that he had farre to goe, that he was olde, and weake, and was every day called for by death, which was also his owne phrase. . . . This Topiawari is helde for the prowdest and wisest of all the Orenoqueponi, and soe he behaved himselfe towards mee in all his answers at my returne, as I marvelled to find a man of that gravitie and judgement, and of soe good discourse, that had no helpe of learning nor breede."

This sketch of the old Cacique is executed with a significant relish. Quite plainly, the savage has become literary material; his type is becoming fixed; he already begins to collect the accretions of tradition. Just as he is, Topiawari is ready to step into an exotic tale. He is the prototype of Chactas and Chingachgook.

The effect on English writers of such accounts as those we have been examining is shown in Michael Drayton's poem, *To the Virginian Voyage:*

" And cheerfully at sea,
Success you still entice,
 To get the pearl and gold,
 And ours to hold
Virginia,
Earth's only paradise.

" Where nature hath in store
Fowl, venison, and fish,
 And the fruitful'st soil,
 Without your toil,
Three harvests more,
All greater than you wish.

" To whom the Golden Age
Still nature's laws doth give,
 No other cares attend,
 But them to defend
From winter's rage,
That long there doth not live."

Virginia reminds the poet both of the Earthly Paradise and the Golden Age; and the second stanza quoted brings an unconsciously ironical reminder of the *Land of Cockayne*. Here we see that fusion of contemporary observation with old tradition on which the Noble Savage idea depends. But as regards the savage himself this process is illustrated still more explicitly by Montaigne.

The essay " Of the Caniballes " occupies the thirtieth chapter of the first book of Montaigne's essays. The author says: " I have had long time dwelling with me a man, who for the space of ten or twelve years had dwelt in that other world, which in our age was lately discovered in those parts where Villegaignon first landed, and surnamed Antartike France." Now whether this traveller ever existed, or whether the device is a cloak for a new kind of *Utopia*,[7] is not particularly material. The essay, if a *Utopia*, at any rate depends for its existence on the narratives of explorers.[8]

Montaigne has been greatly enlightened by his guest as to the inhabitants of Antartike France. He is surprised to learn that " there is nothing in that nation, that is either barbarous or savage, unlesse men call that barbarisme which is not common to them." Our standards may differ from theirs, but are not necessarily superior.

Indeed, it would seem that our standards are lower, for in that savage country " there is ever perfect religion, perfect policie, perfect and compleat use of all things." The cannibals possess " the true and most profitable virtues, which we have bastardized, applying them to the pleasure of our own corrupted taste." They are blest with all the native goodness which modern sophistication has destroyed.

These idyllic beings seem barbarous to us merely because " they have received very little fashion from humane wit, and are yet neere their originall naturalitie. The lawes of nature doe yet command them, which are but little bastardized by ours, and that with such puritie, that I am sometimes grieved the knowledge of it came no sooner to light." For it is in vain that man tries to improve on nature. " There is no reason, art should gain the point of honor of our great and puissant mother Nature. . . . All our endeavour or wit, cannot so much as reach to represent the nest of the least birdlet, its contexture, beauty, profit and use, no nor the web of a seely spider."

Indeed, the condition of these naked savages transcends

---

[7] More's *Utopia* itself, it is interesting to remember, has the same sort of introduction.

[8] For suggestions as to Montaigne's sources for this essay, see Chinard, *L'Exotisme Américain*, pp. 194-201.

the loftiest dreams of poetry and philosophy. " Me seem-
eth that what in those nations we see by experience, doth
not only exceed all the pictures wherewith licentious Poesie
hath proudly embellished the golden age, and all her
quaint inventions to faine a happy condition of man, but
also the conception and desire of Philosophy. Lycurgus
and Plato could not imagine a genuitie so pure and simple . . . nor ever believe our society might be maintained
with so little art and humane combination."

There comes a time when the wisest man is haunted by
his inability to build a bird's nest. And it is right that he
should be so: we need constantly to be reminded of our
pettiness, and of the bungling use we have made of nature's
gifts. Such warnings, however, too often aim a blow at
man's desire to go forward, and cavil unreasonably at the
ills which inevitably attend his advance. Thus the Brazilian savages surpass the lofty dream of the *Republic*: " It
is a nation, would I answer Plato, that hath no kind of
trafficke, no knowledge of Letters, no intelligence of numbers, no name of magistrate, nor of politike superioritie;
no use of service, of riches or of povertie; no contracts,
no successions, no partitions, no occupation but idle; no
respect of kinred, but common, no apparel but naturall,
no manuring of lands, no use of wine, corne or mettle."
Plato's ideal state is based on acquired wisdom; Montaigne's ideal state is based on natural goodness. The issue is clean-cut.

The literature of any period denies as well as affirms
the ideals of that period. Even at the height of its pride
in the fruits of culture, the Renaissance remembered that
those fruits were often Dead Sea apples. Throughout
sixteenth century literature, the feeling that civilization
is corrupt is plainly evident. We may call the pastoral
a merely superficial convention, but we must not forget

that the author of the *Arcadia* had in good earnest fled the
evils of the court. A scepticism that would be despairing
if it did not so greatly enjoy its disillusionment is a prominent tendency of the period. There was much talk of following nature; and though the naturalism of Rabelais is
not romantic, it may be viewed as a stepping-stone toward
the romantic attitude. At the beginning of the century,
Erasmus had praised ignorance in words which almost
startlingly suggest Rousseau. Folly is made to say:

" School-knowledge ... derives its origin from the
author of all abominations. ... The simple people of
the golden age were furnished with no such school-knowledge. Nature alone sufficed to guide them; instinct, to
prompt them how to live. ... What would have been
the use of the principles of logic to men amongst whom
conflicting arguments never arose? ... What would have
been the advantage of jurisprudence to men amongst whom
bad morals — the sole apology for good laws — had no
existence? ... As then the professional arts prosper in
proportion as they are characterized by folly, so by far
the happiest people in the world are those who are in a
position to dispense with artificial training altogether, and
to follow solely nature as their guide. ... It is clear to
you, I presume, now that those who make wisdom their
study, by so doing, make themselves the most miserable of
mankind. ... On the other hand the least miserable of
mankind — those who are as little miserable as it is possible for men to be — are those who in condition and intelligence are very little superior to mere brutes, who are
content with their lowly lot, and have no ambition for anything beyond it. ... By the immortal gods, then, I solemnly swear to you that no class of men is happier than
that of those whom the world calls simpletons, fools, and
blockheads. ... In the first place, men of this class are

entirely devoid of the dread of death. They have no accusing consciences to make them fear it, and no alarms are excited in their minds by the bugbear stories told about the condition of departed souls. Of ghosts and goblins no terrors daunt them, of impending evils no anticipations crush them; and of coming good no vain expectations buoy them up. Of the thousands of cares which lacerate the minds of other men they are happily without experience. They feel no shame, no solicitude, no ambition, no envy, no love. . . . Ah, ye besotted men of wisdom, if you could only reckon up all the numerous days and nights that your souls have been racked with anxiety; if you could only pile together in a heap all the various ills of life which you have gone through, you would need no further evidence to convince you from what a mass of calamities I have delivered my idiotic favorites." [9] This bears a rather strong resemblance to the paradoxes of Rousseau's first discourse.

We need not be surprised at Montaigne's views, since such authorities stood at his elbow. He himself was quite civilized enough, and quite learned enough, to feel the futility of civilization and learning. Should he be asked to justify his negative conception of human happiness, we can imagine him as replying to this effect: " It is true that the cannibals lack almost everything that we prize. But at least they are free from the manifold evils which accompany our civilization, and which make our vaunted progress mockery. The whole veneer of our civilization, with all its benefits, has covered, stifled and misdirected a hundred natural activities comparable to the instinctive skill of the bird and the spider. Our arts, however grand,

[9] *Praise of Folly*, pp. 116-127, *passim*. The possibility that Rousseau drew upon Erasmus has not previously, I believe, been suggested, but the parallel is certainly very close.

exact a terrible price in their departure from nature. Man suffers much, though he gains much, from civilization. Therefore to say that the cannibals owe their virtue to their ignorance is to make a positive statement, though the terms used be negative. For to compensate for the meagreness of their existence, Nature keeps them good and happy under her own laws — laws which we, to our detriment, have ' bastardized.' "

In the essay " Of Coaches," which is about everything, there is an interesting reference to the natives of the New World. Of the American savage Montaigne says: " It is not yet full fifty yeeres that he knew neither letters, nor waight, nor measures, nor apparell, nor corne, nor vines. But was all naked, simply-pure, in Nature's lap. . . . I feare that by our contagion, we shall directly have furthered his declination, and hastened his ruine, and that we shall too dearly have sold him our opinions, our new-fangles, and our Arts. It was an unpolluted, harmlesse infant world, yet have we not whipped and submitted the same unto our discipline, or schooled him by our . . . justice and integrity, nor subdued by our magnanimity. Most of their answers, and a number of the negotiations we have had with them witness that they were nothing short of us in learning. The wonderfull cities of Cusco and Mexico . . . shew us that they yielded as little unto us in cunning and industrie. But concerning unfained devotion, aweful observance of lawes, unspotted integrity, bounteous liberality, due loyalty and free liberty, it hath greatly availed us, that we had not so much as they."

The ideas of the above passage are curiously discordant. The mention of the savage, " all naked, simply-pure, in Nature's lap," is cancelled by the reference to " the wonderfull cities of Cusco and Mexico." After reproaching the Old World for not putting the New to school, Montaigne asserts the moral superiority of the savages over the unscrupulous Europeans. This confusion is rather characteristic of earlier interpreters of savage life, who do not always distinguish between the primitive state of the Caribs and the advanced barbaric civilization of the Incas and Aztecs. They are uncertain whether to admire the Indian because he is so civilized or because he is so savage. In " Of the Caniballes," Montaigne is definitely primitivistic; in " Of Coaches," he wavers between two points of view. It is interesting, however, to note in the latter essay an interpretation of such reports as those of Las Casas.

The Noble Savage has arrived in literature. Montaigne illustrates the third and final stage in his development. By fusing the more or less objective and irreflective narrations of the explorers with various long-current traditions, the philosopher arrives at important generalizations about the virtue of savage man and the deteriorating effects of civilization.

The process may be made clearer if a single phase of savage life is examined. Consider, for instance, the ease with which savages obtain their food. Raleigh reports of the Orenoqueponi: " They never eat of any thing that is set or sowen: and as at home they use neither planting nor manurance, so when they come abroad, they refuse to eat of aught, but of that which nature without labour bringeth forth."

The philosopher comes upon this passage, or upon one like it, in some explorer's narrative. He is hungry for such corroboration of his disillusioned recoil from the civilized world. His " defeatist " temperament blinds him to the fact that wild beasts obtain their food even more easily than Indians. Sick as he is of the strife entailed by progress, it seems to him wholly admirable to lie beneath a tree until the ripe fruit drops into his open mouth.

Possessing some share of that culture he considers so harmful, the philosopher straightway thinks of the Golden Age. Perhaps such lines as Chaucer's come into his mind:

> " A blisful lyf, a paisible and a swete
> Ledden the peples in the former age:
> They helde hem payed of fruites that they ete,
> Which that the feldes yave hem by usage." [10]

In the savage, all such entrancing dreams have come true.

And finally observation and tradition are combined in an answer to Plato: " It is a nation, would I answer Plato, that hath ... no occupation but idle ... no apparell but natural, no manuring of lands, no use of wine, corne or mettle." Here the simple fact that savages obtain their food without much effort has become an argument against civilization.

We may conclude, then, that the Noble Savage is the creation of a philosopher, who, reacting from contemporary glorification of culture, takes from the explorers a picture of a savage and virtuous being, which becomes associated in his mind with long-current traditions of a corroborative nature, and draws from this material a conclusion casting discredit upon the accomplishments of human intellect.

[10] *The Former Age*, based on Boethius and *The Romance of the Rose*.

CHAPTER II

THE NOBLE SAVAGE IN THE PSEUDO-
CLASSIC PERIOD

DESPITE the temptation exerted by such references to Montaigne's cannibal as Gonzalo's famous speech in *The Tempest*, we must not pause to consider the Noble Savage as he appears in the early seventeenth century. The fortunes of the Noble Savage during the age of pseudo-classicism, however, deserve analysis.

Seventeenth century rationalism gave little encouragement to belief in the essential goodness of untutored humanity. Hobbes compares the life of primitive man to " a time of Warre, where every man is enemy to every man." " In such condition," he says, " there is no place for Industry; because the fruit thereof is uncertain: and consequently no Culture of the Earth; no Navigation, nor use of the commodities that may be imported by Sea; no commodious Building; no Instruments of moving, and removing such things as require much force; no Knowledge of the face of the Earth; no account of Time; no Arts; no Letters; no Society." This list of negatives is not unlike that quoted from Montaigne in the preceding chapter. But mark the difference. Montaigne regards the simplicity of savage life as a crushing " answer " to Plato, while Hobbes concludes thus: " ... and which is worst of all, continuall feare, and danger of violent death; And the life of man, solitary, poore, nasty, brutish, and short." Montaigne and Hobbes, using data of exactly the same nature, arrive at quite antithetical conclusions.

Hobbes goes on to say that some of his readers may

doubt the actuality of his picture of primitive existence. He himself questions whether mankind ever existed as a whole in such a brutish condition. But as proof of the fact that at least certain races have lived, and still do live, as he describes, he points to the American Indian.[1] The illustration is interesting because we shall find that Rousseau also uses the Indian to authenticate his description of primitive, or nearly primitive, society. But far from implying any agreement between Hobbes and Rousseau, the fact simply furnishes another proof of how two opposed *a priori* conclusions can twist the same facts to accord with their respective demands.

In the *Philosophical Rudiments*, Hobbes tells us that when the fruits of the earth were common to all, life was one long squabble. Thus the conception of property signalizes the ascendancy of the " rationall " over the " concupiscable " element in man. For Rousseau, property ruined man's native innocence; for Hobbes, it brought order out of chaos.

The Englishman goes on to say that the laws of nature are " the conditions of Society, or of Humane Peace," and that " the law of nature is not an agreement of men, but the Dictates of Reason." In other words, those laws are natural which are in accordance with right reason. But the *state* of nature, according to Hobbes, is in itself lawless, and therefore evil. " All men in the State of nature have a desire and will to hurt." This, of all Hobbes' statements, is the one most offensive to Rousseau. He attempts to refute it by postulating a natural instinct of pity which has been depraved by civilization.

Hobbes declares that the " will to hurt " arises partly from the " discord from comparison of wits " and partly from " the Appetite many have to the same thing." Hence

[1] *Leviathan*, pp. 93-95.

" the beginning of mutual society is from fear." The
laws of nature, arising from fear, are designed to protect
men from their fellows. " It is the fundamental Law of
Nature to seek Peace where it may be had, and where not,
to defend ourselves." And since in community of goods
there is strife and fear, " the first special Law of Nature is,
That our Rights to all things ought not to be retained."
Government, in short, is based on the resignation by the
individual, through fear of his fellow-men, of the dangerous independence which he possessed in the primitive
state. Such a system has no room for the Noble Savage.

No one philosopher, however, can be held to represent
the thought of this complex age. In Locke's *Treatises of
Government*, Rousseau was to find a view of the Social
Contract very different from that of Hobbes, and by no
means uncongenial with his own. " Locke, like his pre-
decessors, regards the compact as marking the transition
from a ' state of nature,' but his state of nature differs
materially from that of Hobbes. So far from being a state
of anarchy, it has ' a law of nature to govern it, which
obliges everyone '; and that law is reason. . . . Indeed,
Locke's state of nature is almost the ideal state; he speaks
of the ' golden age ' in an apparently historical sense and
regards government as introduced by the ' ambition and
luxury of future ages.' [2] . . . The nearest approach to
a definite statement of Locke's ultimate conclusions seems
to be that this mysterious compact, which is the binding
force of the whole social order, is in fact the tacit consent
of mankind to the inequality of property, as implied in the
use of money, and made necessary by the corruption which
followed the golden age." [3]

[2] Stephen, *English Thought in the Eighteenth Century*, Vol. II,
p. 137.

[3] *Ibid.*, p. 142.

Locke's view is in fact much more primitivistic and sentimental than anything we find in the *Contrat Social*. Where did Locke get these ideas of a golden age, of reason as a natural possession of mankind, of the corruption caused by inequality, ambition and luxury?   In his warfare against the elaborate mathematical game being carried on by his contemporaries, he fell back upon the old Arcadian-classical conception of nature, which had been enthusiastically revived during the Renaissance, and which had been preserved during the seventeenth century as a literary and to some extent as a philosophical convention.   Rationalism could not make men stop thinking of nature as a norm of primitive freshness and simplicity.   At no time did the term cease to be used in connection with " innocent," " uncorrupted," " spontaneous."   When the strictly rationalistic view of nature as a mathematically constructed mechanism decayed, the other view flourished through force of contrast with its rival.   The actual development was of course more delicate and complex than can be expressed in words.   If rationalistic nature was tinged with Arcadianism, romantic nature was tinged with the old tendency to build a neat universal system.   In Rousseau the two conceptions struggle for mastery.

To Locke's belief that reason is a gift impartially granted mankind by nature, the essential goodness of man is a corollary.   This doctrine, though theoretically repugnant to rationalism, was held by more than one philosopher of the age.   The school of Shaftesbury, for example, escaped from the meanness of utilitarian ethics by practically identifying God with the ingenious mechanism of the universe. This installation of God in the world spreads a divine benediction throughout nature, and lends a certain naturalness to the divine.   Hence this group is able to regard the instinctive goodness of man both as a gift of God and a law of nature. Man has a moral sense — a conscience which is genial and inspiring rather than stern and restraining. Shaftesbury's detestation of hard-and-fast systems of philosophy is not unlike that of Rousseau.

But the resemblance should not be pressed too far. Shaftesbury and Rousseau are anything but kindred spirits. To Shaftesbury, philosophy is the study of happiness, and happiness is very largely a matter of aesthetic sensibility. He prefers theism to atheism principally because theism is more harmonious and more pleasing to a refined taste. He has the complete optimism of the dilettante. There is no real evil in the universe: what seems evil is merely due to ignorance. Cultivate the graces, and the world will prove completely amiable. Had Rousseau and he been contemporaries, he would have recognized Rousseau as an " enthusiast," and would surely have subjected him to the mild quizzing which he recommended in such cases. Shaftesbury's ideal man was not the man of nature, but the virtuoso — the elegant savorer of the teacup of life. And one suspects that in his heart he believed that only a man of good taste possessed a moral sense.

Nevertheless, the philosophy of Shaftesbury illustrates the way in which rationalism quietly melted into romanticism. He was imitated by many optimistic thinkers who encouraged belief in the doctrine that man is at heart a well-meaning and even rather sensible creature. When the Arcadian conception of nature regained the ascendancy over the conception of nature as a mathematical system, Shaftesbury's ideas took on new seriousness and dignity.

Even greater was the encouragement furnished the doctrine of natural goodness by Hume. " It is . . . an essential part of Hume's theory to demonstrate the reality of the altruistic sentiments. . . . Powerful as is the

passion of self-love, it is easy to discover instances which
are not resolvable into it; for moral approbation survives
where our private interests are separable from, or even
opposed to, the public interests. Sympathy, in short, is
natural." [4] Hume's opposition to official rationalism took
a direction opposite to Berkeley's: instead of ignoring experience, he ignored everything else; instead of soaring
into the clouds, he burrowed deeply into the earth. He
traced the elaborate structures of intellect back to their
origins in instinct. But one result of this sceptical analysis
was the conclusion that morality, like everything else, must
be derived from feeling. Benevolence, then, is no product
of utilitarian syllogisms, but an instinctive element in the
heart of man. Pleasure is the normal accompaniment of
virtue; pain, the normal accompaniment of vice. If this
is true, men were ready to say, there is indeed much

> " . . . reason to lament
> What man has made of man."

One can understand why Rousseau thought for a time of
Hume as a kindred spirit.

We may conclude, then, that the rationalism which
dominated England from the middle of the seventeenth
to the middle of the eighteenth century was less inimical
to the Noble Savage idea than might be supposed. That
idea depends upon belief in nature as a norm of innocence,
simplicity and spontaneity, and upon belief in the instinctive goodness of man. These beliefs, as old as human
thought, persisted during the rationalistic period. They
were among several destructive elements which caused the
decay of rationalism, and from that decay they gained sufficient strength to become two of the most important conceptions of the succeeding age.

[4] *Ibid.*, pp. 103-104.

Just as it is possible to exaggerate the rationalism of the rationalistic period, it is possible to exaggerate the classicism of the literature produced during that period.   Whatever the critical theories may have been, the actual tastes of readers responded rather warmly to the exotic, to an elegant pastoral primitivism, and to satirical flings cast at civilization by unsophisticated types.   Let us consider a few productions of the pseudo-classical age which deal with the wild man in a way that looks forward to the Noble Savage of romanticism.

So far as I have been able to discover, the earliest use of the term " Noble Savage " occurs in Part One of Dryden's *Conquest of Granada,* where Almanzor declares:

> " I am as free as Nature first made man,
> Ere the base laws of servitude began,
> When wild in woods the noble savage ran."

But Almanzor is not, in the true romantic sense, a Noble Savage.   He is a Noble Barbarian, who seems to descend more or less directly from Marlowe's *Tamburlaine.*   The distinction will be made clearer by a reminder of the confusion, in Montaigne's essay *Of Coaches,* between the naked tribes of Caribbean stock and the much more advanced Incas and Aztecs.   The former are savages, the latter barbarians.   The former appealed very little to the taste of the pseudo-classicists; the latter appealed a good deal.   The two types, however, are closely enough related to justify some consideration of the Noble Barbarian in Dryden's day.

In calling Almanzor a noble savage, Dryden is probably influenced by memories of his own *Indian Emperour,* and of Howard's *Indian Queen,* in which Dryden had some share.

The *Indian Queen* may be briefly dismissed as a dull and weak heroic play whose only bearing on our subject is that the characters are supposed to be Aztecs. They might quite as well be Persians or anything else. Since the action takes place before the coming of the Spaniards, there is no opportunity to contrast the two races. Here is the stage direction for the first scene of Act V: " Scene opens, and discovers the Temple of the Sun, all of Gold, and four Priests, in Habits of white and red Feathers, attending by a bloody Altar, as ready for Sacrifice. Then enter the Guards, Zempoalla, and Traxalla; Inca, Orazia, and Montezuma, bound. As soon as they are placed, the priest sings." In pompous, spectacular, semi-operatic scenes like these, the true Noble Savage can play no part. We may be sure that Zempoalla and Traxalla, in front of that golden temple, will not bear witness to the blessings of primeval innocence and simplicity.

In the *Indian Emperour*, Aztec and Spaniard confront each other. The results, however, are not particularly striking. Though Dryden declares in his preface that he has " traced the Native Simplicity and Ignorance of the *Indians*, in relation to *European* customs," he has really done nothing but write a play of court intrigue and warfare. In two passages only do we catch a glimpse of the Noble Savage idea. When a Spanish soldier says that Mexico seems " untaught and salvage," Cortez replies:

> " Wild and untaught are Terms which we alone
> Invent, for fashions differing from our own:
> For all their Customs are by Nature wrought,
> But we, by Art, unteach what Nature taught."

In this there is a touch of Montaigne. Later Montezuma's daughter, in comparing Spanish with Mexican courtship, says to a Spaniard:

> " Strange ways you practise there to win a Heart,
> Here Love is Nature, but with you 'tis Art."

Yet, after all, any shepherdess might say that to any courtier.

Through both these plays runs a masque-like element. The scenes are evidently intended to be elaborate, and provision is made for songs and dances. A still earlier piece, Davenant's *Cruelty of the Spaniards in Peru,* is more a masque than a play. As is well known, it was presented at the Cockpit Theatre in 1658, and it is interesting that the Noble Barbarian should appear in the very dawn of the revival of English drama. The most convenient way of summarizing the plot will be to quote the " Argument of the whole Designe ":

" The Designe is first to represent the happy condition of the people of *Peru* antiently, when their inclinations were govern'd by Nature; and then it makes some discov'ry of their establishment under the Twelve *Incas,* and of the dissentions of the two Sons of the last *Inca.* Then proceeds to the discov'ry of that new Western World by the Spaniards, which happen'd to be during the dissention of the two Royal Brethren. It likewise proceeds to the Spaniards Conquest of that *Incan* Empire, and then discovers the cruelty of the Spaniards over the Indians. . . . And towards the conclusion, it infers the Voyages of the English thither, and the amity of the Natives towards them, under whose Ensignes . . . they hope to be made Victorious, and to be freed from the Yoke of the Spaniard."

It will readily be observed that this entertainment, through its scenes, speeches, songs and dances, offers several quite distinct attractions. First of all we have a lament for the simplicity of the Golden Age of the Incas. This is followed by a bit of political philosophy and court intrigue; these were to be characteristic elements of the heroic drama. Then comes warfare, which is followed by a grim torture spectacle: " Two Spaniards are . . . discover'd sitting in their cloakes . . . ; the one turning a Spit, whilst the other is basting an *Indian* Prince, which is rosted at an artificial fire." The final appeal is to the belief that one Englishman can whip three Spaniards.

To us, the "first entry" is the most important, for it shows that some at least of the Incas are dreaming of the days when they were Noble Savages rather than Noble Barbarians. The priest of the sun delivers a speech based rather closely on the Golden Age passage in the first book of the *Metamorphoses.* "The Speech being ended, the Priest waves his Verge, and his Attendant, with extraordinary Activity, performs the *Somerset.*" (The Attendant is an acrobat who at the end of each speech displays a sample of his skill.)   Then follows a Peruvian song, "in pursuance of the manner of their Life, before their Incas brought them to live in Cities, and to build Forts":

I

"Whilst yet our world was new,
        When not discover'd by the old;
    E're beggar'd slaves we grew,
        For having Silver Hills, and Strands of Gold.

" *Chorus*   We danc'd and we sung
            And lookt ever young,
    And from restraints were free,
    As waves and winds at Sea.

II

"When wildly we did live;
        E're crafty Cities made us tame:
    When each his whole would give
        To all, and none peculiar right did claim.
. . .   .

V

" When garments were not worn,
  Nor shame did nakednesse resent:
Nor Poverty bred scorn:
  When none could want, and all were innocent."

This song represents very clearly the fusion of the
Golden Age tradition with the reports of the explorers.
And it is interesting to note that Davenant, though he represents the Incas as living in a high state of barbaric civilization, puts the Noble Savage idea into their mouths. He
does so, however, in a merely conventional way. This
canny showman has no intention of holding up the savage
as a model to the Englishman of his time. The pseudo-
classicists of the seventeenth century found a much-needed
emotional outlet in exoticism. Provided the author set
his fable in a vaguely foreign land, he was permitted to
" let himself go " a little. It was in drama, especially
during the ascendancy of the heroic play, that exoticism
reached its greatest vogue. Moorish Spain, in *The Conquest of Granada; * Morocco, in *The Emperor of Morocco;*
Persia, in *Cyrus the Great;* India, in *Aurengzebe;* Siam,
in *The Fatal Vision* — these suggest the varied background
provided for the invariable theme of " love and valor."
On the whole, our Incas and Aztecs are used, just as the
Moors and Persians and Siamese are, to satisfy a demand
for more violent action, more ranting, more elaborate
scenic effects and richer costumes than would be decorous
in plays with Greek or Roman characters. Into the portrayal of the Incas and Aztecs, however, does creep a
slight amount of naturalistic feeling. We may, without
exaggerating the importance of this element, believe
that such plays as these helped to preserve the seeds

of the flower that was to bloom in the Romantic Movement.[5]

To trace in detail the source of every Noble Savage in English literature would require a book in itself. We may say in general, however, that the plays which we have been examining are, like other exotic plays and romances, of French ancestry. In his *L'Amérique et le Rêve Exotique,* Professor Chinard shows that in 1634 and 1653, respectively, Garcilaso de la Vega's *History of the Incas* and Calancha's *History of Peru* were translated from Spanish into French. These histories contained material well adapted to heroic romance and drama. Such works as Gomberville's *La Jeune Alcidiane* and Calprenède's *La Princesse Alcidiane,* or at least the type which they represent, were familiar to Davenant, Howard and Dryden. It seems reasonably certain that the Noble Inca and the Noble Aztec were imported from France as part of the exotic-heroic tradition.

The ancestors of these figures, however, are less interesting to us than their offspring. Of these the most important is Aphra Behn's *Oroonoko.*

Whether the Divine Astraea actually spent part of her girlhood in Surinam or whether the often-praised realism of portions of her novel springs from a diligent reading of Warren's *Impartial Description of Surinam* [6] is a ques-

---

[5] For the sake of completeness I may mention here *The History of Sir Francis Drake,* Davenant's companion-piece to *The Cruelty of the Spaniards.* This work is patriotic in character, and the Peruvians exist only to sing songs in praise of Drake's courage and kindness.

[6] Ernest Bernbaum, in his *Mrs. Behn's Oroonoko* (*Kittredge Anniversary Papers,* pp. 419-434), tries to show that the book is a mere fabrication. Montague Summers, in his edition of the works of Mrs. Behn (Vol. I, pp. xviii-xix), defends the authenticity of the work, but not in a completely convincing manner. The question is still open.

tion which we need not attempt to answer. For us the important thing is the Royal Slave as he appears in her book. Disregarding the problem of his existence in the flesh, does he impress the reader as a genuine savage, as a Noble Savage, or as something different from either?

Mr. Paul Elmer More thinks that *Oroonoko* illustrates " the fancy of the purity and excellence of man in his natural state, untouched by the vitiating hand of civilization," and represents " the type of natural goodness." [7] Such is the prevailing attitude toward this book. Everyone hails it as a prophetic combination of Rousseau's discourses and *Uncle Tom's Cabin*. Is this view well founded?

The opening pages of *Oroonoko* are devoted to the savage natives of Surinam, who, it should be noted, are not slaves, " for those we live with in perfect Amity, without daring to command 'em; but, on the contrary, caress 'em with all the brotherly and friendly Affection in the world."

" And these people," Astraea prattles on, " represented to me an absolute Idea of the first State of Innocence, before man knew how to sin: and 'tis most evident and plain, that simple Nature is the most harmless, inoffensive, and virtuous Mistress. 'Tis she alone, if she were permitted, that better instructs the World, than all the Inventions of Man: Religion would here but destroy that Tranquillity they possess by Ignorance; and Laws would but teach 'em to know offenses, of which they have no notion."

This is good Noble Savage doctrine, and it harmonizes with a strain of naturalistic sentiment which pervades some of her plays. It would be dangerous, however, to make too much of Mrs. Behn's Arcadianism. Had her belief in primitive innocence been very deep or intense, she

[7] *With the Wits*, p. 95.

would have made her hero something like a true child of nature. Let us examine the character of the Royal Slave. Oroonoko, despite his suspiciously Carib name, is not an Indian but a Negro, fraudulently brought from Africa to Surinam. But Astraea would never make a common black her hero. Be assured that Oroonoko is a person of quality: he is the grandson of the King of Coromantien. And Coromantien is anything but a savage community. It has an elaborate system of laws, a well-disciplined army, and a court teeming with plots and cabals. The king, having evidently progressed somewhat beyond " the first State of Innocence," maintains a typically Turkish harem which reminds us very powerfully of the oriental romances of the time.

Oroonoko's appearance betrays his noble origin. " He was pretty tall, but of a Shape the most exact that can be fancy'd. . . . His Face was not of that brown rusty Black which most of that Nation are, but a perfect Ebony, or polished Jet. His Eyes were the most aweful that could be seen, and very piercing; the White of 'em being like Snow, as were his Teeth. His nose was rising and Roman, instead of African and flat: His mouth the finest shaped that could be seen; far from those great turn'd Lips, which are so natural to the rest of the Negroes. The whole Proportion and Air of his Face was so nobly and exactly formed, that bating his Colour, there could be nothing in Nature more beautiful, agreeable and handsome. There was no one Grace wanting, that bears the standard of true Beauty. His Hair came down to his Shoulders, by the Aids of Art, which was by pulling it out with a Quill, and keeping it comb'd; of which he took particular care." Thus does Astraea make her hero acceptable to elegant readers.

Besides being the darling of the court of Coromantien

and a Narcissus in ebony, Oroonoko has acquired many European accomplishments. "The most illustrious Courts could not have produced a braver Man, both for Greatness of Courage and Mind, a Judgment more solid, a Wit more quick, and a Conversation more sweet and diverting. He knew almost as much as if he had read much. . . . He had heard of the late Civil Wars in England, and the deplorable death of our great Monarch; and would discourse of it with all the Sense and Abhorrence of the Injustice imaginable. He had an extreme good and graceful Mien, and all the Civility of a well-bred Great Man. He had nothing of Barbarity in his Nature, but in all Points address'd himself, as if his Education had been in some European Court." This is not the man of nature in all his primeval purity.

The maiden whom Oroonoko woos, wins, loses, recovers and finally slays is named Imoinda. "One need only say," smirks the Divine Astraea, "that she was Female to the noble Male; the beautiful black Venus to our young Mars; as charming in her person as he, and of delicate Virtues. I have seen a hundred White Men sighing after her, and making a thousand Vows at her Feet, all in vain and unsuccessful." Mrs. Behn does not for one moment see her heroine as a negress, but as an ideal exotic woman, possessed of incredible beauty, constancy and virtue.

Oroonoko and Imoinda are to be regarded as the chief figures of an heroic romance. "Love and valor," the two elements of this genre, make up the substance of the tale. The love is that of courtly folk in the fiction of the period. Note the *précieux* tone of the following passage: "When he came, attended by all the young Soldiers of any Merit, he was infinitely surprised at the Beauty of this fair Queen of Night, whose Face and Person were so exceeding all that he had ever beheld, that lovely Modesty with which she receiv'd him, that Softness in her Looks and Sighs . . . and the Sweetness of her Words and Behavior while he stayed, gain'd a perfect Conquest over his fierce Heart, and made him feel, the Victor could be subdued. So that having made his first Compliments . . . he told her with his Eyes, that he was not insensible of her Charms; while Imoinda, who wished for nothing more than so glorious a Conquest, was pleas'd to believe, she understood that silent Language of new-born Love; and, from that Moment, put on all her Additions to Beauty." Such is courtship in the state of nature.

When Oroonoko first loses Imoinda, he remains for two whole days in a trance, in spite of the fact that he is leader of the army, and his country is being invaded. But just as the young prince's men are beginning to waver, valor triumphs over love, and the revived Oroonoko cries to his followers: " Come, if we must die, let us meet death the noblest Way; and 'twill be more like Oroonoko, to encounter him at an Army's Head, opposing the torrent of a conquering Foe, than lazily on a Couch, to wait his lingering Pleasure, and die every Moment by a thousand racking Thoughts, or be tamely taken by an Enemy, and led a whining, love-sick slave to adorn the triumphs of Jamoan that young Victor, who already is enter'd beyond the limits I have prescribed for him." A Roman triumph in Africa is an amusing incongruity. The speech, of course, is the conventional heroic ranting familiar to any reader of *The Conquest of Granada:*

> " It pleases me your army is so great;
> For now I know there's more to conquer yet."

And like Almanzor, Oroonoko wins the field almost single-handed.

There is still better ranting toward the end of the book, where Oroonoko, sorely wounded, addresses his white persecutors thus: " *Look ye, ye faithless Crew, 'tis not Life I seek, nor am I afraid of dying,* (and at that Word, cut a Piece of Flesh from his own Throat, and threw it at 'em) *yet still I would live if I could, till I had perfected my Revenge: but oh! it cannot be.* . . . At that, he ripped up his own Belly, and took his Bowels and pull'd 'em out." Here the fantastic bravado of the seventeenth century hero merges with the defiant stoicism of the " dying Indian," whose behavior under torture becomes a popular poetic theme.[8]

It is true that in the second part of the book, after Oroonoko is brought to Surinam, Mrs. Behn succeeds in creating a livelier illusion of reality than in the completely artificial African episodes. She does so chiefly by inserting a long descriptive passage borrowed, according to Bernbaum, from a traveler's account, and by loosely connecting Oroonoko with some of the details in that description. Except for these pages, the second part is but little less " heroic " than the first.

Criticism of *Oroonoko*, in short, has suffered from the passion for discovering forerunners. An examination of the book in connection with works of its own, rather than of a later, period, will disclose its essential affinity with the " heroic " tradition. It is much more like *The Indian Emperour* than like Rousseau's second discourse or *Uncle Tom's Cabin*.

On the other hand, *Oroonoko* certainly marks an advance beyond the Incas and Aztecs of Davenant, Howard and Dryden. Even though Mrs. Behn may have been attracted to this simple tale of a suffering Negro chiefly by its novelty, it is something that she should have regarded

[8] *Vide infra*, Chap. XIII.

that story as worthy of literary adornment. And though she does not stress the humanitarian implications of her theme as strongly as if she had lived a century later, she does stress them more emphatically than we should expect of a writer of her period. Beneath the trappings of the Royal Slave we faintly discern Montaigne's cannibal, preserved in incongruous guise until the time when he can stand forth as the man of nature.

Popular as Mrs. Behn's work was, a man of the eighteenth century would probably think of *Oroonoko* as a play rather than a novel. It relapses readily into the type from which, as has been suggested, it arose. The first dramatic version, prepared by the elder Southern, was produced in 1696. Unwilling to let the original story stand or fall on its own merits, Southern adds a comic plot, dealing with the amorous and financial schemes of a widow, which occupies a good half of the action. The Royal Slave part of the plot follows Mrs. Behn closely, except that Imoinda is made white. We learn that she was brought as an infant to Coromantien by a white man who became Prince Oroonoko's comrade-in-arms.

This striking change may be due to a sense of the improbability of white settlers' sighing after a black slave-girl. It also, however, enables Southern to imitate *Othello*. In his hands, the Royal Slave becomes something very like the Noble Moor of Venice, and even less like a real savage than Mrs. Behn's character. His princely qualities are almost ludicrously emphasized. In every crisis, he shows himself the warrior, courtier and statesman. Whereas all the other characters speak prose, he speaks proud and sententious blank verse abounding in Shakespearian echoes. There are two or three haughty flings at the contrast between Christian doctrine and Christian practice, but the play certainly brings us no nearer to the real Noble Savage.[9]

In the version of Southern's play prepared by Dr. John Hawkesworth in 1775, the pointless Widow plot is excised, the construction is in other respects improved, and some insignificant verbal changes are made. More is said about the evils of slavery. In 1817 Hazlitt, after seeing this form of the play, wrote: " The story of this *servile war* is not without a parallel elsewhere: it reads a great moral lesson to Europe, only changing black into white." But the slightly greater humanitarian element injected by the reviser has no effect on the character of the hero. Hawkesworth, as we shall see, sympathized rather strongly with the Noble Savage idea, but his Oroonoko is still the royal prince, the exotic hero, the " well-bred great man " who merely happens to be black.

Davenant, Dryden and Aphra Behn deal with savages of tropical climes. The Indian of North America, I believe, first appears as a character in English imaginative literature in John Dennis's *Liberty Asserted* (produced 1704.) The scene is laid in Canada, and the author's purpose is to contrast English liberty with French tyranny. The Indian characters are noble, but merely with the nobility possessed by most figures in the tragedy of the period. The heroic actions and lofty sentiments of Ulamar, the young chieftain, are indistinguishable from those of Beaufort, the English leader. Beaufort, we learn, has " instructed " Ulamar " in European arts." It is no surprise to learn that Ulamar is after all only half an Indian, since his father turns out to be a Frenchman of ex-

[9] Another dramatic version of *Oroonoko*, which I have not felt obliged to examine, is William Walsh's *Victorious Love*, produced in 1698.

ceptional virtue. Dennis, like Davenant before him, uses the Indians as a means of attacking England's enemies. The enemy of course is different, and a stiffer classical quality has replaced the earlier Restoration technique. There is even less attempt at realistic treatment of savage life than in Davenant, Dryden or Southern, and of sentimental naturalism not the slightest trace appears. *Liberty Asserted* is important merely as an early landmark in the history of our subject.

Later chapters will show that the romantic spirit gradually transforms the Incas, Aztecs, Royal Slaves and high-minded Iroquois of the heroic-exotic tradition into something very like Noble Savages. At present, however, we must take up a more profitable line of development — the employment of the Noble Savage in satire. The contrast between savage and civilized life offers a tempting field for satirical treatment. Whether civilized man journeys to the wilds, or the savage journeys to the city, the confrontation of the man of nature and the man of the world gives interesting results.

In April, 1710, four Indian " kings " came to London as representatives of the Six Nations. Dr. Bissell and Professor Farley have shown that their visit attracted a good deal of popular attention.[10] Of literary reflections of the incident, the most important are those which appeared in the *Tatler* and the *Spectator*.[11]

Steele's *Tatler* paper begins with a discussion at the Grecian as to whence arise honors and titles. Timoleon

---

[10] *Cf.* Bissell, *American Indian in the Eighteenth Century*, p. 59 and Appendix; and Farley, *The Dying Indian* (*Kittredge Anniversary Papers*, pp. 251-260.)

[11] *Tatler*, No. 171; May 13, 1710. *Spectator*, No. 50; April 27, 1711. The former paper is by Steele, the latter by Addison.

supposes " that in those ages which first degenerated from simplicity of life and natural justice, the wise among them thought it necessary to inspire men with a love of virtue by giving them, who adhered to the interests of innocence and truth, some distinguishing mark to raise them above the common level of mankind. . . ' Such a man,' continued he, ' without the qualities which should give a man pretence to be exalted above others, does but turn him to jest and ridicule.' "

This just observation reminds Urbanus of the Indian kings. They lodged, he relates, with an upholsterer who was kind to all of them, and particularly kind to one chief who had been taken sick during his stay. This chief was especially impressed by the bed on which he lay, and argued that the maker of so beneficent an object must be a great man. And so " these just and generous princes, who act according to the dictates of natural justice, thought it proper to confer some dignity upon their landlord before they left his house." Accordingly they held a council at the end of which they called in the little upholsterer and conferred upon him the title of *Cadaroque*, " which is the name of the strongest fort in their part of the country."

The moral of this story is not stated, but seems clearly implied. To an Englishman, the idea of conferring a title upon a mere tradesman is ridiculous. But these savages, as Steele has said, " act according to the dictates of natural justice." Their landlord has shown nobility of soul in his treatment of them; and as a maker of beds he is far worthier of honor than rich fops who do nothing to ease the pains of their fellow-men. Why should he not have a title?

Addison's *Spectator* essay is far more pointed and significant, for it purports to be a translation from some papers accidentally left behind by one of the kings. The chief begins by describing St. Paul's with naïve suggestions as to the possible method of erecting so great a structure. Then he throws his shaft: " It is probable that when this great work was begun . . . there was some religion among this people; for they give it the name of a temple, and have a tradition that it was designed for men to pay their devotion in. And indeed there are several reasons which make us think that the natives of this country had formerly among them some sort of worship; for they set apart every seventh day as sacred: but upon my going into one of these holy houses on that day, I could not observe any circumstance of devotion in their behaviour."

The remainder of the paper simply uses the Indian king as a mouthpiece for the criticism of some of Mr. Spectator's pet aversions. The chiefs learn of two strange and terrible beasts — the Whig and the Tory. The dress of the English " is very barbarous, for they almost strangle themselves about the neck, and bind their bodies with many ligatures, that we are apt to think are the occasion of several distempers among them, which our country is entirely free from." Then there are wondering comments on men's wigs, women's *coiffures*, beauty-patches — which are regarded as symptoms of some curious internal disease — breeches and petticoats. Mr. Spectator's conclusion is that " we are all guilty in some measure of the same narrow way of thinking which we meet with in this abstract of the Indian journal, when we fancy the customs, dresses and manners of other countries are ridiculous and extravagant if they do not resemble our own." [12]

A typically mild Addisonian moral. But the sting of

---

[12] *Cf*. Bissell, *op. cit.*, pp. 69–71, for an account of a paper in the *Scots Magazine*, 1742, written as a continuation of the Indian king's letter in *Spectator*. As befits its later date, its satire is much more severe and sweeping than Addison's.

that idea of St. Paul's being a relic of some long-dead religion is not Addisonian at all. Its gravely inverted irony suggests that of Swift, and it may well have originated in the mind of that great satirist.

On April 28, 1711, the day after the appearance of Addison's paper, Swift wrote in his *Journal to Stella:* "The *Spectator* is written by Steele, with Addison's help: it is often very pretty. Yesterday it was made of a noble hint I gave him long ago for his *Tatler*, about an Indian supposed to write his Travels into England. I regret he ever had it. I intended to have written a book on that subject. I believe he has spent it all in one paper, and all the under-hints there are mine too; but I never see him or Addison." There seems to be no doubt that Number 50 of *Spectator* is by Addison; Steele, after making rather feeble use of the four kings in the *Tatler*, must have passed Swift's idea on to his partner. The bit about St. Paul's we may suppose to be one of the "under-hints." What would we not give to have Swift's own book on this theme!

Though Swift never carried out his intention, he has devoted part of his most famous work to a unique treatment of the Noble Savage idea. I refer to his *Voyage to the Houyhnhnms*. The Land of the Houyhnhnms is an ideal realm, set up, for our admiration and shame, in contrast to the sordid and vicious life of man. This part of *Gulliver* is a Utopian Voyage, a form which applies to old visions of an ideal state the technic of the explorers' narratives. It arises from such comparisons as that drawn by Montaigne between the life of the cannibals and the attempts of poetry and philosophy "to faine a happy condition of man." Frequently, though by no means invariably, the Utopias discovered in these explorations of the fancy are peopled by Noble Savages.

Such, beneath their equine disguise, are the Houyhnhnms. The source of their virtues is the lack of everything prized in civilized society. They have, for instance, " not the least idea of books and literature." They have no war, no weapons, no laws or lawyers, no diseases or doctors, no politicians, no ministers of state, no nobility.

In his conversation with the old Houyhnhnm who becomes his master, Gulliver attempts to explain the evils inseparable from civilized activities, but with small success. " During the discourse my master was pleased to interrupt me several times. . . . He was wholly at a loss to know what could be the use or necessity of practising those vices. To clear up which I endeavored to give him some idea of the desire of power and riches, of the terrible effects of lust, intemperance, malice and envy." But this attempt is frustrated by the limitations of the Houyhnhnm vocabulary. " They have no word in their language to express lying or falsehood." [13]   Indeed, they have ordinarily no ideas which could give birth to such expressions. The old Houyhnhnm is simply nonplussed by Gulliver's account of European life. " My master heard me with great appearances of uneasiness in his countenance, because doubting or not believing are so little known in this country that the inhabitants cannot tell how to behave themselves under such circumstances."

For the Houyhnhnms derive knowledge of the distinction between right and wrong directly from nature. " These noble Houyhnhnms are endowed by Nature with a general disposition to virtue." " They will have it that Nature teaches them to love the whole species." Nature,

---

[13] Mrs. Behn says the same thing of the natives of Surinam. Professor Bernbaum, however, finds in the Jesuit missionary Pellepart's *Introduction à la langue des Galibis* (1655) five Carib synonyms for *menteur*. (*Kittredge Anniversary Papers*, pp. 430–431.)

in short, "works all things to perfection." The Houyhnhnms, provided with something like Shaftesbury's "moral sense," simply cannot understand the perplexities of civilized existence.

In several respects the Houyhnhnms recall the Germani of Tacitus. Their government is communistic. Their sexual relations are sternly chaste. "Friendship and benevolence are the two principal virtues among the Houyhnhnms, and these not confined to particular objects, but universal to the whole race. For a stranger from the remotest part is equally treated with the nearest neighbor, and wherever he goes, looks upon himself as at home. They preserve decency and civility in the highest degrees, but are altogether ignorant of ceremony. . . . Temperance, industry, exercise and cleanliness are the lessons equally enjoined to the young of both sexes."

Knowing no evil, the Houyhnhnms take no shame in going naked. Gulliver, indeed, has difficulty in explaining his curious custom of wearing clothes, for his master "could not understand why Nature should teach us to conceal what Nature had given." This is an excellent illustration of what might be called the philosophizing of the explorers' reports.

But though Gulliver, through fear of exposing his Yahooism, retains his garments, he succeeds in sloughing off most other corruptions of civilization. "No man," he says "could more easily verify the truth of these two maxims, that Nature is very easily satisfied, and that Necessity is the mother of invention. I enjoyed perfect health of body and tranquillity of mind; I did not find the treachery or inconstancy of a friend, nor the injuries of a secret or open enemy. I had no occasion of bribing, flattering or pimping to procure the favor of any great man or of his minion. I wanted no fence against fraud or oppression; here was neither physician to destroy my body nor lawyer to ruin my fortune." Another list of blessed deprivations! [14]

The Houyhnhnms, we may conclude, are Noble Savages. They escape the ills of civilization because " their wants and passions are fewer than among us." They are virtuous, because they derive from nature an instinctive propensity toward goodness. Let the reader picture to himself that dialogue between the old Houyhnhnm and Gulliver. The former, child of nature, listens with pained surprise while the latter, perplexed with doubt and burdened with a thousand vices, vainly attempts to explain the meaning and purpose of books, lawyers, doctors, wars and politics. There is a typical confrontation of Noble Savage and civilized man, a scene we shall meet with again.

One cannot think that Swift seriously believes in the Noble Savage. No one cherishes fewer illusions about human nature than he. The Houyhnhnms are not men: mankind is represented by the filthy Yahoos. The Houyhnhnms are simply ideal creations of satire through whom Swift pours out his scorn upon the human race.

This use of the Noble Savage as a satirical vehicle is characteristic of the age. Voltaire's *L'Ingénu* represents a variant of the same practice, for in his story the supposed savage visits civilization, and the technic is therefore inverted. Neither Voltaire nor Swift believes in the Noble Savage, but both are willing to use him for their purposes.

[14] Such lists were so common as to be subject to parody. As early as 1635, Scarron thus pokes fun at an expedition about to start for Guadeloupe: " Adieu France, adieu Paris. . . . Je renonce aux vers burlesques, aux romans comiques et aux comédies, pour aller dans un pays ou il n'y aura ni Mazarins, ni faux béats, ni filoux de dévotion, ni inquisition, ni hiver, ni saison, ni fluxion qui m'estropie, ni guerre qui me fasse mourir de faim." (Chinard, *L'Amérique et le rêve exotique*, p. 34.)

This adaptability of the Noble Savage idea to satire must have been an important influence in preserving it throughout an age with which it was not in harmony. Thus Swift's friend, John Gay, though he cannot by any stretch of the imagination be regarded as an apostle of nature, makes use of it in *Polly*.

That Polly Peachum should marry a Noble Savage is one of the most incongruous facts in literature, but marry a Noble Savage she does. The heroine of the sequel to the *Beggar's Opera* is brought to the West Indies by Mrs. Trapes, a bawd in the guise of an agent for servants, and is turned over to Mr. Ducat. From his brutal advances she escapes to a pirate camp in male attire. Her sojourn among the pirates gives her a chance to warn the English settlers that the buccaneers are about to make a raid upon them. The Indians of the island support the English against the pirates, who are defeated. The leader of the pirates, Morano, proves to be none other than our old friend Macheath. Polly discovers his identity just as he is led away to be executed. She is not inconsolable, however, for she has already developed an interest in Cawwawkee, the young Indian chief.

" Allow me," sobs Polly, " to give a decent time to my sorrows."

" Fair princess, for so I hope shortly to make you," is the chief's reply, " permit me to attend you, either to divide your griefs, or, by conversation, to soften your sorrows." There seems little doubt, as the curtain falls, that Polly's sorrows will soon be softened.

This courtly and elaborate speech of Cawwawkee's imperfectly represents his character. Elsewhere he approaches much more closely the familiar Indian of tradition — stern, stoical, laconic, scornful of the whites. I quote excerpts from the scene that takes place when he is led a prisoner into the pirate camp. Observe that his answers are turned into broadly satirical points by the comments of other characters.

"*Morano* [Macheath]: Do you know your danger?

"*Cawwawkee*: I am prepared to meet it. [Here he breaks into a song about the indestructibility of honor.]

. . .   .

"*Mor.*: Mere downright barbarians, you see, lieutenant. They have our national honour still in practice among them.

"*Vanderbluff*: We must beat civilizing into 'em, to make 'em capable of common society, and common conversation.

"*Mor.*: . . . Can you feel pain?

"*Caw.*: I can bear it.

"*Mor.*: I shall try you.

"*Caw.*: I speak truth, I never affirm but what I know.

"*Mor.* [Asking about English troops]: . . . How are they disposed? . . .

"*Caw.*: What, betray my friends! I am no coward, *European*.

. . .   .

"*Vanderbluff*: What, neither cheat nor be cheated? There is no having either commerce or correspondence with these creatures.

"*Jenny* [Morano's doxy]: We have reason to be thankful for our good education. How ignorant is mankind without it!

. . .   .

"*Polly* [Aside]: How happy are these savages! Who would not wish to be in such ignorance."

Gay employs Cawwawkee, as Swift employs the Houyhnhnms, to cast scorn upon the cowardice and treachery of the English. But whereas Swift's bitterness seems brutally genuine, Gay's seems merely superficially and journalistically violent. He is trying to do, one feels, what Drevetière had done so delightfully in *Arlequin Sauvage*.[15] But forgetting the fun of the situation, Gay

[15] Chinard, *L'Amérique et le rêve exotique*, pp. 221 ff., gives an account of this jolly play and of other French satirical comedies of the

permits himself to become indignant, and his indignation, unlike Swift's, is not strong or deep enough to be impressive. Such satire, neither cutting nor merry, trembles on the verge of sentimentality.

What we may call the satirical Noble Savage continues into the early part of the Romantic Period. One of Lyttelton's *Dialogues of the Dead* (1760) presents an argument between the shades of a Duellist and of a Savage. The Savage, although he was killed after scalping women and children, refuses to cross the Styx in the same boat with the Duellist, who had slain on the field of honor a friend who had asked him to pay a debt. The Indian may be brutal to his enemies, but he is not treacherous to his friends.

Mercury, who has guided the pair to Styx, thus sums up the case: " How far the Barbarism of the Mohawk will excuse his horrid Acts I leave Minos to judge. But the Englishman, what Excuse can he plead? The Custom of Duelling? A bad Excuse at the best! but in his case it cannot avail. The Spirit that made him draw his Sword in this combat against his friend is not that of *Honour;* it is the Spirit of Alecto herself. To her he must go, for she hath long dwelt in his merciless bosom." [16]

The judgment of Mercury is representative of the less enthusiastic type of Noble Savage literature. The Indian can be forgiven his cruelty, since he knows no better; but

---

same type. Bissell, *op. cit.*, pp. 130-133, describes *Art and Nature* (1738), an imitation of *Arlequin*, and refers to two other English adaptations of Drevetière's play.

[16] The idea of introducing a savage into Lucianic imitations was probably suggested to Lyttelton by Fontenelle's dialogue between Cortez and Montezuma. (*Nouveaux Dialogues des Morts,* Part II, Section iii, Dialogue 6.)

the European, who knows the right and chooses the wrong, is to be condemned.

The reader may wonder where the line is to be drawn between the satirical Noble Savage and the genuinely romantic Noble Savage. The distinction is not easy to explain, though it may become clearer as we progress. In the 1790's, we find Bage, a writer of undoubted romantic tendencies, treating the Indian in a manner suggestive of Voltaire. Still later, Byron's use of the Noble Savage is partly satirical. But on the whole, the rationalistic satirist uses the savage as a convenient weapon; the romanticist sees him as an embodiment of a creed. Therein lies the essential distinction.

Before passing on to definitely romantic literature we must turn back to Defoe, who occupies an intermediate position between the satirical and the romantic attitudes. In him the stripping down of human nature to its common denominator is entirely sympathetic. Without thinking of *Robinson Crusoe* as a philosophical tract, we may recognize that the adventures of this shipwreck-story are permeated with philosophy. The book shows Man, bare of all unnecessary trappings, building up a virtuous and reasonable life with the hands and the mind and the heart that God gave him. Precisely in being isolated from the rest of mankind, Crusoe discovers the common elements of humanity within himself — a fact which helps to explain the romantic combination of love of solitude with passionate philanthropy.

In Friday is shown a man lower in the scale of civilization than Crusoe. The sympathy and understanding that spring up between the two represent on a small scale the feelings which would bind all men together if they turned inward to their hearts instead of outward to the world.

The care taken by Defoe to distinguish Friday's appearance from that of Negroes and less attractive Indian tribes is worthy of notice. The following passage is distinctly reminiscent of Mrs. Behn's attempt to glorify her black hero: "He was a comely, handsome fellow, perfectly well made, with straight strong limbs, not too large, tall, and well-shaped, and, as I reckon, about twenty-six years of age. He had a very good countenance, not a fierce and surly aspect, but seemed to have something very manly in his face; and yet he had all the sweetness and softness of an European in his countenance, too, especially when he smiled. His hair was long and black, not curled like wool; his forehead very high and large; and a great vivacity and sparkling sharpness in his eyes. The colour of his skin was not quite black, but very tawny, as the Brazilians and Virginians, and other natives of America are, but of a bright kind of a dun olive colour, that had in it something very agreeable, though not very easy to describe. His face was round and plump; his nose small, not flat like the negroes; a very good mouth, thin lips, and his teeth well set, and white as ivory." Defoe was evidently afraid that Friday, unless carefully described, would suggest to the reader's mind a negroid type. Friday's speech, which resembles that used in representations of negro dialect in early American literature, makes it a little hard to remember that he is a Carib.

Carib — the word from which "cannibal" is derived. Crusoe's island, the reader will recall, is a sort of picnic-ground for a neighboring tribe of cannibals; and only the white man's intervention saved Friday from the gluttony of his enemies. Crusoe's own attitude toward cannibalism is disapproving but broad-minded: "It is certain these people . . . do not commit this as a crime; it is not against their own consciences' reproving, or their light reproaching them.   They do not know it to be an offence, and then commit it in defiance of Divine justice, as we do in almost all the crimes we commit.   They think it no more a crime to kill a captive taken in war, than we do to kill an ox; nor to eat human flesh, than we do to eat mutton."   This recognition of relativity in ethics is destined to become the favorite romantic explanation of savage vices.

Friday himself is a cannibal, and Crusoe at first finds great difficulty in persuading his new comrade not to eat the bodies of his enemies.   With surprising quickness, however, Friday abandons his appetite for human flesh. The loathsome habit forms no part of his natural equipment as a man: it is an unnatural social convention to be sloughed off, as Crusoe has sloughed off his, when the pressure of society is released and he can be himself.

For a time Crusoe does not realize Friday's true character, and elaborately guards himself against being murdered by his servant.   " But," he finds, " I needed none of all this precaution; for never man had a more faithful, loving, sincere servant than Friday was to me; without passions, sullenness, or designs, perfectly obliged and engaged; his very affections were tied to me, like those of a child to a father; and I dare say he would have sacrificed his life for the saving mine, upon any occasion whatsoever."

Indeed, the virtues of Friday fill Crusoe with wonder that God should give to ignorant savages " the same powers, the same reason, the same affections, the same sentiments of kindness and obligation, the same passions and resentments of wrongs, the same sense of gratitude, sincerity, fidelity, and all the capacities of doing good, and receiving good, that he has given to us; and that when he pleases to offer them occasions of exerting these, they are as ready, nay, more ready, to apply them to the right uses for which they were bestowed than we are.   And this

made me very melancholy sometimes, in reflecting . . .
how mean a use we make of all these, even though we have
these powers enlightened by the great lamp of instruction,
the Spirit of God, and by the knowledge of His Word
added to our understanding; and why it has pleased God
to hide the like saving knowledge from so many million
souls, who, if I might judge by this savage, would make a
better use of it than we did."

Hoping for rich results when to Friday's natural virtues
should be added the blessings of the Christian faith, Crusoe tries to impart religious instruction to the Indian.   The
details of this attempt must be reserved for a later chapter.
Suffice it to say here that Friday, with artless but searching
questions, strips away the formal husk of creeds which
has almost smothered Crusoe's religion; while Crusoe is
able to rescue Friday from the superstitions of his savage
cult without destroying the true reverence which lies at its
heart.   Restored to nature and to natural faith, man and
master accept with joy the few simple conceptions necessary to a religious life.   " We had the sure guide to heaven,
viz., the Word of God; and we had, blessed be God, comfortable views of the Spirit of God teaching and instructing
us by His Word, leading us all into truth, and making us
both willing and obedient to the instruction of His Word:
and I cannot see the least use that the greatest knowledge
of the disputed points in religion, which have made such
confusion in the world, would have been to us if we could
have obtained it."

Careful readers of Defoe will hesitate to call him a romanticist.   The nature to which Crusoe returns is a nature
of health, temperance, wholesome work, common-sense,
good-will, and Biblical fundamentals.   Later generations,
on stripping man down to his essential equipment, were
to find not only these things, but other things much more

exciting. Crusoe remains unmoved by wild scenery. For him, storms are simply wet and dangerous, hills are to be ascended only in the hope of sighting a passing sail, trees are to be hacked into shelters, and animals are to be classified into edible and inedible. Crusoe's experience " made a man of him " in a sense which Kipling, rather than Wordsworth, would have understood and approved. It made him strong and resourceful, and enabled him to forget a great many silly and unnecessary things. As for Man Friday, he is just a good, honest fellow, with virtues that a modern city-dweller might discover, with foolish surprise, in a guide or farmer. If Oroonoko is the Noble Savage of heroic romance, and the old Houyhnhnm the Noble Savage of misanthropic satire, Friday is the Noble Savage of early eighteenth century " common sense."

Though none of these figures predicts in a wholly satisfactory way what the Noble Savage was to become, each gives a hint of the romantic attitude. The Noble Savage never quite lost the fustian grandeur of Oroonoko; he never lost the satirical sting of the Houyhnhnm; and he never — thank heaven! — lost the quaint wholesomeness of Friday.

Chapter III

EARLY ROMANTICISM

A FTER two chapters of fidgeting on the brink we are ready to plunge into the deep and turbid waters of the Romantic Movement. The term "Early Romanticism" is here applied to those preliminary and often only half-conscious symptoms of romanticism which begin to appear about 1730 and reach full development about 1790. During this period, interest in the literature of past ages, in humble life and in external nature steadily emerge, along with sensibility, subjectivity and the temper of reform. How do writers who manifest these tendencies feel toward the Noble Savage?

If scholars continue to push romanticism further and further back into the eighteenth century, the pseudo-classic period will, to the great embarrassment of literary historians, disappear entirely. Without denying that certain elements connected with the development of romanticism appeared before the publication of *The Seasons*, it seems best to begin our consideration of the new movement with James Thomson. Says Professor Beers: "Thomson's denunciation of the slave trade, and of cruelty to animals . . . ; his preference of country to town; his rhapsodies on domestic love and the innocence of the Golden Age; his contrast between the misery of the poor and the heartless luxury of the rich; all these features of the poem foretoken the sentimentalism of Sterne and Goldsmith, and the humanitarianism of Cowper and Burns. They anticipate, in particular, that half-affected itch of simplicity which titillated the sensibilities of a corrupt and artificial society in the writings of Rousseau, and the idyllic pictures of Bernardin de St. Pierre's *Paul and Virginia*." [1]

After all this, we shall surely expect to unearth a Noble Savage or two; and we shall not be disappointed. After a denunciation of war, for example, occurs the following passage:

> " Not such the sons of Lapland: wisely they
> Despise the insensate, barbarous trade of war;
> They ask no more than simple Nature gives;
> They love their mountains and enjoy their storms.
> No false desires, no pride-created wants,
> Disturb the peaceful current of their time,
>
> . . . .
>
> Thrice happy race! by poverty secured
> From legal plunder and rapacious power,
> In whom fell interest never yet has sown
> The seeds of vice, whose spotless swains ne'er knew
> Injurious deed, nor, blasted by the breath
> Of fruitless love, their blooming daughters woe."

Here the conception of the Noble Savage has been extended to include not only the physically attractive natives of tropic climes, but the ugly, blubbery folk of the bleak northern wastes. Lapland, indeed, becomes a surprisingly popular locality in eighteenth century poetry, at least as far as short flattering allusions are concerned. And the Laplanders' love of their mountains and storms points forward to the union of the cult of the savage with the cult of scenery.

Thomson does not, however, forget the American Indian. In a passage about birds, he speaks of " the gaudy robes they lent proud Montezuma's realm." Later he says of the waters of the river " Oronoque: "

[1] *English Romanticism in the Eighteenth Century*, p. 112.

> " O'er peopled plains they fair-diffusive flow,
> And many a nation feed, and circle safe
> In their soft bosom many a happy isle,
> The seat of blameless Pan, yet undisturbed
> By Christian crimes and Europe's cruel sons."

In the background of this bit of humanitarianism hover the shades of Las Casas, Montaigne, Du Tertre and Aphra Behn. But the dragging in of Pan makes the passage seem conventional and decorative.

In fact, although Thomson toys with the Noble Savage idea, his serious opinions lie in a different direction. An examination of *The Seasons* brings to light enthusiastic praises of philosophy, industry and organized government — three shibboleths of the Enlightenment — together with the most definite repudiation of natural man. The poet declares that without the fruits of reason man would be a mere fur-clad, beast-hunting savage,

> " . . . devoid of every finer art
> And elegance of life."

Primitive man was a wretched and unhappy creature until Industry "roused him from his miserable sloth" and showed him how to curb and guide nature by means of the arts and sciences. The beneficent power of "active government" is embodied in Peter the Great:

> " . . . . He
> His stubborn country tamed — her rocks, her fens,
> Her floods, her seas, her ill-submitting sons;
> And, while the fierce barbarian he subdued,
> To more exalted soul he raised the man."

In such declarations one finds no "rhapsodies . . . on the Golden Age," no "itch of simplicity." These far from primitivistic "big bow-wow" passages probably ex-

press Thomson's true philosophy. Yet though it would
be dangerous to take too seriously his praise of the Lapps
and of other simple folk, he undoubtedly had a certain
emotional affinity for naturalism; and it is interesting to
see him toying with the child of nature in the half-genuine,
half-artificial manner that characterizes his treatment of
nature in general.

Joseph Warton, much more consciously a romanticist
than Thomson, is much more consistently a champion of
the savage. His *Dying Indian* is perhaps the earliest example of a genre which has been studied by Professor
Farley.[2] He appears to have thought of himself as a
bard of nature whose muse was some sylvan spirit, for in
another poem he invokes Fancy as a

> " . . . nymph with loosely-flowing hair,
> With buskin'd leg, and bosom bare,
> Thy waist with myrtle-girdle bound,
> Thy brows with Indian feathers crown'd." [3]

Joseph Warton's chief poem, *The Enthusiast, or The
Lover of Nature,* is a perfect Christmas stocking of romantic ideas. Both its titles, even, are challenges flung
down before the age. It is almost inevitable that in such a
work the Noble Savage should play a part. Here, for instance, is the customary reference to Saturn's reign, reminding us again of Chaucer's " Former Age ":

> " Happy the first of men, ere yet confin'd
> To smoky cities; who in sheltering groves,
> Warm caves, and deep-sunk vallies liv'd and lov'd
> By cares unwounded; what the sun and showers,
> And genial earth untillag'd, could produce,
> They gathered grateful."

[2] *Vide infra,* Chap. XIII.
[3] *Ode to Fancy. English Poets,* Vol. XVIII, p. 163.

This passage is more than mere ornament: we shall not find it contradicted by any long-winded Thomsonian praise of industry.

Warton does not assert that primeval men were entirely serene and blissful. They had, he admits, troubles of their own. But our distresses are worse than theirs, because they are unnatural, and brought upon ourselves by our own corrupted desires:

> " . . . but us,
> Diseaseful dainties, riot, and excess,
> And feverish luxury destroy. In brakes
> And marshes wild unknowingly they cropp'd
> Herbs of malignant juice; to realms remote
> While we for powerful poisons madly roam."

Thus far, the poet has spoken merely of imaginary figures of the Golden Age. But just at the close he makes the natural transition to the American Indian:

> " O, who will bear me then to western climes,
> (Since virtue leaves our wretched land) to fields
> Yet unpolluted with Iberian swords:
> The Isles of Innocence, from mortal view
> Deeply retir'd, beneath a plantane's shade,
> Where Happiness and Quiet sit enthroned,
> With simple Indian swains, that I may hunt
> The boar and tiger through savannahs wild,
> Through fragrant deserts, and through citron groves?
> There, fed on dates and herbs, would I despise
> The far-fetched cates of luxury, and hoards
> Of narrow-hearted avarice; nor heed
> The distant din of the tumultuous world."

America will soothe the wounded feelings of the enthusiast. A wigwam in the citron-groves among living reminders of the Golden Age, far from "the lays of artful Addison," artificial landscape-gardening and urban

vices — such is the Chateaubriandesque dream of this mid-
eighteenth century scholar.   Joseph Warton, to be sure,
seems to have been a comfortable, contented and well-
nourished person whom it is difficult to picture as frater-
nizing with "simple Indian swains" or hunting "the
boar and tiger through savannahs wild."   But are a poet's
dreams less significant than his acts?   This rather important pioneer of the Romantic Movement at least
dreamed of playing Indian.

A still more important precursor of romanticism,
Thomas Gray, expresses in his famous *Elegy* views har-
monizing with the Noble Savage idea.   There is a connection between the rudeness of the "rude forefathers of
the hamlet" and the poet's admiration for them.   Their
lot "circumscribed their growing virtues," but in so doing ensured for them a permanent innocence.   Better oblivion with peace than ambition with misery.

But this poet's connection with our subject is not restricted to the note of retreat which he sounds in common
with many admirers of natural man.   We shall find that
one of the merits of the Noble Savage is his spontaneous
poetic ability.   The researches of scholars like Percy and
Herder became fused with the impostures of MacPherson
and the naturalistic philosophy of Rousseau to form a sort
of bardic legend, in which primitive man is good because
he sings and sings because he is good.   Gray was influential
in the growth of this legend because he not only inves-
tigated primitive poetry but sought in some of his own
works, such as *The Bard*, to reproduce the spirit of that
poetry.   He helped to increase popular interest in the
Noble Savage by making known the nobility of primitive
art.   In the chapter, *Natural Man and Natural Poetry*,
this subject will be discussed more fully.

The opinions of William Collins are elusive, for he avoided self-exposition in his poetry. But evidence provided by his ode, *The Manners*, shows that his ideas on education were such as Rousseau would have approved. He speaks of science as the bride of doubt, and commends instead a direct, clear-eyed observation of nature.

> " O thou who lov'st that ampler range,
> Where life's wide prospects round thee change,
> And with her mingling sons allied,
> Throw'st the prattling page aside,
> To me, in converse sweet, impart
> To read in man the native heart;
> To learn, where science sure is found,
> From nature as she lives around."

This is an idea that was later to be expressed in *Émile*.

If at times this discussion appears to go beyond its legitimate boundaries, it will be because of a desire to show how closely interwoven is the cult of the savage with the general fabric of romanticism. Thus, along with Collins' characteristically romantic feeling against rationalistic pedantry goes an interest in primitive peoples which appears in his *Ode on the Popular Superstitions of the Highlands of Scotland*. He speaks enthusiastically of the natives of Kilda,

> " On whose bleak rocks, which brave the wasting tides,
> Fair nature's daughter, virtue, yet abides.
> Go! just, as they, their blameless manners trace!
> Then to my ear transmit some gentle song,
> Of those whose lives are yet sincere and plain,
> Their bounded walks the rugged cliffs along,
> And all their prospect but the wintry main.
>
> . . . .
>
> Thus, blest in primal innocence, they live
> Sufficed, and happy with that frugal fare
> Which tasteful toil and hourly danger give."

The association of mountains with the freedom and benevolence of those who dwell among them is quite typical.
Observe that the privilege of being regarded as genuinely
Arcadian is here accorded not to Indians, or Lapps, but to
Scotch peasants. The circle of the Noble Savage is widening to include South Sea Islanders and Negroes; and at the
same time narrowing to include indigenous examples of
simplicity.

Goldsmith is here included among the poets because it is
in his verse that he connects himself most closely with our
subject. Not to me alone has the proper placing of this
writer been difficult. Mr. Gosse says of him: " In that
mechanical and dusty age he did not set up to be an in-
novator. We search in vain, in Goldsmith's verse or prose,
for any indication of a consciousness of the coming change.
He was perfectly contented with the classical traditions." [4]
There are few who would not, with varying degrees of
warmth, dispute the accuracy of that statement. But those
who claim Goldsmith for romanticism on the basis of his
mild sentimentality and his sympathy for the lowly err to
an almost equal extent. Goldsmith is hence a border-line
case, and it will be interesting to apply to his work the
touchstone of the Noble Savage.

In the *Deserted Village*, we find a sanguine representation of the simple life. The poem is important in that it
opposes rural innocence not merely to the conventional
urban corruption, but to the great economic changes of the
period — the rise of the factory system and the consequent
breaking up of the village community. Against the all-
powerful forces of the industrial revolution Goldsmith
presents a series of pictures of " sweet Auburn," of those

[4] Garnett and Gosse, *English Literature: an Illustrated Record*,
Vol. III, p. 342.

"dear lovely bowers of innocence and ease" in which his youth was spent. Here the poet sharply contrasts nature and art — of course to the disadvantage of the latter.

> "Yes! let the rich deride, the proud disdain,
> The simple blessings of the lowly train;
> To me more dear, congenial to my heart,
> One native charm, than all the gloss of art."

The baneful influence of commerce is driving from England the "rural virtues," which include "contented toil," "hospitable care," "kind connubial tenderness," "piety," "steady loyalty," and "faithful love." Of these the country has a positive monopoly. Things are very different in the city, where one sees

> ". . . ten thousand baneful arts combined
> To pamper luxury and thin mankind; "

and where pleasure is to be gained only through the misfortune of others.

To be logical, Goldsmith should have regarded America as a land of refuge where the virtues of the emigrant rustics might flourish unhindered. But alas! he does no such thing. Instead, he imagines them as struggling with an environment composed of intolerable heat, tigers, murderous savages and tornadoes. Goldsmith, we are forced to conclude, would have indignantly denied that his peasants were savages at all, much less Noble Savages. And Johnson's mouth-filling conclusion to the poem is as good as a guarantee that the *Deserted Village* is not, after all, a treasonably romantic work.

A passing glance may be directed toward one of Goldsmith's obscure admirers — Miss Susanna Blamire, "the Muse of Cumberland." This very bad poet's *Stoklewath, or The Cumbrian Village* is a laborious imitation of the

Deserted Village. "His long vexations passed," an old soldier returns to the hamlet and relates his experiences. He has been captured by Indians, who treated him well:

> "Tho' different in their manners, yet their heart
> Was equal mine in every better part.
> Brave to a fault, if courage fault can be;
> Kind to their fellows, doubly kind to me."

Their kindness, to be sure, may be accounted for by the fact that the soldier taught them to build houses and cultivate the soil — which shows that Miss Blamire does not preach the gospel of nature in all its purity. At least, however, she feels that benevolent Indians are not out of place in a poem of the *Deserted Village* type.

But let us return to Goldsmith. His prose rather than his poetry will disclose to us his real opinions. To his edition of the *Citizen of the World*, Mr. Gibbs prefixes a note: "The plan of the work . . . does not properly belong to Goldsmith. No doubt 'The Turkish Spy' (1684), Montesquieu's 'Lettres Persanes' (1721), Madame de Grafigny's 'Lettres d'une Péruvienne' (about 1747), D'Argen's 'Lettres Chinoises' (1750), Voltaire's 'Asiatic' in the 'Philosophical Dictionary' (1752) . . . and Horace Walpole's 'Letter from Xo Ho, a Chinese Philosopher at London, to his friend Lien-Chi, at Peking' (1757), some one of these, and particularly, perhaps, the last . . . suggested to our author his plan."[5] To the ideal observers in this *genre* the term "Noble Savage" has frequently, but rather loosely, been applied. The form is really the converse of the Utopian Voyage: a Utopian comes to England, and makes satiric-didactic comments upon what he sees. But this Utopian, though he may be a Noble Savage, is not necessarily one, and before

[5] *Works*, Vol. III, editor's preface.

we apply the title to Goldsmith's stalking-horse we must examine his views.

Letter VII. provides the age-old but at this time especially popular doctrine that " men may be very learned, and yet very miserable; it is easy to be a deep geometrician . . . but very difficult to be a good man." This fling at the Enlightenment, with its half-implied opposition of learning to virtue, is significant.

In Letter VI, which bears the promising caption, " Happiness Lost by Seeking after Refinement," we find our travelling philosopher warning his friend not to cultivate his intellect to the exclusion of the joys of sense. " All our pleasures, though seemingly never so remote from sense, derive their origin from some one of the senses. The most exquisite demonstration in mathematics, . . . if it does not ultimately tend to increase some sensual satisfaction, is delightful only to fools, or to men who have by long habit contracted a false idea of pleasure." This reduction of intellect to sense-impressions seems to derive from Hume.

The reader of Goldsmith, if he uses Mr. Gibbs' edition, is now at the bottom of the page. Half expecting to find a Noble Savage between the sheets, he turns over, and is faced by:

" He who separates sensual and sentimental enjoyments, seeking happiness from mind alone, is in fact as wretched as the naked inhabitant of the forest, who places all happiness in the first. . . . There are two extremes in this respect: the savage who swallows down the draught of pleasure without staying to reflect on his happiness; and the sage, who passeth the cup while he reflects on the conveniences of drinking." Here is a compromise in which natural man receives no more approval than the rationalist. Goldsmith is wise enough to see that the desirability of returning to the instinctive plane of behavior is not proved by the fact that reason can be reduced to terms of sense.

Letter X describes a wretched Siberian tribe; wild, degraded, little better than beasts. In Letter XI the philosopher asks his correspondent: " From such a picture of nature in primeval simplicity . . . are you in love with fatigue and solitude? Rather tell me; has not every kind of life vices peculiarly its own? . . . Am I not better pleased in enjoyment, than in the sullen satisfaction of thinking that I can live without enjoyment? . . . Luxury . . . as it increases our wants, increases our capacity for happiness." Probably this very sensible passage — with so much of Dr. Johnson in it — is a conscious retort upon Rousseau.

Goldsmith's Chinaman, then, is no more a Noble Savage than the ideal observer in G. Lowes Dickinson's *Letters of John Chinaman*. He is a philosopher,[6] and a member of a more enlightened race than the English. He criticizes his hosts not as an unsophisticated child of nature, but as a being of superior intelligence.

The fact that Goldsmith is not powerful or original in speculation makes his mind a battlefield for the tendencies of the time. In the *Deserted Village,* romantic sentiment strives with pseudo-classic technic. The *Vicar of Wakefield* exudes a sensibility just prevented from liquefying by a touch of Johnsonian discipline. The *Citizen of the World* shows a mind veering between Rousseau and his opponents of the encyclopedia group, but finally siding with the latter. Goldsmith is certainly not a romanticist, and quite as certainly not a pseudo-classicist. He exhibits a characteristic paradox of the age in that he espoused

---

[6] The title, indeed, reads *The Citizen of the World, or Letters from a Chinese Philosopher, etc.*

emotionally that which he rejected intellectually. He doubted the power of knowledge to give happiness; he shrank from the roar of commerce. He half believed that the country had a monopoly of virtue and the city a monopoly of vice; he suspected a causal connection between ignorance and virtue. In these respects, he approaches the Noble Savage idea. But all this was in his heart. His mind, though not without some wavering, was on the side of the Enlightenment. Thus he epitomizes a period not quite certain of its own ideals.

James Grainger, a poet known to Goldsmith and Johnson, has left a poem in which he attempts to lend the artless simplicity of the ballad to the sorrows of an Indian maiden. *Bryan and Pereene, a West Indian Ballad* is said to be based on fact. Pereene, "the pride of Indian dames," loves Bryan, a young white sailor. As his returning vessel approaches the shore, he ardently leaps overboard the sooner to reach his Pereene, but is bitten in two by a shark.

Despite this affecting story, we need not ascribe to Grainger any earnest sympathy for savages. Toward black ones, at any rate, his attitude was severely practical. Witness these excerpts from the Argument of Book IV of *The Sugar-Cane:* "Invocation to the Genius of Africa. . . . Negroes when bought should be young and strong. . . . The marks of a sound Negro at a Negro sale. . . . The Minnahs make good tradesmen, but addicted to suicide. The Mundingos, in particular, subject to worms; and the Congas, to dropsical disorders. . . . How salt-water, or new Negroes should be seasoned. . . . Negroes should always be treated with humanity. Praise of freedom. . . . Praise of commerce." Such callous husbandry of human beings was not long to prevail.   Soon even the Negro will qualify as a Noble Savage.

The humanitarian strain, though still restricted to the Indian, is taken up by James Beattie in his *Ode to Peace*. Peace, sings the bard, has fled from England.   Where is she now?   In Siberia?   Description of Siberia.   In Lybia? Description of Lybia.

> " Or does some isle thy parting flight detain,
>   Where roves the Indian through primeval shades,
>   Haunts the pure pleasures of the sylvan reign,
>   And led by reason's light the path of nature treads? "

The connection of reason with nature is symptomatic.

The next stanza tells us that Peace was last seen in Cuba, but left when the cruel Spaniards came.   The allusion is of course to the Virgilian notion that Justice, on the downfall of the Golden Age, was last seen among the innocent tillers of the soil.

In his love of rural life and scenery, his religious fervor and his hatred of slavery, William Cowper, an admirer of Beattie, is associated with romanticism.   What was his attitude toward the Noble Savage?

The *Progress of Error* passes upon the evils of the age a judgment not unlike Rousseau's.   After a bitter tirade against " Petronius " (Chesterfield), Cowper exclaims:

> " Accomplishments have taken virtue's place,
>   And wisdom falls before exterior grace;
>   We slight the precious kernel of the stone,
>   And toil to polish its rough coat alone."

This recalls the first discourse, with its attack upon the veneer of manners.

We are not surprised, therefore, to learn from *The Task* that the works of nature are " superior to, and in some cases inimitable by, art." But in the same book of the same poem Cowper sings " the blessings of civilized life," which is " friendly to virtue." It is hard to be good in London, but easy enough to be good in the parlor at Olney.[7] Cowper has no thought of running off with " simple Indian swains," but he does feel that civilization has reached a point where men are too neglectful of nature's gifts. He wants a life that will have simplicity without brutality, and civilized amenities without civilized corruption.

Cowper does not find in the savage an example of this ideal equilibrium. Witness his attitude toward the South Sea Islands, which in Cowper's day were the subject of great interest. The natives of these " favour'd isles," he says, are not more virtuous than other men. Life is too easy for their good, and their morals become lax. Above all, they are shut off from the sciences and arts of civilized lands. Cowper has so strong a Methodist strain that he cannot reconcile virtue with a life of tropical plenty. No doubt, too, he is shocked by reports of the freedom of Tahitian manners.

But Cowper's pity is moved by one " gentle savage " who was given a glimpse of English life, and then sent back to his " homestall thatch'd with leaves." This man is Omai, a native of the island of Huaheine. Captain Furneaux, Cook's associate on the famous Antarctic expedition, took him aboard the *Adventure* and brought him to London. Omai was by no means a person of prominence at Huaheine, and in Cook's opinion " was not a proper sample of the inhabitants of these happy islands, not having any advantage of birth, or acquired rank; nor

[7] *The Task*, Argument of Book I.

being eminent in shape, figure or complexion." The circumnavigator, however, later confesses his error. "Omai has most certainly a very good understanding, quick parts, and honest principles; he has a natural good behaviour, which rendered him acceptable to the best company, and a proper degree of pride, which taught him to avoid the society of persons of inferior rank. He has passions of the same kind as other young men, but has judgment enough not to indulge them in an improper excess." [8] In London, Omai attracted much favorable attention. Even Dr. Johnson, that resolute hater of the Noble Savage, "was struck with the elegance of his behavior, and accounted for it thus: 'Sir, he had passed all his time, while in England, only in the best of company; so that all that he had acquired of our manners was genteel'" — which, considering Ursa Major's own manners, is amusing.

In Cowper's view, however, we have drawn Omai forth from his " native bow'rs " only to show him

> " With what superior skill we can abuse
>   The gifts of Providence, and squander life."

Now that Omai has returned to his " cocoas and bananas," the poet asks,

> " . . . are thy simple friends,
>   Thy simple fare, and all thy plain delights,
>   As dear to thee as once? "

We have spoiled Omai by giving him a demoralizing taste of a life which is no part of his inheritance. But if all we can show a savage is how to " abuse the gifts of Providence," why are the South Sea Islanders to be pitied for their ignorance?

[8] *Voyage Towards the South Pole*, Vol. I, pp. 169-170.

Omai's name, by the way, figures on the title-page of two anonymous publications of the period. *An Heroic Epistle from Omiah to the Queen of Otaheite* (1775) is a conventional satire of what might be called the " savage observer " type. Omai, or Omiah, is disgusted by what he has seen.

> " Can *Europe* boast, with all her pilfer'd wealth
> A larger share of happiness, or health?
> What then avail her thousand arts to gain
> The stores of every land, and every main:
> Whilst we, whom love's more grateful joys enthral,
> Profess one art — to live without them all."

That Omai did not find even England lacking in " love's more grateful joys " is suggested by *Omiah's Farewell; Inscribed to the Ladies of London* (1776.) " The novelty of his figure," says the anonymous author, " drew much attention upon him, and more particularly from the women of quality, for with many of them he was intimate and familiar. Is it not cruel that such generous politeness to a stranger should have such illiberal insinuations put upon it. . . . I have a higher opinion of my fair country-women, than to think they would be so condescending, and yet philosophy cannot reconcile the depravity of female inclinations." In the venomous poem which follows, Omiah thanks asterisked noblewomen for their favors.[9]

The actual facts of Omai's homecoming are not unin-structive. Cook, on his third and last voyage (1776–

---

[9] This satire has an analogue in *A New Humorous Song on the Cherokee Chiefs*. This broadside ballad was written by H. Howard on the occasion of a visit of some Cherokees to London in 1765. Two of the few printable lines are:

> " Wives, Widows and Matrons, and pert little Misses,
> Are pressing and squeezing for Cherokee kisses."

1779), restored the man to his island home. Omai was delighted to return. He was fairly loaded with treasures, consisting largely of precious red feathers, by means of which he expected despite his low caste to gain entrance into the best society of the Society Islands.[10] But the leaders of his people, while accepting the feathers, rejected the man. "I own, I never expected it would be otherwise," [11] says Cook. "He associated with none but vagabonds and strangers, whose sole views were to plunder him." The chiefs disliked him all the more because they found that "they could not procure, from any one in the ships, such valuable presents as Omai bestowed on the lowest of the people, his companions." [12] The primitivist may rejoice in the fact that the South Sea Islanders will not respect a man merely because he has plenty of red feathers. One must regret, however, that children of nature should draw such rigid social lines.

If in Cowper's time the missionaries had established themselves firmly in the South Seas, the poet would have been more enthusiastic. The work of the Moravian missionaries in Greenland excites his admiration. The Greenlanders, he says, live in an intensely uncomfortable region,

> " — Yet Truth is yours, remote, unenvied isle!
> And Peace, the genuine offspring of her smile;
> The pride of letter'd Ignorance, that binds
> In chains of errour our accomplish'd minds,
> That decks, with all the splendour of the true,
> A false religion, is unknown to you."

Cowper's admiration, however, is not for the natives of Greenland, but for the pure religion which the Moravians have brought them. As for the Greenlanders,

[10] Cook, *Voyage to the Pacific Ocean*, Vol. I, p. 6.
[11] *Ibid.*, Vol. II, p. 9.   [12] *Ibid.*, pp. 22-23.

" They were, what base Credulity believes
True Christians are, dissemblers, drunkards, thieves.

.   .   .   .

What are they now? — Morality may spare
Her grave concern, her kind suspicions there:
The wretch, who once sang wildly, danc'd and laugh'd,
And suck'd in dizzy madness with his draught,
Has wept a silent flood, revers'd his ways,
Is sober, meek, benevolent, and prays,

.   .   .   .

Abhors the craft he boasted of before,
And he that stole has learned to steal no more." [13]

Cowper certainly has no desire to fly to some solitary spot, there to be a Noble Savage himself. In this respect the Alexander Selkirk verses are about as primitivistic as Lady Mary Wortley Montagu. This poet inclined toward romanticism. His condemnation of urban society and his sympathy for Omai would seem to place him on the side of natural man. His piety, however, made him feel that despite our sins we are better than those who have never heard the word of God.

The foregoing notes, by no means intended to be exhaustive, may suffice to show that several of those poets who are regarded as precursors of the Romantic Movement refer favorably to the Noble Savage, though just as we cannot call them thorough-going romanticists, so we cannot call them thorough-going partisans of primitive man. Poems devoted entirely to the savage or to some aspect of his life, however, are not common, and very few of them are the work of important writers. In Chapter VI of his dissertation, Dr. Bissell has described or mentioned a number of such poems. It is worthy of note that the Aztecs and Incas who, as we shall see, continue to be

[13] *Hope*, ll. 459 ff.

fairly popular dramatic figures, receive some attention from the poets. An example of this type is Edward Jerningham's *Fall of Mexico* (1775), which deals, of course, with the adventures of Cortez. Las Casas appears, and helps to express the writer's sympathy with the oppressed Indians.[14]

In 1784, Helen Maria Williams, later to become prominent in Jacobin circles, published *Peru,* an epic poem in six cantos. It covers the familiar Pizarro-Ataliba matter, but does so from a more than usually naturalistic viewpoint. Here the Spaniards are not merely greedy, cruel, and fanatical: they are the enemies of Nature. Peru appears as a sort of Arcadia, where

> " The Virtues rose, unsullied, and sublime.
> There, tender Charity, with ardor warm,
> Spread her wide mantle o'er the shiv'ring form,
> Chear'd with the festal Song her lib'ral toils,
> While in the lap of Age she pour'd the spoils.
> Simplicity in each low Vale was found,
> The meek nymph smiled with Reeds and Rushes crown'd:
> And Innocence, in light, transparent Vest,
> Mild Visitant! the gentle Region blest."

This passage follows a fanciful description of Peruvian scenery, the implication being that the virtues of the land are in accord with its beauty.

Ataliba is no longer an Almanzor or even an Oroonoko:

> " In Ataliba's pure, unsullied mind
> Each mental Grace, each lib'ral Virtue shin'd,
> And all uncultur'd by the toils of Art,
> Bloomed the dear genuine offspring of the heart " —

his love for Alzira. With Helen Williams, in short, the Noble Barbarian definitely becomes a Noble Savage of a rather soft and sentimental kind.

[14] For a fuller account of this poem, *cf.* Bissell, *op. cit.,* pp. 167-169.

The idea that the Indian was by nature a poet and orator gave rise to a number of love songs, death songs and versified orations in which the savage was made to speak for himself. Consideration of these, however, will be deferred until the chapter on *Natural Man and Natural Poetry.*

Several eighteenth century dramas are so aptly illustrative of the development of our subject that they demand attention here. In the preface to his tragedy *Alzuma,* Arthur Murphy states that he knows of no plays on Indian themes between Dryden's and his own, which was written in 1762 but not performed until 1773. Murphy has forgotten or is ignorant of Dennis' *Liberty Asserted,* performed and published in 1704. Bissell, also, has shown that a tragedy by Francis Hawling called *The Indian Emperor* was acted in 1728, but not published.[15] Gay's *Polly* was written in the same year, but not produced until 1777. In 1738, *Art and Nature,* an imitation of Drevetière's *Arlequin Sauvage,* appeared on the stage. Its satire of artificial civilization, though pungent, is far from serious. As in the French original, a young savage brought from America passes amusing comments upon the folly of what he sees in the corrupt Old World.[16]

Murphy's intention — to return to *Alzuma* — was at first to adapt *Alzire,* Voltaire's Peruvian drama, but he decided to strike out for himself. The result is an heroic play of the vaguely exotic type which was dealt with in the preceding chapter. A slight increase of naturalistic feeling, however, is noticeable. The prologue, for example, reminds us that Columbus on reaching the western shores found

[15] *Op. cit.,* p. 127.
[16] For a more detailed account of this play, *cf.* Bissell, *op. cit.,* pp. 130-133.

> " A race of men unletter'd, and untaught,
> Strangers to science, yet with virtue fraught.
> No school had they of philosophic pride,
> And simple reason was their only guide.
> That reason in the paths of nature trod,
> And worshipping the Sun, they meant a God;
> Free from the ills in polish'd life that spring,
> And gold with them was a neglected thing."

The opposition of virtue and philosophy, the praise of
" simple " reason, and the scorn of gold are by now exceedingly familiar.

The promise held forth in the prologue, except for
some talk about savage liberty and Christian oppression, is
hardly fulfilled by the play itself. And yet there are a
few symptoms of the newer attitude. Orellana, the heroine, is a very cultivated and eloquent princess; and Alzuma, the hero, makes Oroonoko seem positively primitive.
Yet Orellana astonishingly says to Pizarro:

> " Pardon, Sir,
> If the rough manners of my native clime
> Form'd me in plain simplicity — unskill'd
> In all the studied elegance of feature,
> I only know to look my honest meaning."

And in the crucial scene Alzuma blazes out at the oppressor with

> " And dar'st thou, homicide, alledge the laws?
> The laws of Spain — know there's a prior law,
> To which weak mortals are not train'd, but born;
> Not form'd by science, but endow'd by instinct,
> Great nature's law! — that best, that surest guide."

Hence, though Murphy is working in a conventional *genre*,
he does make some attempt to endow his Peruvians with

the blessings of nature. Instinct *versus* science seems to be the aspect of the subject that most interested him.

Henry Brooke, disciple of the mystic William Law, defender of enthusiasm, and author of *The Fool of Quality*, is a man of some importance in the early history of romanticism, but his Aztec tragedy *Montezuma* [17] is not of much help to us. In the opening scene, Vasquez complains:

> " By science unrefined, this world is laid
> In nature's simple lap. Mechanic arts
> Hold no republic here; but all is wild
> And savage, as the soil."

" Nature's simple lap " is a verbal reminiscence of Montaigne's essay *Of Coaches*. [18]
Cortez replies:

> ". . . Savage and wild
> Are terms we give to fashions not our own.
> Better, perhaps, that man had yet been left
> To the rude dictates of his native virtue;
> Than to be wrought and polished into vice
> By arts too much refined."

Now this colloquy, especially the speech of Cortez, is taken almost verbatim from Dryden's *Indian Emperour*. [19] Comparison, however, will show that Brooke makes Cortez' reproof slightly more emphatic.

After this, we plunge into the old heroic intrigues and battles. Both Aztecs and Spaniards, barring a sprinkling of villains, are made incredibly noble. They are forever rescuing each other or handing back each other's swords.

[17] Published 1778. I find no record of its having been performed. The play follows Dryden's *Indian Emperour* rather closely.

[18] *Vide supra*, p. 20.

[19] *Vide supra*, p. 30.

But just at the close, Brooke remembers his naturalistic
moral and stresses it very firmly.　On Montezuma's death,
Cortez generously suggests that Guyomar, the dead king's
son, shall rule Mexico.　The Aztec prince's reply is that
he has no desire

> " . . . to be versed
> In sciences that teach us to destroy,
> And arts that serve to vitiate and corrupt
> The honesty of nature. — Far from hence
> I, with my willing exiles, will retire;
> While my loved Alibech shall light our way,
> And bless our steps with beauty — there, nor gems,
> Nor gold, nor silver, shall excite the lust
> Of fell invasion; nor insatiate Spain
> E'er come, in search of poverty! — Know, Cortez,
> Where wants are few, a little will suffice
> To furnish nature; and a light content
> Shall make it luxury! "

Thus ends a play which, save for its opening and conclusion, does nothing to advance the cause of nature.

From the fustian grandeur of these Incas and Aztecs,
one turns with relief to a play which, whatever its short-
comings, is not quite like anything else in English literature
— George Colman the Younger's *Inkle and Yarico*, produced and published in 1787.　Because of its incidental
songs, the piece is called an opera, but in reality it is a
farce of sensibility, combining broadly humorous appeal
with a determined and not wholly unsuccessful assault
upon the heartstrings.

Inkle, a young merchant already grown hard and dry
beneath the discipline of Threadneedle Street, sets sail
for the Barbadoes to marry Narcissa, the daughter of
Governor Sir Christopher Curry.　With his comic servant
Trudge, he lands at a vaguely delineated " American

forest " on a foraging party. The crew, pursued by the cannibal natives, make off, leaving Inkle and Trudge alone in the wilds.

Colman's ideas about the natives of this region are not very clear. They are referred to as " Indians," but also as " blacks." Trudge sees three of them " all dancing about in black buff; just like Adam in mourning." Later he describes Yarico as " of a good comely copper . . . quite dark, but very elegant; like a Wedgewood teapot." Although Yarico is termed " a Hotty-pot gentlewoman " by Narcissa's maid, she is of lighter hue than her attendant Wowski, who is definitely black. Both Yarico and Wowski have learned English from a castaway who was subsequently eaten. Yarico speaks correctly except for the occasional omission of a definite article. Wowski's English is decidedly broken; her misunderstanding of long words suggests that Colman thinks of her as a negress. Thus at the end of the play, when Trudge is taken into Governor Curry's service, we find:

" *Trudge:* Wows, you'll be Lady, you jade, to a Governor's Factotum.
" *Wowski:* Yes — I Lady Jacktotum."

That is hardly the speech of an Indian. But George Colman recked little of such refinements.

During this anthropological excursus, Inkle and Trudge have been roaming about, expecting every moment that they will be captured, eaten, and, as Trudge puts it, " stuff'd for a couple of white wonders." At last they come upon Yarico and Wowski. Inkle finds Yarico " wild and beautiful," and Trudge finds Wowski " a nice little plump bit." With the ingenuous savages, it is love at first sight. Yarico vows to protect Inkle from her tribe; Inkle swears that they shall never part.

We are not shown a glimpse of their life in the woods, but Yarico later sings a song reminding her faithless lover of those happy days:

> " Our grotto was the sweetest place!
>   The bending bows, with fragrance blowing,
> Would check the brook's impetuous pace,
>   Which murmur'd to be stopt from flowing.
> 'Twas there we met, and gaz'd our fill;
>   Ah! think on this, and love me still."

When the curtain rises on Act II, the two pairs of lovers, picked up by another ship, have reached Barbadoes. At once the pressure of civilization begins to be felt. Inkle and Trudge are urged to sell as slaves their woodland brides. Here Colman introduces a touch perfectly characteristic of the age of sensibility. Trudge, who hitherto has figured only as a buffoon, proves that he has a heart of gold. Wowski — or " Wows," as he playfully calls her — has atrocious table-manners. She is also so ignorant as not to know the meaning of the word " gratitude," a fact which makes her husband declare, " Ha! this it is now to live without education; the poor devils of her country are all in the practice of gratitude without finding out what it means; while we can tell the meaning of it, with little or no practice at all. — Lord, Lord, what a fine advantage Christian learning is! " But Trudge does himself an injustice: he at least is willing to embody in action his knowledge of the meaning of gratitude. Indignantly he refuses to sell Wows — " my poor, dear, dingy wife! " The planter who proposes the sale may scoff and say that Trudge, the lover of a black, is " not fit to live among us Christians! " The buffoon has a different conception of Christianity. " Plague on't; there it is. I shall be laughed out of my honesty here. — But you may be jogging, friend! I may feel a little queer, perhaps, at shewing her face — but dam'me, if ever I do anything to make me asham'd of shewing my own." Laughter and tears from the audience!

Inkle's reaction is very different. His return to civilization has restored the cool, calculating prudence of Thread-needle Street. It is clearly to his interest to get rid of Yarico, and anything that is to his interest can somehow be justified. After a little virtuous hesitation, he decides to sell the woman who has saved his life.

Poor Yarico cannot believe that Inkle's love is dead. She feels that if she can only get him into the woods again, all will be well. " Come, come, let's go," she pleads. " I always fear'd these cities. Let's fly, and seek the woods; and there we'll wander hand in hand together. No cares will vex us then — we'll let the day glide by in idleness; and you shall sit in the shade, and watch the sun-beam playing on the brook, while I will sing the song that pleases you. . . . In the fresh early morning you shall hunt down our game, and I will pick you berries — and then, at night, I'll trim our bed of leaves, and lie me down in peace — Oh! we shall be so happy! "

But to Inkle this is merely " the trifling of an unen-lightened Indian. Hear me, Yarico," he continues with rather labored unconscious irony. " My country-men and your's differ as much in minds as in complexions. We were not born to live in woods and caves — to seek sub-sistence by pursuing beasts. We Christians, girl, hunt money, a thing unknown to you. But here, 'tis money which brings us ease, plenty . . . and of course happiness. You are the bar to my attaining this." In the literature of the Noble Savage, civilized man often exposes his vile-ness in this naïve fashion.

Thanks to complications which do not concern us, it

happens that the man to whom Inkle is trying to sell Yarico
is none other than Sir Christopher Curry, Governor of
Barbadoes and Inkle's prospective father-in-law.   When
he has heard enough, he denounces the merchant's ingratitude.   Inkle — the play must end somehow — immediately repents, and takes Yarico to his bosom.   Narcissa has obligingly married someone else.   Trudge is
lauded for his constancy.   All forgive, weep, laugh, and
join in the concluding song.

Inkle and Yarico deserves the space which has been
granted it.   If the Noble Savage idea has in no previous
play been treated with such farcical humor, in no previous
play has it been treated with such earnestness.   The intimate fusion of the Noble Savage with the cult of sensibility
is for us decidedly important.   Colman, too, is up-to-date
in selecting the type of civilization to be attacked — not
the gay immorality of courts, but the sordid prudence of
Threadneedle Street.   The popularity of the play is easy
to understand.   Certainly Yarico is worth a dozen Peruvian
princesses.

The plot of *Inkle and Yarico* was not invented by Colman.   It is simply the most popular of a number of tales
dealing with the love of a white man for a savage woman.[20]
The source is Richard Ligon's *True and Exact History
of the Island of Barbadoes* (1657.)   Ligon tells of an Indian slave named Yarico, who was employed as house-
servant at the plantation where he was entertained during
his stay.   She " was of excellent shape and color, for it was
a pure bright bay; . . . this woman would not be woo'd
by any means to wear Cloaths."   On one occasion she
leaves the house, goes to a nearby stream, gives birth to a
healthy infant, washes it in the stream, returns to the house
and resumes her duties almost immediately.   Ten years

[20] *Cf.* Bissell, *op. cit.*, pp. 138-139.

before, this woman was cruelly used by an unnamed white man who had been left defenseless on her native island. " But the youth, when he came ashoar in the Barbadoes, forgot the kindnesse of the poor maid, that had ventured her life for his safety, and sold her for a slave, who was as free born as he. And so poor Yarico for her love, lost her liberty." Now one of her duties is to remove chiggers from the feet of Richard Ligon.

Steele next takes up the theme in the eleventh number of *Spectator*. The story as he knows it is considerably more circumstantial than Ligon's version. Inkle's name is given. His cruelty is ascribed in part to his father, who had trained him to be cold and prudent. Two harrowing details are added. First, Yarico herself signals the ship which by rescuing Inkle dooms her to slavery. Second, Inkle, on being told that Yarico is with child by him, simply raises the price he had put upon her. Neither of these touches is employed by Colman.

Upon Steele's account is based *The Story of Inkle and Yarico, a most moving Tale from the Spectator, Attempted in Verse by the Right Hon. the Countess of* . . . (1738.) The identity of the noble author is unknown. Appended to the narrative is *An Epistle from Yarrico* [*sic*] *to Inkle, After he had left her in Slavery*. Here the Indian slave is made to emulate Pope's Eloisa. She still loves Inkle; his ingratitude hurts her more than slavery. Her despair at being sold caused the death of her baby — a new touch. A priest has told her that good people go to heaven, and bad ones to hell.

> " Think, if this sad conjecture should be true,
> Dear faithless youth, oh think, what wilt thou do! "

Bissell shows that poetical versions of the story, and epistles from Yarico to Inkle, appear at intervals throughout the eighteenth century, and even extend into the nine-teenth.[21]   The incident figures in English drama as early as 1742; and in 1792 [22] Colman's work was imitated in a play called *The American Heroine*.

Steele's *Spectator* story was translated into German verse by Gellert.   Gellert's poem in turn was translated into French by de Riveri and later by Sedaine.   Poetical expansions and continuations of Steele's version were written in German by Bodmer and Gessner.   It is interest-ing to observe that three important figures of early Ger-man romanticism are connected with the story.   A French dramatic version is Chamfort's *Jeune Indienne* (1764.)

The history of the theme subsequent to the appearance of Colman's play in 1787 is not, for us, important.   As a curiosity, a German opera, *Inkle und Yariko: oder, Er war nicht ganz Barbar* (1798) is worth mentioning.   It deals with the return of Inkle to Yariko's forgiving arms. Yariko is provided with a father of the sententious-old-sachem type.   His name is Kaliko.

Dr. Bissell describes a number of Indian plays which appeared during the closing decade of the century, and the reader may safely be consigned to his guidance.[23]   Largely due to the influence of Marmontel's *Incas*, the Peruvian tradition flourished with increased vigor.   The most im-portant example of this type is Sheridan's *Pizarro* — a very popular adaptation of Kotzebue's *Die Spanier in Peru*.

The North American Indian attracts less attention from the dramatists.   In such pieces as O'Keefe's *The Basket Maker* and the anonymous *Catawba Travellers*, the Indian is employed for comic purposes; and to *The Cherokee* he

---

[21] *Op. cit.*, p. 198.

[22] *Op. cit.*, pp. 139-140.

[23] *Op. cit.*, pp. 140-162.   I am indebted to Bissell for most of the following remarks on the drama.

merely adds a superficial picturesqueness. But in *The Indians,* attributed to Professor Richardson of Glasgow, one finds a curious mixture of realism and idealization. On the whole the natives are portrayed as cruel and bloodthirsty, but the wise old sachem Onothio is a Noble Savage if ever there was one. Bissell aptly compares him to Chateaubriand's Chactas. In this work, then, appears an interesting conflict between the actual Indian and the Indian as an embodiment of the conception of natural man.

No such conflict appears in James Bacon's *The American Indians; or the Virtues of Nature.* The play represents love among the Indians as a passion heroic, pure, chivalrous and free; and the contrast between such love and European courtship is persistently stressed. The moral atmosphere is that of Goethe's *Stella* transported to the wilderness, for the heroic chieftain Ouabi is quite willing to turn his wife over to the white man whom she has grown to love. Bacon's drama is based upon an American poem of which Bissell gives an account.[24]

Not unrelated to dramatic representations of the savage are the rather numerous eighteenth century plays, such as Mrs. Inchbald's *Child of Nature,* in which simple-hearted and sophisticated characters are contrasted. Belcour, the significantly named hero of Cumberland's *West Indian,* is English by birth, but he has a tropical soul. When his father summons him to England in order to observe his character, the young man brings a breath of fresh air into a decadent atmosphere, and plays a part very like that of the savage observer of civilized corruptions. Further consideration of this subject would carry us too far afield, but it is evident that the sentimental appeal from civilization to nature had become general in eighteenth century drama.

[24] *Op. cit.,* pp. 207-211.

The great novelists of the eighteenth century contribute little to the history of our subject. At Goldsmith we have already glanced.   The influence of Richardson upon Rousseau is well known, but the conception of natural man was no part of it.   Richardson quite powerfully fostered the doctrine that stupidity and virtue, intelligence and vice, are allied.   Apart from this, his Noble Savagery is nil.

Fielding relates somewhat more closely to our theme. That postilion — later transported for robbing a hen-roost — who gives his coat to the naked and shivering Joseph Andrews has a natural benevolence which the elegant passengers of the coach have lost.   Is not Joseph Andrews himself a monument of ignorant innocence?   And granting that Joseph is a mere parody — though he soon becomes more than that — what shall we say of Tom Jones?   Surely here is a natural man, leading the life of instinct in a world of pedantry, hypocrisy, greed and oppression.   But Tom Jones falls far short of being a Noble Savage in that his portrait is a true one.   Fielding reacted so strongly against the artificiality of his day that he sometimes appears as the champion of nature.   His nature, however, is real human nature, and not an ideal state.   Hatred of cant occasionally betrays Fielding into a cant of his own, but in the main his reaction is thoroughly healthy. Not many police magistrates have believed in the Noble Savage.

One of the episodes of Smollett's *Humphrey Clinker* uses the familiar Indian-captivity theme.   Lismahago and Murphy are captured by the savages and fiendishly tortured.   Murphy dies at the stake, but Lismahago survives the ordeal and lives happily with a squaw for two years. When she dies from a surfeit of raw bear, he returns to England.   In making him relate his adventures, the author puts into his mouth some broad flings at European manners and religion. Smollett's frank animalism leaves no room for the sentimental sort of primitivism. The Indian merely gives him a new field for realistic narrative and for satire.

In the works of Sterne the Noble Savage does not appear, but this writer's character was profoundly sympathetic with emotional naturalism. He preaches the nature cult in its extremest form. He distrusts intellect, and adores sensibility. That he presents us with no example of the figure we are studying is a circumstance dictated merely by his choice of subjects. In the *Sentimental Journey*, indeed, are some French peasants who closely approach the type. One evening Sterne reaches a farm in Anjou, and is welcomed to a feast of bread, wine, and lentil soup. After supper the youths and girls dance with innocent abandon, yet with a curious reverence, their eyes raised heavenward. The old farmer explains that in this manner they render praise to God, since " a cheerful and contented mind was the best sort of thanks to heaven that an illiterate peasant can pay." Happy poverty, virtuous illiteracy, natural love, natural religion — here are some of the blessings of natural man. Certainly the spirit of Sterne powerfully supports the Noble Savage idea. In Mackenzie, the Noble Savage himself enters upon the scene which Sterne has set.

Mackenzie's spirit is akin to Sterne's except that his sensibility is of a more earnest and moralizing strain. Hence we find in his Indian an exquisitely sensitive creature whose passions are regulated by a natural sense of fitness, a being at once intensely emotional and magnificently controlled.

In the *Man of Feeling*, a discharged soldier tells of an old Indian who is taken prisoner by the whites, and shamefully abused. The soldier permits the savage to escape, and is himself court-martialed and imprisoned for neglect of duty. He in turn breaks jail, to be found in the woods and cared for by the same Indian. When they part, the redman embraces him. " You are an Englishman, said he, but the Great Spirit has given you an Indian heart; may he bear up the weight of your old age, and blunt the arrow that brings it rest! " What feeling is here, and what dignity! Mackenzie has caught the cadences — not unlike Ossian — of what passes in English literature for Indian oratory.

This is but a minor incident in Mackenzie's best-known work. In the *Man of the World*, the Indian figures much more prominently. When young Annesley goes up to the university, his father counsels him against too much learning: " The peasant who enjoys the beauty of the tulip is equally delighted with the philosopher, though he knows not the powers of the rays from which its colors are derived." This, of course, is Hume's identification of satisfaction and happiness. The boy, despite this sage advice, goes straight to the dogs, and is forced to flee to America. Toward the close of the book he appears, as the conventional eighteenth century " Stranger," to tell the story of his wanderings.

While a soldier in the colonies, he is captured by the Indians. They torture him, but are so much impressed by his fortitude that they spare his life. " He only is worthy to lift the hatchet of the Cherokees, to whom shame is more intolerable than the stab of the knife, or the burning of the fire," says the venerable chief to whose hut he is assigned.

One may well ask whether the cruelty of the Indians does not conflict with Mackenzie's conception of their virtues. Certainly the two are hardly compatible. But the

Indian appeals to both the Wertheristic and Götzistic aspects of romanticism. He is at once innocent and barbarous, gentle and violent. He is a little like Karl Moor of Schiller's *Die Räuber*, forever committing crimes with the loftiest motives. One is to suppose that he never burns at the stake a captive of genuine sensibility. He who has " an Indian heart " need have no fear of the Indian. And of course the faults of the savage are not natural vices, but the product of European oppression. Thus regarded, the Indian furnishes not only arguments for the primitivist, but thrills for the connoisseur of terror. At one moment he brings tears to the eyes; at the next he makes the flesh creep.

Young Annesley lives with the Indians for several years. Nothing, he declares, could have tempted him to leave his guardian. " When we consider the perfect freedom subsisting in this rude and simple state of society, where rule is only acknowledged for the purpose of immediate utility to those who obey . . . ; where greatness cannot use oppression, nor wealth excite envy; where the desires are native to the heart, and the languor of satiety is unknown; where, if there is no refined sensation of delight, there is also no ideal source of calamity; we shall the less wonder at the inhabitants feeling no regret for the want of those delicate pleasures of which a more polished people is possessed." Annesley declares that his case is no exception. Many other Europeans have found peace in the wilderness.

But eventually the old chief dies, and the wanderer feels that he should go back to his father. When he departs, the tribesmen deliver one of those little lectures on European vices for which the Noble Savage is constantly prepared: " You return to a people who sell affection for money; take therefore with you some of the commodities which their traders value. Strength, agility and fortitude, are sufficient to us; but with them they are of little use. . . . Take as many beaver-skins as you can carry on your journey." Observe the possibly intentional similarity of the closing sentence to the " prayer of Socrates." Mackenzie has caught the trick of making the savages aggressively despise the Europeans. The haughty arrogance of the real Indian is cleverly used as a vehicle for the author's message.

There is an impressive moment when young Annesley pauses at the edge of a frontier settlement to gaze back upon the wilderness in which he has been so happy. He cannot help feeling some elation at the prospect of re-joining people of his own race. And yet his " imagination drew, on this side, fraud, hypocrisy and sordid baseness, while on that seemed to preside honesty, truth and savage nobleness of soul." He sheds a few natural tears, and takes his solitary way from Eden.

Mackenzie assuredly provides us with the most satis-factory Noble Savages encountered up to this point in our study. He draws the Indian with a good deal of realism. Having read deeply in the travelers, he is able to describe such customs as the torture of prisoners, scalping, the war dance and the pipe of peace. His redmen speak in that imaginative, pregnant, compressedly aphoristic way which later writers have taught us to think typical. They are en-dowed with that stateliness, that quiet fortitude, that in-tense passion controlled by innate goodness, which belong to the Indian of legend. And this figure, full in itself of romantic appeal, Mackenzie has suffused with the light of romantic philosophy. The Indian is — always with res-ervations — Rousseau's man of nature, he is Sterne's man of sensibility, he is Mackenzie's own Man of Feeling, op-posed through all the ages to the Man of the World.

Young Annesley, burying himself in the wilderness, has fulfilled the dream of Joseph Warton. His sojourn in the hut of the wise old chief symbolizes the romantic return to nature.

The Noble Savage figures in several minor novels of the period. Of these a careful survey may be found in Dr. Bissell's study,[25] and to analyze them here would be a work of supererogation. I shall, however, draw from Bissell facts tending to show that the portrayal of the Noble Savage in fiction gains in philosophical significance as the century progresses. Thus in *The Voyages of Captain Richard Falconer* (1720), the Indian does nothing but add a thrill to some of the hero's adventures. *The History of the Life and Adventures of Mr. Anderson* (1754), however, uses the Indian not only as a source of excitement and of exotic atmosphere, but as a morally impressive character. The savage Calcathony is represented as a true lover, a loyal friend, and an heroic and chivalrous warrior. The fact that his enemies are French enables the British author to contrast Indian virtues and European vices with particular relish.

John Shebbeare's *Lydia* (1755) carries sentimental primitivism even further. Cannassatego and his beloved — appropriately named Yarico — are idealized out of all relation to humanity, and their goodness is ascribed to the fact that they are ruled only by the laws of nature. The white invaders, on the other hand, have been ruined by the greed of gold. Cannassatego, however, thinks that the Englishmen whom he has seen in America must be only the outcasts of their race, and sails to England in order to lay the wrongs of his tribe before King George. What he sees in London, and his scornful resistance of all attempts

[25] *Op cit.*, Chap. IV.

to make him forget the lessons of the forest, can readily be imagined.

The favorable representation of the savage in *Chrysal: the Adventures of a Guinea* (1760–1765), though less highly colored than in *Lydia,* is all the more impressive in that it has some foundation in fact. Sir William Johnson, of course an historical character who is noted for his influence over the Mohawks, figures in the book. He declares that in the truly essential virtues the Indians stand higher than the English. The author of *Chrysal,* who is probably Charles Johnstone, makes broadly humorous use of Johnson's seignorial relations with the Indian women, but leaves one with the impression that the redskins are very human and likable people.

In *The Adventures of Emmera* (1767), the Noble Savage is definitely associated with naturalistic theories which suggest those of Rousseau. Emmera, the heroine, is reared in the wilderness near Lake Erie. Her father, a man with a past, detests the civilization from which he has fled, and hopes to form a community in which men can live according to the dictates of nature. One thinks of pantisocracy. But the father dies, and is forced to commit his daughter to the care of one Chetwyn, an English rascal of quality. Chetwyn tries to win the girl by a recital of the joys of civilized life, but Emmera — like a true Houyhnhnm — shrinks in horror from his account of European complexities. Colonel Forrester, an enemy of Chetwyn's, kidnaps her, but the redmen rescue her from her white seducer. Eventually, however, the heroine goes with Chetwyn to England, only to be horrified by the greed, cruelty and injustice which surround her. The upshot of the matter is that Emmera and the reformed Chetwyn return to America, there to dwell happily and innocently in the wilds, with only the good Indians for company.

Mrs. Frances Brooke's *Emily Montague* (1769) makes no attempt to thrill the reader with war-whoops and tomahawks. The author deals with the Indian anthropologically and philosophically. She makes much of native customs and beliefs and sets the correspondents whose letters compose her novel to discussing the state of nature. Rousseau is cited as the champion of savage life.[26]

I am not attempting to show that the eighteenth century novels in which the Indian appears display an unflagging crescendo of naturalistic fervor. But when we compare the superficial thrills of *The Voyages of Captain Richard Falconer* (1720) with the polemic earnestness of the captivity episode in *The Man of the World* (1773), or the wildly extravagant and half-affected sentimentality of *Lydia* (1755) with the serious Rousseauism of *Emmera* (1767), we feel drawn to the conclusion that the Noble Savage idea does gain in depth and significance as the century progresses.

As regards poetry and drama, the trend of feeling is not quite so clear. In poetry the mingling of old and new elements was more complex than in fiction; and the theatre, then as now, was incurably theatric. But considering the whole body of eighteenth century literature before the French Revolution, one discerns a fairly steady growth of the attitude that civilization had strayed too far from the simple rules which nature plants in the hearts of all mankind. We have seen that the savage frequently appears as an embodiment of this attitude.

The student of this subject should heed Dr. Bissell's warning not to " force the evidence to some foregone conclusion, some ingenious theory, some novel and startling paradox, calculated to startle rather than to convince judicious readers and critics." [27] The savage is by no means

---

[26] Bissell, *op. cit.*, p. 103.　　　　[27] *Op. cit.*, p. 212.

always a stalking-horse for naturalistic philosophy. To superficial writers eager for new characters and themes his wild environment, his strange customs, his bloodthirsty valor, his naïve wonder at things familiar to civilized people had an obvious journalistic appeal. One should not attach too much significance to a popular fad. One should not, on the other hand, forget that popular fads cannot exist without some relation to the thought of the time. The way in which the Noble Savage becomes associated with other aspects of the return to nature cannot be ignored. Thomson, the lover of scenery, praises the simple Lapps. Joseph Warton, in whom are combined so many early romantic tendencies, dreams of living among the Indians. Gray includes the Indian bard among the primitive poets whom he admired. Brooke, the mystic, speaks through the lips of the Aztecs. Mackenzie, preacher of sensibility, gives us the idealized Indian in all his glory. The most judicious of readers will not be startled by the assertion that though the savage of eighteenth century literature often means nothing at all in the history of romanticism, he still more often means a good deal.

The French Revolution gives yet deeper significance to the Noble Savage as an embodiment of the conception of natural man. Before taking up this phase of the subject, however, we must pause to consider the influence exerted by the accounts of travelers and by the theories of Rousseau.

Chapter IV

EIGHTEENTH CENTURY TRAVELERS
ROUSSEAU

A T this point it will be well to remind ourselves that the process of observation and generalization which produces the Noble Savage did not cease with Montaigne. Throughout the period covered by the preceding chapter, explorers and travelers continued to relate their experiences among wild peoples, and more sedentary men of letters continued to evolve theoretical conclusions from the facts provided by the voyagers. During the eighteenth century, accounts of travel were read with interest. They not only influenced contemporary literature, as in the case of Mackenzie, but formed a rich stock of exotic material upon which the next generation was to draw.

In the first and second chapters of his dissertation, Dr. Bissell has brought together evidence from a large number of historians and travelers. Though I can add little to his findings, I see some advantage in a different method of approach. Whereas Bissell has marshalled his facts under various topics bearing upon savage life, I shall, in the following pages, consider separately a few examples of the literature of travel; and whereas Bissell deals only with observers of the Indian, I shall present glimpses of life in the South Seas and in Africa.

A very influential book of American exploration was Jonathan Carver's *Travels Through the Interior Parts of North America* (1778-1779.) This work is of particular interest in that it is now regarded, not as an authentic personal narrative, but as a compilation from various sources, with perhaps a judicious admixture of pure imagination. The account of the manners and customs of the Indians especially seems to be a combination of Carver's own statements, worked up by literary hacks, with material drawn from other explorers such as Charlevoix, the mendacious Lahontan, and the highly romantic Adair.[1] " Carver's " *Travels* is thus a sort of distilled essence of American exploration, made no doubt with a view to satisfying the public taste in such matters.

It may be added that even in the absence of any intent to deceive, the truth about savages often reached England in a rather impure state. The reports of a good many eighteenth century explorers must have been influenced by naturalistic preconceptions. And when these reports were rewritten by professional men of letters the distortion was all the greater. We shall see later what Hawkesworth did to Cook and Banks, and what Keate did to Captain Wilson.

Carver speaks of the Indians as circumspect, deliberate, undemonstrative and stoical. They are patient under all circumstances, and their manners are tranquil, contented and indolent. Although Indian women are amorous, sexual jealousy is almost unknown. Gambling is the one besetting vice. The Indians have a great respect for old age, a feeling connected with their love of stately oratory. To peaceful strangers they are hospitable and generous. Their memory is wonderful: they never forget either a favor or an injury. With other members of the same tribe they are exceedingly liberal. They have no private ownership of anything save domestic articles.

Indeed, the Indians " can form to themselves no idea of the value of money; they consider it . . . as the source

[1] E. G. Bourne, *The Travels of Jonathan Carver; American Historical Review*, Vol. XI, pp. 287 ff.

of innumerable evils . . . prevalent among Europeans, such as treachery, plundering, devastations and murder. . . . That the want of this useless metal should be the cause of depriving persons of their liberty exceeds their belief. Nor do they fail, on hearing this part of the European system of government related, to charge the institutors of it with a total want of humanity, and to brand them with the name of savages and brutes." It is interesting to imagine as the background of this passage an interview such as that between Gulliver and the old Houyhnhnm. To the romantic temperament the appeal of such an account must have been great.

Another significant contrast occurs in a description of a young chief, of whom Carver says: " Whilst I beheld the artless, yet engaging manners of this unpolished savage, I could not help drawing a comparison between him and some of the more refined inhabitants of civilized countries, not much, I own, in favour of the latter." Such comparisons are ready for home consumption.

But Carver does not represent the Indians in an entirely favorable light. As one who pretends to have escaped from the Fort William Henry Massacre only by amazing good fortune, he testifies to certain faults in the redman. Indian character is a paradox: they are " the worst enemies, and the best friends, of any people in the whole world," " a mixture of ferocity and gentleness. They are at once guided by passions and appetites, which they hold in common with the fiercest beasts, . . . and are possessed of virtues which do honour to human nature." On the whole, the good outweighs the bad. Except when their battle-lust is aroused, they are temperate, sociable, humane and generous.

Carver also has interesting things to say about the religion and the poetical talent of the Indian, but these matters are reserved for subsequent treatment. The book obviously furnished much support to the Noble Savage idea. The Indian's virtues must have seemed a reproach to " more refined nations," his minor faults could be defended by the *tu quoque* argument, and even his ferocity provided a wild and exotic thrill by no means repugnant to one side of the romantic temperament. Above all, such books sketched a background of places and customs against which the man of nature might play his part. We shall see that Wordsworth and Southey used the *Travels* to give substance to their imaginings.

Authorities disagree in their interpretation of Crèvecoeur, the author of the celebrated *Letters from an American Farmer* (1782). Ludwig Lewisohn's view is that Crèvecoeur was " an indomitable optimist. . . . To him the meaning of ' Weltschmerz ' was unknown." [2] Bissell, on the other hand, finds in the *Letters* " a good example of the sentimental longing for the state of nature, reflecting the Rousseauistic theory with a certain melancholy, poetic coloring. . . . Here we can see not only the desire for freedom and independence, but the romantic longings for solace in nature, peace in escaping the restlessness of civilized life." [3]

Though both these statements are somewhat extreme, I take my stand with Bissell rather than with Lewisohn. The most interesting feature of Crèvecoeur's character is that he is at the same time one of the first real Americans, and a Frenchman steeped in the philosophy of nature. The *Letters* are full of a Ben Franklin-like morality in which cheerfulness, honesty, frugality and industry are the chief virtues. But the man is capable of pausing, like

[2] *Letters from an American Farmer*, p. xviii.
[3] *American Indian*, p. 46.

Montaigne, to admire the wisdom with which nature regulates the life of brutes, so different from " the coarse, the imperfect systems of man," who, " though adorned with the additional gift of reason, might learn from the perfection of instinct, how to . . . temper the errors which this second gift makes him commit." This fusion of the cheerfulness and practicality of the pioneer with the disillusion of the romanticist had, and still has, a peculiar fascination for the reader.

Is there no romantic melancholy in the following passage? " Where do you conceive then that nature intended we should be happy? Would you prefer the state of men in the woods, to that of men in a more improved situation? Evil preponderates in both. . . . For my part, I think the vices and miseries to be found in the latter, exceed those of the former; in which real evil is more scarce, more supportable, and less enormous." Here is the pessimism of Rousseau's second discourse: the state of nature is regarded as superior to civilized society, but only in being relatively more endurable.

One must admit, however, that this is not Crèvecoeur's most characteristic mood. The outburst is occasioned by a visit to Charleston, where his feelings are harrowed by the sufferings of the slaves. But for all that, there is plenty of *Weltschmerz* in the man. It crops out in significant passages; and these passages were surely not, to contemporary readers, the least interesting of the book.

But the material relating to the Indians must no longer be postponed. On the outbreak of the American Revolution, Crèvecoeur, divided in his allegiance, contemplates joining an Indian tribe. He hesitates, however, for the sake of his children. Those who experience the savage life in childhood are never willing to return to civilization. He knows of many parents who upon the conclusion of the

French and Indian War sought to regain the offspring that had been captured by the redskins. The children were found, but they had become perfect little Indians. Many did not recognize their own parents; and those who did, refused to follow them. " Incredible as this may seem, I have heard it asserted in a thousand instances, among persons of credit."

To adults also Indian life has a peculiar fascination. Crèvecoeur relates that two Europeans, after several years of captivity in a certain village, were offered their freedom, but preferred to remain among the savages because of the " most perfect freedom, the ease of living, the absence of those cares and solicitudes which so often prevail with us." These are precisely the reasons given by young Annesley for his preference. They err who suppose that civilization would have for a savage charms equally potent. " Thousands of Europeans are Indians, and we have no examples of even one of these aborigines having from choice become Europeans [*sic*]! " A settler adopted an Indian orphan, and cared for the boy in the tenderest fashion; but Mowgli stole away to the jungle.

The American Farmer supposes that among the Indians " there must be something more congenial to our native dispositions, than the fictitious society in which we live. . . . There must be something very bewitching in their manners, something . . . marked by the very hands of nature." In the term " nature," of course, lies the clue. " Without temples, without priests, without kings, and without laws, they are in many instances superior to us; . . . they live without care, sleep without inquietude, take life as it comes, bearing all its asperities with unparalleled patience, and die without any kind of apprehension for what they have done, or for what they expect to meet with hereafter. What system of philosophy can give us so many qualifications for happiness? They most certainly are much more closely connected with nature than we are; they are her immediate children, the inhabitants of the woods are her undefiled offspring." This familiar argument possesses a peculiar insidiousness on the lips of one who poses as a simple, industrious cultivator of the soil. Naturalism is seldom found in one so close to nature.

In 1801 Crèvecoeur published his *Voyage dans La Haute Pennsylvanie, et dans L'État de New-York, Par un Membre adoptif de la Nation Onéida. Traduit et publié par l'auteur des Lettres D'un Cultivateur Américain.*[4] Its three volumes, according to Lewisohn, present "little new or illuminating." I find both novelty and illumination, however, in Crèvecoeur's explicit reversal of his earlier attitude toward the Indian. When someone reminds him of the great writers who have denied the advantages of civilization, he retorts: "What writers have said on this subject . . . was inspired merely by the spirit of censure and singularity: they invented a conception of the savage, of whom they knew nothing, in order to satirize their contemporaries. If, like me, they had accompanied these natives on their devastating war-parties; if their eyes had witnessed the tortures they inflict on their prisoners . . . ; if, finally, they had attended those cannibal feasts, those scenes of drunkenness which I shudder to recall, surely they would have sought the original of their delusive pictures elsewhere than among these men of nature."[5]

From such a source, this attack upon the idealization of the redskin is impressive. It may be that in 1801 Crève-

---

[4] Crèvecoeur pretends that he is merely editing papers rescued from a shipwreck, but the device is transparent.

[5] *Voyage dans la Haute Pennsylvanie*, Vol. I, pp. 95-96. Translation mine.

coeur, like not a few other men of his time, was beginning
to turn from naturalism as the bride of Jacobinism. Another possibility is that his earlier praise of Indians was
written merely in deference to a literary fashion from
which, in this more soberly informative work, he feels himself free. Such a thought troubles our faith in the simplicity of the American Farmer.

The *Voyage* contains a good deal of information about
Indians, in which favorable and unfavorable reports are
mingled.[6] We must not dwell longer upon a book which
was never translated into English, and which seems to
have had no influence upon English literature. It may be
remarked in passing, however, that the whole problem of
Crèvecoeur's relations with the Indians merits further investigation by special students.

The publication in 1773 of the compilation generally
known as *Hawkesworth's Voyages* made the South Sea
Islands a subject of great popular interest, and established
the Polynesian as a Noble Savage. It also presented
scholars with a rather complicated bibliographical situation.

In his first voyage (1768-1771) Captain — then Lieutenant — Cook carried with him Joseph Banks, the naturalist who was later to become president of the Royal
Society, and Dr. Solander, a Swedish botanist. On the
completion of the voyage, the journals of Cook, Banks and
Solander were placed in the hands of John Hawkesworth,
a director of the East India Company and a man of letters. His revision of Southern's *Oroonoko* has been mentioned in a previous chapter.[7] Hawkesworth put these in-

---

[6] The principal sections are: Vol. I, Chap. 1 (General sketch of the
Indians); Vol. I, Chaps. 6-10 (An Indian Council described in great
detail); Vol. II, Chap. 1 (Cherokee mythology); Vol. II, Chap. 5
(An old Indian's life-story.)   [7] *Vide supra*, p. 41.

gredients into his literary mortar and produced a work in
which " it is impossible to know whether we are reading
Cook, Banks, Solander or Hawkesworth himself." [8]   The
real journal of Captain Cook was first published in 1893
by Captain Wharton of the British navy.   In 1896 the
real journal of Joseph Banks was first published by Sir
Joseph Hooker.   The actual journal of Solander has never
been published, but no doubt its substance is incorporated
in his *Observations on Natural History in Cook's Voyage,*
a technical book which we can ignore in the following
pages.   The work entitled *Supplément au Voyage de M.
de Bougainville, ou Journal d'un Voyage autour du
Monde, Fait par Mm. Banks et Solander. Traduit de
l'Anglois par M. de Fréville* (Paris, 1772) is rather a
puzzle.   It is certainly not a translation of Banks' journal,
but shows acquaintance with it.   Since the *Supplément* is
wholly superseded by Hooker's edition of Banks, it may be
left out of consideration, with the passing remark that it
probably suggested to Diderot his work of the same title.

The statement in the *Dictionary of National Biography*
that Hawkesworth changed Cook's journal hardly at all
is decidedly inaccurate.[9]   Cook, Banks and Hawkesworth
differ in several respects, and a comparison of the three
works will tell us much about the voyage-literature of the
eighteenth century.   Let the comparison be restricted to
Tahiti — for us the most interesting point in the voyage.

Cowper writes of Cook that

> " Wherever he found man, to nature true,
>   The rights of man were sacred in his view.
>   He sooth'd with gifts, and greeted with a smile,
>   The simple natives of the new-found isle."

[8] *Captain Cook's Journal*, p. vii (Capt. Wharton's preface).
[9] *D. N. B.*, art. *Hawkesworth, John.*   The statement is made on the
authority of Prior's *Life of Malone*, p. 441.

Cook certainly was always humane, though firm, in his
dealings with the natives. That he should have met
death at their hands is ironic.[10] On arriving at Tahiti he
issued to his crew a remarkable series of orders, of which
the first reads: " To endeavour by every fair means to
cultivate a Friendship with the Natives, and to treat them
with all imaginable humanity." It is impossible to read
the *Journal*, or the narratives of the second and third
voyages, without feeling that England could hardly have
found a more upright representative of her civilization.

But though Cook wins the respect and friendship of almost all the savages with whom he comes in contact, he
displays hardly any enthusiasm for them. They are good
to trade with, to provide fresh food for his men, and to act
as guides; but their natural virtues do not impress him.
Indeed, he finds that though most of them are well-dis-
posed, they are incorrigible liars and thieves. The cool-
ness which pervades his account of Omai [11] well represents
his attitude.

The sexual license of the Tahitians is particularly distressing to Cook. He reports that " More than one half
of the better sort of the inhabitants have enter'd into a
resolution of injoying free liberty in Love, without being
Troubled or disturbed by its consequences." That is, the
offspring of these unions are smothered. The members of
this group hold carnivals of which provocative dancing is
the chief feature. Both men and women " express the
most indecent ideas in conversation without the slightest
emotion, and they delight in such conversation beyond any
other." Chastity is not regarded as a virtue: an unfaith-
ful wife receives at most a beating. " The Men will very

[10] Of course at Hawaii, not at Tahiti. In this connection, see *The
Death of Capt. Cook, A Grand Serious Pantomimic Ballet* (London,
1789.) [11] *Vide supra*, pp. 71–74.

readily offer the Young Women to Strangers, even their own Daughters, and think it very strange if you refuse them."

Cook's reaction to these conditions is that of a practical commander of sailors as well as that of a man of decency. Bougainville's ships, touching at " la nouvelle Cythère " in 1768, had left venereal disease among the natives. The infection was communicated to Cook's men. " All I could do was to little purpose. . . . This distemper very soon spread itself over the greater part of the ship's company."

The native who figures most prominently in the *Journal* is Tupia, chief priest of Tahiti. This man, described by Cook as " very intelligent," has conspired against King Tootaha, and is hence glad to leave Tahiti to become the Captain's guide and interpreter among the islands. He appears to have been quite invaluable to the expedition. Tupia dies of scurvy, with complications, in Batavia harbor. Surely this poor savage, perishing on the English ship so far from his native island, might wring from the least sentimental heart an expression of sympathy. But Cook dryly sets down: " He was a shrewd, sensible, ingenious man, but proud and obstinate, which often made his situation on board both disagreeable to himself and to those about him, and tended much to promote the diseases which put a Period to his Life." There is a certain satisfaction in that capital P.

In order to guard against any misrepresentation of Cook, we shall do well to glance at his *Voyage Towards the South Pole* (1777) and *Voyage to the Pacific Ocean* (1784), in which he describes, respectively, his second and third voyages.[12] On these voyages, having no person like

[12] Volume III of the *Voyage to the Pacific*, describing events subsequent to the death of Cook, was written by Captain James King.

Banks to make scientific and anthropological observations, he came into closer relations with the natives than on his first visit to the islands, when he concerned himself mainly with geography and navigation.   But there is no substantial change in his attitude.   The islanders are much like other folk: some good and some bad.   Here is a typical bit: " To several who called themselves chiefs, I made presents . . . ; and, in return, they promised to bring me hogs and fowls: a promise they never did, nor ever intended to perform."   On the other hand, Oree, King of Huaheine, shows himself an honest man and a true friend; but there is no suggestion that his virtues are due to his closeness to nature.

One feels that Joseph Banks became much more intimate with the Tahitians.   He enjoys them and their carefree life.   On one occasion he takes part, dressed as a native, in a wild funeral ceremony.   He vividly describes a scene in which Tahitians and English sailors regale each other with their national songs.   A village in the interior is compared to Arcadia.   But though Banks likes the natives, he does not wax sentimental about them.   Like Cook, he sees them as amiable, thievish children.   Such children are rather troublesome to Cook, rather delightful to Banks.   Therein lies the difference.

Now to examine the form in which the first voyage was presented to the eighteenth century by the stay-at-home Hawkesworth.   In the *New Voyage Round the World*, the natives are referred to as " noble benefactors."   Their appearance is pleasing, and their agreeable manners are indexes of inward virtues.   " In their motions there is at once vigour and ease; their walk is graceful . . . and their behaviour to strangers and to each other affable and courteous.   In their dispositions, also, they seemed to be brave, open, and candid, without either suspicion or treachery, cruelty or revenge." This is much more highly-colored than anything we find in Cook or Banks.

Hawkesworth further reports that " These people have a knowledge of right and wrong from the mere dictates of natural conscience." It might appear that the thievery of the islanders, which is cheerfully admitted, would run counter to this statement. But no: one must remember that morality is a comparative matter. We can judge these people only by " the conformity of their conduct to what in their opinion is right." If they do not think stealing wrong, one cannot blame them for being thieves. Cook and Banks, who spent much precious time in tracing stolen goods, offer no such extenuation.

Hawkesworth pauses to consider the happiness of the natives — a theme which never inspires Cook. He envies the strength of their passions, the transiency of their sorrows, their freedom from worldly anxieties. " And yet," he muses, " if we admit that they are upon the whole happier than we, we must admit that the child is happier than the man," and that we are losers by the perfection of our nature, the increase of our knowledge, and the enlargement of our views." This foretokening of Wordsworth would make Cook frown, and Banks smile.

Tupia's farewell to his native land furnishes a good point of comparison. Cook makes no mention of it; he does not, as we have seen, greatly care for the savage. Banks writes: " Tupia . . . parted with a few heartfelt tears, so I judge them to have been by the efforts I saw him make to hide them. He sent by Otheothea his last present, a shirt, to Potamia, Dootahah's favourite; he and I went then to the topmast-head, where we stood a long time waving to the canoes as they went off, after which he came down and showed no further signs of seriousness or

concern." [13]   Hawkesworth makes the most of this, saying that Tupia " sustained himself in this scene with a
firmness and resolution truly admirable; he wept indeed,
but the effort he made to conceal his tears concurred to do
him honour." No mention is made of the fact that Banks
stood with Tupia at the mast-head: the savage must have
the spotlight to himself. Hawkesworth also expunges
from the record Tupia's quick recovery from dejection. [14]

Banks, who financed the travels of Tupia, never took
his charge quite seriously. " I do not know," says the explorer, " why I may not keep him as a curiosity as well as
my neighbours do lions and tigers at a larger expense than
he will ever probably put me to." Later he describes
Tupia's efficacious method of praying for wind. " I
plainly saw he never began till he perceived a breeze so
near the ship that it generally reached her before his
prayer was finished." On King George's birthday, " Tupia, to show his loyalty, got most enormously drunk."
Hawkesworth pays no attention to these passages, which
seem deficient in enthusiasm for the man of nature. In
relating the death of Tupia, also, he omits Cook's strictures
on the interpreter's character.

It has been shown that Cook, as a man of somewhat rigid
morals, as well as an efficient captain, is shocked by the sexual habits of the Tahitians. In this matter, Banks is no
precisian. There is not the slightest indication of misbe-
havior on his part, but he seems to have found a certain
pleasure in contemplating the free manners of the islanders. At a native reception, he conducts an innocent flirta-
tion with a pretty girl of low caste, much to the disgust of
the ugly queen to whom he has been assigned as a dinner-
partner.

[13] *Journal of Joseph Banks*, p. 110.
[14] *New Voyage*, Vol. I, pp. 113–114.

Hawkesworth mentions the sexual depravity of the Tahitians in practically the same terms as used by Cook, but with one interesting alteration. Cook describes with horror how a young native has intercourse with a little girl of about twelve, surrounded by a number of islanders who regard the scene with approving interest.[15] Hawkesworth takes over this passage, but adds: "This incident is not mentioned as a subject of idle curiosity, but as it deserves consideration in determining a question which has long been debated in philosophy; Whether the shame attending certain actions, which are allowed on all sides to be in themselves innocent, is implanted in Nature, or superinduced by custom?"[16] That such shame is the product of custom needs no debate. But does not the reader feel the subtle tug of an inference that in such matters nature may well take precedence of custom?

Further citations would support the assertion that in Hawkesworth the attitude toward the savages is much more enthusiastic than in Cook or Banks. Native virtues are emphasized, native faults condoned. Perhaps a disproportionate amount of attention has been given this trio. The comparison does, however, regain for us something of the atmosphere of eighteenth century voyage-literature. Here is Cook, with his honest facts honestly recorded. Here is Banks, with his unsentimental liking for a child-like people. And here is Hawkesworth, the canny man of letters, who knows how to give the explorers' material the popular twist that it requires.

Hawkesworth's "Voyages" set people talking about the South Seas: the topic, we shall find, was often discussed in Johnson's circle. In the popular mind the Tahitian was added to the roll of Noble Savages. He possessed all the virtues of his brethren, with the addition of an extremely

[15] *Journal*, pp. 96-97.   [16] *New Voyage*, Vol. I, p. 79.

picturesque abandon in matters of sex, equally fascinating
to the prude and to the libertine. Thus began a tradition
which has never been more powerful than at the present
time.

Keate's *Account of the Pelew Islands*, though a less
important book than Hawkesworth, shows even more
plainly how the bald facts of a sailor's journal could be
given a romantic aspect. The flavor of the book is so
pleasantly redolent of the age that I may be pardoned for
treating it rather fully. George Keate himself never saw
the Pelew Islands. He simply took the journal of bluff
old Captain Wilson, and turned it into a fine big quarto
(London, 1788) by embroidering with a wealth of sentimental interpretation the interesting story therein contained.

On the night of August ninth, 1783, the Honourable
United East India Company's packet *Antelope*, Captain
Wilson, went aground on Coorooraa, one of the Pelew, or
Palos, Islands. The ship was damaged beyond repair, but
all hands came ashore safely. Thanksgiving changed to
despair, however, when at dawn nude hordes of inquisitive
savages approached.

The fears of the English were baseless. Providence
had arranged that the natives should be a people " who,
although they appeared to be Philosophers in adversity,
Stoics in pain, and Heroes in death, yet, in many of the
more delicate feelings of the human breast, possessed all
the amiable tenderness of a woman." Accepting Max
Beerbohm's classification of mankind into hosts and guests,
one must place the Pelewans under the former head.
Their hospitality is proffered with the most delicate tact.
Observing the white leader's greeting to their chief, they
begin shaking hands with the crew, in order to make them

feel quite at home. Gifts are exchanged — breadfruit for beads. All is goodwill.

Ere long the English are visited by Abba Thule, King of Pelew. This monarch " showed himself firm, noble, gracious and benevolent; there was a dignity in all his deportment, a gentleness in all his manners, and a warmth and sensibility about his heart, that won the love of all who approached him." At the feast given on this occasion, the English are alarmed to observe that every Pelewan chief keeps his eyes intently fixed upon some member of the *Antelope's* crew. They soon find, however, that to every Englishman has been assigned a Pelewan to act as his particular friend and host.

That night, the good Captain is terrified by dreadful sounds issuing from the native stockade, but is relieved to discover that " they were only tuning their voices, in order to begin a song." A sort of glee-club contest is then held, with native and English selections alternating. The King liked the English songs so well " that whenever he met the young lad Cobbledick, who sang them, he would stop him, and make him sing one or two songs." [17]   David and Saul, Cobbledick and Abba Thule!

In such idyllic fashion the days glide by. There are, to be sure, certain merely physical drawbacks. As one of five Chinamen belonging to the crew observes, " This have very poor place, and very poor people; no got clothes, no got rice, no got hog, no got nothing." But however strongly Captain Wilson may have felt the force of this objection, George Keate, writing comfortably in London, repudiates it. " The mind of a speculative reader is far otherwise engaged. He considers human nature, however unadorned, when dignified by virtuous simplicity, as one of the noblest objects of contemplation."

---

[17] *Cf. supra*, p. 108, for a similar incident in Tahiti.

But all this time the English have done more than contemplate primitive virtue. They have constructed a craft stout enough to take them to Macao, and are now ready — not without some twinges of regret — to quit the Fortunate Isles. Shortly before the final preparations are completed, Abba Thule asks for a gift of muskets with which to fight certain enemies of his. The English, incurably suspicious in spite of the repeatedly demonstrated trustworthiness of the Pelewans, refuse. The King reproaches them in a lofty, Indian-sounding speech. What has he done to incur the distrust of the strangers? Consider this confrontation of Noble Savage and civilized man: "The people of Pelew, tutored in the school of Nature, acted from impulse alone, they were open and undisguised; unconscious of deceit themselves, they neither feared nor looked for it in others. — Our countrymen — born and brought up in a civilized nation, where Art assumes every form and colouring of life, and is even perfectioned into a science, were fashioned by education to suspicion and distrust. — Such is the fatal knowledge the world teaches mankind, fencing too often the human heart against the inlets of its own happiness." You may be very sure *that* was never in Captain Wilson's journal!

One young seaman, Madan Blanchard by name, elects to stay at Pelew. His comrades scoff; he remains firm. Wilson reasons with him; he becomes firmer. "He had formed no particular attachment on the island;" he simply loves the place and the people. And so the mariner is left to eat the lotus, or the yams. Two parting bits of advice the Captain gives: always to wear garments, and always to keep the Sabbath. Blanchard's memoirs would be valuable, says Keate, if they were "well digested" by someone — someone like George Keate, no doubt. Indeed, they "might, to all the investigators of simple nature, be

infinitely more interesting than those of half the ministers
and statesmen of Europe." Unfortunately, the sailor can
neither read nor write.

For this imperfectly civilized child of a corrupt civilization is substituted the young Prince Lee Boo, second son of
Abba Thule. The King wishes the boy to go to Europe,
study, and eventually bring back to his native land the wisdom of the English. Abba Thule, you will observe, does
not shrink from civilized vices: he has too lively an appreciation of what muskets may do to his enemies. Also
— to be just — he seems to wish to improve tribal methods
of agriculture. What a contrast is here: Blanchard,
wishing to rot his life out on the beach; Lee Boo, eager to
travel, to see, to learn! Always the complex yearns toward
simplicity; always the primitive aspires to be complex.

The day of parting arrives. With all the tender stoicism of Wordsworth's Michael, Abba Thule commends
his child to the care of Captain Wilson. The natives in
their canoes follow the ship far out to sea, throwing quite
superfluous gifts up on deck. " ' Only this from me!
Only this from me! ' was the general cry; the repetition
of which was urged with such supplicating countenances,
and watery eyes, that this bewitching testimony of
affection and generosity almost overcame everyone
on board." At length, the canoes turn back; Pelew
fades from view; the sailors dry their eyes. Homeward
bound!

But a new life has begun for Lee Boo. This young man
is of handsome appearance and great natural charm. He
has to a high degree that combination of eager vivacity
and delicate tact which characterizes his countrymen. He
assumes toward Captain Wilson the attitude of a dutiful
son; and the old mariner, to his honor, is a kind father
to the youth. He brings Lee Boo to his own home, and

there the savage prince sets himself to the task of self-improvement.

Keate gives us only scraps of information about Lee Boo's life in England. Lee Boo goes to church. He cannot understand the sermon, but he is very attentive — and that is all the eighteenth century demanded. He is much disgusted at seeing a man drunk. Whiskey, he concludes, " it not a fit drink for a gentleman." He attends a *soirée*, is delighted with the music, and obliges with Pelewan songs to the distress of the company. He will give money to old beggars, but not to young ones. He reconciles Captain Wilson and his son after a family tiff. He always calls Mrs. Wilson " Mother," and holds the name in great veneration. From all this and much more one gathers that he was good-natured, docile and affectionate.

Then came the smallpox. Lee Boo was a good patient. He obeyed all the commands of that strange magician, the doctor, but he was doomed. " Good friend," he said on his deathbed, " when you go to Pelew, tell Abba Thule that Lee Boo take much drink to make smallpox go away, but he die."

Upon his tomb was chiselled this inscription:

" To the Memory
of Prince Lee Boo,
A Native of the Pelew, or Palos, Islands;
and son to Abba Thule, Rupack or King
of the Island Coorooraa;
who departed this Life on the 27 of December 1784,
aged 20 years;
This stone is inscribed,
by the Honourable United East India Company,
as a Testimony of Esteem for the humane and kind Treatment
afforded by His Father to the Crew of their Ship
the Antelope, Captain Wilson,

> which was wrecked off that Island
> in the Night of the 9th of August 1783.
>
> Stop, Reader, stop! — let Nature claim a Tear —
> A Prince of *Mine*, Lee Boo, lies bury'd here."

The closing exhortation was more than merely conventional, for at least one reader acknowledged Nature's claim. It was of this very stone that Coleridge writes:

> " Aye as the Star of Evening flung its beam
> In broken radiance on the wavy stream,
> My soul amid the pensive twilight gloom
> Mourn'd with the breeze, O LEE BOO! o'er thy tomb." [18]

Nor, one may conjecture, were other mourners lacking. It would be hard to resist the appeal of this little brown prince of nature, rotting in earth so far from his innocent and benevolent people.[19]

Hawkesworth and Keate will serve to justify my view that the South Sea Islander is a Noble Savage. To establish the Negro upon the same ideal eminence will require more effort. The nobility of black savages will gradually be impressed upon the reader's mind as the work proceeds. As a preparation for the evidence later to be adduced, however, we may glance at Mungo Park's *Travels in the Interior Districts of Africa* (1799).

There is much in this book that would appeal neither to a sentimental naturalist nor to a humanitarian. The savages are constantly pilfering, and are not infrequently hostile. Park, too, is quite callous in regard to slavery.

---

[18] *To a Lady, With a Poem on the French Revolution.*

[19] A popular compilation called *The Interesting and Affecting History of Prince Lee Boo* ran through twenty editions from 1789 to 1850. See also Bowles' *Lament of Abba Thule,* and Joseph Cottle's *Lee Boo, infra,* Chap. XIII.

He travelled chiefly in the company of slave-traders, and returned to England on a slave-ship. He describes with very superficial sympathy the sufferings of an exhausted slave-girl who is unable to keep up with the train. When it is proposed to cut her throat, he retires to the other end of the caravan in order not to see the unpleasant operation. Finally the traders decide to leave her to the wild beasts, and the good Park is much relieved.

Under these circumstances it is the more remarkable that his account of the blacks is on the whole favorable, and not without a certain sentimental enthusiasm. He has something of Hawkesworth's knack for explaining away savage faults. The Mandingoes — the tribe which he describes most fully — steal everything they can lay their hands on. But would a helpless stranger fare any better in Europe than in Africa? He does not think " that their natural sense of justice was perverted or extinguished: it was overpowered only, for the moment." Sometimes one feels, in examining these documents, that the modern tendency to relieve criminals of all responsibility for their actions finds its source in the late eighteenth century.

Park testifies that in many cases he was treated with great kindness. This applies more especially to the women. " In all my wanderings and wretchedness, I found them uniformly kind and compassionate." On one occasion, when he was practically starving, a poor old slave-woman shared with him her little basket of nuts. This made him reflect " with pleasure on the conduct of this poor untutored slave, who, without examining into my character or circumstances, listened explicitly to the dictates of her own heart." A sophisticated European would more probably have kept all the nuts for himself, and passed by on the other side.

This " soft and amiable disposition of nature " is especially strong within the family circle. Mothers and
children display for each other the warmest affection.
Truthfulness is a virtue enjoined upon the young with
particular vigor. It was the sole consolation of one unhappy mother, whose son had been murdered by Moors,
that " the poor boy . . . had never told a lie." Children
honor their mothers. " ' Strike me, but do not curse my
mother,' is a common expression even among the slaves."

Nor does this filial respect cease with maturity. Park
witnesses a meeting between a blacksmith and his blind,
aged mother. It is so affecting as to convince the writer
" that whatever difference there is between the Negro
and the European in . . . the colour of the skin, there
is none in the genuine sympathies and characteristic feelings of our common nature." But what of that little girl
abandoned to the lions?

On the whole, Mungo Park seems to have had a hard
time of it. He was robbed, attacked and churlishly dealt
with quite as often as he was hospitably received. But
he makes a great deal of such decent treatment as fell to
his lot, and persists in basing a favorable judgment upon
very slender grounds. That he did so is probably due to
the spirit of the age. By 1799, no traveller with an eye
to publication would deal very harshly with savages.
Whatever really happened in his wanderings, that summarizing chapter on " Manners and Customs of the Natives " must at all costs praise natural virtue and take a
fling at " more refined nations."

At any rate, Park helped to establish the Negro as a
Noble Savage. In spite of his scanty humanitarianism,
his book appealed especially to opponents of the slave
trade. James Montgomery of Sheffield draws heavily, as
we shall see, upon the *Travels*. An incident described

by Park was versified by the beautiful Georgiana, Duchess of Devonshire, was set to music, and became a popular song. But to this, and to Park's description of Negro bards, we shall return in a later chapter.

During the eighteenth century, the savage did not remain wholly passive beneath the peeping and botanizing eyes of the European traveler. Rather frequently he journeyed to the Old World and made observations of his own. Bissell gives so full an account of " civilization as seen by the savage " [20] that I must content myself with adding to his list of Indian visitors the South Sea Islanders, Omai, Tupia, and Lee Boo. I have not attempted to discover whether any Negro observers came to England during the period in question, but we shall soon find a fictitious one in *Sandford and Merton*. These visits of savages are reflected in eighteenth century journalism, and in minor satirical or sentimental pieces closely connected with journalism. The use made by Steele and Addison of the " four Indian kings " has already been described. But the real importance of such confrontations of savage and civilized humanity lies in the fact that they indirectly stimulated reflection upon " what man has made of man."

Of all the eighteenth century writers who used the Noble Savage in their speculations on man and society, Rousseau was of course the most influential; and he cannot be neglected even in a study nominally devoted to English literature. Definitely to trace and measure that influence, however, is not easy. The consensus of present-day opinion is that he was a thorough-going partisan of the savage. To speak of " Rousseau's sentimentally en-

[20] *Op. cit.*, Chapter III.

thusiastic description of the happy, innocent man of nature " is to make the obviously proper remark. Much the same view was held by most Englishmen of the romantic period. In Lamb's *Pindaric Ode to the Tread-Mill*, for example, we find the lines:

> " In such a place
> Who could expose thy face,
> Historiographer of deathless Crusoe!
> That paint'st the strife
> And all the naked ills of savage life,
> Far above Rousseau? "

Lamb is saying, rather clumsily, that Defoe's picture of savage life is superior to Rousseau's because it is gloomier. But, in so far as Rousseau presents a picture of savage life at all, that picture is rather gloomier than Defoe's. In contrasting Defoe with Rousseau, Lamb forgets that *Robinson Crusoe* is the one book in Émile's boyhood library, and that Émile is to test the value of things by asking whether they will be useful on Crusoe's island.

In fact, the student who turns to Rousseau's actual works will not long remain satisfied with the popular interpretation of his views. Professor Lovejoy goes so far as to say that the *Discourse on Inequality* represents a movement away from, rather than towards, primitivism.[21] A solution of this problem would entail a complete explanation of Rousseau's philosophy — a task for which I lack both space and knowledge. A tentative and partial attempt, however, must be made.

What picture of man in the pure state of nature does the *Discourse on Inequality* present? Primitive man, says Rousseau, is just an animal, " weaker than some, and less

---

[21] A. O. Lovejoy, *The Supposed Primitivism of Rousseau's " Discourse on Inequality" ; Modern Philology*, Vol. XXI, pp. 165-186.

agile than others; but taking him all round, the most advantageously disposed of any." His wants, being concerned almost entirely with subsistence, are easily satisfied. He is hardy and robust. His lack of useful implements is compensated for by his perfect bodily development. Nothing frightens him but the unknown, and his simple world presents few novelties. Natural man is indolent, fond of eating and sleeping. He is far healthier and stronger than we, and his senses are necessarily much more acute than ours.

Rousseau next considers the man of nature on his " metaphysical and moral side." Of the animals, man alone has sufficient mental power to alter his condition by the exercise of his intellect. " In the operations of the brute, nature is the sole agent, whereas man has some share in his own operations in his character as a free agent." And this fact, supposedly man's chief glory, in reality accounts for man's degeneration, " because the mind depraves the senses, and the will continues to speak when nature is silent."

Rousseau expands his idea by saying of this " faculty of self-improvement" that " It would be melancholy, were we forced to admit that this distinctive and almost unlimited faculty is the source of all human misfortune; that it is this faculty, which, successively producing in different ages his discoveries and errors, his vices and his virtues, makes him at length a tyrant both over himself and over nature." In his natural state, however, man had few temptations to alter his condition. Never having experienced the luxurious pleasures of civilization, he could not have felt the need of them, and he was exempt from the bitter price which we must pay for the supposed advantages of progress. We should not, therefore, think of natural man as miserable.

We have already contrasted the ideas of Hobbes and of Rousseau on the question whether man in the state of nature was virtuous or vicious. Hobbes claims " that because man has no idea of goodness, he must be wicked." Now it is true, says his opponent, that natural man has no idea of goodness, but it is equally true that he has no idea of wickedness. Hence it is quite as likely that he is good as that he is bad. Primitive men are kept from evil by " the peacefulness of their passions, and their ignorance of vice: *tanto plus in illis proficit vitiorum ignoratio, quam in his cognitio virtutis.*"

But the case for primitive man can be stated more positively. Against Hobbes' " will to hurt " Rousseau places " an innate repugnance at seeing a fellow-creature suffer." " Such is the pure emotion of morals, prior to all kinds of reflection! Such is the force of natural compassion, which the greatest depravity of morals has as yet hardly been able to destroy! " Pity was stronger in the natural state than now, because then the virtual equality existing among men caused the spectator to identify himself more closely with the sufferer. The influence of reason has been to increase individual differences so greatly that this compassionate instinct has become blunted. No longer recognizing our fellow-men as brothers, we no longer suffer with them.

Rousseau's arguments, however, are largely negative. From statements like the one above-quoted he drops into a pessimistic insistence on the number of evils from which primitive man is exempt. The man of nature was compassionate, but we are given to infer that the chief reason for his mildness is that he had so few incitements to quarrel. Give him a good meal, and he was at peace with the world. Above all, he was free from that most fruitful source of strife — love.

Rousseau distinguishes "between the physical and moral ingredients in the feeling of love." The former is simply the reproductive instinct. The latter is the direction of this instinct toward a single object. " . . . It is easy to see that the moral part of love is a factitious feeling, born of social usage. . . . This feeling, being founded on certain ideas of beauty and merit which a savage is not in a position to acquire, and on comparisons which he is incapable of making, must be for him almost non-existent. . . . He follows solely the character nature has implanted in him, and not tastes which he could never have required; so that every woman equally answers his purpose." This being the case, it was hardly worth while for natural men to fight each other over natural women. The brute part of love is the safest.

The most essential instinct of primitive man was that of self-preservation. "The produce of the earth furnished him with all he needed, and instinct told him how to use it. Hunger and other appetites made him at various times experience various modes of existence; and among these was one which urged him to propagate his species — a blind propensity that, having nothing to do with the heart, produced a merely animal act. . . . Such was the condition of infant man."

Surely the evidence will not permit us to say that natural man is an inspiring or even an attractive figure. Rousseau's " primary object," according to Lovejoy, was " to identify the state of nature with the state of the brute." [22] Except for the redeeming gift of natural compassion, the life of natural man is admirable only in that it is comparatively free from pain. It is easy for natural

[22] *Supposed Primitivism of Rousseau's " Discourse on Inequality*," p. 169.

man to exist. " Food, a female, and sleep " expresses the sum of his needs. His mind is free from the problems of our complex civilization, because in the state of nature those problems do not exist. He is never disappointed, because he never undertakes anything. He has little to fear, because there is no reason for anyone to envy him. He is not jealous, because one woman is no better than another. He can see through other people, because his fellows have yet to learn deception. He is not unhappy, because he has no ambitions; and he is not vicious, because he has never been taught what evil is. It is difficult to discover much sentimental primitivism in these despairing statements. Even primitive man's " repugnance at seeing a fellow-creature suffer " should not be interpreted too sanguinely. Says Professor Lovejoy, " The doctrine of *la bonté naturelle*, so far as the *Second Discourse* is concerned, could best be expressed in English by the proposition that man was originally a nonmoral but good-natured brute." [23]

But man did not long remain in the absolutely natural state. Differences between man and man became more marked, and caused competition among individuals. The necessity for competition made men industrious, and of industry was born property. " The first man who, having enclosed a piece of ground, bethought himself of saying *This is mine,* and found people enough to believe him, was the real founder of civil society." The sum of a number of such primitive capitalistic acts was the beginning of man's life in village communities.

" The first expansions of the human heart were the effects of a novel situation, which united husbands and wives, fathers and children, under one roof. The habit of living together soon gave rise to the finest feelings

[23] *Ibid.,* p. 171.

known to humanity, conjugal love and paternal affection." Thus the rudeness of primitive man became somewhat softened. Corruption, however, soon began to set in. The improvement in manners brought the desire for esteem, with vanity, shame and envy in its train. Since men now had more occasion for strife, they became more pugnacious. "This is precisely the state reached by most of the savage nations known to us." But though not perfect, "this period of expansion of the human faculties, keeping a just mean between the indolence of the primitive state and the petulant activity of our egoism, must have been the happiest and most durable of epochs. The more we reflect on it, the more we shall find that this state was the least subject to revolutions, and altogether the very best man could experience. . . . The example of savages, most of whom have been found in this state, seems to prove that men were meant to remain in it, that it is the real youth of the world, and that all subsequent advances have been apparently so many steps towards the perfection of the individual, but in reality towards the decrepitude of the species." Surely this passage is of great interest for us. Rousseau expressly states that the primitive community life he describes is the same as that of many extant savages, and that this life — the primitive tempered with just a trace of civilized sentiment — is the best life than man has so far enjoyed. Lovejoy observes that "this patriarchal and communistic society . . . was what a number of writers before Rousseau had meant by the ' state of nature,' " and he compares Rousseau's description of this cultural level with Montaigne's.[24]

Yet even this state is ideal only in a restricted sense. If man has shaken off primitive brutality, he is ready to put on sophistication. His blessed equilibrium is theo-

[24] *Supposed Primitivism*, p. 180.

retical, mournful, and fleeting, like the mean between the
defect and the extreme of an Aristotelian virtue. The
true Noble Savage arises from a combination of disillusion about the here and now with illusion about the there
and then. The *Discourse on Inequality* is full of the necessary disillusion, but lacks the necessary illusion. The
dour Genevan Calvinism of Rousseau's boyhood, and the
" encyclopedist " rationalism of his present period, relax
sufficiently to enable him to be enthusiastic about nature
in general, but hold him down to certain unpleasant truths
about primitive man. Lovejoy is quite right in saying
that Rousseau's picture of man in this stage of development is " far less idyllic " than the current view of the
Noble Savage.[25]

It is evident, however, that Rousseau was influenced
by the Noble Savage tradition, and not only in his account of man's happy intermediate state but in his account
of the pre-social state of nature. In what better way
could he reconstruct an image of natural man than by considering, as did Hobbes, the extant human beings who live
closest to the state of nature?

On this point there is a good deal of evidence. Rousseau knows, for instance, Tacitus' *Germania* and Montaigne's *Of the Caniballes*. In the *Discourse on the
Moral Effect of the Arts and Sciences*, after ascribing the
downfall of Greece and Rome to their highly developed
culture, he says " Contrast with these instances the morals
of those few nations which, being preserved from the contagion of useless knowledge, have by their virtues become
happy in themselves and afforded an example to the rest
of the world. . . . Such were the Germans, whose simplicity, innocence and virtue afforded a most delightful
contrast to the pen of an historian, weary of describing

[25] *Ibid.*, p. 181.

the baseness and villainies of an enlightened, opulent and voluptuous nation."

And to this passage is appended a note which should be compared with its source:

Montaigne.	*Rousseau.*
"The very words that import lying, falsehood, treason, dissimulation, covetousness, envie, detraction and pardon were never heard of amongst them.	"I dare not speak of those happy nations who did not even know the name of many vices which we find it difficult to suppress: the savages of America, whose simple and natural mode of government Montaigne preferred, without hesitation, not only to the laws of Plato, but to the most perfect visions of government philosophy can ever suggest."
"Me seemeth that what in those nations we see by experience, doth not only exceed all the pictures wherewith licentious poesie hath proudly embellished the golden age . . . but also the conception and desire of Philosophy. Lycurgus and Plato could not imagine a genuitie so pure and simple."	

Rousseau's fondness for Montaigne is well known, and we may conjecture that *Of the Caniballes* was one of his favorite essays.

Thus on a single page the denouncers of the Augustan Age, of the Renaissance and of the Enlightenment join forces. In support of Rousseau's argument the *Germania* provides an illustration, and *Of the Caniballes* a corroboratory note. But does Rousseau owe anything to the actual narratives of explorers? Let the answer be a setting down of a few typical references to savage peoples.

"The Caribeans, who have as yet least of all deviated from the state of nature, are in fact the most peaceable of people in their amours."

"What a sight would the perplexing and envied labours

of a European minister of State present to the eyes of a Caribean! "

" It would be shocking to regard as a benefactor the man who first suggested to the Oroonoko Indians the use of the boards they apply to the temples of their children, which secure to them some part at least of their imbecility and original happiness."

" The American savages, who go naked, and live entirely on the products of the chase, have been always impossible to subdue. What yoke, indeed, can be imposed on men who stand in need of nothing? "

" When I behold numbers of naked savages, that despise European pleasures, braving hunger, fire, the sword and death to preserve nothing but their independence, I feel that it is not for slaves to argue about liberty."

" It was iron and corn which first civilized men, and ruined humanity. Thus both were unknown to the savages of America, who for that reason are still savage."

" When the relics of humanity left among the Spaniards induced them to forbid their lawyers to set foot in America, what must they have thought of jurisprudence? May it not be said that they thought, by this single expedient, to make reparation for all the outrages they had committed against the unhappy Indians? "

These references, gleaned mainly from the notes, show that Jean-Jacques was not unacquainted with the literature of exploration. Professor Chinard, indeed, calls him " Un Continuateur des Missionaires Jésuites," [26] and gives an impressive array of evidence in justification of this title. I might add that Rousseau certainly knew one of the dramatic versions of *Oroonoko*,[27] and that he

[26] This is the title of Chapter I of Part IV of *L'Amérique et le rêve exotique*, which should be consulted for evidence on this point.

[27] *Confessions*, Vol. II, p. 269.

may well have known Erasmus' *Praise of Folly*.[28]   His
acquaintance with voyage-literature, and with at least
some of the French tales, plays, and satires which drew
material from the explorers and missionaries can hardly
be questioned.

Chinard's conclusion is that " natural man is still the
American savage, but stripped of his individuality, rele-
gated to the past, generalized, so to speak, and thus
becomes the very type of all primitive humanity, and consequently, our ancestor." [29]   This suggestive remark perhaps makes insufficient allowance for the element of de-
ductive speculation in Rousseau's theory.   Is it that he
generalized the Indian, or that he pondered on humanity,
and, like several of his contemporaries, seized upon the
Indian as an example of certain abstract principles he had
evolved?   I incline to the latter opinion.   And though
the discourse is undoubtedly influenced by the Noble
Savage, it presents an unusually grim and pessimistic view
of that figure.   It rejects most of the sentimental enthusiasm of the tradition, instead of, as is generally supposed, increasing its Arcadian element.

The notion that Rousseau wants mankind to return to
the woods and lead the life of savages is utterly absurd
— " a deduction in the manner of my adversaries," as
Rousseau himself calls it.   Such a course, we are told in
the Appendix of *Inequality*, would be neither possible
nor desirable.   That God implanted a disposition towards
virtue in the heart of primitive man shows that He wishes
us to strive toward perfection.   Our duty, then, is to live
as wisely and virtuously as we can in a society that places
every possible obstacle in the way of such efforts.

It is necessary to grapple with still another complica-

[28] *Vide supra,* p. 18.
[29] *L'Amérique et le rêve exotique,* p. 362.   Translation mine.

tion. For Rousseau, as he grew older, changed his conception of natural man. At the outset of the *Social Contract*, he asks his readers to imagine a time when the difficulty of self-preservation in the state of nature has impelled men to combine their forces for the common good. Now according to the discourses, the changes attendant upon such a combination could have only evil results. But Rousseau's ideas have developed. The following passage is of such cardinal importance that I need not apologize for quoting it at length:

" The passage from the state of nature to the civil state produces in man a very remarkable change, by substituting in his conduct justice for instinct, and by giving his actions the moral quality that they previously lacked. It is only when the voice of duty succeeds physical impulse, and law succeeds appetite, that man, who till then had regarded only himself, sees that he is obliged to act on other principles, and to consult his reason before listening to his inclinations. Although, in this state, he is deprived of many advantages that he derives from nature, he acquires equally great ones in return; his faculties are exercised and developed; his ideas are expanded; his feelings are ennobled; his whole soul is exalted to such a degree that, if the abuses of this new condition did not often degrade him below that from which he has emerged, he ought to bless without ceasing the happy moment that released him from it for ever, and transformed him from a stupid and ignorant animal into an intelligent being and a man."

The man who wrote that — when he wrote it — was no believer in the Noble Savage; nor was he that high priest of the cult of the sub-rational who has been painted so luridly by Professor Irving Babbitt.

" The pessimism of the concluding passage of the *Dis-*

course," says Lovejoy, " has thus been overcome by the more hopeful implications of the evolutionistic strain in that writing; and Rousseau, having now ceased to idealize *any* past stage of social development, finds his ideal in the future." [30] This remark applies also to natural man. He is no longer the not unkindly brute of the primeval forest, but man as he will become in a really just and enlightened society.

Now in *Émile* is sketched the education of a natural man in this more mature and optimistic sense. Without detailed analysis of his social and pedagogical theories, we may ask what part the Noble Savage plays in Rousseau's later conception of natural man.

The evidence begins to accumulate from the very outset. Referring to our foolish habit of binding the limbs of infants, Rousseau mentions a more sensible method of swaddling employed by the Peruvians. The information comes from Buffon, and the reader is asked to compare " Le Longue's *Voyage de Siam,* Le Beau's *Voyage de Canada,* etc." Here is testimony of Rousseau's acquaintance with the literature of exploration. The Caribs, on the other hand, swaddle new-born infants even more barbarously than we do. Rousseau neglects to point out that Caribs are closer to nature than Peruvians; but the fact that he is willing to mention the Carib practice shows that he is not a dishonest partisan of the savage.

Infants should not be bathed in warm water. Many races bathe new-born babies in rivers or the sea. This illustration may well be drawn from some voyage to the South Seas, where such Spartan methods are still in force.

Émile above all things must not be coddled; he must have plenty of hard, manly, dangerous play. " The

[30] *Supposed Primitivism,* p. 184.

sports of the young savage involve long fasting, blows, burns, and fatigue of every kind."

Émile's senses are systematically to be sharpened by various exercises. The Canadian Indian's wonderful sense of smell is instanced.

The boy's taste in food is to be kept in a primitive state as long as possible. " Fruit, vegetables, herbs, and then fried meat without salt or seasoning, formed the feasts of primitive man. When the savage tastes wine for the first time, he makes a grimace and spits it out." We are not told the result of the second attempt. A taste for meat is unnatural. Carnivorous races are cruel. " All savages are cruel, and it is not their customs that tend in this direction; their cruelty is the result of their food."

Several more such references might be brought forward. It is impossible to say that Émile as a physical organism is to be a savage, but it is certain that the savage frequently comes to Rousseau's mind when he thinks of making Émile healthy, strong, and temperate. Savages, however, are not even in this respect regarded with sentimental enthusiasm. If some of them swaddle their infants too tight, and if they are all made cruel by meat-eating, Rousseau does not hesitate to say so. He simply admires them for certain qualities which they admittedly possess.

The situation grows more complex when we come to consider Émile's mental and spiritual development. It appears that in training his body we have all along been training his mind. " There are two classes of men who are constantly engaged in bodily activity, peasants and savages, and certainly neither of these pay the least attention to the cultivation of the mind. Peasants are rough, coarse and clumsy; savages are noted, not only for their keen senses, but for great subtlety of mind. . . .

What is the cause of this difference? The peasant has always done as he was told, what his father did before him, what he himself has always done. . . . The case of the savage is very different; he is tied to no one place, he has no prescribed task, no superior to obey, he knows no law but his own will; he is therefore forced to reason at every step he takes. . . . Thus the more his body is exercised, the more alert is his mind." If this is true of the savage, Rousseau implies, it will be true of Émile.

Émile's mind will be like that of the savage in that its keenness, flexibility and freedom will not be clogged by pedantic learning. " Every one knows that the learned societies of Europe are mere schools of falsehood, and there are assuredly more mistaken notions in the Academy of Science than in a whole tribe of American Indians."

Émile has the same psycho-physical adroitness as the savage, but on a higher level. " The philosopher is aware of his own vices, he is indignant at ours, and he says to himself, ' We are all bad alike ' ; the savage beholds us unmoved and says, ' You are mad.' He is right, for no one does evil for evil's sake. My pupil is that savage, with this difference: Émile has thought more, he has compared more ideas, seen our errors at close quarters, he is more on his guard against himself, and only judges of what he knows."

This is for us an important passage. That savage who tells philosophers that they are mad is not the contented animal of the second discourse, but the shrewd Indian chief who comes to Europe to criticize the foibles of civilization — in short, one familiar variety of Noble Savage. " When I want," says Rousseau, " to train a natural man, I do not want to make him a savage and to send him back to the woods, but that living in the whirl of social life it is enough that he should not let himself be carried away by the passions and prejudices of men; let him see with his eyes and feel with his heart, let him own no sway but that of reason. . . . The same man who would remain stupid in the forests should become wise and reasonable in towns, if he were merely a spectator in them."

Now Rousseau has said that the savage, unlike the peasant, does *not* remain stupid in the forests, but on the contrary acquires "great subtlety of mind." The clue to this contradiction is not far to seek. It lies in the difference between the actual savage, seen as little better than a beast, and the Noble Savage, seen as the virtuous and scornful critic of civilization. As a supersensitive pessimist, Rousseau admires the animal peace of the former; as an idealistic prophet, he admires the supposed virtues of the latter.

Both these conceptions enter into the character of Émile, but the latter strongly predominates. We are expressly told that Émile, the natural man, will be like a savage except that he will be more "wise and reasonable" through being a "spectator" in our modern cities. The Noble Savage of the *Arlequin Sauvage* [31] type is just such a spectator. He comes to us a happy, careless child of nature, and our vices sting him into scornful reflection and wring wisdom from his wounded heart.

It seems evident that Rousseau's more mature conception of natural man has influenced his view of the Indian. The savage of *Émile* approaches the Noble Savage more closely than did the savage of *Inequality*, for the increased idealism and optimism of the general theory has tinged with brighter hues the exemplars of that theory. Yet it would be absurd to equate natural man and Noble Savage. Rousseau felt more than he was ever able to say. The ideas that he had to express were novel, but in order to

[31] Rousseau knew and admired Drevetière's play. (Chinard, *L'Amérique et le rêve exotique*, p. 230.)

convey them to his readers he was forced to make use of current formulas. For him, natural man is a great abstract conception embodying everything that nature intended us to be if we did not mar her designs. Of this conception, the idealized Indian is a fairly satisfactory concrete example. In some respects, Émile is like a Noble Savage; but who, after reading the account of his education, does not feel that in mind and soul he far transcends the noblest of savages?

To sum up, the natural man of the mature Rousseau is simply the highest common denominator of humanity — man stripped of all that differentiates one person from another, all that makes this man an Indian chief and that man an eighteenth century pawnbroker. In natural man Rousseau discerns a germ of goodness, a moral sense. This sense is older and deeper than reason, and in very simple stages of society it is in itself an adequate guide. But as man becomes confronted by more complex problems, his moral sense needs the support of reason. Let him beware, however, lest reason stifle his instinctive virtues instead of developing them. The savage has the goodness of stupid innocence. The ideal member of the "civil state" has retained the goodness of the savage, but has made it blossom into wise and strong-nerved virtue by means of art, science and philosophy. When Rousseau speaks of natural man in his maturer works he generally means the perfected, not perverted, natural man of the future. But since this perfected natural man has never existed, Rousseau derives some support for his prophetic vision from the natural man of the past as partially exemplified by the Noble Savage.

Such an interpretation, however, is not likely to be arrived at by any writer's contemporaries: it requires the perspective given by time. Different people, of course,

understood Rousseau in different ways. Perfectibilitarians
like Shelley, for example, rejoiced in the idea of natural
man perfected in wisdom. But the sentimental primitivists
of the Age of Johnson seized upon and distorted Rousseau's conception of natural man in the primitive state.
Having ideas of their own about the savage, they were
quite sure that they understood what Rousseau meant.
He was the man who wanted people to live like bears —
but like Arcadian bears of sensibility. The real Rousseau's Indian is a high, dry, somewhat grim abstraction,
resembling the satirical Noble Savage rather more closely
than the romantic Noble Savage. This prophet of sensibility never endows the savage with the emotions of
St. Preux. This pioneer of scenic description never implies that the heart of the redman is uplifted by the
mountains. This preacher of the religion of instinct never
even hints that the Carib is closer to God for being ignorant of theology. In a word, though Rousseau was in
some respects a sentimentalist, his attitude toward the
savage is almost completely unsentimental. He admires
the savage for being strong, healthy, contented, and un-
pedantically intelligent, and that is all. But the romantic
generation wanted much more than that. It merged
Rousseau's savage with his sensibility, his eroticism, his
love of scenery, his emotional deism, and produced a
quite different figure. The works of Saint-Pierre show
how a disciple could shed a warm haze of illusion over the
gaunt Spartan of Rousseau's imagination.

This sentimentalizing of Rousseau's paradoxes took
place even more easily in England. When Rousseau's
influence began to be felt across the Channel, the Noble
Savage tradition was already thoroughly familiar, and
England's romantic movement had made important advances. From that movement, indeed, Rousseau himself

had derived much. The English, with few exceptions, were unable to appreciate the encyclopedist, the Voltairean side of Rousseau's thinking. Their own rationalism had gone bankrupt, and sensibility was in fashion. They therefore accepted what they were ready to accept — the sensibility of Rousseau.

An author who has a powerful and peculiar personality, and who exhibits that personality as eagerly as did Rousseau, is especially liable to misinterpretation. Rousseau was always, in the journalistic sense of the term, " news." His quarrels, his scorn of society, his love of forest solitude, his Armenian costume, would have gladdened the heart of a modern publicity agent. He became a legendary figure long before his death, and that figure combined the Man of Feeling and the savage critic of civilization.

Our examination of *Émile*, though essential to an understanding of the mature ideas of Rousseau, has probably not helped us to trace the English attitude towards his picture of the savage. That attitude was formed by the *Discourse on Inequality*, and was probably little influenced by *Émile*. It is so much easier to judge an author by his early work than to grow with his mind. And the English were not willing to let the discourse speak for itself. They filled in the gloomy sketch of primitive man with colors derived from their own more sentimental and optimistic Noble Savage tradition. Soon they were able to add elements derived from the personal legend of Rousseau as a savage fellow, and from the later romantic enthusiasm of Rousseau — an enthusiasm which that elusive genius himself never applied to the savage.

Rousseau certainly derived much from the Noble Savage tradition, and he repaid his debt with interest. He exerted a profound influence over many elements of romanticism which, as will be shown in later chapters, became

associated with the idealized Indian. His conception of
natural man, even when imperfectly understood by his
readers, added philosophic dignity to what had been chiefly
a polite literary convention. But the tendency to see in
Rousseau the father of all romantic absurdities and vices
is nowadays so strong that, so far as our small division
of the whole subject is concerned, some corrective is necessary. The fact is that the real Rousseau was much less
sentimentally enthusiastic about savages than many of his
contemporaries, did not in any sense invent the Noble
Savage idea, and cannot be held wholly responsible for
the forms assumed by that idea in English Romanticism.

CHAPTER V

THE relation between Jacobinism and romantic naturalism is not easy to understand. From the prevalence in the revolutionary period of talk about "nature," "natural man," "natural rights," and so forth, one might be tempted to infer that the spirit of the French Revolution was the spirit of the Noble Savage brought from sentimental literature into politics. This would, however, be a reckless generalization. "Our call to liberty is ordained by nature!" cries the Abbé Fauchet in a perfectly typical address.[1] But what does Monsieur l'Abbé mean by "nature"? The neat mathematical system formed in the brains of the *philosophes*, or the life of instinct as preached by those who thought they understood Rousseau?

It would not be merely frivolous to conjecture that while Fauchet may have meant either kind of nature, he very likely meant both kinds at the same time. I find it impossible to make a hard-and-fast division between the revolutionary cult of reason and the revolutionary cult of emotion. The former was undermined by the feeling that reason itself was a sort of instinct; that man might, simply by "letting go," arrive at absolute truth. Now since the term "reason" might be regarded as synonymous with "intuition," it makes very little difference whether one means by "nature," "that state in which men reason," or "that state in which men obey the dictates of the heart."

---

[1] *A Discourse by M. L'Abbé Fauchet*, p. 6.

In his monograph on Thelwall, Charles Cestre attempts to distinguish three main currents of revolutionary philosophy.[2] There was Montesquieu, with his not very radical and very "English" *a priori* science of government. There was Rousseau, with his identification of the natural and civic rights of man. And finally there were the Encyclopedists — Diderot, d'Alembert, Helvétius and Holbach — with their doctrine of mechanical utilitarianism. Although this classification is no doubt allowable, it is much neater than the tangled skein of tendencies which it attempts to unravel. It is not difficult to understand that the old régime might be opposed because it was not reasonable enough, or because it was too reasonable. But the balance of the foregoing sentence tumbles into a muddled chaos, in which rationalism and romanticism seem inextricably confused, when one remembers that "reason" may mean common sense, or geometrical deduction, or heaven-sent intuition.

At the close of the eighteenth century, rationalism had long forgotten empiricism. Finding that facts interfere with speculation, it had thrown facts overboard and gone on speculating. That is why revolutionary rationalism and romanticism are so hard to dissociate: philosophy, at the height of her pride in cold reason, is just on the point of toppling over into the warmest emotionalism. There is no genuine contrast between two things the former of which is in process of becoming the latter.

The foregoing remarks prove merely that the subject under consideration is exceedingly complex. One errs equally in regarding the French Revolution as essentially romantic, and in regarding rationalism and romanticism as two opposite tendencies of the age. A genuinely rationalistic mind might oppose the Revolution because of its

[2] *John Thelwall*, pp. 48-49.

underlying emotionalism; a genuinely romantic mind might oppose it because of its parade of rationalism. The typical confused mind of the period would either support or oppose the revolution for a mixture of both reasons. Burke, for example, takes an attitude in which rationalism and romanticism are mingled, and arouses an equally muddled animosity on the part of certain adherents of the French.

Although the Noble Savage idea can hardly find a place in a genuinely rationalistic philosophy, it is by no means inconsistent with the trend of thought which may be called Jacobin Rationalism. Even in France, the tendency to regard reason as instinctive, and the uncertainty as to the meaning of " nature," made the Age of Reason something very different from an age of clear thinking. This already corrupt rationalism, when imported into England through the medium of revolutionary enthusiasm, was spread in thin and uneven patches over the soil of sensibility; for we must remember that England's romantic movement had already made great headway. The resultant reactions are complex. Some men, like Godwin, seem for a time to abandon naturalism for faith in reason. More, like Thelwall, effect a sort of compromise between heart and head; but with both types, the outcome is a return to a romanticism made all the deeper and stronger through disillusionment. The Man of Feeling sees that he can never become the Man of the World. Arcadianism gives up its temporary rationalistic pretense and becomes once more part of the philosophy of retreat. Throughout this period, the Noble Savage is a convenient example of whatever a writer may wish to prove. The perfectibilitarian can use him to suggest what man, once free, might become; the deteriorationist can use him to show what man formerly was, and never more will be.

That the Jacobin temperament becomes manifest in England before the actual outbreak of the French Revolution is evidenced by the work of Thomas Day. Southey states that Day " has been anathematized as a Jacobin," and that " *Sandford and Merton* will, no doubt, be included in the first English *Index Expurgatorius*." [3] This book contains so vigorous an attack upon the social and economic organization of the eighteenth century that it must indeed have been regarded as rather dangerous. It could hardly have been considered " improving " reading for children until many years after its publication. The Jacobinism of the book is so intense that its dedication to the youth of England and its studiously simple language seem at times mere disguises for the author's more serious purpose.

The importance of the Noble Savage element in *Sandford and Merton* should not be overlooked. Harry Sandford, the poor, ignorant, virtuous, priggish farm-lad, is himself a miniature man of nature. Observe his conduct when he goes to dine with the wealthy Mertons. Mrs. Merton, thinking to dazzle the ingenuous youth, offers him a silver cup. Harry refuses, saying that he has a better one at home. Mrs. Merton is incredulous, and Harry is forced to explain: " We drink at home out of long things made of horn. . . . They never make us uneasy. . . . When the man [a footman] threw that great thing down, which looks just like this, I saw that you were very sorry about it. . . . Now, ours are thrown about by all the family, and nobody minds it." The lad is constantly putting people to shame in this way. No wonder he is able to reform spoiled little Tommy Merton, who thinks himself so fine because he is rich!

But an agent of reformation quite equal to Harry in

[3] *Specimens of the Later English Poets*, Vol. III, p. 308.

importance is the Reverend Mr. Barlow, a country clergyman who is given charge of Master Merton's education. Barlow is imbued with the spirit of Rousseau's *Émile*. He believes in making the child experience the natural consequences of all his actions. Harry works in the garden, and gets a good dinner; Tommy refuses to soil his hands, and goes supperless to bed.

This Spartan régime is punctuated by periods of rest during which Barlow tells stories designed to break down Tommy's snobbishness and artificiality. Most of these deal with primitive peoples. The Laplanders, Tommy learns, are hardy, independent, and simple. They live to a great age. The Greenlanders excel in hunting the whale, and in paddling their frail kyaks. They settle all their disputes by peaceful argument, and regard themselves as superior to the delicate Europeans. The Kamtschatkans are physically so rugged that they put us to shame. Among the Arabs there is no dissension. They do not cultivate the soil, and they scorn all luxury. Courage and truthfulness are their chief virtues. The Highlanders of Scotland are remarkable for their strength, ingenuousness, and honesty. In olden times, the Scythians enjoyed a similar reputation.

Barlow also recites the longer " insert " story of Sophron, a disillusioned Alexandrian Greek who returns to nature with the usual results. He is made to say such things as: " It is surely enough that the stately heifer affords me copious streams of pure and wholesome food; I will not . . . pollute myself with her blood. . . . More wholesome, more adapted to human life are the spontaneous fruits which liberal nature produces for the sustenance of man."

The benefits of this pedagogical method are shown when little Tommy, without the slightest prompting on the part of the teacher, draws his own conclusion from the mass of material which has been presented him. " In all those stories which I have heard," he says, "it seems as if those nations, that have little or nothing, are more good-natured, and better, and braver, than those that have a great deal." A gratifying pupil!

Two important stories are told by other persons. An old soldier provides information about the Indians. Tommy is made to understand that they cannot conceive it possible that one man should serve another for money. " They imagine, that the only just distinctions arise from superior courage and bodily perfections." Thus they re-semble Mackenzie's Indians in refusing to recognize any but " natural " inequality among men.

Day resembles Mackenzie also in his acquaintance with Indian customs. Through his old soldier, he describes a war-dance rather accurately, and gives an Indian oration abounding in stock terms like " Great Father." Their use of the calumet and their general dignity in assembly give occasion for the remark that " though we call them savages, yet, in some respects, they well deserve to be imitated by more refined nations."

The soldier declares that the Indians, when at peace, are hospitable " to a degree that might shame more polished nations." In war, however, they are relentless and cruel, with something terrifying in their very appearance. " Never did I see anything which so completely awed the soul, as the angry scowl and fiery glance of a savage American." How Tommy's sophisticated little heart must have jumped at this!

But the good Barlow feels that a word of interpretation is necessary. It is hard for so young a pupil to reconcile nobility with bestial cruelty. Hence the transplanted Savoyard Vicar states that he cannot " consider, without a certain degree of admiration, the savage grandeur of man in his most simple state. The passion for revenge . . . is certainly to be condemned. But . . . many of those that call themselves refined have more to blush at, in that respect, than they are aware of. . . . I see many around me that are disgraced by the vices of uncivilized Americans, without a claim to their virtues." The *tu quoque* argument can always be relied upon to rehabilitate the reputation of the savage.

Let us turn aside for a moment to consider *The Dying Negro,* a poem written in 1773 by Day in conjunction with Bicknell. The work is said in the "advertisement" to be founded on fact. The Negro slave of a sea-captain commits suicide rather than be separated from a white woman whom he wishes to marry. The poem represents the speech delivered by the black before he stabs himself. It contains a great deal about European greed and oppression, but is noteworthy chiefly for its enthusiastic attitude toward the Negroes.

> "What though no rosy tints adorn their face,
>   No silken tresses shine with flowing grace;
>   Yet of ethereal temper are their souls,
>   And in their veins the tide of honour rolls:
>   .   .   .   .
>   And pity melts the sympathizing breast,
>   Ah! fatal virtue! for the brave distress'd."

Their virtue is "fatal" in that it leads them to be kind to the white explorers, who treacherously and ungratefully enslave them.

The spirit in which the authors write is evidenced by the following note, which they cull from Adamson's *Voyage to Senegal:* "I beheld a perfect image of pure nature, an agreeable solitude bounded on every side by charming landscapes; the rural situation of cottages in the midst of trees; the ease and indolence of the Negroes, re-clined under the shade of their spreading foliage; the simplicity of their dress and manners; the whole revived in my mind the idea of our first parents, and I seemed to contemplate the world in its primitive state." The Ne-groes, in short, are Noble Savages.

With *The Dying Negro* in mind, we may return to *Sandford and Merton,* where a wandering black adds his contribution to Tommy's education. He is natural man brought from Arcadia to testify that in England " there are thousands who live like birds in cages, upon the food provided by others."

The whites are accused of hoarding superfluous treas-ures, of living in houses larger than their needs demand, of cramping their bodies in absurd garments. "When you want to eat, you must have meat enough served up to nourish a whole village; yet I have seen poor famished wretches starving at your gate, while the master has before him at least an hundred times as much as he could con-sume. We negroes, whom you treat as savages, have dif-ferent manners and different opinions."

" The innocent negro," in his African thatched hut, would live content, "provided you did not drag him by fraud and violence away, and force him to endure all the excesses of your cruelty." For Africa is a happy land. Every prospect pleases, and man is there less vile than anywhere else. The Negro women sing merrily in the fields. None refuses the stranger food and shelter. Each town has a sort of common hall. Here, in the evening, the elders "converse upon a variety of subjects," the young men and maidens dance, and the children play games. What has Europe to offer in return for the inno-cent pleasures of which the Negro has been robbed?

In no other work shall we find such a galaxy of Noble Savages. Here are English rustics, Laplanders, Greenlanders, Kamtschatkans, Arabs, Scotch Highlanders, Scythians, Indians and Negroes, all pointing their accusing fingers at " enlightened " civilization. The conception of primitive innocence here influences educational theory, and adds force to the anti-slavery movement. Most important of all, it appears as a phase of the social protest, of the growing revolutionary tendencies of the age.

Those tendencies appear in full force soon after the publication of Burke's *Reflections* in 1790. This work was liable to attack from several sources. Its occasional harsh insistence on expediency made it repugnant to the " men of feeling," and its occasional obscurantist sentimentality enraged the coldly rationalistic group. Among those who leaped into the scrimmage several are interesting to us in connection with the Noble Savage, and none more so than William Godwin.

The Godwin of *Political Justice* (1793) looks forward to a time when abstract justice and wisdom will become concrete entities in social life. He has utter faith in the perfectibility of man. To him perfection implies a state of high cultural civilization combined with Spartan simplicity in material affairs. This ideal is to be attained through reason, and " reason depends for its clearness and strength upon the cultivation of knowledge."

Godwin makes the Socratic identification of knowledge and virtue. Evil is based on, is almost another term for, ignorance. The true is the good; human reason can discover the truth and thus eliminate all weakness and vice. The instincts beloved of Burke are literally non-existent. Nothing is innate; our mental content is the sum of all sense-impressions received since birth. Over this mass of images we must exert rigidly rational control. To succumb to the allurements of the senses, to think or act impulsively, is to be less than a man; for "the perfection of the human character consists in approaching as nearly as possible to the perfectly voluntary state. We ought to be, upon all occasions, prepared to render a reason for our actions." Burke's appeal to nature is hence a meaningless verbal flourish. The maxim, "follow nature," is — as John Stuart Mill was later to point out — generally an apology for perpetuating ancient prejudices. Reason is the only standard.

We may assume that with such views Godwin is no friend to the Noble Savage; and indeed he makes a direct attack upon the whole Arcadian tradition, protesting that "innocence is not virtue. Virtue demands the active employment of an ardent mind in the promotion of the general good. . . . Individuals of exquisite feeling . . . have recurred in imagination to the forests of Norway, or the bleak and uncomfortable Highlands of Scotland in search of a purer race of mankind. This imagination has been the offspring of disappointment, not the dictate of reason and philosophy." In the series of papers entitled *The Enquirer*, Godwin gives another indication of his attitude toward primitivism. The essay styled *Of Learning* rejects the idea that learning and genius are mutually hostile. If this were true, savages would be geniuses. Men rise from the savage state "because they build upon one another's structures." The man who consults his own thoughts rather than those of others "seems to propose . . . to divest himself of this fundamental advantage."

Godwin's general philosophy, together with the two specific passages just cited, would seem definitely to establish him as a hostile critic of the Noble Savage. *The Enquirer*, however, contains a prefatory remark which indicates a decided slackening of revolutionary ardor. Between 1793, the date of *Political Justice*, and 1797, the date of *The Enquirer*, lie the Reign of Terror, war with France, and some vigorous official spy-hunting. Small wonder, then, if Godwin admits that "the friends of innovation were somewhat too imperious in their tone," and that, "with as ardent a passion for innovation as ever, he feels himself more patient and tranquil." Now with Godwin, as with more than one of his contemporaries, this patience and tranquillity bring an attitude much less rationalistic and much more favorable to the Noble Savage idea.

Godwin's novel *St. Leon* (1799), for example, has marked naturalistic elements. The hero loses his last penny at the gaming-table, goes mad, and is taken to the Swiss Alps by his wife. His brain gradually mends, but he cannot share his wife's fondness for peasants and mountain scenery. Suddenly, there comes a terrific hailstorm which reduces the already impoverished family to utter destitution. The effect on St. Leon is psychologically interesting. The loss of every material thing which might distinguish him from less fortunate men seems to awaken in him a sense of the sublimity of fundamental human nature. Recovering sanity, he cries, "Henceforth I desire only to dedicate myself to the simplicity of nature and the genuine sentiments of the heart."

The family moves to the shores of the Lake of Constance, there to begin life anew. "The romantic elevation" of St. Leon's soul "particularly fitted" him to enjoy the scenery. And his domestic life was a renewal of the golden age, a scene from some old pastoral "without its grossness, a situation remote from cities and courts, ... yet not unadorned with taste, imagination and knowledge."

This Eden is lost through the intrusion of the serpent in

the person of a mysterious stranger, who, dying, bequeathes to St. Leon the secret of the philosopher's stone. Assured of eternal life and limitless wealth, St. Leon returns to his old extravagant conduct. But his sudden prosperity awakens suspicion, and he is cast into prison.

At this point appears a genuine Noble Savage. St. Leon attempts to bribe the Negro turnkey, but in vain. The black owes the jailer, his master, a debt of gratitude, and not all the jewels of Golconda will budge him one inch. " He was destitute of knowledge, of intellectual cultivation, and all those exquisite sensations that most distinguish the man from the brute. He passed on quietly in the road of ordinary life, and thought not of the ambition to be wise or great. . . . Kings might have confessed their inferiority to this man. But is he to be regarded as the model of what a human creature should be wished to be? Oh, no! " [4]

It is needless to pursue the story further. This praise of the Negro, with its concluding " Oh, no! " sums up Godwin's attitude toward the Noble Savage at this time. The black is not an ideal man, because his intellect has not been developed; but he does prove the potentialities of the human race.

This attitude, however, is merely an intermediate stage in the development of Godwin's thought. In *Fleetwood*, which was published in 1805, he appears as an almost complete sentimental naturalist. The sub-title, " The New Man of Feeling," implies a decided relaxation from Godwin's early insistence on cold reason and voluntary conduct. The story, indeed, is so permeated with the Noble Savage idea as to demand a running summary.

Young Fleetwood is reared in the romantic fastnesses of Merionethshire, in North Wales. From his scholarly

[4] Note the echo of Gray's *Elegy*.

father he derives a love of books, but nature is his supreme passion.   Constant familiarity with precipices and water-falls gives his character a sort of wild earnestness.   He has never seen the city, but shrinks with instinctive horror from the grossness, the craft, the contentiousness of " the noisy mart."

The wildness of the lad does not imply any lack of benevolence.   On the contrary, he is always doing good deeds among the simple cottagers.   Once he not only saves a peasant from drowning, but gives the man enough money to enable him to marry his sweetheart.   Nor are these " little, nameless, unremembered acts of kindness and of love " dictated by a coldly selfish morality.   " My own heart . . . gave the lie to this execrable doctrine. . . . I experienced a disinterested joy in human relief and human happiness."   This instinctive kindness extends, as in *Sand-ford and Merton,* even to dumb animals, and makes him refuse to hunt or fish.   His favorite companion is a noble dog.   When Fleetwood goes down to the university, this faithful creature breaks his chain, follows his master to Oxford — a matter of one hundred and seventy miles — and, not finding him in his chambers, intelligently trots down to the chapel and waits until the service is over.

The trusty dog, alas, finds that Oxford has worked a sad change in his benefactor.   " In Merionethshire," Fleet-wood tells us, " I had been a solitary savage"; and for the first few weeeks of his university life he behaves precisely like the typical Noble Savage in contact with civilization. He finds it impossible to adapt his phrases, which " were those of enthusiasm and the heart," to the thin sharpness of undergraduate wit.   His smile, on the rare occasions when he condescends to smile, is that " of elevated senti-ment, not that of supercilious contempt, of petty triumph, or convivial jollity."   The picture is singularly like that of

Wordsworth at Cambridge. Not for long, however, does Fleetwood withstand the contagious influences of his environment. Gradually he sinks in the mire of hazing, drunkenness and debauchery. "O divinity that presidest over the constellations. . . ! how was your pupil fallen! how the awestruck and ardent worshipper . . . changed into . . . the shameless roarer of a licentious catch!" Yet the lad is still sound at the core. Inwardly, in the romantic fashion so irritating to Professor Babbitt, he holds himself aloof.

This essential integrity does not, however, prevent him from pursuing in Paris, after his graduation, a career of sexual dissipation. The surprising discovery that his mistress is inconstant produces a Byronic malady for which mountains are the remedy. " I loathed existence and the sight of day. . . . I fled from Paris and sought the craggy and inhospitable Alps; the most frightful scenes alone had power to please, and produced in me a kind of malicious and desperate sentiment of satisfaction."

But the mountains, while satisfying Fleetwood's bitter mood, gradually fill him with softer, loftier feelings. He is soothed. In the simplicity of the Swiss peasants, too, is balm for one who has lost faith in humanity. Who could stand before Tell's chapel, a cynic? Not Fleetwood; his reaction is remarkable: " I thought of William Tell . . . ; I thought of the simple manners which still prevail in the primitive cantons; I felt as if I were in the wildest and most luxuriant of the uninhabited islands of the South Sea. I was lost in visions of paradise, of habitations and bowers among the celestial orbs . . . of the pure rewards and enjoyments of a happier state."

Fleetwood's father has died, and the boy, feeling that he needs the advice of an older man, visits his father's friend, M. Ruffigny. M. Ruffigny dwells in the Canton of Uri, at the foot of Mt. St. Gothard. He is the typical good old man of the period, mildly didactic, consciously benevolent, vaguely and broadly religious, and a vegetarian. One thinks of the Savoyard Vicar. He prefers " the great and living volume of nature " to " cold, insensible, mechanically constructed " books. Books are valuable as a sort of commentary on human life, however, and are not utterly to be neglected. Godwin in his most romantic moments never quite forsakes his love of learning.

Ruffigny points out to Fleetwood the " happy contrast " between " the simplicity of man, and the exuberance of nature." He reawakens in the youth all the virtues of his Welsh boyhood. The old Houyhnhnm is so venerable in appearance, so " primitive and patriarchal in his manners and modes of thinking, that it was perhaps impossible to converse intimately with him and yet continue whelmed in the mire of licentiousness."

In any novel of the period, so important a character must have a story of his own to tell, and Ruffigny is no exception. An orphan child, he is handed over by a wicked uncle to a silk-manufacturer of Lyons, who sets him to work in the mill. Here occurs a very early attack on child labor, with the comment: " The children of gypsies and savages have ruddy cheeks and a sturdy form, can run like lapwings, and climb trees with the squirrel." The children in manufacturing towns are pale and spindly, and have never seen a squirrel.

> " If we cared for any meadows, it were merely
> To drop down in them and sleep."

So little Ruffigny runs away to Paris. In that city, the rich and well-born treat him either with indifference or positive brutality. His only friends are Noble Savages of

the modified Fielding type — a barmaid and a private
in the Swiss Guards. He meets at last the grandfather of
the present Fleetwood, and by him is adopted. Thence-
forth all goes well. When Grandfather Fleetwood dies,
Ruffigny becomes the friend and counsellor of our hero's
father.

We now return to the main channel of the narrative.
Ruffigny and Fleetwood go to London. Fleetwood is
never quite at ease in literary, political or polite society.
The old savage strain will out. " I was the spoiled child
of the great parent, Nature. . . . What aspired to please
me must be as wild as the artless warblings of the choris-
ters of the woods." His unrest is like that of Wordsworth in the same situation.

Fleetwood has reached the age of forty-five when he
hears of the virtues of Mr. Macneil, the recluse of Cumberland. Since Macneil had been a friend of Rousseau's
during the great man's visit to England, Fleetwood begs
the honor of his acquaintance in an amusing letter: " In
my youth I was a wild roe among the mountains of Wales:
as I grew up, I entered upon the scenes of active life, foolishly, not criminally. I contracted an early distaste for
the practices and the society of the world." Macneil is not
the man to refuse such an appeal, and invites Fleetwood
to his rustic home.

Although the two men become fast friends, their temperaments are at variance. Fleetwood is impatient at the
discrepancy between the capacities of human nature, as
evidenced by a few men of genius, and the stupidity and
brutality of the great mass of men. Macneil dwells rather
upon the essential divinity of the average. " In every man
that lives . . . there is much to be commended. . . . I
feel my heart swell within me, when I recollect that I belong to a species, almost every individual of which is en-

dowed with angelic virtues." Fleetwood admires these sentiments, though he cannot share them. Since the hero of every Godwin novel is Godwin himself,[5] it is interesting and rather pathetic to see this frustrated perfectibilitarian envying the mental peace of the primitivist.

Macneil has a lovely daughter, Mary. "Her delight was in flowers; and she seemed like one of the beauties of her own parterre, soft and smooth and brilliant and fragrant and unsullied." Fleetwood weds her. The rest of the book is a study of the psychology of conjugal jealousy, and uses the Othello theme with a happy ending.

It is almost gratuitous to point out the contrast between the Godwin of *Political Justice* and the Godwin of *Fleetwood*. The former is a thorough-going revolutionary rationalist; the latter, a thorough-going romanticist. In place of the old scorn of all things primitive now appears a persistent glorification of the man of nature. The Noble Savage idea, expressly repudiated in the tractate, forms the very backbone of the novel, and Fleetwood himself is something of a Noble Savage. Thus in *Political Justice*, *St. Leon* and *Fleetwood* are respectively illustrated the shallow pride, the wavering, and the final collapse of Jacobin Rationalism.

We now turn from Godwin to the remarkable woman who became his wife. Mary Wollstonecraft's *Historical and Moral View of the Origin and Progress of the French Revolution* resembles *Political Justice* in several respects. The author is, for instance, a perfectibilitarian who hails

---

[5] *Collected Works of William Hazlitt*, Vol. IV, p. 209: " The reader identifies himself with the author, and the secret of that is, that the author has identified himself with his personages." Hazlitt adds other remarks expressive of his opinion that Godwin's novels are wholly sincere.

the revolution as the embodiment of the lofty doctrines of the *philosophes*. At last, she says, we have reached the " point when sincerity of principles seems to be hastening the overthrow of the tremendous empire of superstition and hypocrisy, erected upon the ruins of gothic brutality and ignorance."

But there is a distinction to be made between the two books. *Political Justice* appeared in 1793, just at the beginning of the Terror; *Origin and Progress of the French Revolution* in 1794, after a year of butchery which appalled all but the most ardent of the English Jacobins. Mary Wollstonecraft must therefore adjust her theory to some rather grim facts. In concluding her argument she tries to assure the reader that France is merely ridding itself of " excrementitious humours," but in the body of the book she grapples with the problem in more genuine fashion.

Her thesis is that the old régime has caused a degeneracy in morals. Thanks to the luxury and extravagance provoked by the examples of courts, " the genial current of natural feelings has been poisoned." Even worse than the aristocracy of birth is the newer aristocracy of commerce, which only makes mankind " exchange savageness for tame servility, instead of acquiring the urbanity of improved reason." Reason is man's goal, but utter savagery is a finer state than the present cringing servitude. " Those miserable wretches who crawl under the feet of others are seldom to be found among savages, where men . . . are, in general, brave, hospitable and magnanimous; and it is only as they surrender their rights, that they lose those noble qualities of the heart."

Far from being an opponent of the Noble Savage, as she has sometimes been called, Mary Wollstonecraft makes him the mainstay of her argument for perfectibility.

She contrasts the vices of savage man with those of civilized man, and finds that the former " is an angel, compared with the refined villain of artificial life." And what causes have produced this degeneracy? Plainly, "those unjust plans of government, which have been formed by peculiar circumstances in every part of the globe." The evident remedy is, then, a government which would allow the natural virtues of man to develop, a government " more simple than has hitherto existed." In the same year in which this book appears, we find Mary, in a letter to the rascal Imlay, saying of Rousseau, " I have always been half in love with him." To Rousseau her discussion of the Revolution certainly owes much.

The reader who thinks of the Noble Savage as a glorified American Indian has grown restive. He will ask what has become of the redman since *Emmera, The Man of Feeling, The Man of the World*, and *Sandford and Merton*. He is now to be assured that the tradition steadily continues, influenced by and in turn influencing the theories of the English Jacobins.

Since Mrs. Charlotte Lennox published her first book, *The Life of Harriot Stuart*, in 1751, and was fêted by Dr. Johnson at the Club, she may be irreverently styled an "old-timer." It is not surprising, therefore, that in her *Euphemia* (1790) the Indian should be seen in the mild glamor of sensibility rather than in the lurid glow of revolutionary enthusiasm. The distinctive thing about Mrs. Lennox is that, as the daughter of a colonial official,[6] she passed her girlhood in American frontier posts. When she describes garrison life in Albany and Schenectady she is putting on paper part of her early life. This spark of

[6] Her father was Col. James Ramsay, Lieutenant-Governor of New York.

verisimilitude, however, is almost totally extinguished by her desire to give her readers that romantic view of the American wilderness necessary to obtain popularity for her book. She provides a rich background of scenic beauty through which stalk picturesque and virtuous Indians. Her good characters imbibe inspiration from the Arcadian atmosphere; her bad ones are either reformed or frustrated by its influence.

The hero's mother, but recently come to the wilds, is so badly scared by the Indians that her son, upon his subsequent entrance into the world, bears upon his left breast a perfectly formed bow and arrow. The lady's terror was needless, but providential; for it furnishes the youth a talisman which gives him a claim on the friendship of the Indians. In particular it secures the loyalty of a fine old Mohawk chief — stern and relentless in revenge, but brave, hospitable, grateful for kindness, honorable, sagacious and with the usual talent for sententious oratory. But since Mrs. Lennox adds nothing to Mackenzie's portrayal of similar figures, the sachem's virtues had best be taken for granted.

The earlier portions of Mrs. Lennox's first novel, *The Life of Harriot Stuart*, take place in the neighborhood of Albany, but Indians play practically no part in the book. The heroine says of them that they " had an air so savage and frightful that I could not look on them without trembling." We may assume that Mrs. Lennox had no real affection for Indians, but that by the time she came to write *Euphemia* she realized the fashionableness of sentimental primitivism.

Of the next generation is Mrs. Charlotte Turner Smith, whose *Elegiac Sonnets* (1784) preceded by five years the work of Bowles in the same form. *Emmeline* (1788) is her first novel.   Her prose works were animated by two purposes: to oppose ideals of restrained, rational and virtuous conduct to what she considered the dangerous cult of sensibility then prevalent, and to spread the doctrines of the Revolution.   She is thus a disciple of the coldly rationalistic Godwin of *Political Justice*.   Her *Desmond* (1792) is full of Jacobin philosophy, but it is *The Old Manor House* (1793) that uses the Noble Savage as a stalking-horse for her ideas.

The story is set in the period of the American Rebellion. Orlando, the hero, is forced to enlist in the army which is being sent against the colonists.   Mrs. Smith sympathizes with America; she represents the war as unjust in its origin and brutal, corrupt and inefficient in its conduct. Burgoyne's army is almost wholly composed of sordid wretches eager to butcher their brothers for the King's shilling.   In such a crew, the brave but gentle Orlando is out of place.   It is almost a relief for him to be captured by Indians of the American party.   The savages, enraged at English brutalities, are about to put him to death; but Wolf-hunter, an admirable chief, sees that he is more than a vulgar mercenary and saves his life.   Orlando's sojourn among the Indians gives Mrs. Smith an excellent opportunity to contrast, chiefly through the actions and speech of Wolf-hunter, savage and civilized life.   The general nature of this comparison has already been observed in Mary Wollstonecraft's *French Revolution*.   The Indians are not immaculate, but we are worse, having through complexity and sophistication forsaken their virtues and magnified their vices.   Wolf-hunter is not an ideal man, but he is a better man than such a drunken, bloodthirsty slave of kings as General Burgoyne.

The Indians employed by the British are portrayed with much less enthusiasm.   Mrs. Smith attempts to show that they are sound at heart, but have been corrupted by lies, false promises and bribes. She is not quite able, however, to reconcile the Noble Savage with the actual Indian, and leaves one uncertain as to whether the redman is a gentle child of nature or a skulking, cruel monster. Does not somewhat the same confusion pervade the novels of James Fenimore Cooper? Do not Uncas and his Huron foes belong, not merely to different tribes, but to different literary traditions? As in the case of Charlotte Lennox, Cooper mingles the realism of his own knowledge with the cult of the heroic redman handed down to him from Mackenzie.

A true Jacobin in the height of revolutionary fervor would seldom need to present his readers with an actual savage; for the man of nature was now to be sought, not in the American forests, but in redeemed and liberated Europe. A favorite figure of Jacobin fiction is therefore the virtuous young radical. Though this type of hero is not literally an Indian, his theories and actions are often inspired by the example of the Noble Savage. Holcroft and Bage provide the best illustrations of this tendency.

Frank Henley, the hero of Holcroft's *Anna St. Ives* (1792), is the son of a baronet's gardener, but has the temerity to love his master's daughter. "Pshaw! What is a Baronet? — Away with such insolent, such ridiculous distinctions." That remark typifies his character. He is very severe with the nobility, sneers at laws, and disbelieves in private property. In the opinion of his rival, he behaves like "the legitimate son of Cato's eldest bastard."

Frank's life is one chain of remarkable deeds. He rescues Anna from a highwayman, then rescues the highwayman from jail and reforms him. He is constantly relieving the poor or saving the lives of his enemies. Nor can he understand why his heroism should be admired. He simply has a " system " and follows it consistently. That system is what distinguishes him from a mere Man of Feeling or Fool of Quality. He is benevolent " by the book," and his sensibility is the outgrowth of severely rational principles.

Fortunately Anna St. Ives shares the opinions of her lover. In fact, this pair have acquired the complete God-winian doctrine of perfectibility a year before the appearance of *Political Justice*. But their love, if the term can be applied to their calm mutual esteem, is thwarted by Coke Clifton, a young aristocrat whom the Baronet regards as a more suitable candidate for his daughter's hand.

Clifton is represented as a clever youth whose fundamental goodness has been spoiled by selfishness and frivolity. In every respect he is the antithesis of Frank, and he expresses amusingly his opinion of his rival. " I scarcely know," he writes his sister, " what to make of him; except that he seems to have quite conceit enough of himself. Every other sentence is a contradiction of what the last speaker advanced. This is the first time he ever ventured to cross his father's threshold, and yet he talks as familiarly of kingdoms, governments, nations, manners and other high sounding phrases, as if he had been secretary of state to King Minos. . . . He is the Great Mogul of politicians! And as for letters, science, and talents, he holds them all by patent right."

Clifton later comes to understand that Frank's self-confidence rises not from conceit, but from philosophy. The knowledge to which he lays claim has nothing to do with wealth, breeding or worldly experience: it is acquired simply by following the dictates of reason — the reason which provides the common denominator of all mankind. "He is one of your levellers! Marry! His superior! Who is he? On what proud eminence can he be found?

. . . Dispute his prerogative who dare! He derives from Adam; what time the world was all 'hail fellow well met!' The savage, the wild man of the woods, is his true liberty-boy; and the ourang-outang, his first cousin. A lord is a merry Andrew, a duke a jack-pudding, and a king a tom-fool; his name is man! "

The vivacity of Clifton's remarks indicates that Holcroft does not wholly admire the intolerable prig whom he has selected for a hero. Some of his own feeling must enter into Clifton's remark that there is nothing "so nauseous as an over-dose of wisdom; mixed up, according to the modern practice, with a quantum sufficit of virtue, and a large double handful of the good of the whole." But Frank Henley, despite even Holcroft's limited affection for him, rises from pinnacle to pinnacle of virtue until at last he wins Anna; while Clifton becomes more and more a thwarted Richardsonian villain.

We have seen that Clifton associates Frank with "the wild man of the woods." Frank himself admits, by implication, a sympathy with savages. In a moment of discouragement he writes to a friend: "I have studied to divine in what land or among what people, whether savage or such as we call polished, the energies of mind might be most productive of good. . . . I think of sailing for America, where I may aid the struggles of liberty . . . and at the same time may form a society of savages, who seem in consequence of their very ignorance to be less liable to repel truth than those whose information is more multifarious." This recoil of the perfectibilitarian is significant; the pantisocracy of Coleridge and Southey has the same psychological basis.

The hero of Robert Bage's *Hermsprong, or Man As He Is Not* (1796) has a still closer connection with the Noble Savage. This book is a curious mixture. It has

something of the satirical sting of Voltaire, the whimsi-
cality of Sterne, the sensibility of Mackenzie, the paradoxical quality of Rousseau and the geometrical relentlessness
of Godwin.   With this compound, as with some caustic
acid, Bage attacks the constituted order of things — government, law, economics, religion, war, the conventions of
marriage and parental authority.   He sets before us a
typical English rural community.   There is surly, tyran-
nical, unscrupulous Lord Grondale, the Lord of the
Manor.   He has a lovely daughter, Caroline Campinet,
oppressed but dutiful.   Her friend and adviser is Miss
Stuart, a witty vixen of unbending spirit.   The clergy is
represented by Dr. Blick, the pompous and hypocritical
rector, and by his curate Woodcock, a pretty bad imitation
of Parson Adams.   A Man of Feeling named Glen tells
the story, and takes some part in the action.   Add to these
a dishonest lawyer who helps Grondale in various unsavory projects; Mr. Sumelin, a stupid but well-meaning
merchant of the nearby industrial town; a hazy chorus of
poor tenants; another hazy chorus of artisans — and the
cast is complete save for the hero.

  One morning Miss Campinet's horse becomes unman-
ageable, and is just about to dash over a cliff with his fair
rider, when a total stranger, with infinite strength and
courage, effects a rescue.   It is the mysterious Hermsprong, who has suddenly arrived in the community from
goodness knows where.   At all events his motives seem
honest, for he follows his rescue of Miss Campinet with a
series of benevolent deeds which would make Pollyanna
or the hero of *The Passing of the Third Floor Back* choke
with envy.   When a storm causes suffering among the
poor, he relieves their distress.   He saves a nice girl from
marriage to a mercenary.   He gives Lord Grondale's
neglected old cousin a roof for her gray hairs.   When the

tenants are oppressed, he lends them his support; and when a mob of artisans seem likely to smash things, he calms them with words of reason.

But Hermsprong is more than a professional benefactor. All who meet him are impressed by a strangely individual quality in his manners and speech. The man is not especially handsome, and yet his face has a peculiar distinction. His behavior is " rather open and engaging, than graceful. There is an ease about him, but it is an unstudied, unimitated ease. It seems his own." This pleasing naturalness, however, sometimes borders on the outlandish. The host of the inn complains that the stranger, after a forty-mile hike in shoes " as soft and pliable as silk," will dine upon a cold round of beef, " seasoned . . . with a quart or two of good spring water." Hermsprong traces many diseases of civilization to intemperance in eating and drinking, and his outspokenness on this theme is sometimes embarrassing to those who invite him to dinner.

Mine host did not exaggerate Hermsprong's pedestrian exploits. The man walks everywhere, even to London. The reason is not merely love of healthful exercise, but unwillingness to be encumbered with petty obligations to others. " I must be independent," he says, " as far as a social man can be independent. . . . I must be free from the necessity of doing little things, or saying *little* words, to any man." Another of his strange notions is that it is possible for a man to be too much favored by fortune. When Miss Campinet expresses surprise at " such youth and such philosophy," and asks, " Can the alliance be natural? " he responds, " I should think it was, since it was of the sons of nature I learned it." Now what did he mean by that?

Hermsprong's independence makes him open-minded toward the Revolution. Its aims, " to make mankind wiser and better," are admirable. The means employed are partly good and partly bad. " It is left to the loyal Englishman . . . to approve by the lump." A sane man must discriminate. " All the malignant, as well as the better passions, are afloat in France; and malignant actions are the consequence. Many of the acts of the Assembly are acts of necessity, and some, no doubt, of folly." Here is a man whose reason rises above the blind prejudice of partisanship.

Such a being is not likely to defer to men who have no other claims to respect than coronets and fat purses. When Lord Grondale upbraids him for his attentions to Miss Campinet, he replies: " My fortune . . . kings might envy; it is equal to my desires. As to rank — I have been taught only to distinguish men by virtue." Later he begs Miss Campinet's pardon for being unable to show toward her father a respect which he does not feel. "Whether the frankness I have learned in my youth be, in highly polished countries, a virtue or a vice, I know not." What sort of training could account for such proud stiffness of neck?

The lovely Caroline, though she admires her strange suitor's spirit, and cordially detests her father, is too meek to be undutiful. Timidly she urges the wisdom of humility.

" Humility to a proud man," comes the retort, " is a price I cannot pay — even for life."

" Do you know any country in the world . . . where this price is not paid? "

" Amongst the Aborigines of America, Miss Campinet. . . . I was born a savage."

At this disclosure, " Miss Campinet felt the strangest sort of fear; she never could tell what it was like." The story of Hermsprong's boyhood is not fully told at this point, but the clue here given is sufficient to explain, not merely the wild naturalness of his manners, but his habit of illustrating his conversation by references to savage life. Thus when told that his presence of mind in rescuing Miss Campinet was almost superhuman, he cheerfully admits that few civilized Europeans could have equalled it, but asserts that many American Indians would have made nothing of such a feat. "Man may be in a situation betwixt a state of nature and extreme civilization, such that intrepidity and possession of mind, in sudden danger, may be necessary even for existence." We are reminded of Rousseau's intermediate state.

Later, in discussing with the Reverend Dr. Blick the fear of death, Hermsprong avers that the savage does not dread death "with the timidity of nations who are taught from infancy to fear it." And when Dr. Blick insists that it is unnatural not to fear death, he is met by " Man cannot be taught anything contrary to nature. However he acts, he must act by nature's laws." Which shows that the Noble Savage can on occasion adopt Godwin's necessitarian philosophy.

Glen, the Man of Feeling who tells the entire story, grows a little weary of Hermsprong's praise of savages, and points to certain fruits of progress not possessed by the Indians. Hermsprong grants the progress, but questions whether material advances have wrought much genuine improvement. The great question is whether men are happier than they formerly were, and it is doubtful whether any causal connection exists between happiness and wealth. Progress has brought riches to a few, dire poverty to many. The delights of art and science never reach the common people, and eventually pall even upon the small group rich enough to enjoy them. Luxury brings satiety, and yet renders forever impossible the old delight in simple pleasures. Now the savages have no such artificial cravings, but enjoy every moment of their simple existence. And this is true happiness — " not indeed so high raised as yours sometimes, but more continued, and more uninterrupted."

Hermsprong, though he would not himself give up literature for the games, dances and songs of the Indian, observes that these primitive sports *always* give the savage wholesome pleasure, whereas reading *often* causes headache and boredom. Many men read simply because they have nothing else to do. The study of books, also, does not necessarily lead to knowledge, but rather to empty religious and philosophical disputes which " are calculated rather to confound than enlighten the understanding. Your infinite variety, does it not tend to render you superficial? . . . In variety of knowledge, the Aborigines of America are much your inferiors. What they do know, perhaps they know better." Opposition to the early theories of Godwin on the connection between learning and knowledge, and between knowledge and virtue, is noticeable in this argument. The brief day of rationalistic enthusiasm is spent, and we have returned once more to the atmosphere of Rousseau's discourses.

Like Rousseau, Hermsprong does not admire savage life so much in an absolute sense as in comparison with any other state. Indians, he says, are not perfect. Although they are not to be improved by European rum and diseases and pomp, they do need more objects of reflection. " That, to me, should seem the happiest state of society, in which all its members had the power to alternate the employments of the mind and body, that the operations of each might be enjoyment." But since such a state nowhere exists, and since attempts to attain a similar ideal have failed in the United States and in France, he cannot help yearning back toward the limited but self-sufficient existence of the Indian. Disillusionment has caused a revival of the earlier Rousseau's paradoxical deteriorationism, and the Noble Savage idea, which in *St. Leon* supports the doctrine of perfectibility, here buttresses the opposite theory.

But let us drop Hermsprong's philosophy and turn to the story of his boyhood as imparted to Mr. Glen. His father, a German merchant, incurs the displeasure of his own wealthy parents by marrying beneath him. He — Hermsprong's father — therefore goes to America, where he enters into partnership with Mr. Germersheim, a Philadelphia fur merchant. The son of a Nawdoessie chief comes to Philadelphia on a trading embassy, and " my father, fond of seeing man in a less civilized state, was delighted to converse with him." The white man returns with the Indian to Michillimakinac as Germersheim's agent. He is well received by Great Beaver, the head man of the village, and by all the tribe.

Hermsprong's mother, after staying some time in Philadelphia, comes west to join her husband. An offensively religious woman, she sets out to convert the savages. She begins on Great Beaver's squaw but is repulsed, and next seeks the chief himself. Great Beaver listens courteously to her exhortations; then by way of exchange tells her one of his own myths, dealing with white bears that speak to one another. This tale the woman scorns as incredible.

" A serpent . . . spoke to the first woman," Great Beaver reminds her.

" But . . . they were inspired."

" So was the white bear."

" But this is so excessively absurd."

" I have not called your wonders absurd. I thought it more decent to believe." [7]

Thus urbanely he exposes her bigotry; and she, greatly to her husband's amusement, huffily abandons proselytizing. She now turns to the more useful task of giving birth to the hero of our tale.

Hermsprong grows up among the coppery children of the tribe, imbibing the strength, the courage and the proud independence which are later to startle the pampered sons of luxury. But when he is sixteen, his father dies, and his mother, who has never loved the wilds, returns to Europe. Hermsprong is forced to learn book-keeping and dancing; but, finding himself " too wild and rude " for such tame pursuits, runs away, travels about seeing Europe, and finally winds up in England, where we now behold him.

One further surprise is in store for the reader of Bage's novel. Lord Grondale, eager to ruin Hermsprong, commands his attorney to devise a treason case against him. The hireling reports: " He has read the Rights of Man — this I can almost prove; and also that he has lent it to one friend . . . , which . . . is circulation. . . . I know also where he said, that the French constitution, though not perfect, had good things in it; and that ours was not so good but it might be mended. Now, you know, my Lord, the bench of Justices will not bear such things now." (A shrewd thrust at anti-Jacobin agitation, and perhaps at the Thelwall case in particular.) The trial of Hermsprong not only results in acquittal and complete vindication, but brings to light the fact that Hermsprong's real

---

[7] Bissell (p. 75) quotes from Franklin's *Remarks Concerning the Savages of North America* a passage which appears to be the source of this dialogue. A close parallel appears in Lahontan's *Dialogues*, pp. 16-17.

name is Campinet, and that his father was the elder brother of Lord Grondale.

Even after this disclosure, Caroline feels a sense of duty to her father, and refuses to marry Hermsprong. Discouraged, he thinks of migrating to America with some of those whom he has helped. " I have sixty thousand acres of uncleared land upon the Potowmac. . . . I have imagined a society of friends within a two mile ring; and I have imagined a mode of making it happy." This pantisocratic scheme, like Frank Henley's, is never carried out. Miss Campinet finally revolts against her father, and marries Hermsprong. Grondale soon dies, everybody forgives everybody else, and the curtain falls.

Hermsprong has had so much to say for himself that he requires no gloss. Bage uses the theme, and to some extent the story, of Voltaire's *L'Ingénu,* and his intentions, like Voltaire's, are in part at least satirical rather than didactic. But on the whole Bage writes more in sadness than in mockery. It is 1796, and the romantic reaction to the revolution has set in. " Man as he is not," man as he should be, is this son of nature whose tutors have been Noble Savages.

In this chapter an attempt has been made to show the connection between the Noble Savage idea and that curious compound of rationalistic romanticism and romantic rationalism which makes up the mentality of the Jacobin. An understanding of Jacobinism is essential to an understanding of the Lakists, to whom the next chapter will be devoted. Wordsworth, Coleridge and Southey pass through a stage of youthful radicalism in which they remind us of Fleetwood, Frank Henley and Hermsprong.

CHAPTER VI

WORDSWORTH, SOUTHEY, AND COLERIDGE

IF we may accept the *Prelude* as a reliable autobiographical document, William Wordsworth at Cambridge may be compared to Fleetwood at Oxford.[1] Like Godwin's hero, Wordsworth has passed his boyhood among the lakes and hills. Fleetwood was "a wild roe among the mountains of Wales," and Wordsworth never forgets the time

> " . . . . when like a roe
> I bounded o'er the mountains, by the sides
> Of the deep rivers, and the lonely streams,
> Wherever nature led." [2]

"In Merionethshire," says Fleetwood, "I had been a solitary savage;" and Wordsworth's boyhood was

> " . . . . as if I had been born
> On Indian plains, and from my mother's hut
> Had run abroad in wantonness, to sport,
> A naked savage, in the thunder shower." [3]

Wordsworth, however, differs from Fleetwood in that, barring a few minor lapses from primitive virtue such as the Miltonic drinking-bout, he resists the debasing influences of college life and remains the rather solemnly dutiful child of nature. Hence we cannot say that when Wordsworth, in 1790, sets out for Switzerland with

---

[1] Hugh Trevor, in Holcroft's novel of that name, has a similar experience at college. (Vol. I, pp. 195 ff.)

[2] *Tintern Abbey*.

[3] *Prelude*, Book I, ll. 297 ff.

Robert Jones, he goes in the Byronic, sin-laden mood of Fleetwood. He simply hates study, and wants a holiday among the mountains.

Switzerland is one of the most important spots on the map of romanticism. In the " Swiss School," the first glimmerings of German romanticism appear. Rousseau himself was Swiss. The Alps offer inspiration to the enthusiast and solace to the disillusioned. Switzerland, too, is important for romanticism not only through her scenery, but through the virtues of her inhabitants. As early as 1732, the scientist Albrecht Haller had made an Alpine botanizing tour which resulted in the discovery that the Swiss mountaineer is a Noble Savage — so simple, so innocent, so naturally virtuous that he rivals the legends of the Golden Age and puts to shame the pretensions of civilization.

> " Zwar die Gelehrtheit feilscht hier nicht papierne Schätze,
> Mann misst die Strassen nicht zu Rom und zu Athen,
> Man bindet die Vernunft an keinen Schulgesetze,
> Und niemand lehrt die Sonn' in ihren Kreisen gehn.
> O Witz! des Weisen Tand; wann hast du ihn vergnüget?
> Er kennt den Bau der Welt und stirbt sich unbekannt;
> Die Wollust wird bei ihm vergällt und nicht besieget,
> Sein künstlicher Geschmack beeckelt seinen Stand;
> Und hier hat die Natur die Lehre, recht zu leben,
> Den Menschen in das Herz, und nicht ins Hirn gegeben." [4]

Haller believed that the good qualities of the Swiss were the product of constant strife against an environment which, beautiful as it might be, offered no encouragement to laziness. The more common view, however, was that there was a positive rather than a negative relation between mountains and mountaineer. Mountains had been associated with the spirit of liberty long before Milton sang

[4] Haller, *Die Alpen. Versuch Schweizerischer Gedichten*, pp. 4-5.

" the mountain nymph." In the eighteenth century, the notion was exceedingly popular. Consider Thomson's Lapps and Collins' Highlanders. Consider Corsica, that rocky island which stirred the romantic feelings of Boswell.[5] But the abode of mountain liberty *par excellence* was Switzerland, never more appealing than in 1790, with

> " France standing on the top of golden hours,
> And human nature seeming born again."

Wordsworth's reaction to Switzerland as expressed in the *Descriptive Sketches* is wholly conventional. He pays his respects to mountainous liberty, and says the proper things about Tell's chapel. His references to the Golden Age are also in the right traditional manner. Man's guilt has forever banished that time of constant sunshine and plenty, but nature has not entirely averted her face. To those whose hearts are uncorrupted, like the Swiss, she gives some measure of her original joys.

> " As man in his primeval dower arrayed
> The image of his glorious Sire displayed,
> Even so, by faithful Nature guarded, here
> The traces of primeval man appear;
> The simple dignity no forms debase;
> The eye sublime, and surly lion-grace."

But the Noble Savage that Wordsworth found in Switzerland is a merely literary figure. In a letter written to Dorothy during the tour, William bluntly confesses that the Swiss are a great disappointment to him.[6] In *Descriptive Sketches* he says about the Swiss the things that a

[5] For an excellent discussion of the Corsica fad, not without bearing on the Noble Savage, see Professor Tinker's *Nature's Simple Plan*, Chapter II.

[6] *Letters of the Wordsworth Family*, Vol. I, p. 17.

young romantic poet should say, without much regard to his actual observations. His real interest is not in the people, but in the scenery and in the mystery behind the scenery.

How, through the influence of the French Revolution, nature temporarily gave place to man in Wordsworth's affections; how the excesses of the Terror and the reactionary policy of his own country discouraged and appalled him; how he sought and failed to find satisfaction in Godwinian rationalism; how his restlessness was aggravated by the Annette Vallon affair; how at last, guided by his sister and fortified by Raisley Calvert's legacy, he returned to the true sources of his being — all this is a familiar story. Wordsworth's early sensibility, his brief rationalistic interlude, and his disillusioned flight to nature parallel the experience of many of his contemporaries. But like all great men, he added to this typical development an individual contribution. He had by 1798 evolved from his reaction to the hills and valleys of Dorset a distinctive philosophy.

From the basic principles of Wordsworth's naturalism it follows that, other things being equal, the excellence of human beings is in proportion to the number and richness of their contacts with nature. Hence the child, with his fresh and lively perceptions colored by unconscious memories of his heavenly home, is to be envied. And of adults, those are most blest who dwell uninterruptedly among beautiful and awe-inspiring scenes, as do the shepherds of the Lake Country.

We are told in the *Prelude* that as a boy Wordsworth was dismayed by the hard and dangerous life of the dalesman, which compared but ill with that of the Arcadian shepherd of literature. Soon, however, the lad began to feel the dalesman as a sort of subordinate spirit of nature,

arising from and always associated with his majestic surroundings. When seen through the fog, or outlined
against the horizon, he took on an almost unearthly sublimity. That this figure was in fact a quite ordinary man
idealized by boyish imagination is admitted, but admitted
rather defiantly.

> ".   .   .   Call ye these appearances —
> Which I beheld of shepherds in my youth,
> This sanctity of Nature given to man —
> A shadow, a delusion, ye who pore
> On the dead letter, miss the spirit of things;
>
> .   .   .   .   But blessed be the God
> Of Nature and of Man that this was so;
> That men before my inexperienced eyes
> Did first present themselves thus purified."

If a rustic fell ill and died because of sleeping on the damp
ground, the poet demands of Coleridge, what was the
harm of ascribing his demise to unrequited love?

The adult Wordsworth's views on this point are more
sober, but still enthusiastic. The dalesmen are free; they
labor quietly and cheerfully, attaining ends

> "Unwooed, unthought-of even — simplicity,
> And beauty, and inevitable grace."

They are exempt from urban temptations, and from the
perils of intellectual ambition. Most important of all,
their families have not yet been broken up by the industrial revolution. This last point is emphasized in the letter
written in 1801 to Charles James Fox, accompanying the
second edition of *Lyrical Ballads*. Commerce, says the
writer, is exerting an evil influence upon social feelings.
" In the two poems, *The Brothers* and *Michael*, I have
attempted to draw a picture of the domestic affections as

I know they exist among a class of men who are now almost confined to the north of England. . . . Their little tract of land . . . is a fountain fitted to the nature of social man, from which supplies of affection, as pure as his heart was intended for, are daily drawn." The Lake Country is the last stronghold of nature.

The poet believes that the shepherds are unconsciously influenced by their environment. It would be a great mistake, he says, to suppose that the valleys and streams and rocks meant nothing to Michael:

> "Those fields, those hills —what could they less? Had laid
> Strong hold on his affections, were to him
> A pleasurable feeling of blind love."

Peter Bell, of course, is an exception; but he fairly has to fight in order to resist the benign influences.

> " There was a hardness in his cheek,
> There was a hardness in his eye,
> As if the man had fixed his face,
> In many a solitary place,
> Against the wind and open sky! "

The mere inarticulateness of the dalesmen is no argument against their sensitiveness to the message of nature, for

> " Their's is the language of the heavens, the power,
> The thought, the image, and the silent joy;
> Words are but under-agents in their souls;
> When they are grasping with their greatest strength
> They do not breathe among them." [7]

Are Wordsworth's peasants Noble Savages? What are we to call Michael, nature's venerable patriarch; Leonard and James, the idyllic brothers; the sensitive

[7] *Postscript to the Edition of 1835.*

protagonist of *The Last of the Flock;* Andrew, mild
student of the woods and hills; Simon Lee, the varicose,
the grateful; the pensive and didactic Matthew; the
stoical and eloquent leech-gatherer? Before we attempt
to answer this question, let us ask what, during the period
when the idealized peasant was taking shape, Wordsworth
has to say of Indians.

The Complaint of a Forsaken Indian Woman is a
" dramatic " lyric put into the mouth of a sick squaw who
has been left to die in the snow. The suggestion for the
poem, together with some of the imagery, comes from
Hearne's *Journey from Hudson's Bay to the Northern
Ocean.* Since the *Complaint* was composed and published
in 1798 it is evident that Wordsworth gave at least some
thought to Indians at the time when he was evolving his
ideal shepherds. This poem, however, certainly cannot be
construed as a glorification of savage life.

Ruth belongs to the following year. The young adventurer from America who comes to seek Ruth's hand describes life in an Indian village as one prolonged picnic.
In the morning the girls leave the town, dancing and
shouting; they " gather strawberries all day long," and
return at twilight " with a choral song." Love in the
forest is even more delightful:

> " Sweet Ruth! and could you go with me
> My helpmate in the woods to be,
> Our shed at night to rear;
> Or run, my own adopted bride,
> A sylvan huntress at my side,
> And drive the flying deer! "

But the suitor turns out to be a rascal, and none of those
promises is fulfilled. Quite possibly Wordsworth intentionally makes them extravagant.

Besides these two poems, the work of Wordsworth between 1798 and 1806 presents only scattered references to Indians. In *Her Eyes Are Wild* an " Indian bower " is mentioned; in *A Farewell*, an " Indian shed." Such fragments of evidence show that Wordsworth was mildly curious about Indians, and that he had obtained some knowledge of their customs from travelers' accounts. But although generally favorable in tone, they do not establish him as an ardent admirer of the savage at this period of his career.

It would be pleasant to be able to trace a connection between Wordsworth's interest in Indians and his philosophy of nature. In Book VII of the *Prelude*, such a link is certainly forged. After a characteristic statement of the uplifting power of scenery, he urges the reader to

> " Think, how the everlasting streams and woods,
> Stretched and still stretching far and wide, exalt
> The roving Indian, on his desert sands." [8]

We remember, too, that he compares his own early environment to that of an Indian child. On his walking-tour of 1790, the scattered huts of the Swiss remind him of "tents or Indian cabins." [9] The Lake Country woodman sleeps on the ground in his cabin, like an Indian.[10]

This evidence is far from sufficient to prove the point. Except for the really significant hint as to the power of scenery to " exalt " the Indian, there is no positive indica-

---

[8] *Prelude*, Book VII, ll. 740 ff. De Selincourt's variorum edition shows that the reference to the Indian is not in the 1805-6 version of the poem. One may be permitted to guess, however, that it was added not long afterward. The thought is certainly more characteristic of the earlier than of the later Wordsworth.

[9] *Ibid.*, Book VI, l. 520.

[10] *Ibid.*, Book VIII, ll. 437 ff.

tion that the Noble Savage enters into Wordsworth's philosophy of nature. On the whole, the same must be said of the relation between the Noble Savage and Wordsworth's idealized peasant. [Wordsworth was never an admirer of actual wildness in men or in human institutions. His romanticism was always restrained by conservative scruples; it had a Burkian cast. That a twentieth century scholar should compare his peasants to savages would deeply shock him.

Nevertheless, the comparison is tempting. One may at least say that the dalesman and the Noble Savage are similarly motivated. They spring from the same revulsion against corrupt civilization, and preach fundamentally the same gospel of innocent simplicity. That Rousseau's conception of natural man influenced Wordsworth's conception of the shepherd seems evident; and we have seen that the Noble Savage influenced Rousseau's conception of natural man. Thus the savage and the shepherd are after all connected, if only through Rousseau. And there may have been a certain amount of direct connection. Michael is more like a wise old sachem than like any figure of the pastoral tradition.

To borrow the language of mathematics, the Noble Dalesman is to Wordsworth somewhat as the Noble Savage is to Rousseau in the sense that these figures provide examples of two similar though not identical conceptions of natural man. The differences, however, are quite as important as the similarities. The savage, as we have seen, supports chiefly the pessimistic side of Rousseau's earlier philosophy. He has the contentment which comes from having no desires above the animal plane. The dalesman also illustrates the " defeatist " aspect of romanticism. But he means far more than mere ignorance of civilized complexities. His direct contact with the " wisdom and spirit of the universe " gives him a *positive* happiness and a *positive* goodness. Far from being free, his spirit is constantly chastened by the discipline of nature. " Food, a female, and sleep " does not summarize the life of the Lake Country shepherd.

It must be remembered that Wordsworth's character underwent marked changes as he grew older. He suffered from a gradual hardening of the spiritual arteries. From the first a Calvinistic strain had curbed the exuberance of Wordsworth's nature-worship. He had been forced to recognize that not all hearts were fitted to receive the lessons of nature, that her influence might even be dangerous to an undisciplined spirit. The young scamp in *Ruth* is an example:

> " Whatever in those climes he found
> Irregular in sight or sound
> Did to his mind impart
> A kindred impulse, seemed allied
> To his own powers, and justified
> The workings of his heart."

Now, as his early visions " fade into the light of common day," the poet himself feels the need of a steadying element external to himself. Nature had promised to be to Lucy " both law and impulse," but to his dulled and timid eyes his old teacher seems dangerously quick to " kindle," dangerously slow to " restrain." [11] Hence in his *Ode to Duty* he resigns himself to the " stern lawgiver," and finds her a sure guide.

A symptom of this change as it applies to the Indian is seen in the *Address to My Infant Daughter Dora* (1804). The poet suggests that if the child had been " of Indian birth " her natal day would have been stamped upon the

[11] *Three Years She Grew.*

memory of her parents through either the hostility or the
benignity of the elements on that occasion.   But he continues:

> ".   .   .   .   Mother's love
> Nor less than mother's love in other breasts,
> Will, among us warm-clad and warmly housed,
> Do for thee what the finger of the heavens
> Doth all too often harshly execute
> For thy unblest coevals, amid wilds
> Where fancy hath small liberty to grace
> The affections, to exalt them or refine;
> And the maternal sympathy itself,
> Though strong, is, in the main, a joyless tie
> Of naked instinct, wound about the heart.
> Happier, far happier is thy lot and ours! "

That is certainly not favorable to the Noble Savage.   Yet
one wonders why he should have thought of Dora's " un-
blest coevals " at all.   If there had not been something in
the life at Dove Cottage that reminded him of Indian life,
would he have troubled to draw so careful a distinction?

Although the *Excursion* was begun in 1802, it was not
finished until 1813; and there can be no doubt that
the completed poem represents the later rather than the
earlier Wordsworth.   One need only compare it with the
Prelude to be aware of the changes which have taken place.
In the *Excursion* he confronts his old self with his present
self and sets them to debating.   Solitary is Wordsworth,
the disillusioned Godwinian of 1794; the Wanderer is
Wordsworth, the conservative, optimistic nature-poet of
1813.   That intermediate Wordsworth of 1797–1802,
mystical and impassioned worshipper of stream and flower
and dalesman, is almost entirely absorbed by the mild,
sententious pedler.

Solitary's character might be summed up by the single
statement that he reads *Candide* in the Lake Country.

But the man is sound at heart; his morbid perversity is merely the result of his sorrows. He had been a popular preacher in London. He hailed the French Revolution with idealistic enthusiasm, and developed

> " A proud and most presumptuous confidence
> In the transcendent wisdom of the age."

Later, appalled by the excesses of the Terror, he turned from practical radicalism to abstract philosophy of the Godwinian stamp. His religious faith departed, and he became dissolute. Finding happiness neither in general speculation nor in the cold analysis of his own corrupted emotions, he fled to America in order to find the true man of nature. He imagines the Indian as " Primeval Nature's child " and supposes that, although he is soon to be crushed by civilization,

> " .   .   .   contemplations, worthier, nobler far
> Than her [social art's] destructive energies, attend
> His independence, when along the side
> Of Mississippi, or that northern stream
> That spreads into successive seas, he walks;
> Pleased to observe his own unshackled life,
> And his innate capacities of soul,
> There imaged; or, when having gained the top
> Of some commanding eminence, which yet
> Intruder ne'er beheld, he thence surveys
> Regions of wood and wild savannah, vast
> Expanse of unappropriated earth,
> With mind that sheds a light on what he sees;
> Free as the sun, and lonely as the sun
> Pouring above his head its radiance down
> Upon a living and rejoicing world."

But this attempt to make Joseph Warton's dream come true is a melancholy failure. Instead of " that pure archetype of human greatness "

> ".   .   .   .   .   appeared
> A creature, squalid, vengeful and impure;
> Remorseless, and submissive to no law
> But superstitious fear, and abject sloth."

The conclusion of this passage has sometimes been brought forward as evidence of Wordsworth's entire lack of sympathy with the Noble Savage. Such an interpretation overlooks the fact that these words are spoken by Solitary, and that Solitary exists to be lectured into a more wholesome view of things. Is it too fanciful to suppose that in 1794, Wordsworth, like Solitary, felt a wistful attraction toward the ideal Indian, mingled with a cynical fear that this ideal was illusory? Even in 1813 the attraction of the savage is still strong. Solitary, who loves not nature, associates the virtues of the Indian with the inspiring scenes amidst which he moves. Notice, too, that this vision of savage freedom and happiness is written with a fervor and spirit hardly matched elsewhere in the *Excursion*. For a moment Wordsworth indulges whole-heartedly in one of his earlier dreams, only to remember that Solitary is a cynic, and that the dream must be shattered.

To our disappointment, the Wanderer says nothing in refutation of Solitary's opinion of the Indian. It is rather against Solitary's whole view of life that he directs his sermon, "Despondency Corrected." But, strangely enough, at the conclusion of the Wanderer's exhortation occur the lines:

> " Here closed the Sage that eloquent harangue,
> Poured forth with fervor in continuous stream,
> Such as, remote, 'mid savage wilderness,
> An Indian Chief discharges from his breast
> Into the hearing of assembled tribes." [12]

[12] *Excursion*, Book IV, ll. 1275–1282.

Too much significance should not be attached to the fact that Solitary, who has rejected the savage, is rebuked in a savage oration. No doubt the simile is a merely formal one. Yet even formal similes do not enter the mind of a poet except through the laws of association, and the occurrence of this simile at this point must be more than sheer accident. Surely if Wordsworth were wholly antipathetic to the Noble Savage he would not have capped with this comparison the Wanderer's reply to Solitary.

The heartsick hermit sees the dalesman through the same bilious haze as that through which he saw the Indian. They seem quite unworthy of their surroundings. The callous attitude of an old woman towards her aged husband, who was lost in a storm, makes him say to his visitors:

> ". . . . . . . Pity 'tis
> That fortune did not guide you to this house
> A few days earlier; then would you have seen
> What stuff the Dwellers in a solitude,
> That seems by Nature hollowed out to be
> The seat and bosom of pure innocence,
> Are made of; an ungracious matter this! "

Here also he is to be " corrected." The defense of the dalesman is entrusted chiefly to the Pastor, who uses the tombstones of his churchyard as the texts of his discourse. It cannot be said that he makes a satisfactory witness. Unfortunately he is a staunch though liberal churchman, and for him mere contact with nature, unless reinforced by piety, is not sufficient to mould human character. He relates a few mild stories which indicate that on the whole rural simplicity is desirable. Of one especially humble and happy pair, Solitary pertinently asks whether such a vegetable existence can be held truly virtuous, and receives no adequate answer. Then there is young Oswald, who entered the militia out of sympathy for Switzerland, but caught cold from washing sheep when overheated by his military exercises, and perished.   But the tombs hide ugly stories as well as fair.   This the Pastor cheerfully admits, but feels that he should say little about the seamy side of the life of his flock.

> "   .   .   .   I willingly confine
> My narratives to subjects that excite
> Feelings with these accordant; love, esteem,
> And admiration, lifting up a veil,
> A sunbeam introducing among hearts
> Retired and covert; so that ye shall have
> Clear images before your gladdened eyes
> Of nature's unambitious underwood,
> And flowers that prosper in the shade."

Since half the evidence is suppressed, no possible conclusion can arise from the Pastor's annals of the parish. Wordsworth's dalesmen were once something like Noble Savages, believed in perhaps extravagantly, but genuinely. They are now portrayed as admirable only at the expense of suppressing half the evidence.   Herein lies the real apostasy of Wordsworth.

In the last fourteen lines of the poem, Wordsworth indicates his intention of tracing further the " renovation " of Solitary.   There are excellent reasons for the non-fulfillment of this promise.   The *Excursion* was finished in a totally different spirit from that in which it was begun. Wordsworth's original plan must have been to confront Solitary with a genuine prophet of nature such as he himself still was in 1802.   The Wanderer, however, rapidly develops into a prosy teacher of piety and conservative optimism.   Again, the poem shows traces of a wish to inspire Solitary, through stories of the dalesman, with an appreciation of the fundamental human virtues.   We have already noted the collapse of this intention. In the same way ecstatic praise of nature, enthusiasm for childhood and the mystic thrill of pantheism dwindle down to fumbling discourses on the factory system, national education and the Church of England. The conversion of Solitary cannot be completed because there is no longer anything sufficiently interesting and poetic to convert him to.

Apart from the references to Indians, what chiefly concerns us in the *Excursion* is the dimming of Wordsworth's illusions about the dalesman. In this poem the old and the new attitudes are somewhat in conflict, and the latter may better be understood by examining it in its pure state. Since *The Westmoreland Girl* was composed in 1845, it may be assumed to be reasonably free from traces of the early Wordsworth. Part I of the poem, addressed to his grandchildren, relates how a cottage maiden, ten years old, rescues a lamb from a rushing stream. In Part II the poet turns " to a maturer audience," and describes

> ". . .   this brave child
> Left among her native mountains
> With wild Nature to run wild."

This running wild would have seemed in 1799 the ideal education, for the situation is precisely that which gave Lucy her beauty and her goodness.[13] And even in 1845 the influence of nature operates:

> " Time passed on; the Child was happy,
> Like a Spirit of air she moved,
> Wayward, yet by all who knew her
> For her tender heart beloved."

But even though a child may be happy and tender-hearted, she must not be wayward. Is the Westmoreland Girl

[13] *Cf. Three Years She Grew.*

an example of what a child should be?   In the words of
Godwin, "Oh, no! " [14]

> "What then wants the child to temper
> In her breast, unruly fire,
> To control the froward impulse
> And restrain the vague desire?
>
> Easily a pious training
> And a steadfast outward power
> Would supplant the weeds, and cherish
> In their stead each opening flower."

In *Three Years She Grew*, Nature had provided both impulse and restraint.   Now her province is merely that of
impulse, and the restraint must come from some " stead-
fast outward power."

If, in 1799, Wordsworth had been asked, " Do you
literally mean that Lucy shall have nothing but the education of nature; that the scenes amidst which she moves
will provide all the intellectual, spiritual and moral nourishment that her character needs? " he would no doubt
have reminded the inquirer that *Three Years She Grew* is
a lyric poem and not a pedagogical treatise.   In it Wordsworth expresses an ideal.   His sense of nature's benign
influence makes him imagine a child who shall be wholly
under the tutelage of nature.   He would have been the
first to admit that actual children need education, provided
that it is of a sort to develop rather than warp the natural
virtues.   *The Westmoreland Girl* is also a poem — but
with what a difference!   Here all the prosaic qualifications
which are brushed aside in 1799 flood with their chill
waters the warmth of imagination.   Lucy may have
needed a good board-school training in real life, but in
art she is nature's own.   The Westmoreland Girl, even as

[14] *Vide supra*, p. 151.

a poetic figure, is not long to be allowed to play in the woods.

It was Wordsworth's misfortune to live on into a period which was at variance with all his deeper feelings. In his old age, the things from which he had recoiled in his youth seem more powerful than ever. The industrial revolution has triumphed, and in so doing has given rise to a new form of slavery. The sceptical spirit of analysis, too, has been steadily growing. Tragic, that Wordsworth should have survived the French Revolution, the Napoleonic wars and the Tory reaction only to die amidst the perplexities of the Victorian Era! As he turns his tired eyes about him he sees

> ".   .   . a chilled age, most pitiably shut out
> From that which *is* and actuates, by forms,
> Abstractions, and by lifeless fact to fact
> Minutely linked with diligence uninspired,
> Unrectified, unguided, unsustained
> By godlike insight." [15]

Yet he has himself been false to nature, and it is too late now to return to her in the spirit of his youth. The chill of the age has crept into his own bones. Nothing is left for him but to gather up his feet into the bed.

In the hesitant, pessimistic naturalism of the later Wordsworth the Noble Savage idea plays a small but harmonious part. The Indian is to be envied because he is free from the perplexities which harass the poet. Sonnet XV of the *River Duddon* series expresses uncertainty as to whether a certain chasm is the work of prehistoric man or merely the result of erosion. In the next sonnet we find that

[15] *Musings Near Aquapendente. Memorials of a Tour in Italy,* No. 1; 1837.

> " Such fruitless questions may not long beguile
> Or plague the fancy 'mid the sculptured shows
> Conspicuous yet where Oroonoko flows."

The Indian has positive evidence of the flood, for is he not able to point to sculptures on cliffs which could not have been reached except by water?

Savages, too, can maintain their natural intuitions unperturbed by the harsh claims of reason. In *Presentiments* (1830) occur the lines:

> " Star-guided contemplations move
> Through space, though calm, not raised above
> Prognostics that ye [presentiments] rule;
> The naked Indian of the wild,
> And haply too the cradled Child,
> Are pupils of your school." [16]

The association of the Indian and the child is significant, but to this cluster of ideas still other elements may be added. Michael is surely a contemplative person. The Wanderer, both as a lover of nature and as a pedler, is contemplative. So is Wordsworth himself. Thus on this single thread may be strung the Indian, the child, the dalesman, the Wanderer and the poet of nature. Although Wordsworth has comparatively little to say of the Indian, such clues as this point to an underlying connection between the Noble Savage idea and the poet's philosophy.

Besides these instances there are a few miscellaneous references which show some familiarity with the literature of travel. *A Morning Exercise* (1828) mentions " naked Indians," and cites in a footnote Waterton's *Wanderings in South America*. In the *Excursion*, certain mountain plants are compared to " Indian mats." Earlier in the poem,

[16] Observe that Solitary had imagined the Indian as a contemplative being. (*Excursion*, Book III, 1. 928.)

Solitary, the scorner of Indians, is willing to accept the " American " notion that the first men jumped out of a cave as as good an explanation of the origin of humanity as any other. Like many other romantic writers, Wordsworth drew from tradition and from travelers' narratives [17] information which he found accordant with his belief in the benefits of a natural life. Most of his illustrations he gathered from sources nearer at hand, but he recognized to some extent the value of more exotic evidence. When the fervor of his naturalism chilled, he yet retained a saddened longing for simplicity and occasionally thought of the savage as an example of the mind's lost innocence.

The Balliol men of 1793 found Robert Southey a rather interesting young radical. What few of them perceived was a curious conflict in his spirit. A youth of turbulent feelings, he craved, and soon gained, the ability to control himself. Wordsworth did not consciously turn from impulse to duty until the effervescence of youth had subsided; but in Southey the *frein vital* curbed the *élan vital* almost from the first. In 1793 his guiding star is Rousseau — as an authority on education, as a limner of nature's beauties, and as the great apostle of sensibility.[18] Yet in the following year he deliberately tries to check this aspect of his nature. As an antidote to the sweet and subtle wine of Rousseau, he drains the astringent cup offered him by Epictetus and Godwin. When William Taylor, in 1799, charges him with excessive sensibility, he replies, " Once, indeed, I had a mimosa sensibility, but it

---

[17] For evidence on this point *cf.* two articles by Lane Cooper: *Wordsworth's Sources*, *Athenaeum*, April 22, 1905, pp. 498 ff.; and *A Glance at Wordsworth's Reading*, *Modern Language Notes*, March, 1907, pp. 83-89; April, 1907, pp. 110-117.

[18] Letters of March 16, Easter, and April 4, 1793.

has long ago been rooted out. Five years ago I counter-
acted Rousseau by dieting upon Godwin and Epictetus." [19]

Neither sensibility nor stoicism brought peace of mind.
Unitarian influences made him shrink from taking holy
orders, even at the price of estranging the uncle who had
made his education possible. Added to his religious doubts
was his disappointment over the outcome of the French
Revolution. His first reaction to the upheaval was the
same as Wordsworth's: "A visionary world seemed to
open upon those who were just entering it. Old things
seemed passing away and nothing was dreamt of but the
regeneration of the human race." [20] But to his kind heart
the excesses of the Terror were repugnant. His idealism
thwarted, he began to believe that virtue can be obtained
only by withdrawing from the world. And yet what spot
is so obscure as to provide a refuge from tyranny? "There
is no place for virtue. Seneca was a visionary philosopher;
even in the deserts of Arabia, the strongest will be the
happiest, and the same rule holds good in Europe and in
Abyssinia." [21]

This cloud of disillusionment is at its blackest and
heaviest in the fall of 1793. "O," he cries, "for emancipation from these useless forms, this useless life, these
haunts of intolerance, vice and folly!" [22] As a child he
had dreamed of running away to an island, a little boy's
Land of Cockayne, studded with mountains of ginger-
bread and candy; [23] now, in a not very different mood,
he indulges in Utopian fancies. He would like to found
an ideal city, "her palaces all hovels," and govern it after

---

[19] *Life and Correspondence of Robert Southey*, p. 111. *Cf.* also the
letters of May 2, 1808, and Nov. 8, 1814.

[20] *Correspondence with Caroline Bowles*, p. 52.

[21] *Life and Correspondence.* To Grosvenor Bedford, Oct. 26, 1793.

[22] *Ibid.*, p. 71.   [23] Haller, *Early Life of Robert Southey*, p. 15.

the manner of Plato.[24] Or why not repeople Greece with
men of feeling, and found an ideal university? He would
build a Doric house in the midst of a garden " like Wolmer's " [*sic*]. That notion of a cool classic dwelling surrounded by Rousseau's untamed " English " garden is an
apt symbol of Southey's dual character, as indeed it is of
Rousseau's.

These suggestions are of course more than half playful.
In the same letter, however, he refers quite seriously to
Cowley's desire to retire to America. Southey would
gladly make this dream a reality. " I should be pleased
to reside in a country where . . . man was considered as
more valuable than money; and where I could till the
earth, and provide by honest industry the meat which my
wife would dress with pleasing care." [25] But this strange
youth is able to prick his own bubbles. In December of
the same year he invites his chum Bedford to imagine him,
"building a nice, snug little dairy . . . ; three rooms in
my cottage, and my only companion some poor Negro
whom I have bought on purpose to emancipate. After a
hard day's toil, see me sleep upon rushes. . . . So this
your friend will realize the romance of Cowley, and even
outdo the seclusion of Rousseau; till at last comes an ill-
looking Indian with a tomahawk, and scalps me — a most
melancholy proof that society is very bad. . . . So vanity, vanity will come from my lips, and poor Southey will
either be cooked by a Cherokee or oysterized by a tiger." [26]

In the winter of 1794 no such exotic reveries are either
seriously or humorously set forth. They seem to have
been subdued by the Godwin-Epictetus tonic. The malady is shortly to break out again, and in more virulent

[24] *Life and Correspondence.* To Grosvenor Bedford, Oct. 26, 1793.
[25] *Ibid.* To Horace Walpole Bedford, Nov. 13, 1793.
[26] *Ibid.* To Grosvenor Bedford, Dec. 14, 1793.

form; but while we are waiting for its reappearance we
may ask whether the Noble Savage idea formed part of
Southey's mental baggage at this period.

The jocular reference to the "ill-looking Indian with a
tomahawk" does not necessarily preclude a theoretical
admiration of the redman; and though Southey's Utopias
seem Platonic, one senses in the "palaces all hovels" and
the "garden like Wolmer's" a desire for natural simplicity. From boyhood, in fact, Southey had been deeply
interested in savages. At the age of thirteen he had
"composed a satirical description of English manners, as
delivered by Omai, the Taheitian, to his countryman at
his return." [27] No doubt the boy made the savage say
some scathing things — one can imagine them. At about
the same time he began to dabble in the mythology of
primitive peoples, "and soon became as well acquainted
with the gods of Asia and America as with those of Greece
and Rome." [28] Thus early he began to amass a store of
curious learning which was to become the background of
his most distinctive literary works. It is significant also
that Ariosto and Spenser formed part of his boyish reading; for as Ariosto, followed by Spenser, fused classic
machinery and medieval content to form the romantic epic,
so Southey fused the machinery and spirit of the romantic
epic with his primitive lore to form what might be called
the savage romantic epic — *Madoc, Thalaba,* the *Curse of
Kehama.* Perhaps the best illustration of the type, however, is *A Tale of Paraguay,* a romantic epic about South
American Indians written in Spenserian stanzas. [29] But

[27] *Ibid.* To John May, June 29, 1824. *Vide supra,* p. 73, for two
other cases in which Omai is used as a vehicle for satire.

[28] *Ibid.* To the Rev. John Martyn Longmire, Nov. 4, 1812.

[29] In evolving the "savage romantic epic," Southey had before him
the precedent of Ercilla's *Araucana. Vide infra,* p. 274.

we are looking too far ahead. At present it is enough to know that this young Balliol man is already an enthusiastic student of savage religions and customs.

It was in the spring of 1794 that Samuel Taylor Coleridge, a youth of twenty-one, came from Cambridge to Oxford to visit his old schoolmate Robert Allen. Allen, in the course of entertaining his friend, introduced him to Southey. The two young poets found that they had much in common. Southey's early reading of romances found a parallel in Coleridge's early reading of fairy-tales. By means of such literature the mind of the latter " had been habituated to *the Vast.*" " I never," he told Thomas Poole, " regarded *my senses* in any way as the criteria of my belief. I regulated all my creeds by my conceptions, not by my *sight.*" [30] This tendency to regard reality as coincident with the wide sweep of his imagination made Coleridge a lover of impossible projects, to one of which Southey was shortly to fall a victim.

Up to this time Coleridge and Southey had developed along somewhat similar lines. Each had undergone a period of Bowlesian sensibility. If Southey had chided civilization through the lips of Omai, Coleridge had " mourn'd with the breeze " over the tomb of Lee Boo.[31] For a time the vague visions of both poets had been fulfilled by the Revolution. Samuel had positively gloated in his *Destruction of the Bastille*. To both had come disillusionment, though Coleridge still tried to regard " the blasphemies and horrors during the domination of the Terrorists . . . as a transient storm, and the natural consequences of former despotism and of the foul superstition of Popery." [32] Moreover, Coleridge and Southey

---

[30] *Letters of S. T. C.*, Vol. I, p. 16.
[31] *Vide supra*, p. 117.
[32] *France: an Ode*, note on stanza 3.

were under the same intellectual domination. As Unitarians, both were admirers of Priestley. Both were also disciples of Godwin, though from somewhat different viewpoints. From what must have been a happily fervent comparison of ideals they evolved the plan of pantisocracy — " a scheme," says Joseph Cottle, " perfectly harmless in itself, though obnoxious to insuperable objections." [33]

The clearest statement of the principles of pantisocracy is found in the eleventh issue of *The Friend*. " What I dared not expect from constitutions of governments and whole nations," says Coleridge, " I hoped from religion and a small company of chosen individuals, and formed a plan, as harmless as it was extravagant, of trying the experiment of human perfectibility on the banks of the Susquehannah; where our little society, in its second generation, was to have combined the innocence of the Patriarchal Age with the knowledge and general refinements of European culture; and where I dreamed that in the sober evening of my life I should behold the cottages of independence in the undivided dale of industry."

The cornerstone of this plan is Godwinian perfectibility. But the doctrine is modified by certain features which the Godwin of *Political Justice* would hardly have approved. The Terror had convinced Coleridge and Southey that the world was not yet ready for systematic righteousness; but, like Frank Henley and Hermsprong,[34] they felt that a just society might be established on a restricted scale and under specially favorable conditions. This position is, in fact, almost identical with the one later reached by Godwin in *St. Leon:* it is necessary to fly from a perverted civilization in order to found a true one.

Since the original scheme of pantisocracy entailed emigration to the American wilderness, and since the plan

---

[33] *Reminiscences*, p. 142.   [34] *Vide supra*, pp. 163, 171.

certainly owes something to the tradition of America as a sort of terrestrial paradise, one is tempted to connect it closely with the Noble Savage idea. The movement, however, was permeated by so profound a distrust of human nature that we cannot pigeon-hole it as a phase of sentimental primitivism. " Wherever men *can* be vicious," writes Coleridge, " some *will* be. The leading idea of Pantisocracy is to make men *necessarily* virtuous by removing all incentives to evil." [35] Evil is so deeply rooted in the human heart that it is the children of the pantisocrats, rather than the pioneers themselves, who are to combine patriarchal simplicity with philosophic wisdom. Pantisocracy was quite as much an offshoot of the rationalism as of the romanticism of the age. If Wordsworth, in his brief period of analytical Godwinism, had met Coleridge and Southey, he might well have become a pantisocrat.

But the rationalism of these youths, like that of the age in which they lived, was thin and fragile. Beneath it, and constantly breaking through to the surface, was the sentimental naturalism of the early romantic period. To the head, pantisocracy was cold and mechanical; but to the heart, it was warm and spontaneous. From one point of view, retirement to the wilderness was merely a device to shut out selfishness and inequality; yet from another, it was less a retreat to a rationalistic incubator than a romantic quest for primitive goodness. Thus the Noble Savage philosophy does enter, though perhaps only to a slight extent, into pantisocracy. It appears, as might be expected, chiefly in the poems written by Coleridge and Southey between the formation of their plan and its abandonment. For the present let us concentrate upon the lesser poet.

During 1794, Southey wrote comparatively little. In

[35] *Letters of S. T. C.*, No. XXXVII. To Southey, Oct. 1794.

the previous year he had completed the first draft of *Joan of Arc*, a poem chiefly interesting to us in its later form. At *Wat Tyler*, written in 1794,[36] a glance may be directed. " A good critic might take it," says Saintsbury, " for a deliberate and very happy parody of the cruder and more innocent utterances of sentimental republicanism." [37]   Indeed, the play springs more from Southey's earlier revolutionary enthusiasm than from the disillusionment from which he at this time suffered.   To young Piers, who declares that wealth is to be despised, and that the plowman sleeps more soundly than " the rich slave of pride and indolence," Wat Tyler sensibly replies that the boy will think otherwise when he knows more of the world. But Wat is only being ironic.   The birds, he goes on to say, manage these things better:

> " No fancied boundaries of mine and thine
> Restrain their wanderings: Nature gives enough
> For all; but Man, with arrogant selfishness,
> Proud of his heaps, hoards up superfluous stores
> Robb'd from his weaker fellows."

This praise of beasts at the expense of man is a corollary of the Noble Savage idea.

During 1794 the anti-slave-trade movement engaged Southey's sympathies.   Since this aspect of humanitarianism caused the Negro to be admitted to full status as a Noble Savage, Southey's four slave-trade sonnets, all written at the height of the pantisocratic bustle, are worth mentioning.   The last of the series portrays the slave as a Man of Feeling.   The labors of the day, the cruel lash of the overseer, have wrung no groan from his lips.   But at night, when he wakes to think

---

[36] First published, without Southey's knowledge, in 1817, as part of a plan to brand him as a political turn-coat.

[37] *Cambridge History of English Literature*, Vol. XI, p. 175.

> " .   .   .   .   . that far away,
> While happy negroes join the midnight song
> And merriment resounds on Niger's shore,"

his beloved yearns for him in vain — then at last he weeps.

There was no particular originality in writing poems on the slave-trade: many others were doing it. To give poetic treatment to the penal settlement in Australia, however, was daring. The lecturer on Southey glibly mentions, among the poet's youthful crudities, the *Botany Bay Eclogues*. But let us stop to consider the boldness of the conception; to think what Botany Bay meant in 1794, and what the term "eclogue." In *Elinor*, first of the series, we see the exile calling out in thankfulness to the trackless woods, silent save for "the kangaroo's sad note":

> " .   .   .   . Welcome, wilderness,
> Nature's domain! for here, as yet unknown
> The comforts and the crimes of polished life,
> Nature benignly gives to all enough,
> Denies to all a superfluity.
> What though the garb of infamy I wear, —
> Though day by day along the echoing beach
> I gather wave-worn shells, yet day by day
> I earn in honesty my frugal food,
> And lay me down at night to calm repose."

The judge thought that he was condemning Elinor to punishment, but he was only giving her a chance to be a Noble Savage. Is it not possible that this feeling colored Southey s dreams of pantisocracy, that he sometimes saw himself on the banks of the Susquehanna, crying "Welcome!" to the wilderness?

At this time, also, Southey began to write his *Madoc*, a poem simply crammed with savage lore. His work during the pantisocratic period is therefore devoid neither of naturalistic sentiment nor of interest in primitive man.

Evidently pantisocracy had a romantic side which found
a voice in the poems of Southey. The " back-to-nature "
part of the movement made better poetic material than its
perfectibilitarian aspect. This fact has an important bearing on the future development of Southey. Wordsworth
never quite forgot nature, and returned to her unreserv-
edly when Godwin proved a false guide. In almost
exactly the same way Southey, upon the collapse of pantisocracy, for a time gave free rein to his naturalistic inclinations. Roughly speaking, from 1796 to
1799 is for him a period of nature-worship in which
it is not surprising that the Noble Savage should
cut a larger figure than in the quasi-rationalistic years
1794–1795.

Southey's state of mind in 1796, after his return from
Lisbon, is shown in the series of short bits of blank verse
entitled *Inscriptions*. Of these the general burden is that
for happiness and innocence there is nothing like a " woodland cot." In the wilderness, the stream runs pure; it
becomes polluted only when it passes through the haunts
of men. He asks us to compare the loveliness of Nature
with " the city's crowded streets," and then to

> "   .   .   .   .   . reflect
> That Man creates the evil he endures."

For a brief period, Southey's affection for Rousseau
returns. The " giddy throng " revere his relics with the
same " blind idolatry " they accord those of the " scoffer "
Voltaire. The wiser pilgrim will turn from " the Man of
Nature's " cenotaph to explore the woodland scenes about
Ermenonville.

> "   .   .   .   . ROUSSEAU
> Loved these calm haunts of Solitude and Peace;
> .   .   .   .

> .   .   .   Here, if thy breast be full,
> If in thine eye the tear devout should gush,
> His SPIRIT shall behold thee, to thine home
> From hence returning, purified of heart."

In the *Hymn to the Penates*, Southey represents himself as a disillusioned idealist who heals his soul by cultivating the domestic affections in their appropriate environment of natural simplicity. And this simplicity is not, as in pantisocratic days, regarded as an initial step toward a higher perfection: it is in itself perfection. " There was a time," Southey tells John May, " when I believed in the persuadibility of man, and had the mania of man-mending. Experience has taught me better. . . . The ablest physician can do little in the great lazar-house of society. . . . He acts the wisest part who retires from the contagion."

Such a state of mind provides a fit soil for the growth of the Noble Savage idea. Southey, however, already knows too much about actual savages to regard them as satisfactory examples of primal blessedness. " The savage and civilized states," he declares, " are alike unnatural, alike unworthy the origin and end of man." [38] This attitude appears still more strongly when Southey's enthusiasm for nature wears off. At present his craving for simplicity is such that his emotions counterbalance his knowledge. The Indian may not live in the true state of nature, but he comes so much closer to doing so than civilized man that he deserves approval. To the rule that one can hardly recoil from organized society without espousing the cause of the savage, Southey is no exception.

One would like to see that " seditious ode in the ludicrous style, addressed to the cannibals " which appeared in the *Courier and Telegraph* in one of the early months

[38] *Life and Correspondence.* To John May, June 26, 1797.

of 1796. Southey acknowledges that he is " Caius Grac-
chus," its author.[39] The piece may have no connection
with our subject, but to imagine it as a satirical contrast
between the sins of the cannibals and those of the Pitt
administration is tempting. Possibly a hint was provided
by Montaigne's essay.

Southey's habits of composition make difficult any
chronological treatment of his works. His longer poems
were generally planned several years before publication,
and once published were often altered in subsequent editions. Thus the first draft of *Joan of Arc* was completed
in 1793, but Joseph Cottle did not publish it until 1796.
In this early edition, Joan is impelled to save France by
the supernatural agencies of the traditional legends. This
" machinery " was discarded in the second edition of
1798, when for it were substituted the inspiring influences
of scenery. The Maid of Orleans is portrayed as a simple
child of nature. More will be said of her in a later chapter. Here it is sufficient to hint that she represents innocent
intuitiveness striving against corrupt sophistication. Her
interview with the doctors of the church — her untutored
spirituality shaming their erudite bigotry — is like the
familiar confrontation of Noble Savage and civilized man.

The year 1799, passed by Southey in the little village
of Westbury, near Bristol, is described by the poet as " one
of the happiest portions of my life. I never before or
since produced so much poetry in the same space of
time." [40] Among the fruits of this bountiful season were
the *Songs of the American Indians*. In them, Southey's
knowledge of Indians, both North and South American,
becomes lyrical. The series comprises five poems: *The
Huron's Address to the Dead, The Peruvian's Dirge Over*

---

[39] *Ibid.* To Grosvenor Bedford, June 26, 1796.
[40] *Poetical Works*, Vol. IV, preface.

the Body of His Father, *Song of the Araucans During a Thunder-Storm*, *Song of the Chikkasah Widow*, and *The Old Chikkasah to His Grandson*. That more familiarity with savage lore is displayed here than ever before in English literature is important, but still more important is Southey's attempt to treat the actual life of savages in an imaginative spirit.

The *Songs* give no express laudation of Indian life. They are dramatic lyrics, and with one exception the writer's personality does not obtrude itself. Their romantic quality is not imposed externally, but is extracted from the natural romance inherent in Indian customs. Instead of palliating barbaric cruelty and vengefulness by comparing them with European vices, Southey tries to purify them by giving them poetic dignity. He would have us recognize the similarity between the emotions felt by his Indians and those felt by the heroes of legendary poetry, of Homer and of Ossian.

The Chikkasah widow is haunted by the spirit of her husband, and promises vengeance upon his slayers:

> " Tomorrow thy widow shall wield
> The knife and the fire: be at rest! "

But we are made to see that this bloodthirstiness has its source in true conjugal love.

> " The vengeance of anguish shall soon have its course,
> The fountains of grief and of fury shall flow;
> I will think, Ollanahta! of thee,
> Will remember the days of our love."

Here speaks a copper-skinned Andromache. Similarly, in *The Old Chikkasah to His Grandson*, the bloody scalps of victory are viewed, in a correct psychological spirit, as glorious trophies appropriate to

> " The day of the warrior's reward;
>   When the banners sunbeaming were spread,
>   And all hearts were dancing in joy,
>   To the sound of the victory-drum."

This self-justification of savage feelings sets the *Songs* quite apart, so far as the romantic period is concerned, from most other poetic representations of the Indian.

The one instance in which Southey forsakes dramatic realism for the sake of a personal thesis is *The Peruvian's Dirge Over the Body of His Father*. The bereaved son, evidently a slave to the Spaniards, thinks of his father's happy boyhood, when the Peruvians were free and equal, and led a communal existence.

> " In the fields of the nation, thy hand
>   Bore its part of the general task;
>   And when, with the song and the dance,
>   Ye brought the harvest home,
>   As all in the labor had shared,
>   So justly they shared in the fruits."

These are less the words of a Peruvian than of a thwarted pantisocrat. They indicate a more than aesthetic sympathy with the Indian.

The *Songs* were mere by-products of Southey's wide reading in the accounts of explorers and missionaries. For a more substantial — if not entirely too substantial — poetic outgrowth of these researches, we must turn to *Madoc*. This poem, first pondered in schoolboy days, was finished in the happy year at Westbury, and though it was laid aside for revision and not published until 1805, it seems best to consider it here.

The greatest obstacle in the way of reading Southey's longer poems with the appreciation which they frequently deserve is his practice of basing his plot upon a mass of unfamiliar legend and mythology. When the copious notes are digested, it seems unnecessary to read them all over again in versified form. Hence the reader will not be inflicted with the very complicated details of a poem on which the writer himself would not care to be examined. It is necessary to know that according to an old legend, Madoc, a Welsh prince of the twelfth century, founded a colony in America. He settled in Florida, which at that time was inhabited by the Aztecas, a tribe later to migrate to Mexico as the famous Aztecs. The contact between the Welsh and the Indians sets the epic-romantic story in motion.

Whether Southey had any reason to make Florida the original home of the Aztecs is doubtful. Probably he employed this device in order to combine his knowledge of the great barbaric civilization of Mexico with his knowledge of more primitive tribes. The poem as we have it must be very different from the first draft of 1799, but just how different it is impossible to say. He has hardly finished *Madoc* when he writes his brother Thomas: " It was my design to identify Madoc with Mango Capac, the legislator of Peru: in this I have totally failed, therefore Mango Capac is to be the hero of another poem; and instead of carrying Madoc down the Marañon, I shall . . . land him in Florida: here, instead of the Peruvians, who have no striking manners for my poem, we get among the wild North American Indians. On their customs and superstitions facts must be grounded." [41] This illustrates perfectly Southey's method of writing his poems to fit his footnotes. The design here set forth is not, however, carried out to the letter in the final version of *Madoc*. We do, to be sure, " get among the wild North American Indians," but they mingle with

[41] *Life and Correspondence.* To Thomas Southey, July 12, 1799.

their simple wildness the complex religion, art and social organization of those Aztecs which they are destined to become. No doubt the temptation to draw at the same time upon the accounts of Spanish, Portuguese, French and English explorers was irresistible,[42] but the resultant mixture of Noble Barbarians and Noble Savages is confusing.

The latter appear plainly enough in Madoc's first meeting with the Indians:

> ".   .   .   Of dark-brown color, tinged
> With sunny redness; wild of eye; their brows
> So smooth, as never yet anxiety
> Nor busy thought had made a furrow there;
> Beardless, and each to each of lineaments
> So like, they seemed but one great family.
> Their loins were loosely cinctured, all beside
> Bare to the sun and wind; and thus their limbs,
> Unmanacled, displayed the truest forms
> Of strength and beauty."

There can be no doubt here of Southey's intention to portray the Indian as happy, free and beautiful.

The Aztecas resemble Keate's exemplary Pelewans in that in their curiosity about the whites they do not forget the obligations of the host. Each savage, according to his means, brings the wayfarers food and drink. And lest this be taken for mere poetic fancy, Southey assures the reader that " There is in every village of the Susquehannah Indians a vacant dwelling called the Stranger's House. When a traveller arrives . . . they . . . bring tobacco after they are refreshed, and then ask questions whence they come and whither they go. — Franklin." [43]

[42] Southey refers in his notes to: Franklin, Carver, Lafitau, Charlevoix, Mackenzie, Oviedo, Torquemada, Bernal Diaz, Padilla, Garcia, Clavigero, Bartram, Garcilaso de la Vega, Herrera, Heriot, Timberlake, Pietro Martire, Brainerd, Roger Williams, Priest, and Pero Nino.

[43] In 1796, upon his return from Portugal, Southey mentions this

As a further illustration of Southey's method of using his authorities, an Aztec woman's grief over the loss of her child is supported by " Carver's " account of the behavior of an actual squaw in the same situation: " Expression so replete with unaffected tenderness, and sentiments that would have done honor to a Roman matron . . . tended not a little to counteract the prejudices I had hitherto entertained, . . . of Indian insensibility and want of parental tenderness."

In *Madoc* the simplicity of the Noble Savage is marred by the more sophisticated Aztec strain, and Southey's approval of him is mingled with disgust for the bloody and cruel rites of Aztec religion. But so far as the "wild North American Indian " appears in the poem, he appears as the virtuous child of nature. Southey's wealth of fact is still expended in the cause of romantic sentiment.

That Southey's return to nature is paralleled by an enthusiasm for the Noble Savage which his knowledge of the real Indian restrained, but could not crush, is perhaps a legitimate conclusion. The later development of his feeling toward the Noble Savage must now be considered. We reminded ourselves that by 1806 a combination of factors had caused Wordsworth to desire a firmer guide than his own emotions. Can a similar evolution be observed in Southey?

In 1799, the very year in which the *Songs of the American Indians* were composed, Southey writes to William Taylor: " I have a dislike to all strong emotion, and avoid whatever could excite it. A book like *Werter* [*sic*] gives me now unmingled pain." [44] It is in this letter that

fact to Bedford in connection with the difficulty of finding lodgings in England. (*Life and Correspondence*, p. 97.)

[44] *Life and Correspondence*, p. 111.

he refers to Godwin and Epictetus as having been his diet in 1794.   For a time, as we know, Rousseau had been restored to his old leadership, but now the spirit of Epictetus is once more in the ascendant.

The change here noted would alone have been sufficient to make Southey forsake the Noble Savage; but besides this the influence of his studies must be taken into account. The fascination of primitive religions never lost its hold on him.   His research in Spanish and Portuguese literature, also, gave him a wide knowledge of the writings of the missionaries, whose accounts he supplemented by copious readings in contemporary travelers.

His letters abundantly attest his absorption in this special field.   In 1801, he wants to go to Ireland with Coleridge " to study savage life." [45]   We find him gloating over a " huge lot of . . . books of voyages and travels, and the Asiatic researches." [46]   He urges his naval brother, Lieutenant Thomas Southey, to send him information about the West Indian natives.[47]   An obscure fact about Villegaignon — the discoverer of Montaigne's " Antartike France " — is gleefully exhumed.[48]

In 1803 he reports that he is "about a curious review of the Mission of Otaheite." [49]   From this time onward, he becomes — first for the *Annual Review*, then for the *Quarterly* — in a sense the official critic in England of reports of missionary societies and of travelers' books.   This soft impeachment is admitted by Southey himself when he writes to Grosvenor Bedford, " Out of pure conscience, I have promised Gifford to take all these South American

---

[45] *Ibid.*   To. S. T. C., October 16, 1801.
[46] *Ibid.*   To Thomas Southey, April 22, 1803.
[47] *Ibid.*   To the same, December 7, 1805.
[48] *Ibid.*   To the same, January 10, 1809.
[49] *Ibid.*   To John Rickman, December 23, 1803.

travellers myself, because I can not bear that the Edinburgh should gain credit upon this subject, when I am so much better versed in it than any other man in England possibly can be." [50] Southey has a wholesome endowment of self-confidence, but is so little given to boasting that this statement can probably be accepted at its face value. At all events, Gifford was glad enough not only to let him " take all these South American travellers," but travelers to North America, the Nicobar Islands, the Tonga Islands, Sumatra, Polynesia, Tamar and Tavy.[51]

As might be expected, the more Southey knows about the real savage the less he believes in the Noble Savage. As early as 1799 he hears "a man read an essay upon the comparative evils of savage and civilized society; and he preferred the first, because it had not the curses of government and religion! " The exclamation-point is eloquent of amused contempt. " He had never," continues Southey, " read Rousseau "— a circumstance probably not rare among those who claimed to represent his theories. "What amused me was to find him mistaken in every fact he adduced respecting savage manners." [52] Southey's researches have spoiled him for essays on primitive virtue.

The coffee-house orator probably "amused " Southey by speaking of savages as if they were real natural men. As early as 1797, in a moment of disillusionment, our poet had acknowledged the fallaciousness of this analogy. After 1800, he frequently insists that savages are degenerates. " As for a state of nature, the phrase, as applied to man, is stark nonsense." [53] " The Tahitians are the

[50] *Ibid*. To Grosvenor Bedford, January 4, 1812.

[51] See the list of books reviewed by Southey as given in the appendix of *Life and Correspondence*.

[52] *Life and Correspondence*. To S. T. C., fall of 1799.

[53] *Ibid*. To John Rickman, January 15, 1806.

most degraded of the human species. . . . They have induced me to think it probable that the Spaniards did less evil in Hispaniola than we suppose." This last remark seems to refer to Las Casas, with whose humanitarianism Southey would have been in complete sympathy a few years earlier. Of course he exaggerates: he looks forward to the civilization, not the extirpation, of the savages. " I want English knowledge and the English language diffused to the east, and west, and the south." [54] Naturally he is delighted, therefore, when the King of Tahiti is converted. " His letters are in my last evangelical magazine. . . . This conversion may, very probably, lead to its [Tahiti's] complete civilization. . . . His majesty himself writes a remarkably good hand." [55] This from the man who was glad to sing through the lips of Indians!

But before deciding that Southey forsook the Noble Savage as completely as he forsook Jacobinism, one must consider the duality of his nature. Southey is a Tory in politics, but his Toryism is never rigidly absolute. Similarly, he never, either at this time or later, completely loses his sympathy with the savage. He can call the South Sea Islanders degraded, and yet praise a Birmingham banker's " sweet poem upon the Otaheitian girl." [56]

Rousseau and Epictetus, in fact, battled for the possession of Southey's mind to the end of his days. The latter gained the ascendancy, but not to the complete exclusion of the former. Thus as late as 1837 he writes to Caroline Bowles of the South Sea Islanders: " I like such people as little as you do; but magnanimity and matured affections are found in all stages of society, except where men are thoroughly corrupted in the rottenness of civili-

[54] *Ibid.* To the same, December 23, 1803.
[55] *Ibid.* To the Rev. Herbert Hill, December 28, 1813.
[56] *Ibid.* To Neville White, March 11, 1810.

zation." Here is not that glib acceptance of things as they are which might be expected of " my Tory, ultra-Julian." If the Tahitians are no longer admirable in themselves, they are admirable in contrast with European evils.

The letter just quoted is somewhat too violent, however, to be truly characteristic of the later Southey. Like Wordsworth, he effected a compromise with the spirit of the age. And for him it was easier to form and maintain his compromise than for Wordsworth. Southey, being less deeply romantic, intense, introspective and metaphysical than Wordsworth, was able to write about whatever interested him without being disturbed by the philosophical implications of his subject-matter. His evolution from *Minnesinger* to *Meistersinger* was hence comparatively painless.

In the post-Waterloo work of Southey are to be found only two poems dealing with Indian life, and of these one is left half-told.[57] *A Tale of Paraguay*, begun in 1814, received the poet's intermittent attention up to 1825, when it was completed and published. The poem is a metrical by-product of his *History of Brazil* in particular, and in general of his interest in all accounts of the contact between Christian missionaries and savages. The immediate source is a passage, said to be based on actual fact, in Dobrizhoffer's *De Abiponibus*. In embroidering his theme, Southey draws material from several other explorers and missionaries.

A Tale of Paraguay is interestingly related, also, to contemporary literary tendencies. Wordsworth's theory of the benign influence of scenery is taken over bodily. Bowles, in his *Missionary of the Andes*, provides his old

[57] *Thalaba* and the *Curse of Kehama* show some indebtedness to the Noble Savage tradition, but it seems best to postpone consideration of them until the group of topical chapters at the end of this study.

disciple with some useful suggestions. It seems not unfair
to suppose that had it not been for the success of Campbell's *Gertrude of Wyoming*, Southey's poem might not
have been cast in the Spenserian stanza. The resemblance
to Chateaubriands's *Atala* arises more probably from similarity of source and theme than from direct indebtedness.

The story of the poem is simple. Pestilence drives a
Paraguayan tribe further and further into the wilderness.
All perish except Quiara and his wife Monnema. For
them, forest solitude proves a blessing. The tribe to which
they belong had departed rather far from Arcadian virtues,
especially in succumbing to debased superstitions and barbarous rites. Thus the two survivors present the unusual
spectacle of Indians returning to nature.

The relations of Quiara and Monnema resmble those of
Milton's Adam and Eve — intense, innocent love, pro-
tective and masterful in the man, compliant and tender in
the woman. " Benignant Nature made the burden light."
Their union is blessed with a son and a daughter, Yeruti
and Mooma. Over these children is shed the light that
beamed upon Wordsworth's Lucy.

> " .   .   .   The boy *in sun and shower*
> Rejoicing in his strength to youthhead grew;
> And Mooma, that beloved girl, a dower
> Of gentleness from bounteous nature drew,
> With all that should the heart of womankind imbue." [58]

This idyll is shattered by the death of the father,
Quiara, at the paws of a wild beast. In seeking consolation for her husband's death, Monnema recalls certain
vague accounts, heard in her youth, of the Christian religion. To her children she tells the story of the Virgin,
and arouses in their innocent hearts a longing for things

---

[58] Italics mine; *cf.* Wordsworth's *Three Years She Grew.*

spiritual. Finally all three leave Eden to find God in Dobrizhoffer's settlement. They reach their goal and are converted, but die as a result of the hardships which they suffered on their long journey through the wilderness.

Southey gives an interesting sketch of the Guaranies, the tribe which has accepted the Jesuit message and leads a life of meek agriculture under the control of the missionaries. Instead of despising their " low estate," he says, we should "look round the world," and observe the " injurious passions," the tyranny, the greed, the deceit, the " jarring interests that engross mankind "; and

> " The low pursuits, the selfish aims of life;
> Studies that weary and contract the mind, —
> That bring no joy, and leave no peace behind."

After this survey of civilization, our eyes will rest with delight upon the simple Guaranies.

> " Obedience in its laws that takes delight
> Was theirs; simplicity that knows no art;
> Love, friendship, graceful duty, in its height;
> Meekness and truth, which keep all strife apart;
> And faith and hope which elevate the heart
> Upon its heavenly heritage intent.
> Poor, erring, self-tormentor that thou art,
> O Man! and on thine own undoing bent,
> Wherewith canst thou be blest, if not with these content? "

At first glance, this appears to be characteristic Noble Savage jargon; but an important distinction must be made. These Indians are to be envied not for their closeness to nature, but for their closeness to the God of orthodoxy; not for their wild freedom, but for the whole-heartedness of their submission to religion. In the *Songs of the American Indians*, savages are esteemed for their savagery; here they are esteemed for their ability to absorb spiritual instruction.

A Tale of Paraguay combines two favorite ideas of Southey. In the first place, savages are not truly men of nature: they have degenerated from a happy primal state. Thus Quiara and Monnema are liberated from the vices of their tribe and brought into direct contact with natural influences. But Southey also believes that religion and a little — not too much — civilization are necessary for the welfare of savages. His close study of missionary activities never made him suspicious of their beneficence. And so Monnema and her children, in order that the seeds of natural virtue may grow, are transplanted to the soil of the church.

The uncompleted poem earlier referred to is *Oliver Newman, a New England Tale*. This work is first mentioned in 1811, when Southey writes to Landor: " I am brooding a poem upon Philip's War with the New Englanders. . . . One of my main characters is a Quaker, an (ideal) son of Goffe the regicide." [59] This " brooding," however, came to nothing until 1815, when the poem was begun. The work received its last additions in 1828. The end of the poem is not in sight, and the existent portion is fragmentary.

Oliver Newman — not, it seems, a professing Quaker, but a youth of Quakerish tendencies — comes to the Massachusetts Bay Colony full of visionary ambitions to convert the Indians and ameliorate their lot. Leverett, the Governor, mocks him:

> " .   .   . Thou dream'st
> Of peopling some Arcadian solitude
> With human angels, — ignorant, alas!
> Of time, place, circumstance and men and things —
> The Indians, and thy father, and thyself." [60]

[59] *Life and Correspondence.* To W. S. Landor, January 11, 1811.
[60] Newman does not know who his father is — hence the last line.

Is this Southey the Tory answering Southey the pantiso-crat?

Newman is not to be dissuaded from his aims, but becomes more and more indignant at the colonists' treatment of the Indians. He buys from her brutal owners the slain chief Kawcanon's squaw, with her little son and daughter. Since gratitude is a cardinal virtue of the Indian, it is safe to predict that when King Philip's War breaks out the bread thus cast by Newman upon the waters will return to him buttered. But the poem breaks off too early to permit verification of this guess, and we shall never know the outcome of Newman's attempt to help the Indian through faith and love.

There is an evident resemblance between the *Tale of Paraguay* and *Oliver Newman*. The latter does not possess the naturalistic element of the former, but does display the same interest in missionary effort. *Oliver Newman* might, indeed, be regarded as an attempt to adapt the Dobrizhoffer theme to an English and Protestant setting, and the extreme difficulty of doing this may very well account for the abandonment of the work.

Here, then, are two poems both of which show strong sympathy for the Indian combined with an equally strong desire to improve him. The savage of Southey's later work is like Wordsworth's Westmoreland Girl:

> " Easily a pious training
> And a steadfast outward power
> Would supplant the weeds, and cherish
> In their stead each opening flower."

In order to discover whether Coleridge's attitude toward the Noble Savage underwent a development similar to that of Wordsworth and Southey, it is necessary to turn back to the pantisocratic period. The poems dealing with pantisocracy written during 1794 and the early months of 1795 are all rather feeble and sentimental. *On the Prospect of Establishing a Pantisocracy in America* represents the movement as nothing but a discouraged retreat from European strife. *Pantisocracy* dwells in a more positive tone upon the pleasures to be enjoyed in

".   .   .   the cottag'd dell
Where virtue calm with careless step may stray,
And dancing to the moonlight roundelay,
The wizard Passions weave an holy spell." [61]

But there seems to be little connection between moonlight roundelays and Godwinian perfectibility. *To the Rev. W. J. Hort (while Teaching a Young Lady Some Song-Tunes on His Flute)* [62] assures the recipient that Coleridge,

" Far from folly, far from men,
In the rude romantic glen,"

will often think of Mr. Hort's pipings, and will "ponder" on the piper. Most famous of all is *To a Young Ass*, which hails Peter Bell's victim as " *Brother* — spite of the fool's scorn." Equality could no further go. Surely something of " the innocence of the patriarchal age " is here; but where are " the knowledge and general refinements of European culture? "

To the pantisocratic poems may be added Numbers III and IV of the *Sonnets on Eminent Characters*. In Number III we see NATURE — that is, Religion stripped of all her mummery — lifting her veil to smile fondly upon her son, Dr. Priestley. Number IV hails Godwin as he who

[61] The authorship of the poem is not absolutely certain, but Ernest Hartley Coleridge assigns it to S.T.C.

[62] The " young lady " is Sara Fricker.

> " Bade the bright form of Justice meet my way —
> And told me that her name was HAPPINESS."

One doubts whether the Godwin of 1794 would have liked so soft a notion, or would have agreed with Coleridge on a definition of happiness.

Thus with Coleridge, as with Southey, the Godwinian rationalism of pantisocracy tends to become naturalistic when it is expressed in poetry. Except for Lee Boo, however, no poem published by Coleridge in the pantisocratic period mentions the savage. Of poems written in these years but not published until later, *Lewti* deserves mention. Although this poem did not appear until 1798, one of the manuscript drafts can hardly be later than 1794, for in the text the name " Mary " appears instead of " Lewti," a fact which implies that Miss Evans was still in the ascendant. Not everyone remembers that another manuscript of this puzzling poem was at first entitled *The Wild Indian's Love-Chaunt* instead of *The Circassian's Love-Chaunt,* and that " Tamaha's stream " is simply the Altamaha River of Georgia. Lewti's lover, it seems, was originally a redman.

After the collapse of pantisocracy, Coleridge, like Southey, turned to nature for peace and consolation. His feeling for nature was developed in large measure by his contact with Wordsworth, whom he had met late in 1795 just when both poets were trying to find spiritual anchorage.

As in the case of Wordsworth and Southey, Coleridge's growing naturalism implies the repudiation of Godwin. In 1796 we find him trying, chiefly on religious grounds, to free John Thelwall from his old leader's influence. Godwin's " very heart is cankered by the love of singularity," and he advocates sincerity that he may give vent to his " misanthropy." [63]   " It is not his atheism that has prejudiced me against Godwin, but Godwin who has, perhaps, *prejudiced* me against atheism." [64]   The dropping of this pilot of revolutionary days was an essential part of the romantic reaction.

Coleridge's view of the ethical influence of nature is at first an outgrowth of the old pantisocratic theory. Since his " almost visionary fondness " for woods and mountains has given him "benevolence and quietness," he desires "to be the means of planting it in others, and to destroy the bad passions not by combating them but by keeping them in inaction." [65]   This idea of obtaining virtue by shutting out incentives to vice is essential to pantisocracy, but only as a prerequisite to further progress. Now, on the contrary, the only possible progress lies in retrogression. The positive element in pantisocracy has vanished; the negative element is pushed to its extreme conclusion. But from all extreme conclusions there is an avenue of escape, and in this instance one is provided by the Wordsworthian doctrine. Nature offers not only refuge, but inspiration. Thus out of the nay of retreat emerges the yea of him who responds to the impulses emanating from the vernal wood.

The poems of 1797 and 1798 in which Coleridge expresses his love of nature are well known. They are embodiments of the Wordsworthian philosophy, but with less didactic motive, a more intense sensuous thrill, and a greater element of " strangeness added to beauty." Detailed exposition of Coleridge's return to nature would be superfluous. But did this phase of his development include any enthusiasm for the savage?

[63] *Letters of S.T.C.*, LVII. To John Thelwall, May 1796.
[64] *Ibid.*, LIX. To the same, June 1796.
[65] *Ibid.*, LXXX. To the Rev. George Coleridge, April 1798.

As early as 1793 Coleridge had shown, in two metrical paraphrases from Ossian, [66] an interest in primitive poetry. During the period of nature-worship, the same tendency appears in *Lewti, Kubla Khan* and the *Ancient Mariner.* The connection between natural man and natural poetry is, however, a subject reserved for treatment in a later chapter.

More apposite to the present theme is the influence of primitive legend and folk-lore. *The Destiny of Nations* refers sympathetically to

" .   .   .   those legends terrible, with which
The polar ancient thrills his uncouth throng."

Wild and barbarous tales as they are, they yet contain the germ of true religion in that they teach reliance on God's goodness. The materials of the poem, a foot-note informs us, are drawn from Leemius' *De Lapponibus* and Crantz's *History of Greenland.* Coleridge shares the interest of his contemporaries in travel-literature.

The Three Graves, a Monk Lewis sort of spook-poem begun in 1797, but not finished until much later, is also based upon books of travel. " I had been reading Bryan Edwards' account of the effects of the Oby witchcraft on the Negroes in the West Indies, and Hearne's deeply interesting anecdotes of similar workings on the imagination of the Copper Indians . . . ; and I conceived the desire of shewing that instances of this kind are not peculiar to savage or barbarous tribes." It is Hearne, we remember, who provides the stimulus for Wordsworth's *Complaint of a Forsaken Indian Woman.* In *The Road to Xanadu,* Professor Lowes demonstrates that Coleridge's imagination drew much from the literature of travel and exploration.

[66] *Imitated from Ossian,* and *The Complaint of Ninathoma.*

The comparison between savage and rustic superstitions is very characteristic of Coleridge, but not of Wordsworth. When young Hazlitt visited Coleridge at Nether Stowey, the poet " lamented that Wordsworth was not prone enough to believe in the traditional superstitions of the place, and that there was a something corporeal, a *matter-of-factness* . . . in his poetry, in consequence." [67] This statement does something to justify the assumption that the savage and the peasant were more closely connected in Coleridge's mind than in Wordsworth's.

There can be no question of Coleridge's deep interest in magic during the period of his most enthusiastic naturalism. *Christabel* is rooted in folk-lore much more primitive than the medieval; and any reader of Frazer knows that the scapegoat theme of the *Ancient Mariner* is as old and as widely diffused as priestcraft itself. Hardly less universal are the bringing down of a curse by killing a sacred beast and the release from a spell through the utterance of magical words. Coleridge's two greatest poems are woven of such tales as Hottentot warriors might tell around the fire.

But a penchant for folk-lore does not necessarily imply — is often opposed to — enthusiasm for the Noble Savage. Coleridge's love of nature does not lead him to use Indians or Negroes to illustrate the beneficence of the natural life. Perhaps a trace of the Noble Savage idea appears in the *Ancient Mariner*. Though Coleridge was later to regard the moral of the poem as a blemish, that moral — the unity under God's love of all created things — is not merely a caudal appendage but the backbone of the whole work. This Unitarian doctrine is put in the mouth of a simple, ignorant sailor, who buttonholes the worldly wedding guest to tell him that when everything

[67] *Collected Works of William Hazlitt*, Vol. XII, p. 270.

else is dead, one sees beauty in ugliness, and that therefore one should love everything indiscriminately. There is something of the Noble Savage philosophy in all this, and the mariner himself is something of a Noble Savage.

With *Osorio* (1797), we stand on firmer ground. In this drama, the persecuted Moors are presented as a proud and vengeful race, haughtily scornful of their Spanish oppressors. The atmosphere of the piece recalls that of the Peruvian tragedies from which we had vainly thought to have parted company. The scene is of course not Peru, but Spain. Otherwise the plan is very similar: the cruel, greedy, fanatical Spaniards, the abused heathens, the resultant flings at Christian civilization. Alhadra, a Moorish woman who pretends to be a Christian convert, says to the heroine, Maria:

> " O gentle lady!
> You have no skill to guess my many wrongs,
> Many and strange. Besides, I am a Christian,
> And they do never pardon, 'tis their faith! "

Later, when the long-lost Albert, disguised as a Moor, addresses Maria in passionate language, Alhadra thinks that he intends some insult, and sneers:

> " These renegado Moors — how soon they learn
> The crimes and follies of their Christian tyrants! "

This heavy-footed satire is familiar to us.

The Peruvian tradition, however, is mingled with the new doctrine of scenic inspiration. Of Ferdinand, the high-souled Moor, it is said that

> " Unfit for boisterous times, with gentle heart
> He worships Nature in the hill and valley,
> Not knowing what he loves, but loves it all! "

This suggests Michael's "pleasurable feeling of blind love."

Two fragments from *Osorio* were included in *Lyrical Ballads*. One, *The Dungeon*, is a soliloquy of which the following lines are typical:

> " With other ministrations thou, O Nature!
> Healest thy wandering and distemper'd child;
> Thou pourest on him thy soft influences,
>
> .   .   .   .
>
> Thy melodies of woods and winds and waters,
> Till he relent, and can no more endure
> To be a jarring and a dissonant thing."

Here is a new note in Peruvian tragedy.

The other fragment, *The Foster-Mother's Tale*, has almost no connection with the plot, and was excised when the play was revised and produced as *Remorse*. Maria's foster-mother relates the story of an infant who was reared by a hermit in the woods, and who

> ".   .   .   .   .   grew up a pretty boy,
> A pretty boy, but most unteachable —
> And never learnt a prayer, nor told a bead,
> But knew the names of birds, and mock'd their notes
> And whistled, as he were a bird himself."

Growing older, the lad takes up witchcraft, and is imprisoned by Count Velez. In the dungeon, he sang

> ".   .   .   .   .   a doleful song about green fields,
> How sweet it were on lake or wild savannah
> To hunt for food, and be a naked man,
> And wander up and down at liberty."

He has his wish, for Velez, who loves the boy, releases him. He goes to America,

" And all alone set sail by silent moonlight,
Up a great river, great as any sea,
And ne'er was heard of more; but 'tis supposed
He liv'd and died among the savage men."

One wonders whether Shelley, in writing *Alastor*, thought of this passage. At any rate, it is tempting to see in these lines some reflection of Coleridge's own spiritual experiences. Like the boy in the story, he had — or thought he had — been reared a child of nature. He had practiced the witchcraft of poetry, and had been thrown into the dungeon of a corrupt civilization. Now he longs to escape to the wilds — not to found a Godwinian community, but to be " a naked man." It is the old dream of Joseph Warton — and of Solitary.

Even supposing this allegorizing to be unjustified, *Osorio* certainly shows the influence of the Noble Savage idea. We must recognize, however, that it is exceptional. Coleridge is almost always the intellectual aristocrat. His mind remained complex even in its adoration of simplicity. For a brief space he shared Wordsworth's passion for scenery, but he never, like Wordsworth, credited the peasant with susceptibility to his majestic surroundings. With Wordsworth, love of nature led to love of man; but with Coleridge, love of nature tended gradually to draw him away from man into private conference with the infinite. This unsociable mysticism does not fully appear until his transcendental period, but even at this time it prevents him from accepting the goodness of man as an inevitable corollary of the goodness of nature. The most one can say is that at the period when Coleridge is most absorbed by naturalism he is more attracted by primitive poetry and legend, and in general more favorable to the Noble Savage, than at any other period of his career.

Coleridge's jottings in the *Gutch Memorandum Book*,

which cover the three-year period from the spring of 1795
to the summer of 1798, should also be admitted in evidence.   They suggest that the Noble Savage formed part
of that mass of unfulfilled projects which constantly fermented in the poet's mind.   Thus he considers as a possible
subject: " The Life of the Siminole [*sic*] playful from
infancy to Death compared to the Snow, which in a calm
day falling scarce seems to fall and plays and dances in
and out, to the very moment that it reaches the ground."
He meditates also a treatment of the famous mutiny of
the *Bounty*, a theme into which, as we shall see, Miss
Mitford and Byron inject plenty of Noble Savagery.   If
Coleridge had carried out either or both of these projects,
our results would be less negative.

Southey became his later self through scholarship;
Coleridge, through opium and through transcendental
philosophy.   Although transcendentalism made impossible his old belief in a mechanistic unity, it left him free
to achieve an even more pleasing sort of unity — that imposed upon the flux of things by his own creative mind.
By 1801 he has begun to erect a system of intuitive metaphysics.   Unless a metaphysical conception appeals to the
heart, he insists, it is to be held suspect.   It is not so much
logical dialectic that links ideas together as " the soul, the
state of feeling." [68]   By such Bergsonian arguments Coleridge paves the way for his new synthesis.   No metaphysical feat is difficult for him who glorifies the passional
element in his thought.

This cardiac kind of thinking is not inherently unfavorable to the Noble Savage.   In an interesting letter to
Southey, Coleridge brings together the poet, the philosopher, and the Indian.   " A great poet must be . . . a
profound metaphysician.   He may not have it in logical

[68] *Letters of S.T.C.*, CXVII. To Thomas Poole, March 1801.

coherence in his brain and tongue but he must have the ear of a wild Arab . . . , the eye of a North American Indian . . . , the touch of a blind man." This exquisite sensitiveness is the prime requisite of both poet and philosopher. " I have read no French or German writer who appears to me to have a *heart* sufficiently pure and simple to be capable of this or anything like it." [69] In this there is much of Jacob Boehme and Blake, and of Saint-Pierre's good pariah, who finds truth by means of the *coeur simple*.[70] The Noble Savage may be your true metaphysician.

Such an attitude is not, however, really characteristic of the later Coleridge. It marks a sort of transition between the old naturalism and the new intuitive mysticism. Coleridge would seek truth intuitively, but his intuitions are not those emotional stirrings common to all mankind. They are the intuitions of an intellectual aristocrat, a philosopher, and a genius. By 1809 Coleridge has found in German metaphysics an abstruse and weighty justification of his own half-formed ideas. The fusion of Schelling and Kant with his personal philosophy appears in *The Friend*. His praise of emotion as against logic is embodied in his Kantian conception of reason, a half-mystical faculty which rises above mere understanding as the myths of Plato rise above the dialectic of Socrates. Into these dim mazes of thought we need not follow. The intuitions of the Noble Savage exclude ratiocination; the intuitions of Coleridge are meant to include and transcend it. Possibly Coleridge fell below logic in seeking to soar above it, but to him at least his system had not the slightest tincture of primitivism. Instead of retreating from the revolutionary spirit in primitivistic disillusionment, Coleridge criticizes it from a distinctive viewpoint. The age is not

[69] *Ibid.*, CXXV. To William Sotheby, July 1802.
[70] *Cf.* Bernardin de Saint-Pierre, *La Chaumière Indienne.*

too reasonable; it is not, in the Coleridgian sense, reasonable enough. It needs the deep faith, the high seriousness, the imaginative fervor which true reason implies.

Coleridge the transcendental Tory has lost such slight affection as he once had for the Noble Savage. Anyone who examines himself, he declares, knows " that there is Evil in our nature as well as Good," " from Pascal in his closet . . . to the poor pensive Indian, that seeks the missionary in the American wilderness." [71] And the remedy for evil is not simplicity, but high thought illumined by faith. For improving the Tahitians, indeed, Coleridge has a more practical device. He would, Southey reports, destroy all the breadfruit trees and thus make the natives work for their living." [72] That such a step would, from the Noble Savage point of view, automatically set going the whole chain of vices which have corrupted man, does not distress S.T.C. He sees the Tahitians as a set of degraded rascals who might be helped, and who certainly could not be harmed, by a little honest work. The time has come, then, to part company with Coleridge. By 1809 he has adopted a philosophical position so peculiar to himself that it sets him apart from his contemporaries; and so opposed in intention, if not in reality, to any sort of naturalism, that it makes approval of the Noble Savage impossible.

An attempt has been made to trace the relation of the Noble Savage idea to the intellectual evolution of Wordsworth, Southey and Coleridge. These three poets differed widely, but all represented certain phases of thought and feeling which are typical of the Romantic Movement in

[71] *The Friend*, pp. 4–5.

[72] *Life and Correspondence of Robert Southey*. To John Rickman, December 23, 1803.

general. In considering them, therefore, one considers the spirit of their generation. Their lives fall into six periods, which may be summarized as follows:

(1) A period of "early romantic" sensibility. All three poets are vaguely favorable to the Noble Savage as an emanation of eighteenth century sentimentalism. Wordsworth wishes to find the Swiss better than they are; Southey satirizes civilization through Omai; Coleridge mourns over Lee Boo's tomb. This adolescent stage merges into

(2) A period of revolutionary enthusiasm. Faith in practical reform runs too high for dalliance with the Noble Savage idea. Our poets are disillusioned by terroristic excesses, and pass into

(3) A period of Godwinian rationalism. Wordsworth is the most consistent disciple of the three, and hence the most unhappy. In pantisocracy, Coleridge and Southey combine Godwinism with naturalistic elements not unfavorable to the Noble Savage. All three find Godwin a blind leader of the blind, and in reacting from Jacobin rationalism enter

(4) A period of naturalism. In each case love of nature is paralleled by sympathy with the Noble Savage. Wordsworth invents a closely analogous figure — the Noble Dalesman — and shows interest in Indians. Southey's knowledge of savage customs has not yet dampened his enthusiasm for ideal primitive virtues. Coleridge is strongly attracted by "natural" poetry and by savage legends. Gradually, however, nature proves an inadequate ideal, as the three poets undergo

(5) A period of hardening. The term inadequately expresses the gradual growth of Wordsworth, Southey

and Coleridge into their later selves. As they turn from nature, they turn from the Noble Savage. At last they enter

(6)   A period of merely " official " romanticism, in which their conservatism is either maintained or increased, but in which Wordsworth and Southey show, chiefly in a conventional way, flashes of the old naturalistic philosophy combined with the Noble Savage idea. This does not apply to Coleridge, who draws deeper and deeper into the mists of transcendentalism.

Such a schematized treatment is necessarily abstract and artificial. One cannot but be struck, however, by the way in which the fortunes of the Noble Savage rise and fall with the fortunes of romantic naturalism.

Chapter VII

BYRON, ROGERS, CAMPBELL AND MOORE

> "Scott, Rogers, Campbell, Moore and Crabbe, will try
> 'Gainst you the question with posterity."

SUCH is Byron's challenge to the Lake Poets. The army that he arrays against the foe is diversified. Scott is a lovable, conservative gentleman, able to satisfy the craving for romance without offending good taste by any eccentric "simplicity." Crabbe is included because of his realistic attitude toward the subjects idealized by Wordsworth. Rogers, Campbell and Moore compose a more nearly homogeneous group. They represent what may be called the "urban circle." In this group Byron, had he not been a great genius, would himself be included; and his relations with its members, especially Rogers and Moore, were always close. There is therefore some justification for considering these four poets together.

In our attempt to fix the position of Byron in relation to the Noble Savage, we may imagine the poet's shade as mocking the earnestness of our efforts. He would be especially amused by our sober application of the chronological method to his works. Yet that method, after all, provides the only practicable trail through the forest of Byron's mind.

In *Hours of Idleness*, the youthful Byron looks back yearningly to those years when, "a careless child," he roamed through Deerside, Lochnagar, and the Gram-

pians.[1]   This "young Highlander" of Byron's retrospective longings was like the savage in being

> " Untutored by science, a stranger to fear,
>   And rude as the rocks where my infancy grew." [2]

We are reminded of Wordsworth, who compares his own
boyhood to that of " a naked savage in the thunder-
shower," and of Fleetwood, the " solitary savage " of
Merionethshire.

Wordsworth carried with him to Cambridge, as Godwin's Fleetwood to Oxford, traces of this early wildness.
He found himself too much the enthusiast to share the
levities of student life, too proud to conform to the example
of the herd.   Young Byron is similarly at odds with his
environment.   The Reverend J. T. Becher advises him
" to mix more with society," and receives a turbulent reply.   Within his soul, says Byron, terrific fires of ambition
are seething.   He would give anything to live like Fox,
and die like Chatham.   But the petty round of social
trivialities is galling to him.

> " Yet why should I mingle in Fashion's full herd?
>   Why crouch to her leaders, or cringe to her rules?
> Why bend to the proud, or applaud the absurd?
>   Why search for delight in the censure of fools? "

The illusions of his boyhood have grown dim:

> " My passion the matrons of prudence reprove;
>   I have found that a friend may profess, yet deceive."

But he will preserve so far as possible the integrity of his
spirit.   Though deceived by others, he is not yet deceitful

---

[1] *I Would I Were a Careless Child.   Cf.* also *The Adieu, Written on
Leaving Harrow.*
[2] *When I Roved a Young Highlander.*

—" I still am unpractised to varnish the truth." And why, finally, should he run the risk of corruption by taking the Reverend Mr. Becher's advice?

Thus early are we given a glimpse of that intense pride and ambition, that disillusioned idealism, and that desire to shun the face of mankind which combine to form the Byronic hero. This figure of course makes his first actual appearance in the exotic verse-tales written after the Mediterranean tour of 1809–1811. Explanations of the Byronic hero have often left out of account the thwarted naïveté which is the basis of this character. Take a young Noble Savage with a passionate desire for distinction. Bring him to a great city, and plunge him deep in sophistication. He will emerge a Byronic hero — a medley of natural man, city rake, and misanthrope. *Lara* is an imaginative projection of the melancholy young Highlander who wrote *Lines to the Rev. J. T. Becher.*

A more important result of the Mediterranean tour is the first half of *Childe Harold.* For us the second canto is especially interesting, for it adds to the Noble Savage tradition a new race — the Albanians. Byron's voyage carries him to

> " Climes, fair withal as ever mortal head
>   Imagined in its little schemes of thought;
>   Or e'er in new Utopias were read,
>   To teach man what he might be, or he ought:
>   If that corrupted thing could ever such be taught."

But why should one read Utopias when one can return to the bosom of Nature, " the kindest mother " ? Byron is

> " Her never-weaned, though not her favored child.
>   Oh! she is fairest in her features wild,
>   Where nothing polished dares pollute her path."

It is Albania that inspires these reflections — Albania, "rugged nurse of savage men." Byron's love of this wild land is partly due to its resemblance to Scotland. "Their very mountains seemed Caledonian, with a kinder climate," and the inhabitants remind him of Highlanders "in dress, figure and manner of living. . . . The kilt, though white; the spare active form; their dialect, Celtic in its sound, and their hardy habits, all carried me back to Morven." Albania would no doubt have seemed less Arcadian had it been less like the scenes of the poet's lost childhood.

This Utopia, far from being meek and pastoral, is full of interesting violence. The Arnaouts, or Albanese, are a fierce, predatory race, whose favorite occupations are brigandage and bloodshed. A something Ishmaelitish clings to them: "the Greeks hardly regard them as Christians, or the Turks as Moslems." [3] Their chief, Ali Pasha, is a picturesque and cruel thug whose rule

> " Is lawless law; for with a bloody hand
> He sways a nation, turbulent and bold."

Whether imaginatively or actually, Byron's disillusionment has made it impossible for him to return to Nature with the happy heart of a child. He carries into her mountains the turbulence of a disorganized spirit. He has "sought her more and more, and loved her best in wrath." Thus Nature herself assumes a sort of Byronic gloom, and her Albanian children are not innocent Arcadians, but noble outlaws.

And yet, in accordance with the conflict in Byron's own character, these fierce men

> " .   .   .   .   lack
> Not virtues, were those virtues more mature."

[3] Note B, appendix to Canto II.

Their good points are almost identical with those of the American Indian.[4] They possess great courage and physical endurance. Though terrible in vengeance, they feel the claims of gratitude and the obligations of hospitality.

Byron, "himself awhile the victim of distress," and in a situation which gave every opportunity for ill treatment, saw the softer side of Albanian character. In 1810, after Hobhouse had left him to return to England, the poet came down with a severe fever, and was at the mercy of a wholly incompetent European physician. Two native servants saved Byron's life by frightening away this quack, "whose throat they threatened to cut if I was not cured within a given time." Byron was alone and helpless. "I had left my last remaining English servant at Athens; my dragoman was as ill as myself, and my poor Arnaouts nursed me with an attention which would have done honor to civilization." "Less barbarians," indeed,

> ". . . would have cheered him less,
> And fellow-countrymen have stood aloof."

On another occasion, Byron is driven by a storm "full on the coast of Suli's shaggy shore." The natives of this alliterative region have such a reputation for ferocity that the mariners dread their refuge almost more than the perils of the sea. But the Suliotes prove as amiable as the Pelewans who gave Captain Wilson's crew so kindly a reception. They

> ". . . stretched the welcome hand,
> Led them o'er rocks and past the dangerous swamp,
> Kinder than polished slaves though not so bland,

[4] Byron quotes Gibbon to the effect that Albania, though "within sight of Italy is less known than the interior of America." (Appendix to Canto II, Note B.)

> And piled the hearth, and wrung their garments damp,
> And filled the bowl, and trimmed the cheerful lamp,
> And spread their fare; though homely, all they had."

That the Albanians, whatever their vices, are "kinder than polished slaves" is further evidenced by Dervish and Basili, the two servants who, as stated before, nursed Byron through his fever. The former, though a Mohammedan, is a better man than his nominally Christian colleague. When the servants were paid off at the close of Byron's sojourn in the Morea, Basili took his share with a few perfunctory words of regret at his master's departure. " Dervish took the money, but on a sudden dashed it to the ground; and clasping his hands, which he raised above his forehead, rushed out of the room weeping bitterly. From that moment to the hour of my departure he continued his lamentations, and all our efforts to console him only produced the answer, 'μαφείνει , He leaves me'." Byron, with certain guests who witnessed this scene, " melted." Indeed, who could fail to " sympathize with the simple and unaffected sorrow of this barbarian? " The poet is ashamed for civilization when he contrasts this ferocious but faithful creature with a " noble and most intimate associate," who, shortly before Byron left England, " had excused himself from taking leave of me because he had to attend a relation ' to a milliner's '." Again the old contrast of the corrupt with the primitive! [5]

Albanians satisfy almost perfectly the requirements of the Noble Savage type. They are discovered by a traveler to whose mind their environment and their character suggest Utopia. They illustrate the benefits of a rugged,

---

[5] Canto II, stanzas lxvi-lxviii, and Appendix, Note B. The same note, to show the feudal pride of Dervish on another occasion, quotes a speech which has exactly the ring of Amerindian oratory.

natural life. Their virtues, of the proper traditional sort, are contrasted with European vices in the proper traditional way.

But in one respect a divergence from the pattern is to be noted. Byron does not attempt to gloss over the savagery of the savage; instead, he glories in it. His Albanians are somewhat like Indians in their combination of ferocity and mildness, but he differs from almost all other writers in that he admires the former quite as much as the latter. To him the wild and rebellious spirit of the Albanians is quite as interesting as their Arcadian simplicity. These children of a nature less mild than wrathful exhibit the Götz-Werther complex of the Byronic hero himself.

In 1816 Byron's four years of popularity reached a tragic close under circumstances too familiar to be related. How thin the line between fact and fiction! Godwin's Fleetwood, who had been " a wild roe among the mountains of Wales," gradually lost the innocence of his childhood and sank deeper and deeper into the mire until a final revelation of human baseness made him flee to Switzerland in an attempt to regain his earlier kinship with nature. All these feigned circumstances are equally true of the flesh-and-blood Byron. It is easy to say that the flight up the Rhine, through Switzerland and into Italy was a mere histrionic gesture; but can one be sure that life had not made Byron, in sober earnest, the proud and stricken creature which he had earlier set up as a quite imaginary embodiment of the prophetic feelings of his heart?

In Canto III of *Childe Harold*, the hero " wanders forth again," having found

> " .   .   . himself the most unfit
> Of men to herd with Man; with whom he held

> Little in common; untaught to submit
> His thoughts to others, ...
>
> .   .   .   .
>
> He would not yield dominion of his mind
> To spirits against whom his own rebelled."

The "young Highlander" strain makes him, when "in Man's dwellings," "restless and worn, and stern and wearisome," like a wild falcon with clipped wings. The mountains are his true friends, to whom he now turns for companionship; the ocean his true home, in which he now seeks consolation.

As has often been noted, Byron in this mood approaches the nature-philosophy of Wordsworth. Yet the two intersecting orbits do not coincide. Wordsworth generally gives nature a voice which speaks to all humanity. His belief in her is dependent on his belief in the essential goodness of the human heart. Only a very few marred and disorganized spirits are unfitted to receive her message. It is for her glorious inhumanity, on the contrary, that nature is prized by Byron. She, with him her son, stands out in majestic revolt against the herd. This anti-social naturalism is unfriendly to the Noble Savage idea.

It is true that Byron's misanthropy becomes tempered with a gentler attitude toward mankind which was perhaps stimulated by his intercourse with Shelley, and which appears in *Manfred* and in the lyric *Prometheus*. But Byron has in him too strong an admixture of the flesh to thrive on the thin, pure air that sustained Shelley. On reaching Venice in 1817, he feels the need of a complete moral and intellectual holiday, and he takes it.

In *Beppo* he flings out what can only be interpreted as a conscious repudiation of Arcadian thought:

> "Oh, Mirth and Innocence! Oh, Milk and Water!
> Ye happy mixtures of more happy days!

> In these sad centuries of sin and slaughter
>   Abominable man no more allays
> His thirst with such pure beverage. No matter,
>   I love you both, and both shall have my praise.
>
> Oh, for old Saturn's reign of sugar-candy!
>   Meantime I drink to your return in brandy."

It is not too fanciful to see in this passage a jibe at Shelley. Byron's early primitivism was not of the milk-and-water sort. He valued simplicity for its wildness, not for its meekness. The gentle Shelley, whose loftiest thought was permeated by dreams of a Golden Age, did, however, think of natural man as a being of mildness and love. The notes to *Queen Mab* present the theory that a diet of flesh and fermented liquor is largely responsible for the deterioration of the race. When the two poets met in Switzerland, Shelley was in a state of transition between this boyish notion and the maturer Arcadianism of *Prometheus Unbound* and *Hellas*, both of which hold forth a vision of Saturn's reign restored. Byron mockingly deplores the passing of vegetarian innocence, and drains his brandy to the return of " the world's great age."

The period which Byron spent at Ravenna with the Countess Guiccioli (December, 1819–October, 1821) is marked by a resurgence of his classical tastes. At no time in his career is the poet more ready to bring reason to bear upon problems which he has previously regarded through a thick haze of emotion. In *Cain*, Byron's revolt is all on the side of intellect.

> " The snake spoke *truth:* it *was* the tree of knowledge,
>   It *was* the tree of life; knowledge is good,
>   And life is good; and how can both be evil? "

To attack the myth of man's downfall is inevitably to attack the Noble Savage; for what is Adam but the man of nature, virtuous and happy because of his ignorance?

In the autumn of 1821, the poet fled with the Gambas to Pisa. The Pisa-Genoa period is chiefly noted for a return to satire, less vivacious and harder in tone than that of the Venetian days. Once more the pendulum swings back to irony, and *Don Juan* is resumed.

Götzistic bombast, Wertheristic shrinkings, Shelleyan idealism, rationalistic scepticism — all these attitudes have grown stale and unprofitable. Nothing remains but to expose " the nothingness of life."

> " And the sad truth which hovers o'er my desk
> Turns what was once romantic to burlesque.

> " And if I laugh at any mortal thing,
>   'Tis that I may not weep; and if I weep,
> 'Tis that our nature cannot always bring
>   Itself to apathy   .   .   .   .   .
> .   .   .   .
> Thetis baptized her mortal son in Styx;
> A modern mother would on Lethe fix."

In the above passage one suspects a certain histrionic affectation, for *Don Juan* holds but little sorrow. In it are mingled the irresponsible mockery of an Italianate wit and the *saeva indignatio* of a Swift. Each type of satire makes use of the Noble Savage idea: the former ridicules the primitive; the latter employs it as a weapon.

The spirit of Venetian libertinism is of course better exemplified by those portions of the poem which were written before La Guiccioli interrupted the work. In Canto I the affair between Juan and Julia gives Byron an opportunity to dissect some of his own early illusions. Juan's reveries in the heart of the woods — so like those of Childe Harold — are associated with adolescent eroticism.

> " He pored upon the leaves, and on the flowers,
>   And heard a voice in all the winds; and then
> He thought of wood-nymphs in immortal bowers,
>   And how the goddesses came down to men."

In the fourth canto of *Childe Harold*, Byron had longed to dwell in the desert

> "With one fair Spirit for my minister,
>   That I might all forget the human race,
>   And, hating no one, love but only her! "

This Shelleyan aspiration is burlesqued in the story of Juan and Julia when Byron quotes Campbell's

> " Oh, Love! in such a wilderness as this,
>   Where transport and security entwine,
> Here is the empire of thy perfect bliss,
>   And here thou art a god indeed divine; " [6]

and sneeringly questions the exact connotation of the words " transport " and " security."

The Juan-Haidee episode of Cantos II, III and IV is, however, related with a tenderness which verges on the idyllic.

> " They should have lived together deep in woods,
>   Unseen as sings the nightingale; they were
> Unfit to mix in these thick solitudes
>   Called social, haunt of Hate, and Vice and Care."

Surely there is a trace of the Noble Savage in that. But Byron does not hesitate to sully the purity of this idyll with descriptions and comments which would be exceedingly discomforting to Paul and Virginia.

The Noble Albanian type of *Childe Harold II* reappears half-parodied in Lambro, Haidee's pirate father;

[6] *Don Juan*, Canto I, stanza lxxxviii. The first four lines are quoted from *Gertrude of Wyoming*, Part III, stanza i.

and the daughter herself displays a flash of her sire's wildness when he is about to shoot her lover:

> " How like they looked! the expression was the same,
> Serenely savage, with a little change
> 　In the large dark eye's mutual-darted flame;
> For she, too, was as one who could avenge,
> 　If cause should be — a lioness, though tame,
> Her father's blood before her father's face
> 　Boiled up, and proved her truly of his race."

Byron in his most sophisticated moments is never quite impervious to the charms of wildness.

From utterly cynical and half-cynical presentations of the primitive we turn to Leila, the little Turkish girl who is rescued from the Russians in Canto VIII. Don Juan takes " the little wild Asiatic " with him to London, and upon the advice of the "Society for Vice Suppression" selects Lady Pinchbeck as her guide and monitress. The London cantos are aimless, and the end of the poem is a mere place of leaving off instead of a real conclusion. Hence it is difficult to determine what Byron intended to do with Leila. She is certainly a Noble Savage, though portrayed with the inevitable spice of mockery.

> " .　.　.　Like a day-dawn she was young and pure,
> 　Or like the old comparison of snows,
> 　　Which are more pure than pleasant to be sure."

She is set in the midst of a society which includes the burnt-out dowager Lady Pinchbeck; Miss Reading, a blue-stocking; "Miss Raw, Miss Flaw, Miss Showman, and Miss Knowman " — all appropriately named; " the two fair co-heiresses Giltbedding " ; the under-sexed Miss Milpond; the title-hunter Miss Audacia Shoestring. Lady Adeline Amundeville is " the fair most fatal Juan ever met " — beautiful, proud, imperious. But Aurora

Raby, a younger, colder, shyer, more ingenuous maiden, also plays upon his heartstrings. She is very different from Haidee,

> " Yet each was radiant in her proper sphere;
> The island girl, bred up by the lone sea,
> More warm, as lovely, and not less sincere,
> Was Nature's all: Aurora could not be,
> Nor would be thus; — the difference in them
> Was such as lies between a flower and gem."

Now what is to be the fate of Leila among these surroundings? One can imagine three possibilities. Her natural innocence may, first of all, put to shame the artificial society in which she is placed. She may, that is, provide a vehicle for straightforward satire. Or secondly, she may in spite of herself be corrupted by her environment, and thus become not merely a satirical but a tragic figure. Or finally Byron may sardonically make Leila, as she grows older, prove that she has been dowered by nature with precisely those vices possessed by her more cultivated sisters, and that to educate her in womanly wiles is but carrying coals to Newcastle. The reader must take his choice. What will become of Leila we shall never know.

Up to this point all material drawn from *Don Juan* concerns love and the character of woman. In a later chapter the relation between romantic love and the Noble Savage idea will receive closer attention. But the eighth canto of the poem presents an entirely different aspect of primitivism.

Byron pauses in his description of the siege of Ismail to quote Cowper's " God made the country, and man made the town." Thinking of the fall of great cities of antiquity, Byron is inclined to agree with the earlier poet, and " to deem the woods shall be our home at last." Certainly Daniel Boone, " backwoodsman of Kentucky," was the happiest of men.

> " Crime came not near him — she is not the child
>   Of solitude; Health shrank not from him — for
> Her home is in the rarely trodden wild."

Boone lived to the age of ninety, and in spite of his obscurity left behind him a stainless reputation:

> " An active hermit, even in age the child
>   Of Nature, or the man of Ross run wild."

Although he shrank from crowds and moved further into the woods as houses sprang up about him, he was always kind to " the individual man." His life was not wholly solitary:

> " . . . around him grew
> A sylvan tribe of children of the chase,
>
> . . . .
>
> The free-born forest found and kept them free,
> And fresh as is a torrent or a tree.
>
> . . . . . .
>
> Corruption could not make their hearts her soil;
> The lust which stings, the splendor which encumbers,
>   With the free foresters divide no spoil;
> Serene, not sullen, were the solitudes
> Of this unsighing people of the woods." [7]

To what extent is this remarkable passage serious? The account of the siege, though full of indignation against war, is permeated by a cynicism of which the anxiety of the spinsters as to the beginning of the customary atrocities is the best example. This levity does not leave untouched

---

[7] The source of the passage may quite possibly be the *Topographical Description of Kentucky*, compiled by Captain Imlay of odious memory. Moore mentions it as influential in spreading illusory ideas about America. *Vide infra*, p. 269.

Byron's praise of the backwoodsman. A scholar-friend has insisted in conversation with the present writer that the lines are an ingenious, an almost too faithful, parody of the typical back-to-nature gush. But in view of the naturalism which appears elsewhere in the poem, this opinion seems extravagant. A chief mark of sophistication is the ability to say serious things in a frivolous way. Let us read the stanza which caps the Kentucky passage:

> "So much for Nature:— by way of variety,
>   Now back to thy great joys, Civilization!
> And the sweet consequence of large society,
>   War, pestilence, the despot's desolation,
> The kingly scourge, the lust of notoriety,
>   The millions slain by soldiers for their ration,
> The scenes like Catherine's boudoir at three-score,
> With Ismail's storm to soften it the more."

Then follows the terrible scene of slaughter from which Leila is snatched only just in time. This contrast between natural goodness and civilized viciousness is at bottom seriously ironic; only its overtones are carelessly cynical. Daniel Boone is not, however, a typical Noble Savage of romanticism. He represents disillusion, not illusion; hate, not love. He is an ideal figure set up to shame mankind, not to illustrate the essential worth of humanity. We have already met with a similarly bitter use of the Noble Savage. Byron's backwoodsman, like Swift's Houyhnhnm, is a device through which this world of Yahoos may be satirized.

At Genoa in 1823, just before his idealism rose in that half pure, half histrionic flame of service which was extinguished at Missolonghi, Byron wrote his last poem. *The Island* is often referred to as unimportant except in showing that Byron had never lost his fondness for the romantic verse-tale. The poem is, to be sure, a romantic verse-tale, but one that shows all the influences of the years which had elapsed since *Mazeppa*, the poet's last production in this *genre*. It is laden with satirical implications, and has several incongruously humorous touches. But in the main it seriously represents the struggle of bold men and a faithful woman for liberty, love, and the right to lead a free, untrammelled life.

The chief source of the poem is Lieutenant Bligh's *Narrative of the Mutiny and Seizure of the Bounty, in the South Seas, in 1789*. To the story of this famous mutiny, which accorded well with his penchant for rebellious violence, Byron added a few descriptions and incidents drawn from Mariner's *Account of the Natives of the Tonga Islands*, a popular book of South Sea travel. The specific details of the plot, and of course the interpretation of the action, are original.

The first canto relates the circumstances of the mutiny itself, with the setting adrift of the captain and a few supporters in a small boat. The sailors were mad to return to Tahiti,[8] for reasons which may be explained in Lieutenant Bligh's own words: " The women of Otaheite are handsome, mild and cheerful in manners and conversation, possessed of great sensibility, and have sufficient delicacy to make them to be admired and beloved. The chiefs were so much attached to our people, that they rather encouraged their stay among them than otherwise, and even made them promises of large possessions. Under these and many other concomitant circumstances, it ought hardly to be the subject of surprise that a set of sailors, most of them void of connections, should be led away, where they had the power of fixing themselves, in the midst of plenty, in one of the finest islands in the world, where there was

[8] The *Bounty* was carrying a cargo of bread-fruit trees from Tahiti to the West Indies, where it was hoped they might be naturalized.

no necessity to labour, and where the allurements of dissipation are beyond any conception that can be formed of it." [9]

A conscious or sub-conscious attraction toward a life of indolent lasciviousness has pervaded the South Seas cult from Hawkesworth in the eighteenth century to O'Brien in the twentieth. It seems strange that Byron, with his appreciation of John Hookman Frere, should have ignored the *Anti-Jacobin's* satire on this aspect of Tahitian life. [10] He persists, however, in sublimating the motives of the mutineers. Under his pen they become

> " Men without country, who, too long estranged,
> Had found no native home, or found it changed,
> And, half uncivilized, preferred the cave
> Of some soft savage to the uncertain wave —
> The gushing fruits that nature gave untilled;
> The wood without a path but where they willed;
> The field o'er which promiscuous Plenty poured
> Her horn; the equal land without a lord;
> The wish — which ages have not yet subdued
> In man—to have no master save his mood."

The passage follows Bligh closely, but with a subtle shift of interpretation which makes these simple sailors rather like Byronic heroes in quest of natural liberty.

Not all the mutineers settle in Tahiti. Fearing reprisals, a small band, led by one Christian, a man of a certain high-minded wickedness, establishes itself on the more secluded island of Toobonai. It is here that Canto II opens with a native song,

> " .   .   .   . the harmony of times
> Before the winds blew Europe o'er these climes.
> True, they [the natives] had vices — such are Nature's growth —
> But only the barbarian's — we have both."

[9] Quoted by Byron as note to Canto I, stanza ii.
[10] *Vide infra*, Chap. IX.

Upon landing, the sailors "found beauty linked with many a dusky form," and received answering admiration for their white skins. The consequent alliances are, perhaps strangely, neither casual nor brutal. The carefree life, the beauty of the surroundings, the hospitality of the Toobonians

> " Tamed each rude wanderer to the sympathies
> Of those who were more happy, if less wise,
> Did more than Europe's discipline had done,
> And civilized civilization's son! "

Of all these happy unions the happiest is that between Neuha,

> ".   .   .   the gentle savage of the wild,
> In growth a woman, though in years a child,"

and Torquil, "the fair-haired offspring of the Hebrides." If we deprive Haidee of her feudal status as a pirate princess, and remove from her portrayal all traces of cynicism, we shall have a character identical with Neuha. Except for that tinge of outlawry which seems inseparable from Byron's primitive types, Neuha is a perfect female specimen of the Noble Savage. In person, voluptuously beautiful; in temperament, animated, generous and faithful. Her little moods of anger were like squalls which hardly ruffle a placid lake. "She feared no ill, because she knew it not." Yet, as the sequel will show, her almost childish innocence does not render her incapable of wise and courageous action when danger threatens her beloved.

For this fair exotic, Torquil is the ideal mate. Both are children of nature, but with a difference. Neuha has imbibed feminine softness from the tropic breezes; into Torquil's body and mind has entered the storminess of the Highland gales. In him is typified the dauntless adventurer of all countries, of all ages. In Arabia he would have been a haughty Ishmaelite; in Chili,

> ".   .   .   a proud cacique;
> On Hellas' mountains, a rebellious Greek;
> Born in a tent, perhaps a Tamerlane."

The mention of Tamerlane provides an interesting clue: Marlowe's " Scythian Shepherd " has much in common with Byron's Noble Savage. But indeed the whole passage unites several strands of our subject. Torquil is bred amid the very scenes toward which Byron yearns in *Hours of Idleness*. Both the mutineer and his creator remember with affection the scenes of their youth; for the poet interrupts his description of Torquil to express his own love of the Highlands. Their images have colored his observations of Switzerland, of Italy, and of Greece.

> " The infant rapture still survived the boy,
> And Lochnagar with Ida looked o'er Troy,
> Mixed Celtic memories with the Phrygian mount,
> And Highland linns with Castalie's clear fount."

Here, in Byron's last poem, is explicit testimony that throughout all the alterations of his character, the nature-loving child of Morven remained a constant element. This retrospective primitiveness, also, links the poet with some of his most interesting creations. " The fair-haired Torquil, free as ocean's spray," might not only have been an Arab chieftain, a Chilian cacique, a Greek outlaw, a Tamerlane: he might have been Lord Byron.

After this picture of Neuha and Torquil against an idyllic tropical background, the narrative moves rapidly to its close. A warship comes to Toobonai, bent on the capture of the mutineers. All of Christian's band are killed except Torquil, who is rescued by Neuha. She

bears him away in her canoe to a cave which can be reached
only by diving beneath the waves.[11]   When the pursuers,
thinking their prey drowned, withdraw, Neuha and Torquil return to Toobonai, evermore to enjoy

> "   .   .   such happy days
> As only yet the infant world displays."

It would be unwise to burden *The Island* with an excessive load of interpretation.   The poem is primarily a story,
in which the modern reader will recognize the now familiar outlines of South Sea fiction.   Yet this tale, far from
being purely objective, rises from the depths of Byron's
mind.   For one last time his naturalism, often submerged
but never quite lost, breaks forth.   Nor is it surprising that
a period of satirical writing should close with a reaffirma-
tion of youthful ideals, for one may indict society either
by mocking civilization or by holding up an image of a
better world.   The reader who refuses to take Torquil
seriously may be reminded that Byron became what he
says the mutineer might have been, " a rebellious Greek ";
that Byron died a Byronic hero.   He had, alas, reason to
revise his earlier opinion of the gallant Suliotes.

Of the three fashionable poets who remain to be discussed, Samuel Rogers deserves the title of Dean.   He
was born in 1763, early enough to imitate Gray and Goldsmith in his first poems; and in 1850, at the death of
Wordsworth, he refused the laureateship on the score of
old age.   Tennyson received the honor which the palsied
old hands were too weak to hold, but Rogers lingered on
for six years more.   The reputation which he enjoyed as a
poet is simply amazing to those who now have the curiosity

[11] The cave is borrowed from Mariner's *Account of the Natives of
the Tonga Islands.*

to glance at his dull works. He was not a good poet, even of his own inferior sort. Yet he was a gentleman, a man of respectable though outmoded taste, a true friend, and a charming host.

What traces of the Noble Savage idea are to be found in the works of this cultivated, popular, well-fed banker-poet? Not many, it will probably be assumed. But Rogers, an Augustan who somehow found himself living in the age of romanticism, could seldom afford to write as he chose. Most of his poems are drearily conscious imitations of current literary fads. Like the good banker that he was, he never imitated any tendency while it was unpopular: always he waited until it had become quite safe and sane. Then he published his poem — sometimes, in the first edition, anonymously. In a few of these attempts to follow literary fashion at a safe distance, the Noble Savage may be discerned.

At the age of eighteen, young Rogers, like his master Pope, desired to form a " correct " style, and accordingly gave his days and nights to the study, not of Waller or Addison, but of Gray, Goldsmith and Johnson. In 1786 appeared his first published poem, the *Ode to Superstition*, an imitation of Gray, although the title suggests Collins. Rogers' theme is that throughout the centuries superstition has gradually developed into true religion. The " fur-clad savage " of the north heeds the spell of superstition, as does the Hindu Brahmin. But while Gray has a genuine romantic interest in primitive superstitions, Rogers sees in them only crude symptoms of higher spiritual yearnings to come. He discloses no sympathy with the Noble Savage idea.

Rogers' next production is modelled upon such didactic poems as Goldsmith's *Traveller*. The *Pleasures of Memory* is the cornerstone of this poet's reputation.

Though published in 1792, it serenely ignores the Revolution in order to sing the beauties of Hartley's laws of association. Since Noble Savages are in style, the ready poet produces several specimens. The universal love of home is illustrated by " the mild Tupia," the Tahitian who became Captain Cook's guide and interpreter.

> " So, when he breathed his firm yet fond adieu,
> Borne from his leafy hut, his carved canoe,
> And all his soul best loved — such tears he shed,
> While each soft scene of summer-beauty fled.
> Long o'er the waves a wistful look he cast,
> Long watched the streaming signal from the mast."

Rogers' note on these lines refers to a passage in Hawkesworth with which we are already familiar.[12] " Another very affecting instance of local attachment," says the poet, " is related to his [Tupia's] fellow-countryman Potaveri, who came to Europe with M. de Bougainville. — See *Les Jardins*, chant ii." [13]

The Negro slave is consoled in his captivity by memories of the homeland. He believes that when he dies,

> " Then will he wake on Congo's distant shore;
> Beneath his plantain's ancient shade renew
> The simple transports that with freedom flew."

A footnote shows that Red Indians, too, are passionately devoted to their native soil. One Canadian tribe, when asked to move elsewhere, replied, " What! . . . shall we say to the bones of our fathers, Arise, and go with us into a foreign land? "

---

[12] *Vide supra*, pp. 109–110.

[13] *Les Jardins* was written by the Abbé Delille, a French imitator of Thomson.

The "Intrepid Swiss" so love their mountains that their national folk-song, the *Ranz des Vaches*, cannot be played among Swiss troops in the field or in a foreign service, because it makes them weep and want to go home. In fact,

> " Undamped by time, the generous Instinct glows
> Far as Angola's sands, as Zembla's snows."

Though written in the revolutionary period, the *Pleasures of Memory* uses the Noble Savage in the conventional and sentimental fashion of Early Romanticism. These South Sea Islanders, Negroes, Indians and Swiss mountaineers are after all but typical bits of poetic decoration. Instead of showing the essential worth of human nature, they merely provide exotic instances of the universality of the laws of association.

Southey published his *Madoc* in 1805, and five years later the cautious Rogers issued privately the *Voyage of Columbus*, a production of his own in the same *genre*. His friends received the poem so well that in 1812 it was offered to the public. In view of the unpopularity of *Madoc*, one may ask why Rogers should have chosen to imitate the work of the Lakist. Southey, however, was trying to subject primitive material to epic technic; and in such a task Rogers, with his classical tastes, doubtless felt himself well qualified to succeed. In 1809 Campbell had sung the Wyoming Massacre in the measure of the *Faerie Queene*, and in 1813 Bowles was to publish the *Missionary of the Andes*, a redaction of Ercilla's *Araucana*. Why should not Rogers try his hand at an American epic?

Private publication is an insufficient veil for the coyness of our poet. He pretends that the poem is a translation of parts of a Castilian manuscript " found in an old religious house near Palos. . . . The Writer describes himself as having sailed with Columbus, but his style and manner are evidently of an after-time." They are indeed! The pretense of translation, though few could have taken it seriously, relieves Rogers from some of the responsibilities of his experiment. His real sources are a miscellaneous list of explorers. Compared to those of today, almost all writers of Rogers' time were amazingly familiar with the literature of exploration. Rogers need not, however, be credited with a knowledge even approaching Southey's in this field: he probably "read up" for this particular production.

A large part of the "Castilian manuscript" is summarized in prose, with a few striking scenes selected for "translation" into heroic couplets. On board the ships of Columbus all is despondency. Will land never be sighted? Meanwhile, in proper Homeric fashion, the Indian gods hold a council. The Zemi, deities of the Caribbean Islands, warn the gods of the mainland that the Spaniards are approaching. This news is conveyed through an ode in Gray's bardic vein. To the Zemi is assigned the task of repelling the invader. For a time they cause panic and mutiny in the Admiral's fleet, but "Columbus restores order; continues on his voyage; and lands in a New World. Ceremonies of the first interview. Rites of hospitality." After two months an angel appears to Columbus and tells him that his work is done. For a period the New World will be a scene of bloodshed, but "in due time, all things shall be made perfect." [14]

This use of primitive deities and Christian angels to provide the supernatural machinery of an epic poem illustrates Rogers' desire to be up-to-date without sacrificing

[14] Rogers knew the American poet Barlow, and may have been influenced by that writer's *Vision of Columbus*.

his neo-classical standards. Somewhat closer to the romantic manner is his account of the first meeting between
the Indians and the Spaniards:

> " But what a scene was there? Nymphs of romance,
>   Youths graceful as the Faun, with eager glance,
>   Spring from the glades, and down the alleys peep,
>
>   .   .   .   .
>
>   And clap their hands, exclaiming as they run,
>   ' Come and behold the Children of the Sun! '
>   .   .   .   .   .   Statue-like they stood
>   As worshipped forms, the Genii of the Wood! "

Yet when this passage is compared with Southey's treatment of the same theme,[15] two facts clearly emerge.
First, Rogers is trying to emulate Southey. Secondly, he
is trying to better his predecessor by being more "classical." Southey sees splendid naked men in a real forest;
Rogers sees "nymphs" and "fauns" capering and peeping in a wilderness which, with its "glades" and "alleys,"
is strangely like a park. Southey's Indians have the
beauty which comes from a free and natural life; Rogers'
Indians must be dignified by being compared to statues.
This comparison, too, must be supported by a citation
from Benjamin West, who, " when he first saw the Apollo
of the Belvidere, was struck by its resemblance to an
American warrior."

When we leave this curious attempt to reconcile the
tastes of two periods, we find no more savages in Rogers.
He turns to other fashions. We may glance, however, at
a Swiss mountaineer who appears in the second part of
Italy (1828).

> " Jorasse was in his three-and-twentieth year;
>   Graceful and active as a stag just roused;

[15] *Vide supra*, p. 206.

> Gentle withal, and pleasant in his speech,
> Yet seldom seen to smile. He had grown up
> Among the hunters of the Higher Alps;
> Had caught their starts and fits of thoughtfulness,
> Their haggard looks, and strange soliloquies,
> Arising (so say they that dwell below)
> From frequent dealings with the Mountain-Spirits."

Whence comes this meditative mountaineer, and why is he described in such prosaically simple and uninverted blank verse? There seems little doubt that Rogers is here attempting to delineate, in the Wordsworthian manner, a Wordsworthian child of Nature.

Jorasse says that his father and grandfather have died " among these wilds " and that he is destined to share their fate.

> " And he spoke truth. Within a little month
> He lay among these awful solitudes,
> ('Twas on a glacier — half-way up to heaven),
> Taking his final rest."

The smart epigrammatic snap of " 'Twas on a glacier — half-way up to heaven " shows what chasms of thought and feeling lie between Wordsworth and Rogers.

The urbane and generous host of St. James' Place, in short, had no genuine affection for the Noble Savage, but used him as he used other literary fads. For us the importance of Rogers' work lies in the spectacle of an intensely Augustan mind striving to assimilate romantic material.

Thomas Campbell was less liberal in his politics than Rogers, but more romantic in his poetry. For several years previous to the poet's birth his father was a merchant in America; and at that time such an experience was often an antidote for "republican" ideas. Thomas, too, was born in 1777 — too late, as Rogers was born too early, to receive inspiration from the French Revolution. When Campbell had reached the age when young men's minds are most open to great idealistic conceptions, France was no longer the champion of freedom, but the cruel and formidable enemy of his country. He dreamed therefore of defending national honor, not of establishing the rights of man. These dreams were to color all his later thought: to the end of his days he hated France, and John Bull found in him a lyric voice. Posterity remembers Campbell chiefly as a writer of vigorous patriotic poems like *Hohenlinden*.

But one cannot forever be singing battle-songs. Posterity, in her careless way, has forgotten an important aspect of Campbell's character. Though he must be classified as a "London Poet," he was much less urban in spirit than the other members of the group. His Scotch ancestry, birth and early rearing stood in the way of his complete sophistication. He visited London only periodically, and brought with him to Holland House a faint but unmistakable Lakist atmosphere. In his poems he uses romantic material with much greater personal zest than the timid Rogers. Nature he loves true-heartedly. His mind is tinged with a genuine melancholy, a genuine desire to retreat from a harsh, noisy and artificial world, and a genuine hankering for the primitive.

Campbell's *Pleasures of Hope* (1799) obviously invites comparison with *Pleasures of Memory*. Both poems glorify, in pompous and inflated style, an abstraction; both established the fame of their authors. Campbell's, however, is potentially the more romantic of the two. Rogers merely tricks out eighteenth century psychology in the ribbons and ruffles of conventional poetry. The scientific skeleton of his poem is almost as obtrusive as that of Darwin's *Loves of the Plants.* In the *Pleasures of Hope,* on the contrary, the inspiration is imaginative and emotional; the material of the piece, indeed, is more poetic than the way in which it is treated.

One of the distressingly numerous aspects of Hope set forth in this poem is hope for the progress of the human race. The following apostrophe to " bright Improvement " at first suggests Thomson's praises of science, industry and good government:

> " Thy handmaid arts shall every wild explore,
> Trace every wave, and culture every shore.
> On Erie's banks, where tigers steal along,[16]
> And the dread Indian chants a dismal song,
> Where human fiends on midnight errands walk,
> And bathe in brains the murderous tomahawk,
> There shall the flocks on thymy pasture stray
> And shepherds dance at Summer's opening day."

Strange lines, surely, to be written by the future author of *Gertrude!* Yet observe that the dread Indian is to be improved, not into an ordinary civilized man, but into the silly Strephon of a pastoral.

Another hope, and one more favorable to the Noble Savage, is that of oppressed races for freedom. Nature, says Campbell, has been " degraded," and must assert her rights.

> " Hark! the stern captive spurns his heavy load,
> And asks the image back that Heaven bestowed!
> Fierce in his eye the fire of valor burns,
> And, as the slave departs, the man returns."

[16] We can forgive the tiger, because that name was in the eighteenth century applied to members of the cat family, including the puma, which was then frequently found in the mountains of the East. Campbell, however, has panthers in Australia, hyaenas in South America, and flamingos in Pennsylvania. That is going too far.

The present reality, the poet admits, provides small warrant for this vision. In a passage which certainly gave Montgomery a useful hint, Campbell tells how, " on his boundless plain," an African chief,

> " Strength in his arm, and lightning in his eye,
> Scoured with wild feet his sun-illumined zone,
> The spear, the lion, and the woods his own!
> Or led the combat, bold without a plan,
> An artless savage, but a fearless man! "

As a slave in the West Indies, this unfortunate is

> " For ever fallen! no son of Nature now,
> With Freedom chartered on his manly brow!
> Faint, bleeding, bound, he weeps the night away."

Rogers consoles his slave with memories of the past; Campbell, with hopes of future freedom for the black race. Conservatives are frequently ardent champions of the liberty of other nations than their own. Campbell always supported little Poland; and in this poem he appears as one of the earliest denouncers of oppression in India. This humanitarian spirit brings him into a much closer sympathy with the Noble Savage than was felt by Rogers.

In some of Campbell's later works the confident belief in " improvement " is submerged by the feeling that civilization has committed terrible crimes against the human spirit. When he revisits the banks of his native Clyde, and sees the ugly factories rear their heads amidst the playgrounds of his boyhood, he wonders where all the wealth is going, and whom it is intended to benefit.[17] " Is this improvement? " he asks:

[17] *Lines on Revisiting a Scottish Stream.*

> " Is this improvement?   Where the human breed
>   Degenerates as they swarm and overflow,
>   Till Toil grows cheaper than the trodden weed,
>   And man competes with man, like foe with foe.
>
>   .   .   .   .
>
>   To gorge a few with Trade's precarious prize,
>   We banish rural life, and breathe unwholesome skies."

Campbell insists that the reader should not accuse him of merely sentimental Arcadianism:

> " Nor call that evil slight; God has not given
>   This passion to the heart of man in vain
>   For Earth's green face, th' untainted air of Heaven,
>   And all the bliss of Nature's rustic reign.
>   For not alone our frame imbibes a stain
>   From foetid skies; the spirit's healthy pride
>   Fades in their gloom."

This is the attitude of the later Wordsworth, as it was to be the attitude of Ruskin.

Although *Gertrude of Wyoming* (1809) may seem to the present-day reader an intensely artificial poem, the evidence already given establishes a presumption in favor of its sincerity.   In any case it is the best English poem in which the Noble Savage plays an important part.   If Mary Mitford was over-enthusiastic in referring to it as " that most exquisite of all human productions," [18] Professor Saintsbury is almost equally uncritical in terming it " the clumsiest caricature of the Spenserian stanza ever achieved by a man of real poetic power." [19]   So discriminating a critic as Hazlitt did not hesitate to write: " There are passages in the *Gertrude of Wyoming* of so rare and ripe

[18] Quoted by Pierce, *Currents and Eddies in the English Romantic Generation*, p. 121.

[19] *Cambridge History of English Literature*, Vol. XII, p. 109.

a beauty, that they challenge, as they exceed, all praise." [26]
Just what these passages are, it would be difficult to state;
but even today the poem makes faintly pleasant reading.
The stuff of the work is thoroughly romantic, as is the
Spenserian stanza in which it finds expression. The story,
however, is told in a conscious, high-flown, polished and
periphrastic fashion which constantly suggests an earlier
period. Although more genuinely romantic than Rogers,
Campbell had almost equally fatal notions of the "grand
manner" in poetry. When he tries to elevate his style he
generally relapses into pseudo-classicism. It must not
be forgotten that this half-romanticist defended Pope
against Bowles.

The historical basis of the poem is the Wyoming massacre of 1778, of which Brandt, familiar to readers of
Cooper, is supposed to have been the leader. In his note
to the first edition, Campbell described Brandt as a vil-
lainous German-Indian half-breed. Later, however, the
poet was visited by Brandt's son, "a most interesting and
intelligent youth," who assured him that Brandt was not
present at the massacre, and had tried to restrain the
Indians. Campbell described this incident in a letter
written to the *New Monthly Magazine* in 1822.

The massacre brings to a tragic close an idyll of young
love in the wildernesss. *Gertrude of Wyoming* is not
what Hazlitt hastily terms it, "a kind of historical paraphrase of Mr. Wordsworth's poem of *Ruth*." The first
stanza of *Gertrude* is indeed a paraphrase of the ninth
stanza of *Ruth*, and there are other points of similarity.
But in *Ruth* the glowing promises of woodland joys are
inherently deceitful, while in *Gertrude* the blessings of a
natural life are thwarted only by a catastrophe from with-

[26] *The Spirit of the Age; Mr. Campbell and Mr. Crabbe. Works
of Hazlitt*, Vol. IV, p. 345.

out. Perhaps because his love of nature is shallower than Wordsworth's, Campbell is entirely untroubled by the greater poet's fear that wild scenes may make a wild temperament wilder.

At intervals Outalissi, the Oneida chief, comes in and out of the story. He represents the human side of the untamed but kindly environment which surrounds the Wyoming settlers before the outbreak of the American Revolution. " Mr. Campbell's savage," to quote Hazlitt again, " never appears but on great occasions, and then his punctuality is preternatural and alarming. He is the most wonderful instance on record of poetical *reliability*." [21]

The poem is conscientiously documented; scarcely a fact about life in Wyoming is allowed to stand without the support of a note. Especially is this true of information concerning the Indians — their physical endurance, stoicism, taciturnity, gratitude, hospitality, social customs, dress, oratory, figurative language, superstitions and religious beliefs. Campbell refers to the following authorities: Ashe, *Travels in America; Travels Through America by Capts. Lewis and Clarke, in 1804–5–6;* Cadwallader Colden, *History of the Five Indian Nations;* Rogers, *Account of North America;* Clarke, *Travels Among the Indians;* Adair, *General Observations on the American Indians;* Charlevoix, *Journal of a Voyage to North America;* Bertram [*lege* Bartram], *Travels in North America;* Weld, *Travels in North America;* Jefferson, *Notes on Virginia.*

Outalissi is probably a synthetic Indian, a mass of facts drawn from the travelers, and held together by the poet's creative imagination. That he closely resembles the Indians of Henry Mackenzie may well be due to the fact that Mackenzie drew his materials from sources similar to

[21] *On the Living Poets. Works,* p. 150.

Campbell's. If Campbell had any actual Indian in his mind as he wrote, it was perhaps Chief Logan, the account of whom in Jefferson's *Notes on Virginia* he summarizes in his appendix. Logan had lived in amity with the whites until, in 1774, a party of settlers brutally slew his wife and children. Then he led his tribe on the warpath and shed much Yengeese blood, but was eventually defeated. He refused to attend the parley which followed the cessation of hostilities, but sent an oration which, after contrasting his faithfulness with the treachery of the whites, concluded: " There runs not a drop of my blood in the veins of any living creature: — this called on me for revenge. . . . I have fully glutted my vengeance. — For my country I rejoice at the beams of peace, — but do not harbor a thought that mine is the joy of fear. Logan never felt fear. He will not turn on his heel to save his life. — Who is there to mourn for Logan? not one! " While there is no resemblance between the stories of the real and the fictitious chief, Outalissi suggests Logan in his picturesque language, his tenderness toward children and ferocity toward his enemies, his faithfulness to savage ideals and his ability to impose dignified restraint upon violent emotions.

At the opening of the poem, we are shown such a settlement on the banks of the Susquehanna as the Pantisocrats, in their more romantic and less Godwinian moments, must have imagined. There is not much intellectual activity, and no hard work at all. " The happy shepherd swains had nought to do " except pasture their sheep and go canoeing

> " From morn till evening's sweeter pastime grew,
>   With timbrel, when beneath the forests brown,
>   Thy [Wyoming's] lovely maidens would the dance renew;
>   And aye those sunny mountains half-way down
>   Would echo flageolet from some romantic town."

Since Wyoming is free from those extremes of wealth and poverty which generate crime, no complicated system of law is needed.

> " One venerable man, beloved by all,
>   Sufficed, where innocence was yet in bloom,
>   To sway the strife, that seldom might befall:
>   And Albert was their judge in patriarchal hall."

This primitive legislator is the typical benevolent old man of Romanticism — Rousseau's Savoyard Vicar, Saint-Pierre's *Vieillard* in *Paul and Virginia*, Godwin's *M. Ruffigny*. Historically he is perhaps the kind hermit, with nature-worship substituted for the traditional faith.

Albert is mildly proud of his daughter Gertrude, a lovely little creature of nine. Their life moves on in quiet bliss until one day an Indian, leading a white boy of about Gertrude's age, comes to the door of their cabin. Outalissi, for that is the redman's name, tells a pathetic story.

It should first of all be understood that to English writers the Hurons, allies of the French, are not Noble Savages, but cruel monsters. Probably Campbell is thinking of the Hurons when in the *Pleasures of Hope* he refers to those " human fiends," who

> " .   .   .   on midnight errands walk,
>   And bathe in brains the murderous tomahawk."

James Fenimore Cooper makes a similar distinction between good and bad Indians. Voltaire, on the other hand, finds a good deal of primitive virtue in the Hurons.[22]

Outalissi, as an Oneida and an ally of the English, indignantly relates that the Hurons had descended on a

---

[22] *Cf.* his *L'Ingénu.*

far-distant white settlement and massacred the inhabitants. The Oneidas came to the aid of the English, and managed to rescue a widow, Mrs. Waldegrave, and her little son.

> " Our virgins fed her with their kindly bowls
> Of fever-balm and sweet sagamité:
> But she was journeying to the land of souls." [23]

Now it chances that Mrs. Waldegrave is a childhood friend of Albert, and on her death-bed she charges the patriarch of Wyoming, through Outalissi, to see that her child is restored to certain relatives in England. Outalissi, out of the purest benevolence, has led — and often carried — the boy to Albert. His duty done, he puffs stolidly at his calumet, while Albert indulges in a tearful transport of sensibility.

> " Far differently the mute Oneyda took
> His calumet of peace, and cup of joy;
> As monumental bronze unchanged his look;
> A soul that pity touched, but never shook;
> Trained from his tree-rocked cradle to his bier
> The fierce extremes of good and ill to brook
> Impassive — fearing but the shame of fear —
> A stoic of the woods — a man without a tear."

Yet as an oak rises in soft verdure from the barren rock, goodness rises from Outalissi's savage heart. " He scorned his own, who felt another's woe." Before he leaves he sings to his erstwhile charge a restrainedly tender song of parting, adjuring the lad that if he meets his dead mother in dreamland he should tell her that Outalissi has done his duty. The chief will now retrace the long trail alone:

[23] Sagamité, according to the notes, is a kind of broth for invalids.

> " While I in lonely wilderness shall greet
> Thy little footprints — or by traces know
> Thy fountain, where at noon I thought it sweet
> To feed thee with the quarry of my bow.
>
> .   .   .   .
>
> So finished he the rhyme (howe'er uncouth)
> That true to nature's fervid feelings ran,"

and plunged into the wilderness.

Part II of the poem shows us Gertrude grown to maid-enhood. She has imbibed beauty and goodness from her environment.

> " It seemed as if those scenes sweet influence had
> On Gertrude's soul, and kindness like their own
> Inspired those eyes affectionate and glad,
> That seemed to love whate'er they looked upon."

Like a Radcliffe heroine, her chief delight is to read Shakespeare in the woods. While she is thus indulging her sensibility, a handsome youth comes upon her.

> " Iberian seemed his boot — his robe the same,
> And well the Spanish plume his lofty looks became; "

but in spite of his costume, an Aristotelian recognition scene proves him to be Young Waldegrave. Of course they marry.

In Part III, the wilderness honeymoon is interrupted by the outbreak of the American Revolution. While Young Waldegrave is balancing his love of freedom and his loyalty to England, Outalissi comes to warn his white friends that Brandt's crew of bad Indians and renegade whites is approaching. Fifteen years have changed the chief's appearance so greatly that Albert fails at first to recognize him. The faithful redman reproaches the white:

> " Oh! hast thou, Christian chief, forgot the morn
> When I with thee the cup of peace did share?
> Then stately was this head, and dark this hair
> That now is white as Appalachia's snow;
> But if the weight of fifteen years' despair
> And age hath bowed me, and the torturing foe,
> Bring me my boy — and he will his deliverer know! "

The boy is brought, and another recognition scene ensues.
Led by Outalissi, the family now attempts to escape —
in a manner which suggests the second book of the *Aeneid*.
But the recognition scene has lasted too long. Albert is
shot dead, and Gertrude perishes on her father's breast.
Young Waldegrave pours out his grief without restraint:
" the spirits of the white man's heaven " do not forbid
him to weep. Outalissi is less fortunate. The shades of
his ancestors will permit him to sing his death-song in
iambic tetrameter instead of the Spenserian stanza, but he
must not give vent to his emotions in tears.

> " But hark, the trump! — tomorrow thou [Waldegrave]
> In glory's fires shall dry thy tears;
> E'en from the land of shadows now
> My father's awful ghost appears,
> Amidst the clouds that round us roll;
> He bids my soul for battle thirst —
> He bids me dry the last — the first —
> The only tears that ever burst
> From Outalissi's soul;
> Because I may not stain with grief
> The death-song of an Indian chief! " [24]

We have dwelt at some length on *Gertrude of Wyoming* because it presents the Noble Savage against the

[24] Outalissi has not been wounded, and expects to take vengeance.
Campbell must be using " death-song " to mean a dirge over the body
of another.

background of the whole tradition which produces him. The influence of the pastoral upon the poem is clear: Wyoming is a community of the Golden Age. Arcadian fancies are reinforced by the accounts of travelers. The benefits of a withdrawal from a corrupt civilization are shown in the early part of the work. Gertrude illustrates what scenery can do for a girl. In her fresh and innocent love for Waldegrave the *leit-motiv* of *Paul and Virginia* is repeated.

These various tendencies blend and find a symbol in the figure of Outalissi, whose character serves to summarize the appeal of the Noble Savage to the romantic temperament. Rousseau directed the illustrator of the *Nouvelle Héloïse* to depict Milord Bomston with " un maintien grave et stoïque sous lequel il cache avec peine une extrême sensibilité." Here is the " spleenful " English nobleman who enjoyed such a rage in the continental fiction of the period. For the romanticist is not always unbridled in his expression of emotion. Often, like Bomston, he finds a deeper pride and enjoyment in hiding an extreme sensibility beneath a stoical mask — which of course is lifted frequently enough to make the beholder aware of the seething passions behind it. Byron could on occasion assume this character.

Does not Outalissi resemble Milord Bomston in his combination of intense feeling and stolidity? He is well fitted to the tastes of an age which loved to find strength in weakness, and weakness in strength. This simple and innocent child of nature can, when wronged, be a fearsome enemy. Conversely, this grim and impassive warrior can display the loftiest virtues and the most delicate feeling. Götz without, Werther within, Outalissi unites two important aspects of romanticism — titanism and sensibility.

Yet a schoolboy might turn from the *Last of the Mohicans* to *Gertrude of Wyoming* with no great shock of surprise. He would be disgusted to find that he was reading poetry, and bored by some, to him, unintelligible talk about nature; but in Outalissi he would recognize an old friend. To anyone not familiar with the history of his type, this savage would appear simply as a rather over-drawn Fenimore Cooper Indian. Campbell's naturalism is too limited — or his deference toward popular taste too great — to permit him to emphasize the social and philosophical import of his creation. He presents his Indian, not in support of a thesis, but as intrinsically good poetic material. Traits which would once have been indictments of civilization are now little more than conventional qualities of a stock type. In *Gertrude of Wyoming* the whole Noble Savage tradition is gathered up, purged of its paradoxical outlawry, and delivered into the admiring hands of the same refined readers who slept with *Lalla Rookh* beneath their pillows.

The author of the gingerbready poem mentioned in the foregoing sentence may be briefly dismissed. In his topical satires, his light verse, his sentimental lyrics and his rococo narrative poems, Moore moves in an atmosphere generally inhospitable to the Noble Savage. Diligent search of his voluminous works might disclose a few insincere praises of the simple life, a few conventional portraits of pseudo-primitive beings. He has, for example, a short lyric called *The Young Indian Maid:*

> " There came a nymph dancing
> Gracefully, gracefully,
> Her feet a light glancing
> Like the blue sea; "

and more to the same trivial purpose. But this nymph is the vaguest wisp of an Indian — quite as likely a Hindu as a redskin. We may be fairly sure that any savage folk who may lurk in Moore's poems are exotic decorations and not embodiments of naturalistic philosophy. Though genuine feeling sometimes shows through the glossy finish of his work, few poets of the time are further from nature. In fact, except for one special group of poems, Moore has no bearing on our subject.

That exception, however, is an important one. Beginning in September 1803, the poet spent fourteen months in the United States, and *Poems Relating to America* is the fruit, the bitter fruit, of his sojourn among us.[25]

Moore "went to America with prepossessions by no means unfavorable, and indeed rather indulged in those illusive ideas, with respect to the purity of the government and the primitive happiness of the people, which I had early imbibed in my native country." He finds that the people certainly enjoy " a close approximation to savage life, not only in the liberty which they enjoy, but in the violence of party strife and private animosity which results from it." They have achieved all the vices but few of the virtues of civilization.[26]

From Norfolk he confides to Miss Moore his hopes of finding in America a land of freedom, peace and plenty.

> " Oh! Ask me not, if Truth have yet
>   Her seal on Fancy's promise set;
>   If ev'n a glimpse my eyes behold
>   Of that imagin'd age of gold; —
>   Alas, not yet one gleaming trace! "

[25] These poems were first published in the *Odes and Epistles* volume, 1806. In the final collected edition of 1841 they were made a separate division.

[26] *Poetical Works*, p. 94. Moore's preface.

In a sneering footnote to this poem, Moore ascribes the popularity of the American legend to " such romantic works as *The American Farmer's Letters* and the account of Kentucky by Imlay," which " would seduce us into a belief, that innocence, peace and freedom had deserted the rest of the world for Martha's Vineyard and the banks of the Ohio." [27]

Moore is not speaking at random, for in the course of the poems he has occasion to mention: Weld, *Travels in North America*; Morse, *American Geography*; Charlevoix, *Letters on the Traditions and the Religion of the Savages of Canada*; Hennepin, *Voyage into North America*; Mackenzie, *General History of the Fur Trade*; Anburey, *Travels*; *Voyages du Baron de Lahontan*; Bossu, *Voyages aux Indes Occidentales*; Imlay, *Kentucky*; Lafitau, *Moeurs des Sauvages Américains*. These are used chiefly for notes on the geography and fauna of the country, but also to reinforce a few references to savage superstitions in poems later to be mentioned.

Of the French travelers Moore says that they, "too, almost all from revolutionary motives, have contributed their share " to the blowing of the great American bubble. He sees in the highly-colored accounts which he is attacking not merely sentimentality, but insidious propaganda. Let those who are attracted by French revolutionary doctrines come to America, land of "slaving blacks and democratic whites," and behold

> " .   .   .   the piebald polity that reigns
> In free confusion o'er Columbia's plains."

[27] The reference to Martha's Vineyard shows that Moore is thinking of Crèvecoeur's *Letters from an American Farmer*. The *American Farmer's Letters* was written by J. Dickinson. I have already suggested that Imlay's *Topographical Description of Kentucky* may be the source of the Daniel Boone passage in *Don Juan*. *Vide supra*, p. 242.

Here is the perfectibility of the *philosophes* in practical operation!

But Moore is too canny a poet to ignore the popular appeal of the wilder side of American life. He pauses in his diatribes to tell the story of the deranged youth who wanders off into the Dismal Swamp to find his dead sweetheart. He never returns,

> " But oft, from the Indian hunter's camp,
>   This lover and maid so true
> Are seen at the hour of midnight damp
> To cross the Lake by a fire-fly lamp,
>   And paddle their white canoe! "

A more elaborate treatment of Indian superstitions was suggested to Moore by a difficult journey " through the very dreary wilderness between Batavia, a new settlement in the midst of the woods, and the little village of Buffalo upon Lake Erie." The forest seemed animated by a malicious intelligence determined to bar his path. Charlevoix and Hennepin provided material to show that the poet's feeling was supported by savage beliefs. In the resultant poem, the guardian deity of the woods urges his attendant spirits to hamper, exhaust and bewilder the Christian invader of the Indians' domain.[28]

Yet this dramatic lyric, after all, represents Moore's ingenuity in making literary capital out of real or fancied hardships rather than any real feeling for the savage. When Moore, in spite of the Evil Spirit of the Woods, finally reaches the little village of Buffalo, he unburdens his mind to W. R. Spencer in the most unflattering of his American epistles.

> " Take Christians, Mohawks, Democrats and all
>   From the rude wigwam to the congress hall,

[28] *Song of the Evil Spirit of the Woods.*

> From man the savage, whether slaved or free,
> To man the civilized, less tame than he, —
> 'Tis one dull chaos, one infertile strife
> Between half polished and half barbarous life."

Here both red and white Americans are included in a single condemnation which will suffice to sum up the poet's opinion.

One may well doubt the sincerity of the expectations with which, according to his own statement, Moore came to America. It is conceivable that his purpose was from the first one of exposure, and that the Golden Age and primitive happiness are brought forward merely for the sake of rhetorical effect. One of the best means of attacking the real is to contrast it with an intentionally illusory ideal. On the other hand, the warm sentimentality of Moore's nature and his sympathy with Irish nationalism make it just possible that his disappointment was not gleeful, but sorrowful. For us the question is not a pressing one. Whatever the answer may be, the fact remains that Moore, an exceedingly popular writer, definitely threw his influence against the Noble Savage idea. He set sail for the Earthly Paradise, and landed on Penguin Island.

Our three "London Society Poets," being after all three distinct human beings, make three distinct contributions to our subject. Rogers tried to bring the Noble Savage into agreement with his own polite and belated tastes. Campbell, in spite of his romantic sympathies, fixed the traits of the Indian in a conventional mould. Moore helped to destroy the Utopian conception of America. In the hands of this group, the Noble Savage fared badly. If the Lakists ended by trying to convert him, the London Poets did still worse in classicizing him, prettifying him, and attacking the sublimity of his habitat.

Chapter VIII

MINOR POETS. NEGATIVE AND DOUBTFUL
RESULTS

THIS chapter has two purposes: to give an account of
some minor romantic poets in relation to the Noble
Savage; and to explain the less favorable reactions of a
number of more important writers both of poetry and of
prose. The resultant material may be somewhat lacking in
unity. It seems not illogical, however, to deal in a single
chapter with writers who, although in sympathy with the
savage, are not of great significance; and with those who,
though they are of great significance, have little or no
trace of primitivism.

A. Minor Poets, 1790–1830

Like some other poets whom posterity has stamped as
"minor," William Lisle Bowles was in his day a fer-
tilizing influence. A pupil of Joseph Warton and an idol
of the young Lakists, he provides a not unimportant link
between pre-revolutionary and post-revolutionary romanticism. The reader who thinks of Bowles merely as a
writer of melancholy sonnets will be surprised to find how
large a part the Noble Savage plays in his poems.

Bowles loves to obtain a vicarious thrill by speaking
through the mask of some wild man. In the *Song of the
American Indian*, the "stranger" is urged to bide and
share the carefree Indian life, listening to the birds' songs,
hunting, canoeing, and in general enjoying an ideal vaca-
tion. In *Abba Thule's Lament for his Son, Prince Le* [*sic*]

Boo, we meet two old friends. Bowles has read with some care the *Account of the Pelew Islands*, for he refers to the knotted string which, according to Keate, Abba Thule prepared to keep a record of Lee Boo's absence. The poem describes the old king's grief at the failure of his son to return to Pelew.

In view of the influence exerted by Bowles upon Southey and Coleridge, it would be interesting to know whether Bowles' *Song of the American Indian* was composed before Southey's series of dramatic lyrics, and *Abba Thule's Lament* before Coleridge's *To a Young Lady*. I am unable to date with certainty either of the Bowles poems; but in *Scenes and Shadows of Days Departed,* in which the pieces are arranged chronologically, Bowles places them at the beginning of the volume, even before the 1789 sonnets. Since, however, the two poems seem not to have been published until 1837, in *Scenes and Shadows,* it is very unlikely that Southey and Coleridge knew them.

The Dying Slave is addressed by his fellows in a congratulatory song. At last, as they suppose, he is going back to Africa,

> " Where thy father's hut was reared,
> Where thy mother's voice was heard;
> Where thy infant brothers played
> Beneath the fragrant citron shade."

They too hope soon to die — to rest from toil, and follow their comrade to his happy home.

Here then are American, Polynesian and African savages. To the list might be added Antonio, the faithful Javanese body-servant of the wandering Camoëns, who is referred to by his master as " My sable slave (ah, no! my only friend)." [1]

[1] *The Last Song of Camoëns.*

More important than these dramatic monologues and
stray references is *The Missionary of the Andes*, which was
first published anonymously late in 1813.[2] On January 29,
1814, Southey writes to Grosvenor Bedford: " Some
unknown author has sent me a poem called the Missionary,
not well arranged, but written with great feeling and
beauty. . . . It is Ercilla's ground-work, with a new
story made to fit the leading facts." Later we shall see
that *The Missionary* influenced Southey's *Tale of Paraguay*. The latter poem was begun in 1814, the year in
which Southey read the " unknown author's " work. As
for Bowles, it is not likely that he went back to the original
Spanish of Ercilla's *Araucana*.[3] He could have found
the story, for example, in the appendix to the second
volume of Hayley's poems of 1785, where a detailed account of it is given, with translations of several passages.
At all events here is a poem related in matter and spirit to
an old Spanish work, to Chateaubriand's *Atala*, to Campbell's *Gertrude of Wyoming* and to Southey's *Tale of
Paraguay*.

The confused story may be outlined as follows. Lautaro and his sister Olola, two Araucan Indians of Chile,
grow up in the woods with their father, Attacapa. Their
life, like that of Paul and Virginia, is full of happy innocence, good health, and love of nature. Comes an evil
day when Lautaro is captured by the Spanish and sold as a
slave. A good missionary of the Las Casas-Savoyard
Vicar type buys and converts him. He adds to the boy's

---

[2] Gilfillan, Bowles' editor, assigns it to 1815, but I have inspected
the anonymous 1813 edition in the British Museum. That it was
published *late* in 1813 is indicated by the Southey letter quoted above.

[3] Alfonso de Ercilla y Zuniga was a soldier of fortune sent to Chile
in 1554 to help suppress a revolt of the Araucan Indians. The
Araucana, a pseudo-classical epic in twenty-seven books, was the result.

natural goodness the goodness of simple piety. But ambition stirs within Lautaro's breast. He manages to get to Spain, where he becomes a page to Valdivia, a high-minded Spanish noble. Later, as a young esquire at arms, he returns to the land of his birth. There is war between the Spaniards and the Araucans, Lautaro's own tribe. His position is delicate. He is, in successive layers, an Araucan Noble Savage, a pantheistic-Catholic devotee, and a Spanish soldier. The conflict within him results in a number of long antithetical speeches and in attempts to make Araucans and Spaniards recognize a common bond of humanity. The war, however, continues. In a great battle, the Indians repulse the invaders. The good missionary is discovered, and his life, thanks to Lautaro, is spared. Olola, the long-lost sister, is restored to her brother's arms.

A less complex character, a purer type of Noble Savage, is Caupolican, chief of the Araucans. His name is evidently a traditional one, for it is borne today by an opera singer of some note. Bowles' Caupolican does not sing, but he is an excellent orator. There is a quite serious parody of Milton's council in hell. Various chiefs give their views — rash, cowardly or politic — upon the war with Spain, and Caupolican represents Satan. He even has the temerity to begin his speech with " Friends, fathers, brothers, dear and sacred names! " Joseph Warton had imitated Milton, and had dreamed of the Noble Savage. His admiring pupil manages to unite both interests.

Caupolican spares the life of a captive white woman, asserting that the Indians wish not to harm the innocent, but to defend themselves against the oppressor. Several other incidents show his dignity, wisdom and magnanimity.

In one case Bowles displays definite familiarity with savages more recent than those of the sixteenth century.

When young Lautaro is captured by the Spanish, his father, Attacapa, is grief-stricken. Who now will mourn for him when he dies? This pathetic thought, says Bowles, is taken from the speech of the American Indian chief, Logan. The passage also bears many resemblances to the *Lament of Abba Thule*. The more one follows the subject, the more one feels the unity binding all Noble Savages together, be they red, brown, black or even white.

A less important figure connected with the Lakists was the worthy but not very talented Bristol publisher, Joseph Cottle. Like Bowles and Coleridge, Cottle responded to the pathetic story of Lee Boo, and composed a poem with that name as a title. The scene is Pelew on the evening before the departure of the English. Abba Thule tells Lee Boo that he is to sail to the land of the white men. The old king is entirely ignorant of science,

> " Yet Heaven enrich'd him with a princely mind,
> Her noblest gift — the milk of human kind."

Lee Boo, as befits his heady youth, is rather insular in his attitude toward the English:

> " I should have judg'd the waves had given them birth!
> Their skins so foully white! unknown their tale,
> Their limbs so fetter'd, and their teeth so pale! "

Let this be a rebuke to the pride of Englishmen. But Lee Boo suddenly drops satire for a sentiment worthy of Frank Henley:

> " Yet, why should colour change the feeling mind?
> In being men, I love my fellow-kind."

Unless the printer has erred, Cottle's syntax is sadly at fault; but one understands what is meant.

Lee Boo now goes to break the news to Dorack, his sweetheart. To his grief, she strongly opposes the project. " We want no stranger's artificial aid " is her answer to the argument that Lee Boo can acquire valuable learning in England. " We know enough," she insists, " for happiness." But her lover departs, and the poem closes with a very Bowles-like picture of Abba Thule's fruitless waiting.

A Cossack Noble Savage also emerges from Joseph Cottle's pages.[4] Markoff lived contentedly in Siberia with his wife and children.

> " No rapturous hope or rankling care he knew,
> His means were simple, as his wants were few."

But in an evil day he is seized with a mad ambition to explore the lonely wastes to the north. He loses his way, almost freezes to death, and is brought home by a band of sable-hunters, quite satisfied henceforth with his humble cabin. The moral of the piece, of course, is that in order to avoid " rankling care," one had better do without " rapturous hope," or, as the cockney in Mr. Galsworthy's *Windows* expresses it, " Don't 'ave 'igh 'opes; 'ave low 'opes."

These two poems are thoroughly in keeping with the general tone of *Malvern Hills*, Cottle's chief work, which is full of diatribes against the wickedness of city life and the folly of civilized ambitions. As always, the Noble Savage comes readily to the mind of the disciple of naturalism.

After considering two writers, the first of whom influenced the poetry of the Lakists and the second their

---

[4] *Markoff, a Siberian Eclogue.*

practical affairs, we pass by a natural transition to one of their followers. That John Wilson, " Christopher North," was successively an accomplished literary critic and an inspiring if not very erudite professor of moral philosophy is common knowledge. His fame in these two fields has rightly obscured his earler attempts to practice poetry. As a young man he lived in the Lake Country, was a devoted admirer of Wordsworth and Coleridge, and wrote verses in frankly humble imitation of their greatness.

Wilson did not need to project his mind into exotic regions in order to find examples of primitive innocence. Such examples were at his very door. On one occasion he takes a fishing-trip with Wordsworth and a party of friends " among the mountains of Westmoreland, Lancashire and Cumberland." These delightful days, and in particular one evening when a party of rustics visited the camp of the excursionists, have made upon him an impression that he " wishes to preserve in poetry." The result is *The Angler's Tent*, a poem obviously patterned after Wordsworth in its ideas. Wilson writes for " those who delight in the wilder scenes of Nature, and who have studied with respect and love the character of their inhabitants." The association of the dalesmen with their dales swells the evidence already adduced to show the harmony between the cult of nature and the Noble Savage idea.

The anglers are resting in their tent after the day's sport when they are hailed from the lake by a band of natives. The hospitality of the camp is offered and accepted. Wilson is delighted by the simple courtesy and frankness of the men, the artless modesty of the maidens. He is reminded of old tales about simple shepherds in the age of gold. Such poems were not false figments of the imagination, for

" .   .   .   still in many a favour'd spot of earth,
The virtues that awoke their voice endure!
Bear witness thou! O, wild and beauteous dell,
To whom my gladden'd heart devotes this strain;
— O! long may all who in thy bosom dwell
Nature's primeval innocence retain."

This passage is not representative of the eighteenth century pastoral tradition. That tradition accepted the Golden Age as an elegant literary convention to which the contemporary rustic might be fitted by carefully disregarding his real character. In this poem the Golden Age is regarded as a spiritual truth of which the dalesman as he actually exists is an illustration. Wilson in Westmoreland, like Amadas and Barlow in Virginia [5] and like Albrecht Haller in Switzerland,[6] finds a race of men so free from civilized vices that they make Arcadian dreams come true. Wordsworth may not have regarded his peasants as Noble Savages: the greatest poets first absorb and then transcend the conventions of their time. But that some lesser men who followed in his footsteps did see the simple dalesmen in much the same light as the simple Indian or the simple Negro is suggested by *The Angler's Tent*.

In *The Isle of Palms*, Wilson turns from Wordsworth to his other idol, Coleridge. Here the imitation, however, is chiefly technical: the metre makes rather successful use of *Christabel's* syllabic equivalence, and the expression makes a much less successful attempt to attain Coleridge's weird intensity of imagery. At the opening of the poem a ship is speeding over the ocean. On board are a youth and a maiden, both children of nature. Mary has grown up " like some solitary mountain-flower," " far from the haunts of men." Fitz-Owen, by a happy coincidence, is

[5] *Vide supra*, p. 13.   [6] *Vide supra*, p. 173.

" a mountain youth." Mary has been exposed chiefly to
nature's softer influences, Fitz-Owen chiefly to the storm
and tempest. Since, like Torquil and Neuha, the couple
respectively represent the feminine and masculine, or the
Wertheristic and Götzistic, elements of romanticism,
they inevitably fall in love; but the foolish restraints
of civilization prevent their disclosing the fact to each
other.

Then occurs an opportune wreck. Fitz-Owen and
Mary, after an uncomfortable interlude on a barren rock,
reach the beautiful Isle of Palms. Do they, like Robinson
Crusoe, try to scrape together some fragments of civilization in the wilderness? They do not. They welcome the
wilderness as their appropriate environment. Off drop
the tawdry trappings of convention; primal man and
primal woman stand forth together unashamed. They
return joyfully to the nature which brooded over them in
their childhood. They marry — God himself is the
priest. Of their union is born an Ariel-like sprite. At last
they are picked up, and return to Mary's aged mother
in Wales, refreshed and glorified by their contact with the
pure essence of the universe. All this is familiar nowadays to every reader of South Sea fiction, every faithful
attendant at the moving pictures. In Wilson's day the
tradition was fresher. Fitz-Owen and Mary, by escaping
the thwarting influences of society, find love and happiness
as Noble Savages.

Just as fleas are said to suffer from parasites, so minor
poets have minor poets to imitate them. William Glen, a
countryman of Wilson's, published in 1816 *The Lonely
Isle, a South Sea Island Tale*. Perhaps thanks to Campbell, the poem is written in Spenserians, but the plot and
general feeling are much like the *Isle of Palms*. Glen's

ludicrous ineptitude, however, makes Wilson seem a genius. The work is founded on a Tahitian story, reported by Cook, of an island like the Earthly Paradise but never visited because it is said to be haunted.

Monimia's parents die rich. A wicked uncle, to get her money, has her shanghaied with Henry, her betrothed. The lovers are marooned on an island which is uninhabited, and which at first appears to be a mere barren rock. But on passing through a slit in the cliffs, they find themselves in a veritable Eden.

> " The lofty Cocoa towering high was seen,
> And Mountain Cabbage quivered in mid-air:
> Delicious fruits showed Nature's tender care,
> The Sapadillo and the Nectarine,
> The Guava, Shaddock, Pine, the Prickly Pear,
> The Mammee Apple, with the clustering vine,
> And hundreds more were there, all luscious, rich and fine."

In this favorable environment they wed, in a manner reminiscent of Wilson. And their union, like that of Mary and Fitz-Owen, produces a child of nature. Little Edward's eye is blue, as is his mother's,

> " But it was far more piercing, and more wild —
> He was indeed a lovely interesting child."

One morning while Edward, " with his friend the goat," was playing on the shore, he was kidnapped by a band of natives who had paddled over from a neighboring island. His captors, however, possessed unusual sensibility, for when he cried for his mother

> " . . . . even savage pride
> Was humbly melted to a pitying tear; —
> They gave him fruit, and smiled to calm his boyish fear."

After some time, Henry and Monimia are rescued. Later they return for Edward, who is safe and sound.

Glen promises to tell the story of Edward's adventures in another romantic lay, but this sequel was never written. We should certainly have had some very Noble Savages, and some very bad poetry.

Though she presents us with another example of the South Sea Island type, Mary Mitford cannot be accused of imitating either Wilson or Glen, for her *Christina, The Maid of The South Seas* appeared as early as 1811. She draws instead upon that famous story of the *Bounty* mutiny, which, as we have seen, later inspired Byron's *The Island*. The poem mingles fact and fiction, but the following account will not attempt to disentangle the two.

An American vessel, cruising in the South Seas, accidentally comes upon what is now known as Pitcairn Island. The place proves to be inhabited by a people who are leading a most idyllic life. The head of the community is Fitzallan — the poet confesses that his name in real life was Smith — the only survivor of the band of mutineers who set Bligh adrift.

Fitzallan's narrative occupies a large portion of the poem. He was the close friend of Christian, the leader of the mutineers, by whose " gallant and amiable " character Miss Mitford herself was "irresistibly attracted." [7] At Tahiti, Christian takes Iddeah, a native woman, as his wife. When the *Bounty* is about to depart, she discloses the fact that she is with child. Bligh's refusal to let Iddeah sail with the English arouses Christian's enmity, and the mutiny results. After Bligh and his few supporters have been set adrift, the mutineers return to Tahiti. But soon, weary of tropical voluptuousness and shocked by the Tahitian custom of human sacrifice, Christian, Fitzallan and a few others, with their native wives, make their way to Pitcairn Island.

[7] *Christina*, p. vi.

Here for a time all goes well. But remorse for his conduct toward Bligh so works on Christian's mind that he hurls himself over a cliff. Then some Tahitian servants under a leader curiously called Tupia revolt and massacre all the adult whites except Fitzallan, who is badly wounded. But the faithful native wives of the sailors get the murderers drunk and kill them all. Fitzallan, recovering, sets himself to the task of founding a new and better community. Miss Mitford does not enlarge upon the method by which this must have been accomplished, nor does she note the fact that all the inhabitants of Pitcairn Island except Fitzallan are necessarily either Tahitian or half-caste.

Thus Christina Christian, "the maid of the South Seas," the daughter of Christian and Iddeah, is represented as a beautiful English girl reared by the hand of nature. Iddeah herself conveniently dies just before the poem opens. Christina is betrothed to Hubert, Fitzallan's son by the Tahitian princess Avanna. She falls in love, however, with Henry, a young Englishman who happens to be on the American ship. After certain unimportant complications, Hubert generously hands Christina over to Henry, and the happy pair sail away.

The Noble Savage idea pervades Miss Mitford's poem. The innocent happiness of the Pitcairn Islanders is strongly emphasized. Iddeah, Avanna and Christina are female Noble Savages of a type to be discussed in a later chapter. Fitzallan's defence of the Tahitians is a representative passage:

> " O generous people! Thou art call'd
>   A land by vice and folly thrall'd;
>   Immers'd in ignorance and woe,
>   Savage and lowest of the low,
>   And they are great that call thee so!
>   But were some wondrous chance to guide
>   Thy light canoes across the tide,

> To polish'd Europe, free and fair,
> Say what would be thy welcome there?
>
> . . . .
>
> Would she her little all bestow,
> On strangers plung'd in want and woe? "

Of course not!

In her notes, Mary Mitford refers not only to Bligh, but to Bougainville, Dampier, Wallis, Cook, Banks, Hawkesworth and Burney. Captain Burney himself helped her to arrange and revise the notes. The poem is thus a literary product of the *Bounty* mutiny in particular and of South Seas exploration in general. It is interesting to find that the future author of *Our Village* responded in her youth to the appeal of the Noble Savage.[8]

Miss Mitford is but the first of four women who are to provide us with material. To the hunter of Noble Savages, it is especially satisfying to learn that Mrs. Hemans, whose work mirrored all the fashions of her time, was distinctly partial to Indians. Entering into the feelings of John Hunter, who had been reared by the redmen,[9] she imagines the pleasures of his former comrades.

[8] A word here may save trouble for the reader whose eye is caught by the title of the Rev. John Mitford's *Agnes, the Indian Captive*. This poem is not what bibliographers call an " Indian captivity," but a bare-faced imitation of Scott's romantic narratives. The action centers around the wars of Timur the Lame, and there is no Noble Savagery in the piece.

[9] John D. Hunter's *Memoirs of a Captivity Among the Indians of North America*, 1823, is one of the best known of the numerous " captivity " narratives. His parents were killed in a massacre, and he was brought up by the Indians from infancy to the age of nineteen, when he came to England. He gives a favorable, but not a sentimental, picture of Indian life.

> " They rest beside their streams — the spoil is won —
> They hang their spears upon the cypress bough;
> The night-fires blaze, the hunter's work is done —
> They hear the tales of old — but where art thou?
>
> . . . .
>
> They call — wild voices call thee o'er the main,
> Back to thy free and boundless woods again."

This comes very close to Jack London's "call of the wild"
and Kipling's "can't you hear the red gods calling?"
But Mrs. Hemans knows that for "the child of the forests " return is impossible.

> " Thou hast quaff'd knowledge from the founts of mind,
> And gather'd loftier aims and hopes divine.
> Thou knowest the soaring thought, the immortal strain —
> Seek not the deserts and the woods again! " [10]

That Mrs. Hemans herself felt the call of the wild is
evidenced by *I Dream of All Things Free*. She dreams
of a ship, a stag, an eagle, mountain rills, and, in the last
stanza,

> " Of a happy forest child,
> With the fawns and flowers at play;
> Of an Indian 'midst the wild,
> With the stars to guide his way:
>
> . . . .
>
> My heart in chains is bleeding
> And I dream of all things free! "

Felicia's heart was of the sort that bleeds on slight provo-
cation, and we need not take her too seriously. She knew,
however, what people wanted to read, and for us the fact
that people wanted to read this sort of thing is significant.

Poems by this writer in which savages appear fall under

[10] *The Child of the Forests, Written After Reading the Memoirs
of John Hunter.*

two general classes: those in which the savage speaks for himself, and those representing the influence of the Christian religion upon him. At the age of twelve, little Felicia Dorothea Browne penned *Ceba: an Indian Love Song:*

> " Haste, my Ceba, to the bower,
> Love demands one social hour."

Ceba and her lover are East Indians, but any faintly exotic setting would serve them equally well. Later in her career, with a considerable gain in realism, Mrs. Hemans frequently sang through the lips of American Indians. In *The Aged Indian,* for example, an old chief laments the loss of his friends and the decay of his powers. He hears the spirits of his family calling, and begs his fellow-tribesmen to end his life. Poems of this type, however, must be reserved for discussion in the chapter on " Natural Man and Natural Poetry."

We may consider here, however, poems dealing with the relation of Christianity to savage life. *The Forest Sanctuary* provides a familiar contrast between Spanish oppression and Indian freedom. Two victims of the Inquisition take refuge in the American forest. One of them, after relating his horrible experiences, remarks that the savage has no idea

> " Of the dark holds wherewith man cumbers earth,
> To shut from human eyes the dancing seasons' mirth."

The Indians have a natural religious sense. In *The American Forest Girl,* a white youth is about to be burned at the stake when an Indian maid throws herself upon his breast with, " He shall not die! " The savages are abashed.

> " They gazed — their dark souls bow'd before the maid,
> She of the dancing step in wood and glade!
> . . . .

> Something o'ermaster'd them from that young mien —
> Something of heaven, in silence felt and seen,
> And seeming, to their childish faith, a token
> That the great spirit by her voice had spoken."

But to this " childish faith " must be added the light of Christian doctrine. Thus in another poem [11] we are told of Edith, an American child. She survives a massacre, and is cared for by an old Indian couple who, since they have lost their own children, treat her with special tenderness. As she grows older, she converts them to Christianity. Before long, however, she dies of that vague wasting disease which afflicts the maidens of minor romantic poetry. Her foster-parents sing a death-song entirely purged of paganism:

> " Dim will our cabin be, and lone,
>   When thou, its light, art fled;
>   Yet hath thy step the pathway shown
>   Unto the happy dead.

> " And we will follow thee, our guide!
>   And join that shining band;
>   Thou'rt passing from the lake's green side —
>   Go to the better land! "

In *The Cross in the Wilderness*, a traveler finds an aged Indian sitting by a rude cross in the red glow of the setting sun. His bow lies beside him, unstrung.

> " His eyes, that might not weep, were dark with grief,
>   And his arms folded in majestic gloom."

Urged by the traveler, he tells the story of a beloved missionary who died after saving the souls of the tribe. The

[11] *Edith, a Tale of the Woods.* The poem, according to the author's note, is " founded on incidents in an American work, *Sketches of Connecticut.*" Mrs. Hemans seems to have been fond of " captivity " stories.

Indians have buried him by the lake, " where he was wont to pray."

> "We rear'd this Cross in token where he lay,
>   For on the Cross, he said, his Lord had died! "

The Indian's Revenge, sub-entitled *Scene in the Life of a Moravian Missionary,* is one of the dramatic sketches which were then so popular. With surprising ease, Hermann, the missionary, persuades Enonio, an Indian, not to avenge the murder of his brother. The basis of this playlet is Carne's *Narrative of the Moravian Missionaries in Greenland.* Such transference of material from one type of savage to another is by no means uncommon.

It may be objected that this poet's eagerness to improve the Indian is not eloquent of faith in the Noble Savage. One must admit that Mrs. Hemans is no thorough-going champion of untrammeled wildness. She does, however, recognize the innate virtues of the Indian, and, like the later Southey, wishes to see those virtues developed along Christian lines. There can be little doubt, also, that despite her subjection to the fads of the day she had a hankering for " all things free."

There is much less Noble Savagery in Letitia Landon, the celebrated " L.E.L." of album poetry. Yet she had exceptional opportunities to observe the blessings of primitive life, for she married a Mr. Maclean, the Lieutenant-Governor of the Cape Coast Colony in Africa. Before the marriage, the official residence had been graced by the presence of a native mistress, and Letitia consented to wed only upon the most definite assurance that this person had never been united to Maclean by any valid ceremony. One morning Mrs. Maclean was found dead in that official residence with an empty bottle labelled " Prussic

Acid " in her hand. Since the physician who had made up her medicine-chest before her departure for Africa had included no Prussic Acid, the affair was mysterious. There is a pleasant possibility that she was murdered by the discarded mistress, but accident or suicide are unfortunately more tenable hypotheses. One abandons with reluctance the thought that in one instance a savage took revenge upon a minor poet of the period.

In her letters from Africa, L.E.L. makes some patronizingly favorable remarks about the blacks. Stronger sympathy appears in her poem, *The African Prince*. She describes the life of a young black prince, free, proud and courageous, a mighty hunter and warrior. He is captured and sold into slavery. Being noble, he cannot, like his fellow-slaves, become reconciled to his lot. At last, however, he is converted to Christianity by a " seraph child " — an ancestress of Little Eva — becomes patient, and meekly dies in the hope of salvation. The emphasis on the royal nature of the slave suggests *Oroonoko*, but with the Behn influence is mingled Mrs. Hemans' interest in missionary effort.

She Sat Alone Beside Her Hearth tells the story of an Indian girl called The Startled Fawn. A white youth wanders into her village, and she saves his life. They have an Inkle-Yarico affair of the heart. Soon, however, he deserts her. After a period of brooding " beside her hearth," she goes in search of him, but finds him only to be spurned. In despair, she lets her canoe drift over the brink of a cataract.

The feminine heart in relation to scenery, love, friendship, ethics and religion formed the stock-in-trade of L.E.L. Her enthusiasm for the Noble Savage seems to have been slight, though it was not wholly absent from her work.

Amelia Opie, whose poetical ability was somewhat less than her slight skill as a novelist, exhibits the same conventional reaction to the savage that we observed in Letitia Landon. Her humanitarianism is much stronger than her love of nature. *The Negro Boy's Tale*, which will later be examined as a rare example of serious dialect poetry, expresses the idea that at heart the Negro is as white as the white man.

The Lucayan's Song extends to the Indian the same sympathy for the oppressed. It is based on a passage in Bryan Edwards' *History of the West Indies*, which relates that the Spaniards lured some Lucayan Indians to Hispaniola by assuring them that that island was the heaven of their simple mythology, and that the shades of their ancestors would greet them on its shores. Once in Hispaniola, of course, the Lucayans were enslaved and barbarously used. The song is that of a Lucayan slave who escapes to a cavern to die. He tells the story of Spanish deceit. Hungrily he sniffs the wind which has passed over his home. He yearns for Zama, his wife, and for his child. How long they have been waiting for him! The last stanza is delivered with his expiring breath.

We have seen that Bowles, Letitia Landon and Amelia Opie combine varying degrees of interest in the savage with opposition to Negro slavery. There is certainly a close connection between the humanitarianism of the romantic period and the Noble Savage idea. The Negro would have awakened much less sympathy if it had not been possible to regard him as a child of nature. By no means every poetic protest against the slave-trade is an example of romantic primitivism; but when John Wilson, after reading Clarkson's *History of the Slave Trade*, is inspired to praise those

> " . . . . noble shapes,
> Kings of the desert, men whose stately tread
> Brings from the dust the sound of liberty," [12]

he is surely influenced by the Noble Savage idea. I have earlier suggested that the Negro can be a Noble Savage; the following notes may serve to prove this not unimportant point.

As the editor of *Iris*, a Sheffield newspaper, James Montgomery was a leading provincial Jacobin. In 1794 and 1795 his republican views and his opposition to the war against France twice caused his imprisonment. The rise of Bonaparte dampened his revolutionary ardor, but instead of abandoning his liberalism he directed it into humanitarian channels and became an agitator against the slave-trade. The reader who has up to this time been unwilling to regard the Negro as a Noble Savage must now brace himself against a shock, for the thesis of Montgomery's *The West Indies* is that the Negro is every whit as much a Noble Savage as the Indian. Moreover, the poem is in a sense an official embodiment of humanitarian opinion, having been begun in 1807 at the request of a committee which was preparing a memorial to celebrate the abolition of the slave-trade. It was accepted by the committee, and published in 1809. [13]

Montgomery insinuates himself into his subject by describing the West Indian natives before the coming of the Spaniards.

> " Untamed, untaught, in arts and arms unskill'd,
> Their patrimonial soil they rudely till'd,
> . . . .

[12] *On Reading Mr. Clarkson's History*, etc. The fact that Wilson seems to be thinking of Arabs rather than of Negroes does not affect the quality of the sentiment.

[13] *Poetical Works*, Vol. I, pp. 127 ff.

> Their lives in dreams of soothing languor flew.
> No parted joys, no future pains they knew,
> The passing moment all their bliss or care."

But need one continue? It is all so perfectly typical.

Then come the Spaniards. What they did is history, and Montgomery is not forced to exaggerate the facts in order to paint a terrible picture of brutal oppression. The crisis of the poem is now at hand. The Spaniards must have slaves. They have almost exterminated the Indians, and the remnant of the race is too delicate for toil. The oppressor seeks new victims:

> "Abroad he looked, a sturdier stock to find;
> . . . .
> That stock he found on Afric's swarming plains."

In another poem, *The Ocean*, Montgomery represents Africa as an Eden,

> "Where Nature and Innocence dwelt in her youth,
> When pure was her heart, and unbroken her truth."

The West Indies goes further, asserting that "In these romantic regions man grows wild." The Negro is a child of nature, scorned by mankind, but loved by his mother. She "gazes on him from her warmest sky," and fondly sees him as a creature of grace and beauty,

> "Sees in his breast, where lawless passions rove,
> The heart of friendship and the home of love,
> . . . .
> Sees in his soul, involved with thickest night,
> An emanation of eternal light."

But such vague statements are not enough for Montgomery. Home life in Africa, he insists, is a medley of innocent pleasures. The Negro reveres his parents, loves

his wife, and is respected by his children. In the evening
he dances, or " feasts on tales of witchcraft," or delight-
edly listens to

> " . . . . . . the song of elder times,
> When men were heroes, slaves to Beauty's charms,
> And all the joys of life were love and arms."

The last line strangely recalls Dryden's formula for
heroic drama and its embodiment in *Oroonoko*. Add to
these amusements the profuse generosity of the soil, and
what more can one ask? We must remember that Montgomery wrote over a century before the publication of
Maran's *Batouala*, with its horrible picture of Negro
bestiality. Untroubled by the obligations of realism, the
editor of *Iris* draws from Mungo Park and a few other
travelers such details as will support his thesis that the
black is a Noble Savage quite as worthy of the admiration
of true lovers of nature as his externally more attractive
red brother.

Montgomery is not alone in his recognition of Negro
nobility. William Roscoe, though he became the sort of
poet who breakfasted with Rogers and dined with the
Hollands, was in his youth something of a Jacobin. His
Jacobinism, as so often happened, was accompanied by
humanitarianism. In *The Wrongs of Africa*, he shows
how the " healthful native " passes his time. The Negro
rises when he pleases, takes his bow, and goes out " to
pierce the murderous pard." At noon, when the sun is
high, he sleeps in the shade. When evening comes, he
returns to the village and takes part in " the mazy dance."
In his old age he has other resources, for

> " . . . when the active labours of the chase
> No more delighted, in the shady bower

> Idly industrious, sat reclined at ease
> The sable artist; to the javelin's shaft,
> The ebon staff, or maple goblet, gave
> Fantastic decorations; simply carved,
> Yet not inelegant."

Later in the same poem, Roscoe relates the story of Cymbello, the son of the king of Monsol. As a child, Cymbello is kept away from " the flattery of a court." It is a little disheartening to know that the courts even of savage kings are thoroughly corrupt. Just as if he were the son of a romantic European, the black prince is reared in the woods. His instructor is the gentle hermit Matomba, whose black skin does not hide the traits of the " good old man " whom we have met before. Cymbello is taught to love nature and — young Roscoe is a Jacobin — to recognize all men as his equals. Advancing to young manhood, he falls in love with Matomba's daughter, Kiaza. After he ascends the throne, with Kiaza as his queen, he begins a reign of great wisdom and benevolence. But alas, the slave-traders come. On the ship, Cymbello leads a revolt, but the rifles of the whites are deadly. Cymbello and Kiaza are shot down in each other's arms.

Roscoe varies with notes of nature-worship and Jacobinism the *motifs* of savage royalty and savage love set forth in *Oroonoko*. It is probably due to Aphra Behn that so large a percentage of Negro slaves were kings in their native country. In this respect, even the Irish are outdone. The Reverend James Hurdis perfectly represents the tradition in crying to a brutal overseer,

> " . . . . . Inhuman dog, forbear:
> The man who now lies bleeding at your feet
> Was once a monarch; "

and goes on to give the now familiar picture of happy life in Africa. Hannah More, on the contrary, is trying to democratize Mrs. Behn when, after praising the native genius of the Negro and deploring his fate as a slave, she assures us that

> "No individual griefs my bosom melt,
> For millions feel what Oroonoko felt."

Humanitarian feeling influences not only portrayals of the Negro, but of the Indian. Both Mrs. Opie and Montgomery, as we have seen, write with horror of Spanish brutality in the West Indies. But is the record of England perfectly clean in this respect? It is interesting to find that Ebenezer Elliott, the " Corn-Law Rhymer," does not think so. His social conscience is historical as well as contemporary, for it responds to the fate of the Indians in seventeenth century New England.

In *Withered Wild Flowers,* the poet's namesake, Eliot the Puritan missionary, delivers a defence of King Philip:

> "If every White Man aims at him a blow,
> Justly he sees in every White a foe;
> And, doom'd in combat or in flight to die,
> Does he not well to face his enemy?
> Sage, patriot, hero, king! for Nature's rights,
> Brave as our own Caractacus, he fights.
> Reluctant draws the knife, and heaves a sigh;
> Then wars on fate and possibility.
> For, arm'd to extirpate his hated race,
> The Whites shall hunt them o'er earth's blasted face;
> Till, in the ocean of the farthest west,
> The last Red Man shall shroud his bleeding breast."

This prophecy occurs in a narrative poem which otherwise has nothing to do with Indians. *Kerhonah,* a blank verse drama, deals entirely with warfare between red men and white. The plot frequently demands of the reader

what Coleridge calls " a willing suspension of disbelief."
The scene is western Massachusetts and eastern New York
in 1660. On the restoration of the Stuarts, Dixwell, the
executioner of Charles I, lives in fear of his life. His
daughter Mary happens to be the wife of Morton, "an
Englishman in authority," whose duty it is to capture
Dixwell. Morton has no idea that the fugitive is his
father-in-law, but Mary knows the secret.

Kerhonah is a wise old sachem of the Maspataquas.
He has two sons, Toronto and Maskate, and a daughter,
Nidaniss, who loves the missionary Eliot. When Maskate is wantonly slain by the whites, Kerhonah effects an
alliance against the English between the Maspataquas and
their old foes the Mohawks. There is a council scene with
much Indian oratory. While it is in progress, Dixwell
enters and fans the flames by adding his hatred of the
English to theirs. Eliot, who is somehow present, tries
to dissuade them, but only puts his own life in jeopardy.
Nidaniss saves him by the proper " He shall not die! "
method.

In the final scene, Kerhonah and Nidaniss pray to the
Cohoes waterfall as a preparation for the warpath. They
are there surprised by Morton, who has been pursuing
Dixwell in company with his own wife, disguised as a man,
and quite unrecognized by him. Morton shoots Kerhonah
and Dixwell, Toronto kills Morton, and the curtain falls
upon a play which would furnish an ideal libretto for an
Italian opera. Throughout, of course, we hear much of
Indian honor and English treachery.

The appearance of the missionary Eliot in the above
poems will remind us that Mrs. Hemans is not the only
minor poet to concern herself with the effects of Christianity upon savages. The Quaker Bernard Barton,

Lamb's friend and Fitzgerald's father-in-law, tells of a South Seas missionary who wins the respect and confidence of the natives.

> " The savage softened, and the savage place
> A scene of blessedness and love became." [14]

After his death, the islanders, like the old Indian in Mrs. Hemans' poem, reverently point out his grave to strangers.

In a similar spirit, Josiah Conder's *The Star in the East* deals with missionary activity all over the world. Conder is shocked at the sexual license of Tahiti. In the original state of that island,

> " The Paphian Venus, driven from the West,
> In Polynesian groves long undisturb'd
> Her shameful rites and orgies foul maintain'd."

But a great change has come over *la nouvelle Cythère*. Thanks to the missionaries, the traveler now hears, not

> " . . . maddening songs of Bacchanals;
> But, from the rude Morai, the full-toned psalm
> Of Christian praise. A moral miracle!
> Tahiti now enjoys the gladdening smile
> Of sabbaths."

After showing similar results in Greenland and Africa, the poet turns to America. The Indian has within him a pure spark of religion.

> " . . . Noblest of savages,
> In war not quite a demon, and in peace
> Nought less than man, the Arab of the West; —
> In him, yet unextinct, a faint remain
> Of Nature's primal creed, like a sick lamp
> Struggling with noxious darkness, strangely gleams."

[14] *The Missionary.*

Instead of falling down before a multitude of false gods, he,

"... with sublimer faith than erst
Peopled Olympus with vile deities,
Feels the Invisible, invokes his name —
'Giver of Life!' and calls his maker good."

Such people, Conder feels, are already half Christians, and their complete conversion will only be a matter of time.

It is a cardinal principle of scientific method that no experiment is valid without some sort of negative control. Though we have seen that a number of minor poets between about 1790 and about 1830 were interested in the savage, we cannot come to any conclusion until we know how many minor poets were *not* interested in the savage. The reader has already been warned that no portion of this study claims to be exhaustive. I am, however, able to report negative results after examining the poems of the following: Thomas Lovell Beddoes, Robert Bloomfield, Caroline Bowles, John Clare, Hartley Coleridge, Hannah Cowley, George Darley, Erasmus Darwin, Octavius Gilchrist, James Hogg, Thomas Hood, Richard Hengist Horne, Richard Payne Knight, Matthew Gregory Lewis, Charles Lloyd, Thomas Maurice, Henry Hart Milman, John Mitford, Robert Montgomery, Bryan Waller Procter, John Hamilton Reynolds, William Sotheby, W. R. Spencer, Alaric Alexander Watts and Charles Wolfe. Several of these writers express ideas similar to those which underlie the conception of the Noble Savage. Several of them have English or Scotch peasants, medieval warriors and children of nature who in some respects remind us of the figure of our search. They do not, however, present any real savages for our admiration.

True, the favorite themes of some of these poets preclude any possibility of the savage's appearing in their work; but if they had been interested in the savage he would obviously have become one of their favorite themes. And if the negative results can be criticized from the positive viewpoint, the converse process is equally in order. Not many of the minor poets who write of the savage are deeply enthusiastic about him; not many seriously set him up in opposition to civilized vices.

On the whole, then, the Noble Savage is a less important figure in the minor poetry of the period than one would expect. With several exceptions, it may be said that those poets who were born well before the close of the eighteenth century, and who began to write in about 1790, are most likely to feel the true Noble Savage idea. These, like Wordsworth, Coleridge and Southey, gradually abandon the conception. Roscoe's *Wrongs of Africa* appeared in 1787 and 1788; the poems of his maturity are savageless. Bowles' last Noble Savage poem, *The Missionary*, is of 1813, and he clung to the subject longer than most of his generation. Poets who begin to write between 1800 and 1810 have generally lost the philosophy of the savage, but keep him as an interesting conventional figure. In them, also, opposition to the slave-trade and the proselytizing impulse are strong. Poets whose careers begin between 1810 and 1820 generally ignore the savage in favor of other themes, and early Victorians like Darley will have nothing to do with him at all. Though more nearly complete knowledge might alter my opinion, I have a strong impression that the Noble Savage was dead as a philosophically significant figure by 1810, and practically dead as a literary fad by 1820.

Only those who share my own interest in this subject

will be particularly intrigued by the fact that Mrs.
Hemans has more savages than Mrs. Opie, and that
the Reverend Henry Milman has none at all. But there
are writers whose attitude toward the Noble Savage is a
question of real importance in the history of romanticism,
and these must be dealt with in the following section.

B. Negative and Doubtful Results

Up to this point I have avoided any attempt to define
romanticism, and I hope that it will even now not be necessary to pin down the elusive term. It is perhaps safest
and easiest to regard English romanticism as the sum of
the tendencies most prominently displayed in English
literature between 1780 and 1830. To me, the underlying bond between these tendencies is a desire to find the
infinite within the finite, to effect a synthesis of the real
and the unreal. This definition, which is substantially
identical with that of Paul Elmer More, need not be
forced upon the reader. In any case it will be admitted
that the Noble Savage is a sort of by-product of the romantic tendency to return to nature in the hope of finding
more than really exists there.

But there are other aspects of romanticism — other
ways in which the intermingling of finite and infinite may
be attained. The romantic fusion may be sought in earlier
writers who seem to exemplify it: Milton, Shakespeare,
Spenser, the poets of the Middle Ages. It may be sought
in purely sensuous beauty of color, form, sound. It may
be sought in the writer's own mind, wherein resides a
power to bring the real into accordance with the ideal.
Medievalism, aestheticism and transcendentalism, then,
are three important varieties of romanticism which are
only very tenuously, or not at all, connected with the
Noble Savage.

Besides, as has already been stated, not every writer of the romantic period deserves to be called a romanticist. Crabbe was a conscious foe of naturalistic enthusiasm. He did not, however, firmly adopt an anti-romantic viewpoint until his art matured. In *The Library* (1781), he makes a " youthful poet," after a glance at the grim rows of law-books, sigh for the days when such things were not needed. In that imaginary age, all shared wealth in common; since no one was poor, no one was proud of being rich. In this case, the list of blessed negations suggests Warton's *Enthusiast:*

> " No wars or tumults vex'd each still domain,
> No thirst of empire, no desire of gain;
> No proud great man, nor one who would be great,
> Drove modest merit from its proper state;
> Nor into distant climes would Avarice roam
> To fetch delights for Luxury at home:
> Bound by no ties which kept the world in awe,
> They dwelt at liberty, and love was law! "

Law, personified, answers that in the state of nature each man was "a cheerless son of solitude," with nothing to give him pleasure or expand his mind until the arts and sciences raised him to a higher plane. The resultant complexity of society has made laws necessary.

Speaking now in his own person, Crabbe sides with neither party. Luxury, he says, is a flood that sweeps civilized man along with it. The laws are bulwarks constantly rising higher in an attempt to curb the noxious tide. But though we may boast of having controlled luxury by our laws, the waters are seeping under the bulwarks, and rotting them.

> " The basis sinks, the ample piles decay,
> The stately fabric shakes and falls away;
> Primeval want and ignorance come on,
> But Freedom, that exalts the savage state, is gone."

Here we have the true — not the sentimentally interpreted — doctrine of Rousseau's discourses. The savage state is admirable only for a crude simplicity and freedom, but civilization as corrupted by luxury is still worse. The idea that civilization may relapse into a state even worse than savagery, though now rather common, was a bold one in Crabbe's day.

It is in *The Village* (1783) that we get the man whom Byron called "nature's sternest painter." The poem gives not the slightest encouragement to naturalistic illusions. "Its sentiments as to the false notions of rustic happiness and rustic virtue," Boswell tells us, were so pleasing to Johnson that he revised the poem and even furnished a few lines of his own. In the hamlets of the Suffolk coast the poet has vainly sought Arcadia.

> "Here, wand'ring long, amid these frowning fields,
> I sought the simple life that Nature yields;
> Rapine and Wrong and Fear usurp'd her place,
> And a bold, artful, surly, savage race."

Of actual savages, Crabbe says almost nothing. To the reader of books of travel, he grumbles, perils and hardships seem easy enough.

> "He thinks not then of Afric's scorching sands,
> Th' Arabian sea, the Abyssinian bands;
> Fasils and Michaels, and the robbers all,
> Whom we politely chiefs and heroes call." [15]

In *Tales of the Hall*, the Squire archly quizzes his seafaring brother. Has he been shipwrecked? Has he, like Bruce in Abyssinia, cut raw beefsteaks from living cattle?

---

[15] *Edward Shore. Tales*, No. XI. Fasil and Michael are characters, much like Byron's Albanians, in Bruce's *Travels in Abyssinia*.

Has he perhaps left " some swarthy princess," some Yarico, behind him? [16]

Though such evidence is not very significant, there can be no doubt that the whole weight of Crabbe's influence is against the Noble Savage idea. He represents in poetry that realistic tendency which arose in the eighteenth century novel, and which is quite distinct from romanticism.

For a different reason, William Blake has little direct bearing upon our subject. If Crabbe was too realistic to believe in the savage, Blake was too mystical. Yet one or two hints are worth noting. It appears, for example, that this poet once thought of migrating to America.

> " Tho' born on the cheating banks of Thames,
> Tho' his waters bathèd my infant limbs,
> The Ohio shall wash his stains from me:
> I was born a slave, but I go to be free! " [17]

Mr. Sampson assigns this poem to 1793 or thereabouts. Like Wordsworth, Coleridge and Southey, Blake has lost his revolutionary enthusiasm, and wants to escape. He feels the influences which gave birth to pantisocracy.

That Blake hoped to find Noble Savages by the cleansing waters of the Ohio is at least suggested by his conversation with Isaiah and Ezekiel in *The Marriage of Heaven and Hell*. This work, of course, contains his characteristic transcendental ideas, such as that " a firm persuasion that a thing is so, makes it so," and that the first principle of all things is poetic genius. At this prophetic dinner, Ezekiel, when asked by Blake " why he ate dung,

---

[16] *Tales of the Hall*, Book IV. This is interesting testimony to the popularity of the Inkle-Yarico story. As for Bruce, many of his tales were received with incredulity. *Cf.* Peter Pindar's *Complimentary Epistle to James Bruce.*

[17] *Why Should I Care for the Men of Thames?* (*Rossetti MS.*)

and lay so long on his right and left side," made answer: " The desire of raising other men into a perception of the infinite: this the North American tribes practise." These activities suggest Hindu fakirs rather than Amerindian medicine-men, but the question of Blake's accuracy is less important than his desire to support his mystical philosophy by an appeal to the primitive. There are few better illustrations of the curious affinity of the supposedly super-rational for the sub-rational.

Blake, however, is almost wholly lacking in material for us except when his philosophy encourages the fusion of the Noble Savage idea with other elements of romanticism. In this connection he will be mentioned later.

In *Peter Bell the Third*, Shelley contrasts Burns with Wordsworth in their feeling for nature. The former, he says, enjoyed his mistress like a frankly passionate lover; but the latter, merely on touching the hem of Nature's skirt, felt faint, and indulged in vague philosophical sublimations of the instinct he was too timid to satisfy. The distinction, though maliciously drawn, is not without foundation. But it should not make us forget that Burns soon came to realize, if indeed he did not realize from the first, the practical value of being a ploughboy poet in a time when the gentry were looking for poetry in ploughboys. Burns was a conscious artist, and it was part of his art to keep close to nature. He was adroit enough to realize that a genuine ploughboy poet does not wax sentimental over ploughboys — or over savages. Hence, except in a few pieces like *The Cotter's Saturday Night*, where the real Burns struggles with the Burns that Dr. Moore wished him to be, his poems deal with the primitive without being in the least primitivistic.

Burns' democratic spirit might have found expression

in some savage who reminds elegant Europeans that " a man's a man for a' that." One can only say that no such savage appears in his work. Except for *The Slave's Lament*, which will find a place in the chapter on *Natural Man and Natural Poetry*, Burns has nothing for us.

It is a long leap from Burns to Shelley, but the intervening poets have already been considered. One may say of Shelley, as of Blake, that he soared in an atmosphere too rarefied and unearthly for the noblest savage to breathe.

In the immature *Queen Mab*, however, one does discern a rather strong tincture of primitivism. Shelley plainly believes in a Golden Age:

> " Once peace and freedom blessed
>   The cultivated plain:
>   But wealth, that curse of man,
>   Blighted the bud of its prosperity."

Commerce has made men selfish, has polluted the " full fountain " of " natural kindness " ; and since the greed of tyrants is the cause of war,

> " The harmony and happiness of man
>   Yields to the wealth of nations."

Shelley imagines that before the lust for gold raised its head, the world was an Arcadia. " Every heart," he declares, " contains perfection's germ," and the wisest sage of all history would seem " but a weak and inexperienced boy compared to what the humblest slave or criminal of to-day would be if only he could shake off the chains of venality."

A hint of the Noble Savage idea appears in one of several rather conflicting solutions of the problem of evil presented in *Queen Mab*. The Fairy who conducts the celestial tour which constitutes the machinery of the poem bids the Spirit gaze upon the earth. Everything there is full of " peace, harmony, and love " except " the outcast man." Man, " blessed from his birth with all bland impulses," has separated himself from nature by his unnatural habits.

> " He slays the lamb that looks him in the face,
> And horribly devours his mangled flesh."

The " putrid humours " thus engendered are responsible for " misery, death, disease and crime."

The notes on this passage are important. In almost all mythologies Shelley finds support for the belief " that at some distant time man forsook the path of nature, and sacrificed the purity and happiness of his being to unnatural appetites." The Christian allegory of the fall of man " admits of no other explanation than the disease and crime that have flowed from unnatural diet." From Newton's *Defence of Vegetable Regimen* Shelley borrows a similar interpretation of the Prometheus myth. According to Hesiod, physical suffering was unknown before the time of Prometheus. But " Prometheus . . . effected some great change in the condition of his nature, and applied fire to culinary purposes. . . . From this moment his vitals were devoured by the vulture of disease. . . . All vice rose from the ruin of healthful innocence. Tyranny, superstition, commerce and inequality were then first known, when reason vainly attempted to guide the wanderings of exacerbated passion." Here, then, is an explanation of the genesis of evil that plainly demands the assumption of primitive innocence as a standard from which man has fallen away. And this innocence, Shelley believes, will some day be regained by man. He looks forward to a millenium in which awakened reason will banish tyranny.

> " How sweet a scene will earth become!
> Of purest spirits a pure dwelling-place,
>
> . . . .
>
> When man, with changeless Nature coalescing,
> Will undertake regeneration's work."

When the " morn of love " dawns, when earth becomes the " reality of heaven," there will be no false distinction between reason and passion. Both, in this blest reunion, will become parts of nature.

> " Here now the human being stands adorning
> This loveliest earth with taintless body and mind."

Animals and children no longer fear him, for he is purged of blood-lust and sin. Free and happy, from the amiable earth he

> " . . . . . drags the gem of truth
> To decorate his paradise of peace."

As Shelley matures, he leaves behind him most of the crudity and confusion of *Queen Mab;* but he never shakes off the Arcadianism of that work. His loftiest visions of man's final happiness constantly remind us of what Byron, with Shelley almost certainly in mind, called " old Saturn's reign of sugar-candy."

In the *Revolt of Islam,* for example, the temporary practical success of Laon and Cythna is celebrated by a great feast of liberty in which for a moment the hopes of man's future expressed in *Queen Mab* are realized. Cythna hails " the dawn of mind " in the stirring words:

> " My brethren, we are free! the plains and mountains,
> The gray sea-shore, the forests and the fountains,
> Are haunts of happiest dwellers; — man and woman,
> Their common bondage burst, may freely borrow
> From lawless love a solace for their sorrow."

These lawless lovers are now free to make the earth beautiful by means of poetry and science.

The festival is essentially a return of man to "Earth, the general mother".

> ". . . . . . . The fruits are glowing
> Beneath the stars, and the night winds are flowing
> O'er the ripe corn, the birds and beasts are dreaming;"

while man, at peace with the animal world and lord over the vegetable, innocently regales himself with pomegranates, citrons, melons, dates, figs, edible roots, grapes (happily not fermented), corn and pure water. In short,

> "They helde hem payed of fruites that they ete,
> Which that the feldes yave hem by usage;
> They ne were nat forpampred with outrage."

Chaucer would have seen in these happy Jacobins "the peples of the former age," and the author of *The Golden Bough* might more realistically find in savage cults of fertility the origin of their rejoicing. But when is the science to begin? What of reason was left, we wonder, when the love-making and eating had to stop? The feast is, no doubt, symbolical, but only a very bad poet chooses symbols which have no relation to his thought.

The hero of *Prometheus Unbound* is a being very different from him who in *Queen Mab* rashly seduces man from vegetarian innocence. Prometheus is here "the light-bringer" in a much loftier aspect. He supplies the one deficiency of the Golden Age — knowledge, and the fruits of knowledge. In the words of Mrs. Shelley, he "used knowledge as a weapon to defeat evil, by leading mankind, beyond the state wherein they are sinless through ignorance, to that in which they are virtuous through wisdom." Here is a conception that soars far above mere primitivism.

And yet, on completing this poem, one may question whether man has now become " virtuous through wisdom." The world after the fall of Jupiter is more like the Golden Age than like the age of creative intelligence of which Prometheus has been made the symbol. Acts III and IV of *Prometheus Unbound* have the fervidly pastoral atmosphere of the feast of liberty in the *Revolt of Islam*. Prometheus does not renew the civilizing activities for which he was punished by Jupiter. On his release he retires to a cave in a forest to enjoy the embraces of Asia and to hold converse with Earth, Ocean, Sun and Moon. His reunion with Nature is not only the restoration of man to his just place in the universe, but a " return to nature " in something like the usual romantic sense.

Hellas, of course, provides another example of Shelley's Arcadianism. The chorus has nothing to say of Prometheus' gifts — wisdom, science, philosophy. Its thoughts hark back to the Golden Age, to the restoration of " Saturn and Love," who, as Shelley reminds us " were among the deities of a real or imaginary state of innocence and happiness."

Of some significance in connection with our subject are the *Fragments of an Unfinished Drama,* written, according to Garnett, " at Pisa during the late winter or early spring of 1822." Mrs. Shelley is able to give a synopsis of the projected work, which runs as follows: " An Enchantress, living in one of the islands of the Indian Archipelago, saves the life of a Pirate, a man of savage but noble nature. She becomes enamoured of him; and he, inconstant to his mortal love, for a while returns her passion; but at length, recalling the memory of her whom he left, and who laments his loss, he escapes from the Enchanted Island, and returns to his lady. His mode of life makes him again go to sea, and the Enchantress seizes the opportunity to bring him, by a spirit-brewed tempest, back to her island." Unfortunately the only direct information about this " savage but noble " pirate is furnished by his jilted sweetheart in one uncompleted scene. She says of him:

> " . . . He was so awful, yet
> So beautiful in mystery and terror,
> Calming me as the loveliness of heaven
> Soothes the unquiet sea: — and yet not so,
> For he seemed stormy, and would often seem
> A quenchless sun masked in portentous clouds;
> For such his thoughts, and even his actions were;
> But he was not of them, nor they of him,
> But as they hid his splendour from the earth.
> Some said he was a man of blood and peril,
> And steeped in bitter infamy to the lips." [18]

There is evidently something Byronic about this pirate; and Byron himself was a member of the circle for whose amusement, as Mrs. Shelley tells us, these fragments were written. One wonders whether Byron had yet read Bligh's *Narrative of the Mutiny and Seizure of the Bounty* and Mariner's *Account of the Tonga Islands* and had discussed them with Shelley; for *The Island*, which was written early in 1823, suggests a comparison with the *Unfinished Drama*. Each is concerned with love on a South Seas island, and noble mutineers are first cousins to noble pirates. If there is any real connection between the two works, the differences are more interesting than the similarities. It is very characteristic of Shelley to prefer a Circe-like enchantress to an actual Polynesian maiden, and to idealize his pirate almost to Promethean heights.

[18] The pirate's lady is loved by an East Indian youth, but his character is not developed sufficiently to enable one to determine whether he is a Noble Savage.

In these fragments we have Shelley's nearest approach to the depiction of actually savage beings, and the approach is anything but close. One line of *Prometheus Unbound*, to be sure, pays its respects to Southey's *Madoc*. Asia reminds Demogorgon that Prometheus

> ". . . taught to rule, as life directs the limbs,
> The tempest-wingéd chariots of the Ocean,
> And the Celt knew the Indian."

But this allusion appears in a passage glorifying intellectual progress, and has no tincture of primitivism.

The confusion in Shelley's mind between perfectibilitarianism and deteriorationism, between reason and emotion, between determinism and free will, and between nature as a norm of Arcadian innocence and as a Godwinian machine is an inheritance from the philosophy of the revolutionary period, and is hence most evident in *Queen Mab*. In that poem at least something of the Noble Savage idea appears clearly enough. But once recognized there, that something can dimly be traced into his maturer work. His visions of peace and happiness are inseparable from the Golden Age tradition. His belief in perfectibility depends upon belief in the natural goodness of man. His faith in the power of love implies that the human heart is the repository of ultimate truth.

It must certainly be admitted, however, that Shelley was anything but consciously primitivistic. Whatever naturalistic elements exist in his work are so transmuted by Berkleyan, Spinozistic and Platonic influences, and by the genius of Shelley himself, that they have little direct relation to the type of thought that produces the Noble Savage. They disappear entirely in those happy moments when Shelley gives up the task of improving mankind and frankly skims the ether that is his proper element. Shelley did believe in natural man, but his natural man existed in the rosy clouds of his private vision, not in the American forest.

When Keats began to write, the Noble Savage had lost practically all of his philosophical significance, and most of his popularity as a literary fad. The romanticism of this poet points forward to the Victorians rather than backward to the days when natural man was what debaters call a " live topic." It derives much from the older admiration for the Elizabethans, the Middle Ages and the Ancients, but it views those traditions in a new way. It is a romanticism of beauty. It finds in lovely forms, bright colors and soft textures that fusion of the natural and the supernatural, or of truth and beauty, which earlier romanticists sought in other ways.

Keats writes to his brother in the States that he has been reading Robertson's *History of America* and Voltaire's *Siècle de Louis XIV*. " In how lamentable a case," he says, " do we see the great body of the people in both instances; in the first when Men might seem to inherit quiet of Mind from unsophisticated senses . . . even there they had mortal pains to bear as bad, or even worse, than Bailiffs, Debts and Poverties of civilized Life. The whole appears to resolve into this — that Man is originally a poor forked creature subject to the same mischances as the beasts of the forest. . . . If he improves by degrees his bodily accommodations and comforts — at each stage, at each ascent there are waiting for him a fresh set of annoyances." In this dilemma, the best that man can do is to remember that " there is still a heaven with its Stars above his head." [19] Such balanced resignation leaves no room for the Noble Savage.

[19] To George and Georgiana Keats, April 15, 1819.

In the whole body of Keats' poems, there are only four or possibly five references to the American Indian.[20] The doubtful one occurs in *Isabella*, where the vision of the dead Lorenzo is said to come back to his beloved

> ". . . . . like a lance,
>   Waking an Indian from his cloudy hall
>   With cruel pierce, and bringing him again
>   Sense of the gnawing fire at heart and brain."

This I believe to be reminiscent of Southey's *Curse of Kehama*, in which the unfortunate Ladurlad, after a brief respite on a high and hence " cloudy " mountain, must descend to his agony.[21] The last line of the Keats passage suggests the words of the curse itself:

> " Thou shalt live in thy pain,
>   While Kehama shall reign,
>   With a fire in thy heart,
>   And a fire in thy brain."

Of the four references which undoubtedly concern the American Indian, two are merely decorative. The glassy floor of Neptune's hall in *Endymion* is likened to the surface of a lake

> ". . . . . on which the slim canoe
>   Of feather'd Indian darts about, as through
>   The delicatest air."

Another simile, this time in *Sleep and Poetry*, compares life to

> ". . . . . . . a poor Indian's sleep
>   While his boat hastens to the monstrous steep
>   Of Montmorenci."

[20] The " Indian Maid " in *Endymion* is of course not to the point. Diana did not disguise herself as a squaw.

[21] *Curse of Kehama*, XII, 5.

These passages show, as we should expect, that Keats was not insensitive to the picturesqueness of the Indian.

One of the last two references strikes the humanitarian note. The wealth of Isabella's wicked brothers is based upon the suffering of their fellow-men.

> " And for them many a weary hand did swelt
>   In torched mines and noisy factories,
> And many once proud quiver'd loins did melt
>   In blood from stinging whip; — with hollow eyes
> Many all day in dazzling river stood,
> To take the rich-or'd driftings of the flood."

Here Keats pays his respects to the shades of Las Casas.

The last passage which we have to consider occurs at the very opening of *The Fall of Hyperion:*

> " Fanatics have their dreams, wherewith they weave
>   A paradise for a sect; the savage, too,
>   From forth the loftiest fashion of his sleep
>   Guesses at heaven; pity these have not
>   Trac'd upon vellum or wild Indian leaf
>   The shadows of melodious utterance,
>   But bare of laurel they live, dream, and die;
>   For Poesy alone can tell her dreams."

This passage probably epitomizes Keats' attitude toward the savage. The Indian is picturesque; his sufferings are to be pitied; he has his visions. But he is " bare of laurel," and Keats' love is reserved for those who can tell their dreams.

Merely to mention the three principal types of novel which flourished in the first three decades of the nineteenth century — the realistic, the Gothic, and the historical — will indicate that the Noble Savage was not an important figure in the fiction of the period. Jane Austen, the great exemplar of the first type, might well have satirized the cult of primitive man along with the cult of sensibility and the cult of horror. Though explicit evidence is lacking, one can feel sure that she admired the savage even less than her precursor Fanny Burney, who at least found Omai rather amusing.[22] Miss Mitford, though she devoted an early poem to one aspect of the Noble Savage tradition, soon turned to very different fields. The Gothicists, unlike the realists, represent a genuine element of romanticism, but of a sort which has nothing to do with our subject. An exception to this sweeping statement is Maturin's *Melmoth the Wanderer*, for Immalee is a perfect example of the female Noble Savage. Her virtues, however, must be set forth in a later chapter.

It is much more important for us to ask whether the tradition represented by Scott has any connection with the Noble Savage idea. The author of the Waverley Novels was at least " exposed " to the primitivistic contagion, for his brother Thomas, who served in Canada as paymaster of the seventieth regiment from 1813 to his death in 1823, was enthusiastic about the savage.

Two years after his arrival in Canada, we find Thomas telling Walter of his " red brethren." He announces proudly that he is a Mohawk chief by adoption, and that he " preferred the manners of the native Indians to the insipid conversations of our own officers." Captain Norton, a Mohawk chief, is described in some detail. Not only does he speak twelve Indian tongues, but he is fluent in

[22] *Early Diary of Frances Burney*, Vol. I, pp. 321, 330–337; Vol. II, pp. 24–25, 38, 130, 139. Fanny's brother, Captain (later Admiral) James Burney, was a South Seas enthusiast, and one of Omai's intimates.

English, French, German and Spanish. He has translated the *Lady of the Lake* and the Holy Scriptures into
Mohawk. Yet with all this cultivation, he is a true savage. " For, brother, you ask doth he paint himself, scalp,
etc., etc.? I answer yea, he doth; and with the most
polished manner of civilized life, he would not disdain to
partake of the blood of his enemy at the banquet of sacrifice. Yet I admire and love the man, and would cheerfully
give fifty guineas that you could see him for one half-
hour." This remarkable person has written in English a
journal of his travels. He is afraid of the more than
Mohawk savagery of the *Edinburgh Review*. Will
Walter, asks Thomas, arrange to have the book reviewed
in the *Quarterly?* [23]

Thomas's praise of Norton seems in part an answer to
questions which Walter had previously asked. Those
questions, however, with Walter's reaction to his brother's
reply, are lost to us. Scott's published letters indicate that
he was quite aware of the Noble Savage tradition, but had
no strong feelings on the subject. From a burlesque
gazette report in which he announces to Patrick Murray
his approaching marriage we learn that Miss Carpenter
" is no relation whatever to the Indian Chief called the
little Carpenter, late Sachem of the Shawanese, but that
she was born in the south of France, and was a ward of the
present Lord Downshire." [24] Ten years later, Scott com-

---

[23] *Familiar Letters of Sir Walter Scott*, Vol. I, pp. 344–346.
Captain John Norton's Mohawk name was Teyoninhokarawen. His
Gospel of St. John, in Mohawk and English, was published in 1804.
(*Cf. Quarterly Review*, Vol. XXXVI, pp. 9–11.) His travels, and
his translation of the *Lady of the Lake*, do not seem to have been
published.

[24] To Patrick Murray, Dec. 22, 1797. The Little Carpenter was
chief of a South Carolina tribe. The *St. James's Chronicle* of Nov.
19–21, 1761, quotes an oration made by him upon concluding peace
with the British.

pares his literary life to the life of the savage — " absolute indolence interchanged with hard work." [25] He reads with amusement an account of Caraboo, the Devonshire cobbler's daughter who persuaded people to regard her as a kidnapped Malayan princess, but the account suggests to him merely the ease with which such tricks may be played.[26]

Yet though actual Indians and spurious Malayans appealed little to Sir Walter, the Scotch Highlander appealed a great deal; and the Highlander, as Byron realized, is not without traits which suggest the savage. Thus in the *Heart of Midlothian* we read: " One . . . stood upright before them, a lathy young savage. . . . Yet the eyes of the lad were keen and sparkling; his gesture free and noble, like that of all savages." Rob Roy's " ideas of morality were those of an Arab chief, being such as naturally arose out of his wild education." In his character, too, were combined " the wild virtues, the subtle policy, and unrestrained license of an American Indian." In Roderick Dhu, to shift to the poems, we find the same wild virtues, the same craft, and the same lack of restraint.

In fact Scott's Highlander, like Wordsworth's dalesman, and still more like Byron's Albanian, might be called an adaptation of the Noble Savage idea to the writer's own surroundings and temperament. As with Wordsworth and Byron, the special variety differs rather widely from the norm. The wildness of the Highlander, and his rugged good qualities, while they stir Scott's admiration,

[25] To Miss Seward, November 23, 1807.
[26] To Miss Edgeworth, November, 1823. The book referred to by Scott is probably *Caraboo. A Narrative of A Singular Imposition.* For an account of this woman, who really showed astonishing powers of deception, see also Hone's *Every-Day Book*, Vol. II, columns 1631–1634.

do not tempt him to philosophize about the blessings of nature.   Scott's popularity was largely due to the fact that he combined great enthusiasm for certain external manifestations of the romantic spirit with an almost total lack of enthusiasm for romantic doctrine.   He loved the feudal past, he loved to seek ballads and legends in mountain recesses, and he loved the quaint, brave, hospitable folk he met there.   He found them admirable for the limited but real virtues which all savages possess.   No writer of the period, however, is less likely to sentimentalize the primitive than Walter Scott.

From the thin trickle of minor novels which carry into the nineteenth century the Richardsonian sentimentality of the eighteenth, patience might extract a few grains of material.   There are Indians, for example, in Mary Brunton's *Self-Control* (1810), but they are mere tools in the abduction of the heroine.   The villain dismisses them because he suspects them of sympathizing with the unfortunate Laura [27] — a hint of natural goodness which is not developed.   Although Indians may appear in a few other obscure novels, I can state with some certainty that except for *Melmoth* no really important novel between 1800 and 1830 makes use of the Noble Savage.   Perhaps it was felt that the novelists of the preceding generation had worked him to death.

Of the essayists who flourished in the later portion of the romantic period little can be said.   The literary form which they employed did not permit the direct representation of savage virtues, and the themes which they discussed seldom raised the threadbare problem of natural

[27] *Self-Control*, p. 475.   The Indian kidnappers are perhaps derived from Mrs. Lennox's *Life of Harriot Stuart*, Vol. I, pp. 87–92.

man. Leigh Hunt, not only as essayist but as poet, must be passed by with a curt " no reaction."

Charles Lamb says too many amusing things about the savage to be treated so cavalierly. Perhaps because of his urban environment, his romanticism found expression in the study of Elizabethan drama, in the cultivation of odd friendships, in tasting the flavor of London life, in whimsical reminiscence and introspection, in a score of amiable hobbies which never shook the depths of a singularly well-controlled personality. He had Scott's wise ability to love strange old things without regarding them as symbols of the infinite, to enjoy the pleasures of the romantic attitude without committing himself to the romantic philosophy.

It is well known that Lamb was no adorer of scenery. A few citations will show that he feels toward wild people as he does toward wild places. Thus he explains to Southey that he prefers *Roderick* to *Kehama* and *Madoc* because its characters are less exotic. " I am at home in Spain and Christendom. I have a timid imagination, I am afraid. I do not willingly admit of strange beliefs, or out-of-the-way creeds or places. I never read books of travels, at least not farther than Paris, or Rome. I can just endure Moors, because of their connection as foes with Christians; but Abyssinians, Ethiops, Esquimaux, Dervises, and all that tribe, I hate. I believe I fear them in some manner. . . . I am a Christian, Englishman, Londoner, *Templar*." [28]

Lamb's fling at " the naked ills of savage life " in the *Pindaric Ode to the Tread-Mill* has already been cited.[29] Ordinarily, his dislike of savages finds a more broadly humorous expression. His ill-fated farce *Mr. H——* appeared in 1806, when primitive innocence was one of

[28] *Works*, Vol. I, pp. 250–251.
[29] *Vide supra*, p. 121.

those fashionable fads which provide targets for the wit of light comedy. Thus Mr. Hogsflesh, finding himself spurned as a suitor at the disclosure of his unsavory name, yearns " to go where the persecuted syllables shall be no more heard, or excite no meaning — some spot where his native tongue has never penetrated, nor any of his countrymen have landed, to plant their unfeeling satire, their brutal wit, and national ill manners. . . . Some yet undiscovered Otaheite, where witless, unapprehensive savages shall innocently pronounce the ill-fated sounds, and think them not inharmonious." This speech was no doubt intended to evoke the same sort of laughter as would greet an allusion to prohibition in a present-day American farce. Three years before, Lamb had supped at Rickman's with " a merry *natural* captain, who pleases himself vastly with once having made a pun at Otaheite in the O. language." [30]

In 1803 Lamb's friend Manning determines to go to Siberia, there to do missionary work among the Tartars. " For God's sake," Lamb expostulates, " don't think any more of ' Independent Tartary.' " He urges Manning to talk with the Tartar who is on exhibition at Exeter Change — " he is no very favorable specimen of his countrymen! " But Manning's best course will be to banish the idea entirely from his mind by employing Hartley's associative method. " For this purpose repeat to yourself every night, after you have said your prayers, the words Independent Tartary, Independent Tartary, two or three times, and associate with them the *idea* of *oblivion*." By this means, perhaps, Manning will every day, in this respect, be getting better and better.

---

[30] *Works*, Vol. I, p. 178. (Letter to Manning, February 19, 1803.) The sailor was Captain, later Admiral, Burney, who learned the Tahitian language from Omai himself.

" My dear friend," Lamb continues, " think what a sad pity it would be to bury such *parts* in heathen countries, among nasty, unconversable, horse-belching Tartar-people! . . . The Tartars, really, are a cold, insipid, smouchy set. You'll be sadly moped (if you are not eaten) among them." Then follows more curative advice: "*Shave the upper lip.* Go about like an European. Read no book of voyages (they are nothing but lies), only now and then a romance, to keep the fancy *under*." This recommendation of romance-reading as an emotional safety-valve, though offered in jest, tells us much of Lamb's philosophy. Elia is poking fun at himself when he tells Manning, to whom he had earlier described his adventures with a rattlesnake, not to " go to any sights of *wild beasts. That has been your ruin.* Accustom yourself to write familiar letters, on common subjects, to your friends in England, such as are of a moderate understanding. And think about common things more." [31]

All this, though of course merely playful chat, shows that Lamb felt toward the Noble Savage as he did toward the cult of scenery. How much seriousness lay beneath his opposition to primitivism one cannot say, since under the jester's garb Lamb maintained an impenetrable privacy of the mind.

William Hazlitt admires *Oroonoko, Gertrude of Wyoming,* and Crèvecoeur's *Letters.* In one instance, too, his fresh, intense love of nature associates itself with the savage. " Give me the clear blue sky over my head, and the green turf beneath my feet, a winding road before me, and a three hours march to dinner — and then to thinking! . . . I laugh, I run, I leap, I sing for joy. From the point of yonder rolling cloud I plunge into my past being,

[31] *Ibid.*, pp. 177–178.

and revel there, as the sun-burnt Indian plunges headlong into the wave that wafts him to his native shore." [32]

But this simile, though more than superficially decorative, does not imply approval of every aspect of savage life. " The Huron," says Hazlitt, " devours the Iroquois, because he is an Iroquois, and the Iroquois the Huron for a similar reason. Neither suspects that he does it, because he himself is a savage, and no better than a wild beast; and is convinced in his own breast that the difference of name and tribe makes a total difference in the case." [33] These savages are far too human to fit into the tradition we are studying.

Both on his good side and on his bad, Hazlitt was unfitted to be an admirer of the Noble Savage: his love of reason and his emotional perversity were too great. In his day the defense of savages had become a rather outworn fad which no one who adored originality as he did could cultivate with much pride.

In the works of Thomas De Quincey little or no naturalism can be discerned. His refusal to sentimentalize over primitive people is shown in his attack on two popular misconceptions: " that the savage has more imagination than the civilized man " ; and " that Oriental nations have more imagination (and, according to some, a more passionate constitution of mind) than those of Europe." [34] The arguments offered in refutation of these fallacies will be outlined in the chapter on *Natural Man and Natural Poetry*. At present it is enough to know that De Quincey refused to believe that the imaginative power of a race decreases as that race becomes more civilized.

[32] *On Going a Journey.*
[33] *On Party Spirit.*
[34] *Collected Writings,* Vol. X, p. 443 (*False Distinctions*).

In the *Revolt of the Tartars,* the author has an ideal opportunity to write a prose epic on the Noble Savage theme — an opportunity which he ignores. He does not, like Lamb, find the Tartars a " cold, insipid, smouchy set." Instead, they are fascinating; but fascinating as Tartars, not as sons of nature. They are " a people semi-barbarous, but simple-hearted and of ancient descent." The word " but " in the foregoing sentence proves De Quincey to be no true friend of the primitive, for the barbarity and the simple-heartedness of the Noble Savage go hand in hand. "Ancient descent," too, strikes a discordant note.

De Quincey, in fact, loves his Tartars only as a scholar loves the subject on which he is engaged. He speaks of " the natural unamiableness of the Kalmuck disposition," a phrase which a champion of the Noble Savage would brand as self-contradictory. In a note on Gilfillan's criticisms on Keats' sins against the English tongue, De Quincey observes that the Kalmucks are proud of their " hideous language." They are, indeed, very patriotic in every way. " Even the Kalmuck face, which to us foolish Europeans looks so unnecessarily flat and ogre-like, these honest Kalmuckish Tartars have ascertained to be the pure classical model of human beauty; which, in fact, it *is,* upon the principle of those people who hold that the chief use of a face is not at all to please one's wife, but to frighten one's enemy." Except to a determined humanitarian, ugly savages are seldom noble.

In concluding the *Revolt of the Tartars,* De Quincey expresses his gratification at the Kalmucks' having abandoned their wild nomadic life for the settled agricultural environment of China. " But one great disadvantage there was, amply to overbalance all other possible gain: the chances were removed to an incalculable distance for their conversion to Christianity, without which, in these times, there is no absolute advance possible on the path of true civilization." Like the later Southey, De Quincey approves of simplicity only in so far as it makes conversion easy.

Walter Savage Landor, one of the least romantic writers of the romantic period, provides us with more material than we might expect. His poems, of course, must be set aside. Though their classicism may easily be exaggerated, they are certainly free of any primitivistic tinge. The 1795 volume contains a typical " dying slave " passage in which the nobility of the Negro is emphasized,[35] but such juvenile indiscretions hardly deserve notice.

In four *Imaginary Conversations*, however, the savage is used as a means of attacking contemporary evils. Thus the King of the Sandwich Islands, with the help of a somewhat malicious interpreter, addresses uncomfortably naïve questions to Peel and Croker regarding bribery, court influence and the like.[36] In another dialogue, Rao-Gong-Fao describes to his master, the King of Ava, what he has seen in England. The question of Catholic emancipation provides material for broad satire. The savage king is much shocked by what he hears, and decides to send missionaries to the English.[37]

Two of the conversations bitterly assail the colonial policy of France, which even then seemed to fall short of the enlightened ideals of that nation. Polverel, a French captain, comes to Tahiti to " protect " Queen Pomare from the English. His talk of extending the benefits of civilization, as an English missionary points out, is only a

---

[35] *Apology for Satire. Poems of Walter Savage Landor*, pp. 62–63.
[36] *Works*, Vol. I, pp. 446–448.
[37] *Ibid.*, pp. 490–495.

mask for selfish imperialism. The native queen is put in chains and manhandled while the carefully coached French sailors cry " *Vive la reine*." [38] Another dialogue, that between Marshal Bugeaud and an Arab chieftain, deals in a similar spirit with some forgotten massacre in Syria.[39]

It should be noted, however, that Landor concerns himself less with savage virtues than with civilized vices. In his hands, the Noble Savage is merely a satirical bludgeon. Fontenelle, in reviving the Lucianic tradition, had written a dialogue between Cortez and Montezuma,[40] and Lahontan had given the world a whole series of conversations between himself and an Indian.[41] Like these, and like his less remote predecessor Lyttelton,[42] Landor appreciates the usefulness of the savage as a speaker in dialogue. He varies the device by applying the savage's comments to specific events of the day rather than to the general contrast between the primitive and the civilized. But his hatred of corrupt and oppressive politics, though it leads him to champion the savage, does not imply any illusions about the state of nature. His South Sea Islanders and Arabs, like Swift's Houyhnhnms, awaken our scorn of civilization without arousing our admiration for the aboriginal.

Our roll-call of the writers of the romantic period is now tolerably complete. Before summing up the history of the Noble Savage, however, we must consider a few of his enemies. Moore tried to dispel the sentimental haze

---

[38] *Ibid.*, Vol. II, pp. 202–206.

[39] *Ibid.*, pp. 242–243.

[40] *Nouveaux Dialogues des Morts*, Part II, section iii, dialogue 6.

[41] *Dialogues de Monsieur le Baron de Lahontan et d'un Sauvage.*

[42] *Vide supra*, p. 51.

through which many of his contemporaries regarded America, but he himself coquetted with primitivism. Crabbe opposed romantic naturalism, but has so little to say of actual savages that his importance for us is slight. The anti-naturalism of the men to be taken up in the following chapter has more significance. They accepted the Noble Savage as a symbol of sentimental naturalism, and through the savage thrust at the movement which he represented.

CHAPTER IX

ENEMIES OF THE NOBLE SAVAGE

SAMUEL JOHNSON admired form, and detested the slipshod, the sentimental, the eccentric in literature; he believed in a strong government based upon obedience to authority, and frowned upon all that savored of " levelling "; he accepted the doctrines of the Established Church, and viewed with disgust both Wesleyan enthusiasm and deistic scepticism; he sensed a reality outside himself, and repudiated the transcendental philosophy. Had he been able to systematize his likes and dislikes, he might have become one of the great preachers of the philosophy of control. He did not, however, quite perceive the unifying element which might have given coherence and dignity to his prejudices. Instead, his characteristic method was to fly to the opposite extreme from each of his aversions. Hence we find him counting Milton's iambics on his fingers, growling out nonsense about the divine right of kings, keeping a fervid devotional diary and kicking boulders to refute Berkeley. His love of truth was thwarted by his pugnacity. Yet that love of truth, beneath the spluttering and bullying which irritate us, ran clear and strong.

The Lexicographer's remarks on primitive innocence and allied notions exhibit this combination of hot-headed perversity and clear-eyed sanity. Isolated from the rest of his conversation, they show that the Noble Savage was one of the tendencies against which he threw his massive bulk.

As early as 1735, in his translation of " Lobo's " *Voyage to Abyssinia*, Johnson's characteristic attitude appears. The preface to this piece of hackwork states that the peoples described by the apochryphal Lobo are neither " devoid of all sense of humanity, or consummate in all private and social virtues. Here are no Hottentots without religion, polity or articulate language; no Chinese . . . completely skilled in all sciences."

In 1735 the Noble Savage was no very formidable enemy. But let us skip thirty years. Johnson, no longer the down-at-heels writer of prefaces, sits on the throne of English letters. His reign, however, is not untroubled. Boswell tells us that " Rousseau's treatise on the inequality of man was at this time a fashionable topic." Ladies and gentlemen were fascinated by the strange new doctrines; and many of them, with a perversity not without modern parallels, espoused or affected to espouse theories which implied their downfall. At first Johnson belittled Rousseau, calling him a maker of paradoxes, " led away by a childish desire of novelty." Before long, however, he was to compliment Rousseau by taking him seriously. In answer to Bozzy's question, " Do you really think him [Rousseau] a bad man? " the retort is crushing: " If you mean to be serious, I think him one of the worst of men; a rascal, who ought to be hunted out of society. . . . I would sooner sign a sentence for his deportation, than that of any felon who has gone from the Old Bailey these many years." [1]

Of Boswell's answer to this outburst we are not informed. One would like to see his face. He has recently been to France, has written Rousseau letters of the most fulsome flattery, has visited the father of French romanticism, and by an idiotic exposure of his inmost soul has

[1] This was in 1766.

established himself on a rather familiar footing with this "rascal" whom he does not now dare to defend.[2] Poor Boswell! His life held many such awkward moments. His decidedly romantic inclinations were the cause of repeated snubs from his master.

Johnson's violence against Rousseau is no doubt wholly sincere. "The Philosopher" recognizes in Jean-Jacques the foe of all that he prizes. From now on, it is war to the death. At no time did Johnson understand Rousseau's man of nature much better than he did the rhythms of Milton or the idealism of Berkeley. What he splutters at in Rousseau is the notion of the savage as natural man which appears in the half-baked discourses. That he ever even considered the problems dealt with in *Émile* and the *Social Contract* is doubtful. In short, he was quite ready to accept the current English caricature of Rousseau as the man who wanted everyone to return to the life of the savage. This fact does not, however, imply that Johnson would have agreed with Rousseau if he had completely understood him. The two men represent diametrically opposed systems of thought.

Rousseau's first discourse held many ideas which were offensive to Johnson, and which he attacked whenever they appeared in conversation. Thus one evening, when Goldsmith, whose flirtations with the Noble Savage we have examined, supports the notion that knowledge brings unhappiness, Johnson insists that "upon the whole, knowledge, *per se*, is certainly an object which every man would wish to attain." His own feeling is summed up in the saying attributed to Aristotle, "that there was the same difference between one learned and one unlearned, as between the living and the dead." Boswell's contention "that a refinement of taste was a disadvantage" he labels

[2] *Letters of James Boswell*, Vol. I, No's. 28, 30, 32, 47.

as "a paltry notion." "Endeavor," he rumbles, "to be as perfect as you can in every respect." The delights of being satisfied with everything through lack of discrimination never appealed to the Lexicographer.

If the *Discourse on the Sciences and Arts* was repugnant to Johnson, that *On the Origins of Inequality* was doubly so. For his part, he held that "mankind are happier in a state of inequality and subordination. Were they to be in this pretty state of equality, they would soon degenerate into brutes; they would become Monboddo's nation; their tails would grow. Sir, all would be losers, were all to work for all: they would have no intellectual improvement. All intellectual improvement arises from leisure: all leisure arises from one working for another." The aim of life is happiness, of which liberal activities are the symbol. No liberal activities without leisure; if a few are to have leisure, many must toil. The argument, while distressing to the equalitarian mind, is not untenable.

Johnson loved to apply the *reductio ad absurdum* to the ideas of those who considered all men their brothers. He once abashed Mrs. Macaulay, an ardent republican, by suggesting that her manservant sit down to table with them. And yet his goodness to the poor and the unfortunate is familiar to all. His strange houseful of derelicts speaks for itself. To Francis Barber, his negro servant, he was unremittingly kind. Johnson never indulged in absurd protestations of equality which were later to be withdrawn. If he was always the master, he was always the gentle, thoughtful and faithful master.

In keeping with Johnson's relations with Francis Barber was his attitude in the case of the negro Knight. The point at issue was the freedom or slavery of the black, whose father had been a slave but who was himself born in England. It is interesting to recall that Lord Monboddo, the Rousseauist and connoisseur of apes, was one of four Lords of the Session who maintained that Knight was a slave; while Dr. Johnson, the hidebound reactionary, provided arguments in favor of the man's freedom.[3] We sometimes need to be reminded that an extreme Tory may possess a warm and generous heart.

The notion that pity is instinctive is of course intensely distasteful to Ursa Major. " Pity," he insists, " is not natural to man. Children are always cruel. Savages are always cruel. Pity is acquired and improved by the cultivation of reason." Note this anthropologically sound use of children and savages to represent the instinctive level of behavior. On another occasion we find him observing that the reason for the splendid physical development of Indians is that weak and diseased members of the race either do not survive, or are not permitted to do so. " Had I been an Indian I must have starved, or they would have knocked me on the head, when they saw I could do nothing." Boswell suggests that the redmen's love of oratory would have led them to spare Johnson. " Nay, Sir," is the reply, " I should not have lived long enough to be fit to talk; I should have been dead before I was ten years old. Depend upon it, Sir, a savage, when he is hungry, will not carry about with him a looby of nine years old who can not help himself. They have no affec-

---

[3] James Burnett, Lord Monboddo, was an eccentric Scotch jurist and philosopher who anticipated certain aspects of the theory of evolution but at the same time managed to be a primitivist of the extremest type. He drew from the Indians evidence as to the state of nature. One of his theories was that the orang-utan is a primitive form of man; but he endowed the ape with some of the attributes of the Noble Savage and thus reconciled the evolutionary and primitivistic elements of his thought. Monboddo also enlarges upon the advantages of going naked, taking cold air-baths, and eating vegetables raw. *Cf.* Bissell, *op. cit.*, pp. 44–46.

tion, Sir." He admits elsewhere that Indians "help some of their children . . . ; for some of them live, which they could not do without being helped." Pity, he believes, is a product of right thinking and right living. " Sir, natural affection is nothing; but affection from principle and established duty is sometimes wonderfully strong." The conception of natural virtue runs counter not only to his humanism, but to his religious feelings. He says of Lord Kames' *Sketches of the History of Man,* " In this book it is maintained that virtue is natural to man, and that if we would but consult our own hearts, we would be virtuous. Now after consulting our own hearts all we can, and with all the helps we have, we find how few of us are virtuous. This is saying a thing which all mankind know not to be true."

Johnson's attack on Kames is typical of his opposition to English and Scotch supporters of Rousseau. His dislike of Monboddo, whose orang-utan we shall meet again in Peacock, is especially intense. The Scotch judge " talked a great deal of nonsense " about savages. " He attacked Lord Monboddo's strange speculations on the primitive state of human nature, observing: ' Sir, it is all conjecture about a thing useless, even were it known to be true! ' " When he hears that " Lord Monboddo still maintains the superiority of the savage life," he exclaims, " What strange narrowness of mind now is that, to think the things we have not known are better than the things which we have known." And one suspects that Monboddo is " that impudent fellow from Scotland, who affected to be a savage, . . . " and who " maintained that there was no distinction between virtue and vice," of whom the Doctor makes the devastating comment, " If he really does think that there is no distinction between virtue and vice, why, Sir, when he leaves our house let us count our spoons."

No less strong is his opposition to Hume, whose relations with Rousseau are well known. In connection with this philosopher's contention "that all who are happy, are equally happy," he makes a shrewd distinction: "A peasant and a philosopher may be equally *satisfied*, but not equally *happy*. Happiness consists in the multiplicity of agreeable consciousness. A peasant has not the same capacity for having equal happiness with a philosopher."

It was this distinction between satisfaction and happiness which prevented Johnson from giving credence to those enthusiastic notions about the blessings of savage life which sentimentality had engrafted upon the Rousseau-istic doctrine. He would have growled at our modern campers who pretend to prefer bad meals to good ones. "A hungry man," he insists, "has not the same pleasure in eating a plain dinner that a hungry man has in eating a luxurious dinner." When Bozzy "attempted to argue for the superior happiness of the savage life, upon the usual fanciful topics," the Doctor overwhelms him: "Sir, there can be nothing more false. The savages have no bodily advantages beyond those of civilized man. They have not better health; and as to care or mental uneasiness, they are not above it, but below it, like bears. No, Sir; you are not to talk such paradox: it cannot entertain, far less can it instruct." Surely beneath all this spluttering and fuming lies a stratum of right reason. To say that savages are below, not above, care, is not only to make a sharp thrust at naturalism, but also to place oneself on the side of those to whom the pursuit of truth is more important than the avoidance of pain.

Johnson believes that those who wish to live like beasts have in their own natures an element of bestiality. "Philosophers tell you that pleasure is *contrary* to happiness. Gross men prefer animal pleasure. So there are men who have preferred living among savages. Now what a wretch must he be, who is content with such conversation as can be had among savages! You may remember an officer at Fort Augustus, who had served in America, told us of a woman whom they were obliged to *bind*, in order to get her back from savage life." Boswell: " She must have been an animal, a beast." Johnson: " Sir, she was a speaking cat."

On one occasion, " a gentleman " — the term is sometimes a cloak for Boswell's own foolishness — quotes from a traveler as follows: " Here am I, free and unrestrained, amidst the rude magnificence of Nature, with this Indian woman by my side, and this gun with which I can procure food when I want it. What more can be desired for human happiness? " Who could resist being moved to enthusiasm by so romantic a picture? But beneath it Johnson scents Rousseau's " food, a female, and sleep " formula. Instantly he smashes the bubble. " Do not allow yourself, Sir, to be imposed upon by such gross absurdity. It is sad stuff; it is brutish. If a bull could speak, he might as well exclaim, — Here am I with this cow and this grass; what being could enjoy greater felicity? "

Johnson loved thus to lay bare sentimental fallacies concerning the state of nature. In that condition, General Paoli once asserts, " a man and woman uniting together would form a strong and constant affection . . . and the same causes of dissension would not arise between them, as occur between husband and wife in a civilized state." " Sir," is the retort, " they would have dissensions enough, though of another kind. One would choose to go a hunting in this wood, the other in that. . . . Besides, Sir, a savage man and a savage woman meet by chance; and when the man sees another woman that pleases him better, he will leave the first." The Doctor is not here at his best: he should have held to his strongest position — that it is better to be above than below care. But on the whole one must marvel at the vigor and competence with which he parries the arguments of his opponents. Even among his best friends he found traces of hankering for the primitive. At tea one day his beloved Mrs. Thrale quotes with approval Garrick's mutilation of a line from *The Winter's Tale*, "I'd smile with the simple, and feed with the poor." It affects Johnson as a red rag a bull. "Nay, my dear lady, this will never do. Poor David! Smile with the simple. What folly is that? And who would feed with the poor that can help it? No, no; let me smile with the wise, and feed with the rich." This witty, human and wise remark may serve to sum up Johnson's attitude toward the blessings of a primitive existence.

It must be admitted that Johnson's ideas as to the life of savages were of an *a priori* character. The only actual savage with whom he ever came in contact — so far as I have been able to discover — was Omai. We already know that the Doctor "was struck with his behavior," but that he ascribed it to the civilizing influence of genteel company.[4] In 1773 some Esquimaux were in London, and the ever-curious Boswell "carried on a short conversation by signs" with them. This fact Johnson refused to believe. His mind, on such matters, was doggedly closed. When Boswell informs him that an American savage has asked a European whether money "will . . . purchase *occupation*," Johnson is quick to smell a rat. "Depend upon it, Sir," he snorts, "this saying is too refined for a savage."

Yet, curiously enough, Johnson himself once succumbed

[4] *Vide supra*, p. 72.

to the lure of Indian oratory. In Number 81 of the *Idler*, an Indian chief watches a column of English troops marching through the forest to attack the French. Turning to his followers, he denounces the pale-faces: " Their power they have never exerted in our defence, and their arts they have studiously concealed from us. Their treaties are only to deceive, and their traffic only to defraud us. They have a written law among them of which they boast as derived from Him who made the earth and sea. . . . Why is not this law communicated to us? It is concealed because it is violated. For how can they preach it to an Indian nation, when I am told that one of its first precepts forbids them to do to others what they would not that others should do to them." If a little fish can talk like a whale, a Noble Savage can talk like Dr. Johnson. The Indian's appeal to Christian doctrine in rebuking Christian conduct is a familiar device. Either Johnson was willing, for journalistic purposes, to bow to a convention for which he had little sympathy, or his ideas had not in 1759 hardened into their anti-primitivistic bias.

So strong has this bias become in Johnson's period of dictatorship that he has little good to say of the published voyages which made the South Seas a fashionable topic of conversation. Boswell admired Forster's *Voyage to the South Seas*, but his idol " did not like it." Johnson later says of the three-volume collection of *Voyages to the South Sea* which appeared in 1784: " *Who* will read them through? A man had better work his way before the mast, than read them through; they will be eaten by rats and mice before they are read through. There is little entertainment in such books; one set of savages is like another." Evidently he sees in all such works a basis on which readers may erect the theories which he detests.

Johnson's lack of enthusiasm for what Mr. O'Brien

terms the "mystic isles" is a thorn in the side of poor Bozzy, whom a conversation with Captain Cook has inflamed "with the general grand and indistinct notion of A VOYAGE ROUND THE WORLD." "Yes, Sir," says Johnson, "but a man is to guard himself against taking a thing in general." He prides himself on the fact that circumnavigators do not tell to him the astounding stories they tell to other people. When "a gentleman" — Boswell? — "expressed a wish to go and live three years at Otaheité, or New Zealand, in order to . . . be satisfied what nature can do for man," Johnson replies: "What could you learn, Sir? What can savages tell, but what they themselves have seen? Of the past, or the invisible, they can tell nothing. The inhabitants of Otaheité and New Zealand are not in a state of pure nature; for it is plain they broke off from some other people. Had they grown out of the ground, you might have judged of a state of nature."

But Boswell, though often subdued, is never permanently silenced. The South Sea isles have a strong attraction for him. "I am well assured," he observes on another occasion, "that the people of Otaheité, who have the bread tree, the fruit of which serves them for bread, laughed heartily when they were informed of the tedious process necessary with us to have bread." This is a typical Noble Savage observation, and it is interesting to see how Johnson deals with it. "Why, Sir," he growls, "all ignorant savages will laugh when they are told of the advantages of civilized life. Were you to tell men who live without houses, how we pile brick upon brick, and rafter upon rafter, and that after a house is raised to a certain height, a man tumbles off a scaffold, and breaks his neck; they would laugh heartily at our folly in building; but it does not follow that men are better without houses. No,

Sir, (holding up a slice of a good loaf) this is better than the bread tree."

This utterance was delivered in 1773. Eleven years later, we find Tahiti still a subject of dissension. Boswell: " I do not think the people of Otaheité can be reckoned savages." Johnson: " Don't cant in defense of savages." Boswell: " They have the art of navigation." Johnson: " A dog or a cat can swim." Boswell: " They carve very ingeniously." Johnson: " A cat can scratch, and a child with a nail can scratch."

" Don't cant in defense of savages! " His cry, uttered so often and so vigorously, was to go unheeded. For some years at least, the cant grew rather than diminished in volume. Johnson was as powerless to stay the onrush of romantic naturalism as Canute to stay the tides. His was a losing fight, but a gallant one.

Dr. Johnson helps us to feel the atmosphere which enveloped the Noble Savage in the early portion of the romantic movement. That atmosphere is characterized by a half-genuine, half-affected recoil from urban sophistication, cold-heartedness and logic toward woodland innocence, sensibility and intuition. As a topic of parlor conversation, the Noble Savage was perhaps never more popular than at this time. But he represented a desire to withdraw from civilization, not a desire to reform the world. The Noble Savage of the revolutionary period, on the other hand, becomes a symbol of perfectibilitarianism.

The young English Jacobin of the 1790's united early romantic sensibility with Godwinian rationalism. He had advanced literary tastes — felt that Pope was coldly artificial, and admired the sonnets of Bowles. In his own work he cultivated a melancholy either gently pensive or more violently Teutonic. On every page were displayed his sensibility and his love of nature. Through his most fervent outbursts, however, ran a strain of solemn didacticism. He was a reformer, a propagandist, whose poems and novels were *Tendenzstücke*. In the same breath he could be coldly romantic and warmly rationalistic. He yearned for a system of society in which the natural virtues could operate unhindered by priests and kings. Hence the French Revolution appeared to him as a great upheaval of essential humanity beneath the smothering burdens imposed upon it by organized society. He advocated, and sometimes vaguely plotted for, an English Revolution.

Among other peculiarities of the Jacobin may be mentioned religious radicalism. To him, formal religious organizations were agencies of oppression. His own beliefs were earnest but uncertain. Emotional deism and naturalistic pantheism attracted him strongly. He was seldom an out-and-out atheist: he had too much heart for that. If to literary, political and religious heterodoxy we add opposition to the conventions of marriage, and a warm interest in prison reform, the anti-slavery movement and perhaps in vegetarianism, we shall have a fairly accurate cross-section of the Jacobin mind.

The British government, serious, unimaginative and panicky, " viewed with alarm " the opinions and activities of the Jacobins. It developed a persecution mania which soon became a mania for persecution.

The *Anti-Jacobin*, of which the first issue appeared on November 20, 1797, adopted different and more appropriate tactics. Its aim was to laugh the Jacobins out of court by exposing to satire all their foibles, literary, social and political. The editor-in-chief was William Gifford, the veteran satirist whose *Baviad* and *Maeviad* had already smashed the bubble of the Della Cruscans. The new organ, however, gave little scope for his heavy, old-fashioned method of attack, and he confined himself mainly to prose contributions. With him was associated George Ellis, who had already acquired a reputation as a writer of political satire. The Revolution had led this former member of the *Esto Perpetua* club into the Tory camp. As with his friend Walter Scott, his interest in the Middle Ages did not imply approval of romantic politics.

Much of the cutting liveliness of the *Anti-Jacobin* was due to the work of two younger wits destined to be famous in later days — George Canning and John Hookham Frere. Both were Eton boys. Canning had recently come down from Oxford, and Frere from Cambridge. They were young, clever, learned and well-bred. Besides the serious political purpose which actuated their older associates, Canning and Frere had a lively temperamental antipathy toward their foes. To them, Jacobins were "cads" and "rotters." It is the opposition of Coke Clifton to Frank Henley, transferred from literature into real life.

Like most satirists with a practical aim, the *Anti-Jacobin* group did not stop to distinguish levels of merit and fine shades of opinion among their opponents. The term "Jacobinism" was used almost as indiscriminately as "Bolshevism" in our own day. One was either pure Tory or pure traitor. Yet this lumping together of all sorts of people and all sorts of tendencies was carried on with great brilliance. In a sense, the attempt of the Anti-Jacobins was the attempt of modern scholarship — to find unity beneath the various tendencies of the age. They saw the period unsteadily, but saw it whole. Perhaps synthesis can be arrived at in no other way.

The Anti-Jacobins,[5] for instance, felt a connection between the political attitude of the Jacobins and sensibility, that " sweet child of sickly fancy " whom Rousseau carried with him into exile:

> " Mark her fair votaries, prodigal of grief,
>   With cureless pangs, and woes that mock relief,
>   Droop in soft sorrow o'er a faded flower;
>   O'er a dead jackass pour the pearly shower;
>   But hear, unmoved, of Loire's ensanguined flood
>   Choked up with slain; of Lyons drenched in blood;
>
> . . . .
>
>   Of hearts torn reeking from the mangled breast,
>   They hear — and hope, that all is for the best."

In this poem, *The New Morality,* are mentioned as horrible examples Coleridge, Southey, Lloyd, Lamb, Priestley, Whitfield, Thelwall, Paine, Williams, Godwin and Holcroft.   Here we have an excellent illustration of the faults and virtues of the *Anti-Jacobin.*   It is unfair to state that the English radicals were " unmoved " at hearing of " Loire's ensanguined flood" : practically all of them were profoundly shocked and discouraged by the Terror.   It is equally unfair to name Charles Lamb and Tom Paine as disciples of the same philosophy.   On the other hand, the passage is not without validity.   As we have observed in a previous chapter, there was certainly some connection between the cult of sensibility and political radicalism.   It is true, also, that in the early stages of the Terror many young Jacobins did " hope that all is for the best " ; such was for a time the feeling of Mary Wollstonecraft and of Coleridge.   In 1798, when *The New Morality* appeared, the accusation was no longer just; but even the most up-to-date of satires is likely to

[5] In the following remarks, no attempt will be made to specify the contributions of Ellis, Canning and Frere.

have a reminiscent tinge. And those eleven men who are branded as Jacobins were not in the 1790's quite so different from each other as they later became. On the whole, considering the fact that satire without unfairness is a contradiction in terms, the *Anti-Jacobin* scored a high percentage of accurate hits.

Of course the man whom these satirists particularly detested was William Godwin. Through the time-worn device of the "mock correspondent," the revolutionary philosopher figures in the pages of the *Anti-Jacobin* as Mr. Higgins, of St. Mary-Axe. This gentleman combines in his single person every tendency striven against by his creators. He is the arch-Jacobin.

Higgins makes known his beliefs in an illuminating letter. "What you call the new principles," he assures the editors, "are, in fact, nothing less than new. They are the principles of primeval nature, the system of original and unadulterated man." Just here, the impatient reader may be assured, is where the Noble Savage idea enters.

The aim of Higgins "is to restore this first and pure simplicity; to rescue and recover the interesting nakedness of human nature, by ridding her of the cumbrous establishments which the folly, and pride, and self-interest of the worst part of our species have heaped upon her." Apart from the excellence of this as parody, is it not interesting as showing the connection between primitivistic thinking and English radical opinion? But let Mr. Higgins continue:

"Our first principle is, then, the reverse of the trite and dull maxim of Pope — 'Whatever is, is right.' We contend that, 'Whatever is, is wrong': that institutions, civil and religious, that social order (as it is called in your cant) and regular government and law, and I know not what other fantastic inventions, are but . . . so many badges of his degradation from the primal purity and excellence of his nature." So much for Rousseauistic pessimism; now for the other side:

"Our second principle is 'the eternal and absolute perfectibility of man.' We contend that if, as is demonstrable, we have risen from a level with the cabbages of the field to our present comparatively intelligent and dignified state by the mere exertion of our own energies, we should if these energies were not repressed and subdued by the operation of prejudice and folly, by kingcraft and priestcraft, and the other evils incident to what is called Civilized Society, continue to exert and expand ourselves in a proportion infinitely greater than anything of which we have any notion . . . but which would in time raise man from his present biped state to a rank more worthy of his endowments and aspirations; to a rank in which he would be, as it were, all mind; would enjoy unclouded perspicacity, and perpetual vitality; feed on oxygen, and never die but by his own consent." Here is that union of pessimism toward the present with optimism toward the past and toward the future when approached *via* the past — a process of getting ahead by going backward. Somehow, everything would be different if mankind could be given a fresh start.

Nothing so extravagant as this is to be found in the works of Godwin, who, with all his faults, was a man of real intelligence. But we have seen in Holcroft, Bage, and the Pantisocrats this very blend of primitivism and perfectibilitarianism. The satire is at least true to the general tenor of Jacobin thought.

Higgins does not confine to prose the expression of his theories. He sends the editors copious samples of his great didactic poem in forty cantos, *The Progress of Man*.

This, the work of Canning, Gifford and Frere, is one of the finest parodies in our literature. It is dedicated to Richard Payne Knight, and imitates the matter and manner of that savant's *Progress of Civil Society* (1796).

It is only fair to state that Knight, though tinged with Jacobinism, was no friend of the Noble Savage. His perfectibilitarianism was consistent, and, in intention at least, scientific. He applies to anthropology the spirit which Erasmus Darwin, another victim of the *Anti-Jacobin*,[6] applies to botany. Although savages are free from certain ills of modern life, says Knight, they are too bestial to be admired or envied. Men do not deteriorate from a state of primal goodness; they steadily advance from a state of primal animalism. But the *Anti-Jacobin* group were in no mood to discriminate. Knight was a Jacobin, an eccentric, a sceptic, and a very bad poet. He had written a much-abused book on Priapism, and had said in the *Progress of Civil Society* that marriage would be less often unhappy if it were easier to dissolve. Though he did not praise savages, he mentioned them with suspicious frequency. Hence the *Anti-Jacobin* ascribed to Knight a belief in the Noble Savage, which, though common enough among his fellow-radicals, he himself did not happen to entertain. In other respects the parody is very close.

The editors declare that the portion of the first canto which has been submitted to them " contains so happy a deduction of man's present state of depravity from the first slips and failings of his original state, and inculcates so forcibly the mischievous consequences of social or civilized as opposed to natural society, that no dread of imputed imitation can prevent us from giving it to our readers." The delicious argument runs thus: " Man only discontented — born a Savage; not choosing to con-

6 *Cf. The Loves of the Triangles*, a parody of Darwin's *Loves of the Plants*.

tinue so, becomes polished — resigns his Liberty — Priest-craft — Kingcraft — Tyranny of Laws and Institutions. — Savage Life — description thereof. — The Savage free — roaming Woods — feeds on Hips and Haws — Animal Food — first notion of it from seeing a Tiger tearing his Prey — wonders if it is good — resolves to try — makes a Bow and Arrow — kills a Pig — resolves to roast a part of it — lights a Fire — Apostrophe to Fires — Spits and Jacks not yet invented. — Digression. — Corinth. — Sheffield. — Love the most natural desire after Food. — Savage Courtship. — Concubinage recommended. — Satirical Reflections on Parents and Children — Husbands and Wives — against collateral Consanguinity. — Freedom the only Morality, etc., etc., etc."

Like young Shelley in the notes to *Queen Mab*, Higgins sees in a vegetable diet one of the chief sources of the virtues of natural man:

> " Lo! the rude savage, free from civil strife,
> Keeps the smooth tenour of his guiltless life;
> Restrained by none, save Nature's lenient laws,
> Quaffs the clear stream, and feeds on hips and haws.
> Light to his daily sports behold him rise;
> The bloodless banquet health and strength supplies."

The pig whose slaughter marks the end of all this innocence is magnificently apostrophized:

> " Not unrevenged thou diest! — In after times
> From thy spilt blood shall spring unnumbered crimes.
> Soon shall the slaughterous arms that wrought thy woe,
> Improved by malice, deal a deadlier blow;
> When social man shall pant for nobler game,
> And 'gainst his fellow-man the vengeful weapon aim."

This initial act of brutality, indeed, is seen as the root of all civilized carnage:

> " As love, as gold, as jealousy inspires,
> As wrathful hate, or wild ambition fires,
> Urged by the statesman's craft, the tyrant's rage,
> Embattled nations endless wars shall wage,
> Vast seas of blood the ravaged field shall stain,
> And millions perish — that a King may reign! "

Thinking the very liberal-minded attitude of the radical group toward marriage and allied problems worthy of attention, the editors devote the twenty-third canto of Mr. Higgins' poem to a description of " the vicious refinement of what is called Civilized Society in respect to marriage."   Again it would be unjust to deprive the reader of the argument: " Marriage being indissoluble, the cause of its being so often unhappy. — Nature's Laws not consulted in this point. — Civilized Nations mistaken. — Otaheité — Happiness of the Natives Thereof — Visited by Captain Cook, in his Majesty's ship *Endeavour* — Character of Captain Cook. — Address to Circumnavigation. — . . . Arrival at Otaheité — Cast Anchor — Land — Natives astonished. — Love — Liberty — Moral — Natural — Religious — Contrasted with European Manners — Strictness — Licence — Doctors' Commons — Dissolubility of Marriage recommended — Illustrated by a Game at Cards — Whist — Cribbage — Partners changed — Why not the same in Marriage? — Illustrated by a River. — Love free — Priests, Kings. — German Drama — Kotzebue's ' Housekeeper Reformed.' — Moral Employments of Housekeeping described. — Hottentots sit and stare at each other — Query, why? Address to the Hottentots — History of the Cape of Good Hope — Résumé of the Arguments against Marriage. — Conclusion." [7]   What complete malicious understanding!

[7] With " Illustrated by a river " compare Shelley's *Love's Philosophy*:

> " The fountains mingle with the river,
> And the rivers with the ocean."

The editors were shrewd enough to perceive the sensual element in the exoticism of their time. Had they lived to-day, they would have been quick to point out the connection between such works as *Noa Noa* or *White Shadows in the South Seas* and cabaret songs like " My Hula Maid " and " The Beach at Waikiki." There is an identity of desire, differently expressed. Kipling is at least frank:

> " Ship me somewhere east of Suez,
>   Where the best is like the worst;
>   Where there ain't no ten commandments,
>   And a man can raise a thirst."

Of all lands of the Noble Savage, Tahiti is especially fated to stir the imaginations of civilized men who dream of " a neater, sweeter maiden, in a cleaner, greener land." As Mr. Higgins puts it:

> " There laughs the sky, there zephyr's frolic train,
>   And light-winged loves, and blameless pleasures reign:
>   There, when two souls congenial ties unite,
>   No hireling Bonzes chant the mystic rite:
>   Free every thought, each action unconfined,
>   And light those fetters which no rivets bind.
>   There in each grove, each sloping bank along,
>   And flowers and shrubs, and odorous herbs among,
>   Each shepherd clasped, with undisguised delight,
>   His yielding fair one — in the captain's sight;
>   Each yielding fair, as chance or fancy led,
>   Preferred new lovers to her sylvan bed.
>   Learn hence, each nymph, whose free aspiring mind
>   Europe's cold laws, and colder customs bind —
>   O! learn, what Nature's genial laws decree —
>   What Otaheité is, let Britain be! " [8]

Here one pauses to ask whether Dr. Johnson, in his grudging attitude toward accounts of exploration, may not

[8] *Anti-Jacobin*, No. XXVI. I have already queried whether Byron could have known these lines when he wrote *The Island*.

have had some premonition of what was to come. Boswell's vague and hesitant hankerings have crystallized in the cry, " What Otaheité is, let Britain be! " We are dealing, of course, with a parody, but no one who has read thus far will deny the essential accuracy of the thrust here delivered.

If Johnson attacks the Noble Savage of the age of sensibility, the *Anti-Jacobin* attacks the Noble Savage of revolutionary enthusiasm. We know that the individual and collective disillusionment which succeeded the Jacobins' early sympathy for France resulted in an attempt to find peace in nature. This movement, at first merely one of retreat, evolved an optimistic philosophy of which the Noble Savage again served as a symbol. In this stage of the development of our subject, Thomas Love Peacock is the most interesting hostile critic of the savage.

To call Peacock an " enemy of the Noble Savage " is perhaps to speak rashly. His attitude lacked both the uneasy spleen of Johnson and the conscious political animus of the Anti-Jacobins. For the latter, indeed, he felt a strong distaste: his sketch of Mr. Anyside Antijack in *Melincourt* is scathing.[9] Liberty he loved too dearly to approve the " one-hundred-per-cent English " policy. One cannot easily pigeonhole a man who could make merciless fun of Shelley and at the same time be that poet's warm friend. Indeed, Peacock is remarkable for his ability to take a position far removed from the strifes of the time. He puts in Mr. Crotchet's mouth the words, " The sentimental against the rational, the intuitive against the inductive, the ornamental against the useful, the in-

[9] Antijack is probably Canning. *Works of Thomas Love Peacock*, Vol. I, p. 325, and note.

tense against the tranquil, the romantic against the classical; these are great and interesting controversies which I should like, before I die, to see satisfactorily settled." Such was Peacock's wise and humane spirit. There can be no doubt, however, that his own tastes were on the side of the rational, the inductive, the useful, the tranquil — in a word, the classical. He liked to poke fun at the more extravagant aspects of romanticism, especially at melancholy and the nature-cult.

In *Headlong Hall*, the first of the series,[10] we find a number of strange characters assembled at the manor of Squire Headlong. Most prominent among the guests are Foster, the perfectibilitarian, and Escot, the deteriorationist. The former has a boundless belief in human progress; the latter maintains that the world is going to the dogs, and holds forth at great length on the superiority of primitive existence.

Mr. Carl Van Doren, in his *Life of Thomas Love Peacock*, advances in regard to these characters a theory which seems to me untenable. He writes: " The partial identity of Mr. Escot and Mr. Foster . . . with Peacock and Shelley respectively, probably points to an origin for the story in the duels of opinion which the two friends had fought in their walks of the preceding summer and fall." " It is natural at the outset," we read later, " to suspect that Mr. Foster, whose zealous defence of progress is his principal characteristic, must have been in part suggested to Peacock by the similar habit in Shelley; and it is equally natural to suspect further that Mr. Escot, the pessimist, may very reasonably represent Peacock himself, or, rather, the character he would assume in the presence of such a Shelley as Mr. Foster." [11]

---

[10] Published December 1815; dated 1816.
[11] *Life of Peacock*, p.78 and pp. 89–90.

Even with the saving grace of the word "partial," these identifications are questionable. Foster, to be sure, is a perfectibilitarian; so was Shelley. But Foster believes that for things to be perfected they need only progress from where they are, while for Shelley perfection is to be attained only through sweeping changes in the structure of society which will enable the natural goodness of man to develop freely. In 1815, Shelley's doctrine of perfectibility is not unlike that of Mr. Higgins, the *Anti-Jacobin's* mock correspondent, and Shelley's father-in-law in disguise. Foster and Shelley hold very different views.

Escot is a deteriorationist, and Peacock was certainly opposed to the doctrine of perfectibility. But until the querulousness of old age came upon him, he never asserted that the world was going downhill. He simply repudiated the unphilosophic notion of a law of continuous and inevitable progress, and distinguished clearly between activity and accomplishment. Escot, as citations to follow will abundantly prove, believes in the Noble Savage. Peacock certainly does not believe in the Noble Savage, who, leaving *Headlong Hall* out of the question, is broadly satirized in *Melincourt*. It is difficult to see in Escot a mouthpiece for the ideas of Peacock.

Let us hear Escot, who, while eating a hearty breakfast, discourses on the degeneration of the race through flesh-eating: "The natural and original man . . . lived in the woods: the roots and fruits of the earth supplied his simple nutriment: he had few desires, and no diseases. But, when he began to sacrifice victims on the altar of superstition, to pursue the goat and the deer, and by the pernicious invention of fire, to pervert their flesh into food, luxury, disease and premature death were let loose upon the world. *Such is clearly the correct interpretation of the fable of Prometheus, which is a symbolical portraiture* of *that disastrous epoch, when man first applied fire to culinary purposes, and thereby surrendered his liver to the vulture of disease.*" [12] This sounds like Mr. Higgins, in the first canto of the *Progress of Man*. It sounds even more like Shelley, who in his notes to *Queen Mab* devotes a great deal of space to a defence of vegetarianism. We cull the following: " I hold that the depravity of the physical and moral nature of man originated in his unnatural habits of life. . . . The allegory of Adam and Eve eating of the tree of evil . . . admits of no other explanation than the disease and crime that have flowed from unnatural diet. . . . *The story of Prometheus is one likewise which, although universally admitted to be allegorical, has never been satisfactorily explained. . . . Prometheus (who represents the human race) effected some great change in the condition of his nature, and applied fire to culinary purposes; thus inventing an expedient for screening from his disgust the horrors of the shambles. From this moment his vitals were devoured by the vulture of disease.* . . . All vice rose from the ruin of healthful innocence. Tyranny, superstition, commerce and inequality were then first known, when reason vainly attempted to guide the wanderings of exacerbated passion." [13] Compare the passages from *Headlong Hall* and the notes to *Queen Mab*, especially the italicized portions. If Escot is Peacock, why is he made to deliver a close paraphrase of Shelley's own words?

I conclude that Escot is not Peacock, that Foster is not Shelley, and that although Foster and Peacock have little in common, there are various points of resemblance between Escot and the young Shelley. The resemblance, however, should not be pressed too closely. The satire of

[12] *Works of Thomas Love Peacock*, Vol. I, p. 7. Italics, mine.
[13] *Vide supra*, p. 306. Italics, mine.

Headlong Hall is typical, whereas Peacock and Shelley are highly individual. Foster and Escot are embodied theories rather than parodied persons. This matter of identity has been discussed at some length, not because of any inborn contentiousness on my part, but simply because Peacock cannot be opposed to the Noble Savage and be Escot at the same time. We may now drop the subject and examine some of the verbal clashes between Foster and Escot.

The first of these disagreements occurs when Foster and Escot are riding to Headlong Hall in a coach. Foster is delighted by the prosperous appearance of the country through which they are passing. " Everything we look on," he exclaims, " attests the progress of mankind in all the arts of life, and demonstrates their gradual advancement towards a state of unlimited perfection." " These improvements, as you call them," retorts his companion, " appear to me only so many links in the great chain of corruption, which will soon fetter the human race in irreparable slavery and incurable wretchedness: your improvements proceed in a simple ratio, while the factitious wants and unnatural appetites they engender proceed in a compound one; . . . till every human being becomes such a helpless compound of perverted inclinations, that he is altogether at the mercy of external circumstances, loses all independence and singleness of character, and degenerates so rapidly from the primitive dignity of his sylvan origin, that it is scarcely possible to indulge in any other expectation, than that the whole species must at length be exterminated by its own infinite imbecility and vileness."

" You will allow," objects Foster, " that the wild man of the woods could not transport himself over two hundred miles of forest, with as much facility as one of these vehicles transports you and me through the heart of this cultivated country." Escot's answer illustrates admirably that confusion of happiness with satisfaction against which Johnson protested. " I am certain," he says, " . . . that a wild man can travel an immense distance without fatigue; but what is the advantage of locomotion? The wild man is happy in one spot, and there he remains; the civilized man is wretched in every place he happens to be in, and then congratulates himself on being accommodated with a machine, that will whirl him to another, where he will be just as miserable as ever."

Not long after their arrival at the hall, the illuminati whom Squire Headlong has assembled inspect the neighborhood of Mt. Snowdon; and a dispute arises as to whether the scenery might be improved through the services of a landscape architect. Mr. Foster of course takes the affirmative side, but Mr. Escot, equally of course, " did not think that any human being could improve upon it, but had no doubt of its having changed considerably for the worse, since the days when the barren rocks were covered with the immense forest of Snowdon, which must have contained a very fine race of wild men, not less than ten feet high." The great stature of primitive man was one of Lord Monboddo's favorite theses, and is mentioned several times in *Melincourt*, of which Monboddo is the principal butt. To return for a moment to the point of contention, it is unlikely that Peacock, as Escot, should use one of the pet notions of a man whom he thought ridiculous. The idea is much more characteristic of the youthful Shelley.

Foster and Escot would naturally fall out about the effects of knowledge upon morals. It is Foster's belief " that men are virtuous in proportion as they are enlightened; and that, as every generation increases in knowledge, it also increases in virtue " — a position much like Dr.

Johnson's. "I wish it were so," answers the deteriorationist, ". . . but to me the very reverse appears to be the fact. The progress of knowledge is not general: it is confined to a chosen few of every age. How far these are better than their neighbors, we may examine by and bye. The mass of mankind is composed of beasts of burden. . . . Give me the wild man of the woods; the original, unthinking, unscientific, unlogical savage; in him there is at least some good; but, in a civilized, sophisticated, cold-blooded, mechanical, calculating slave of Mammon and the world there is none — absolutely none. . . . Sir, if I fall into a river, an unsophisticated man will jump in and bring me out; but a philosopher will look on with the utmost calmness, and consider me in the light of a projectile." This is a restatement, in concrete form, of the old doctrine of natural pity to which Rousseau had given a new impetus.

Rousseau's influence, also, perhaps accounts for Escot's opinion that reason is destructive of happiness. "On the score of happiness," he says to Foster, "what comparison can you make between the tranquil being of the wild man of the woods and the wretched and turbulent existence of Milton . . . ? The records of literature demonstrate that Happiness and Intelligence are seldom sisters."

But the most characteristic of Escot's speeches is the following combination of Rousseauism with one of the young Shelley's pet theories: "The first inhabitants of the world knew not the use either of wine or animal food; it is, therefore, by no means incredible that they lived to the age of several centuries, free from war, and commerce . . . and every other species of desolating wickedness. But man was then a very different animal to what he now is: he had not the faculty of speech; he was not encumbered with clothes; he lived in the open air. . . .

His first dwellings, of course, were the hollows of trees and rocks. In process of time he began to build: thence grew villages; thence grew cities. Luxury, oppression, poverty, misery and disease kept pace with the progress of his pretended improvements, till, from a free, strong, healthy, peaceful animal, he has become a weak, cruel, carnivorous slave."

Mr. Van Doren is no doubt right in supposing that the debates between Foster and Escot find their origin in actual debates between Peacock and Shelley. The primitivism which Peacock burlesques in *Headlong Hall* is the primitivism of the boy Shelley, whose ideas at this period were much like those of the young Jacobins of the 1790's. It is a remarkable fact that Shelley, until he wrote *Alastor*, was definitely *behind* his own times. In 1810 and 1811, he practices a crude and outworn form of Gothicism. From 1812 to 1817, he subscribes to a Godwinism which Godwin himself had abandoned some years earlier. Thus the Noble Savage idea as it appears in *Headlong Hall* belongs to, say, 1795 rather than to 1816, the date of the book's appearance.

In *Melincourt*, which was published in the following year, Peacock adds to the earlier form of the Noble Savage idea the nature-philosophy of Wordsworth. The new combination is seen in the character of Sylvan Forester. He is described by Sir Telegraph Paxarett as "always railing at civilized life, and always holding forth in praise of savages and original men."

His first appearance sets the key to his conduct throughout the story. Sir Telegraph, meeting him in the mountains of Westmoreland, exclaims, "Who should have dreamed of meeting you in this uncivilized part of the world?" "I am afraid," is Forester's reply, "this part of the world does not deserve the compliment you have bestowed upon it. Within no very great distance from this spot are divers towns, villages and hamlets, in any one of which, if you have money, you may make pretty sure of being cheated, and if you have none, quite sure of being starved — strong evidences of a state of civilization."

Forester, like Escot, holds that mankind is decreasing in size and strength. This is a favorite tenet of Monboddo's, who is one of the chief victims of *Melincourt*. According to Forester, man's physical degeneration is due to the fact that " under the influence of civilization . . . the intellectual are confessedly nourished at the expense of the physical faculties. Air, the great source and fountain of health and life, can scarcely find access to civilized man, muffled as he is in clothes, pent in houses, smoke-dried in cities, half-roasted by artificial fire, and parboiled in the hydrogen of crowded apartments."

From such conditions, Forester loves to flee to the Lake Country, where "Nature seems to have raised her mountain-barriers for the purpose of rescuing a few favored mortals from the vortex of that torrent of physical and moral degeneration which seems to threaten nothing less than the extermination of the human species." Here and elsewhere in Forester's speeches, we are reminded of Wordsworth's letter to C. J. Fox.

To the Lake Country Forester escorts the fair heroine, Anthelia, remarking, "You will find . . . in the little valley we are about to enter, a few specimens of that simple and natural life which approaches as nearly as the present state of things will admit to my ideas of the habits and manners of the primeval agriculturists, or the fathers of the Roman republic." Anthelia observes that she has always longed to see the pastoral pictures of Spenser and Tasso realized " in the actual inhabitants of the country."

Forester replies that even the simple cottagers are doomed to corruption, but that " whatever be the increasing ravages of the Triad of Mammon, avarice, luxury and disease, they will always be the last involved in the vortex of progressive degeneracy, realizing the beautiful fiction of ancient poetry, that, when primeval Justice departed from the earth, her last steps were among the cultivators of the fields." [14] Observe how natural the transition from belief in the Noble Savage to belief in the English rustic. In 1817, savages and peasants are still being compared to shepherds of the Golden Age.

It must not be supposed that Forester is allowed to orate without let or hindrance. He has a dogged opponent in Mr. Fax, who speaks, in some measure at least, for Peacock himself. Mr. Fax has no illusions about the enlightenment, but hopes that good may come from " the general diffusion of moral and political truth." Though there may never be another Homer or Milton, " Lucretius we may yet hope for." The two men hold an argument on progress so serious and fairly-balanced that it rises above the level of burlesque.

Forester admits that the decay of superstition is beneficial, but questions whether the growth of luxury does not counterbalance the benefits. " The corporeal decay of mankind I hold to be undeniable; the increase of general knowledge I allow: but reason is of slow growth; and if men in general only become more corrupt as they become more learned, the progress of literature will oppose no adequate counterpoise to that of avarice, luxury and disease."

Fax retorts that though the progress of reason is slow, " the ground which it once has gained it never abandons."

[14] The reference is to *Georgics*, II, 473.

In spite of self-interest and prejudice, intelligence gradually diffuses itself through society. Forester insists that
the love of truth is " of all qualities . . . the most rare."
Pointing to the evils of public life, he says that retirement from the world is the only recourse open to a virtuous man.

But "if reason be progressive, however slowly," is
Fax's reply, " the wise and good have sufficient encouragement to persevere; and even if the doctrine of deterioration be true, it is no less their duty to retard its
progress." Retirement, then, should be " consecrated to
philosophical labour."

Forester thinks that theoretical knowledge can never
progress rapidly enough to keep pace with the " accelerated
depravation of practical morality." Greed governs the
world as never before, and " blights the blossoms of love."

Fax says that greed is as old as human society. Forester
shifts ground, and asks " how far the security of property
. . . is favorable to the growth of individual virtue."
Wealth, replies Fax, is the means of tranquillity and
leisure, and from these arise many benefits.

But Forester thinks that the leisure gained by wealth is
used for selfish ends. " The *elegant* philosopher is much
too refined . . . to allow such vulgar subjects as the
sufferings of the poor to interfere with his sublime speculations." Fax readily admits that " those *elegant* philosophers are among the most fatal enemies of the
advancement of moral and political knowledge."

Real "public feeling and national sympathy," according
to Forester, exist only among the uncivilized. " The
Canadian savages cannot imagine the possibility of any
individual in a community having a full meal while another has but half a one: still less could they imagine that
one should have two meals, while another had nothing.

Theirs is that bond of brotherhood which nature weaves and civilization breaks, and from which the older nations grow the farther they recede."

Such conditions are possible, says Fax, in a small and primitive community. We are working through a distressing middle period on the far side of which may be a genuinely free and at the same time civilized existence. "I form the best hopes for my country in the mental improvement of my people."

Here, of course, nothing is settled, but the setting forth of the two contrasting types of thought is singularly clear and satisfying.

Another source of dispute between these discordant natures is the supposed beneficent influence of mountain scenery. "A modern poet has observed," says Forester, "that the voices of the sea and the mountains are the two voices of liberty: the words mountain liberty have, indeed, become so intimately associated, that I have never found any one who even thought of questioning their necessary and natural connection." [15]

This sentiment is regarded by Mr. Fax as "a most gross delusion." "I have often seen," he continues, "a young man of high and aspiring genius . . . withdrawn from all intercourse with polished and intellectual society, by the distempered idea that he would nowhere find fit aliment for his high cogitations, but among heaths, and rocks, and torrents." "Mountaineers," he insists, "are for the most part a stupid and ignorant race, and where there are stupidity and ignorance, there will be superstition; and where there is superstition, there will be slavery. . . . All I mean to say is, that there is nothing in the nature of mountain scenery either to make men free or to keep them so. The only source of freedom is intellectual light. The

[15] The reference is, of course, to Wordsworth's sonnet.

ignorant are always slaves, though they dwell among the Andes. The wise are always free, though they cultivate a savannah." Here Wordsworth is quite evidently glanced at.

An important feature of *Melincourt* has till now been withheld. In its pages appears a genuine man of nature. Sir Oran Haut-ton, Forester's boon companion, is an orang-utan, " a specimen of the natural and original man." He is strong, healthy, amiable, simple and pleasing in manner. " He was caught by an intelligent negro very young, in the woods of Angola; and his gentleness and sweet temper winning the hearts of the negro and negress, they brought him up in their cottage as the play-fellow of their little boys and girls." Sir Oran was pur-chased by one Captain Hawltaught, who was " struck with the contemplative cast of his countenance." Though at first homesick almost to the point of death, the noble monkey gradually grew deeply attached to the Captain; and when the latter retired from the sea, accompanied him as gardener.

Although he never learned to speak, Sir Oran acquired most other human accomplishments. He had a pretty taste in music, and performed creditably on the flute and French horn. His taste for strong drink was equally acute, for the Captain corrupted " the amiable simplicity of the natural man by this pernicious celebration of vinous and spirituous orgies." In spite of this vice, however, Sir Oran remains " a much better man than many that are to be found in civilized countries." He plays an impor-tant part in the story, performing many virtuous deeds. He is unanimously elected to Parliament from the borough of Onevote. The noble ape's adventures sometimes recall those of Bage's Hermsprong.

Through Sir Oran, Peacock means to poke fun at the

vagaries of Lord Monboddo, selections from whose *Ancient Metaphysics* and *Progress of Language* are employed as footnotes. Practically all the absurd things said by Forester in praise of Sir Oran were actually written by Monboddo. Why Peacock should grant so much attention to Monboddo is not clear. So far as I can find, the Scotchman was not being much read at this time. Possibly he is selected to represent the highest possible degree of absurdity in the philosophy Peacock wishes to satirize. Probably, too, the eccentric Scotchman was kept fresh in Peacock's mind by the similar opinions of Shelley regarding the physical decadence of man.

But, as we have observed, the rather antiquated primitivism of Monboddo is here mingled with the more recent primitivism which is related to the nature-philosophy of Wordsworth. The virtues of natural man are no longer abstractions floating in the air, but are associated with the healing and inspiring influence of scenery. Peacock is still somewhat behind the times, for by 1816 Wordsworth, Coleridge and Southey had forsaken nature-worship. Yet with the exception of Coleridge, who was coming into his own as a damaged archangel, the Lakists were at this time decidedly unpopular because of their " apostacy." Peacock is not alone in reviving their early theories for satirical purposes. His burlesque applies to the Noble Savage of 1798–1802.

Nightmare Abbey, Peacock's best work, contains nothing which bears directly upon the Noble Savage. Except for Scythrop, who represents a much more Radcliffian youth than the real Shelley of 1818, the characters and their foibles are genuinely contemporary with the satirist. Peacock here glances at sentimentality, Byronic melancholy, and transcendentalism. Even for one who was unusually slow to forget the joke of primitivism, the

Noble Savage was no longer worth satirizing. *Crotchet Castle* (1831) is equally barren of material for us, and *Gryll Grange* (1861) is wholly beyond our ken.

Though by considering the enemies of the Noble Savage we have in a sense reviewed the main features of the whole subject, a brief historical summary will not be out of place at this point. The Noble Savage arises in the Renaissance as the result of the interplay of ancient and medieval primitivistic conceptions, explorers' reports, and the naturalism of the sixteenth century. For the development of the idea in France between Montaigne and the middle of the seventeenth century, the reader must seek the invaluable help of Professor Chinard.

So far as I have been able to discover, the Noble Savage plays no part in English literature until the restoration of the Stuarts, when he is imported from France as a subtype of the exotic genus of the heroic species. The Aztecs and Peruvians of Davenant, Howard and Dryden, while not true Noble Savages, look forward to the figure as he appears in the Romantic Movement. *Oroonoko*, though mainly heroic, is still more suggestive of future developments. The Almanzor type of savage continues to appear in eighteenth century literature, especially in drama, but his original traits become influenced by sentimental naturalism.

The savage makes his first notable appearance as a vehicle of satire in Steele's *Tatler* paper on the four Indian kings. The satirical tradition, increasingly blended with romantic elements, continues throughout the eighteenth and early nineteenth centuries, Byron and Landor being its last exemplars.

What may be called " Early Romanticism " extends from about 1730 to about 1790. The period is characterized by an increasingly conscious repudiation of the ideals of rationalism and of urban civilization. The Noble Savage is gradually adopted as an illustration of the freedom, simplicity and general closeness to nature which the age admired. He also, in his " Götzistic " aspect, satisfies the prevalent hankering for untrammelled wildness. In the 1760's, the growing influence of Rousseau, though his ideas are but imperfectly understood, gives a new seriousness to the Noble Savage, who becomes a genuine warning to the Enlightenment. Then, too, the reports of explorers in America and the South Seas, and the visits of actual savages to England, make the Noble Savage, between 1760 and 1780, a popular social and literary fad.

The outbreak of the French Revolution created in England a curious combination of *philosophe* rationalism and early romantic sensibility. This confusion is reflected in the Noble Savage. He exemplifies one aspect of the doctrine of perfectibility — perfectibility, one might say, through retrogression. In him may be seen that essential human worth which is to provide the basis of the coming Utopia. He justifies condemnation of the old civilization, and hope for the new.

The collapse of revolutionary enthusiasm is followed by a return to nature at first more disillusioned and later more hopeful than the weaker naturalism of pre-revolutionary days. The Noble Savage, though he begins to lose much of his broadly popular appeal, supports for a time the nature-philosophy of the Lakists and their followers.

The history of the Noble Savage from 1810 to 1830 is in the main the history of a dying convention. As we have seen, there are numerous exceptions to this statement. He does rather frequently appear as a picturesque figure, and his appearances are generally accompanied by the time-honored praises of nature. But as science begins to give a true if harsher picture of the universe, the conception of nature inevitably changes. It becomes more and more difficult to think of her as a kind mother to whom one may fly from the buffets of civilization. And the evolutionary conception of man likewise makes it more and more difficult to regard primitive beings as ideal. Hence the Noble Savage, deprived of his philosophical significance, becomes a mere outworn fad, and gradually gives place to other aspects of the romantic spirit. He is as immortal as the phoenix, but he dies one of his many deaths in the neighborhood of 1820.

CHAPTER X

THE CHILD OF NATURE AND THE
NOBLE SAVAGE

THIS chapter, and the three which are to follow it, will employ a topical rather than an historical method. Their object will be to show the relation between the Noble Savage idea and four other important aspects of romantic naturalism. The topics to be treated are: (1) the influence of scenery on the young; (2) ingenuous and unconventional love; (3) the religion of nature; (4) the poetry of primitive folk. Although these are obviously not the only topics which might be considered, to discuss them in connection with the Noble Savage will help to place our particular subject against the general background of romanticism.[1]

In these discussions it will often be necessary to remind the reader of passages which have already been cited in a different context. Most of the material, however, will be fresh: drawn sometimes from authors who have previously been considered, and sometimes from authors who, although they have deserved no place in the general history of our subject, yet shed light upon one or more of these special topics. Free from chronology and biography, we are now able to range at will over the whole field from 1730 to 1830, following wherever the path of thought may lead.

---

[1] The reader will find in Dr. Bissell's study further material on all these topics. My own examples are so copious that I have refrained from drawing upon his stock.

This freedom has the usual perils of liberty. Unless the history of our theme be remembered, the results of the present discussion will be grotesque. Though Wordsworth may resemble Thomson in certain respects, the two poets are quite different in many other respects. The Wordsworth of 1798 and the Wordsworth of 1820, also, are almost two distinct men. A verbal similarity between Shelley and "Della Crusca" does not prove that Shelley was as great a fool as Robert Merry. The trail of the Noble Savage leads deep into the romantic forest, yet the fact that it connects many parts of romanticism should not imply that those parts are identical. In short, the purpose of these chapters is not at all to bring the whole of romanticism under the head of the Noble Savage idea, but simply to show certain points of contact between that idea and other characteristic conceptions of the period.

This explanation given, we may approach our first topic. Every reader of romantic literature is familiar with the child of nature — generally, though not always, a girl — who is born and grows to maturity in the heart of some wild region untouched by civilization, and who imbibes beauty, innocence and an unerring moral sense from the scenery which surrounds her. It is the heroine of Wordsworth's *Three Years She Grew* who best represents the type.

At the age of three, Lucy is adopted by Nature, who intends, by filling her mind with " vital feelings of delight," to make her beautiful and good. Wordsworth's conception of the " Education of Nature " is not, however, one of sheer expansiveness and spontaneity. Nature to Lucy will be " law " as well as " impulse " ; will " restrain " as well as " kindle " her emotions.

Yet in *Ruth*, which was written in the same year (1799), Wordsworth shows that there are persons capable of ab-

sorbing only kindling and impulsive influences from
nature. Ruth, herself a Lucy who

> " Had built a bower upon the green
>   As if she from her birth had been
>   An infant of the woods,"

is deceived by that youth who

> " Had roamed about with vagrant bands
>   Of Indians in the West."

Wordsworth very early began to lose his faith in the
disciplinary power of nature; it was his desire for a
steadier control that made him turn to Duty. The Westmoreland Girl,

> " Left among her native mountains
>   With wild Nature to run wild,"

is as much a weed as a flower, and needs moral and intellectual cultivation.

Lucy nevertheless represents a genuine ideal in Wordsworth and in the romantic movement. In the height of
naturalistic enthusiasm it was easy to imagine an affinity
between the unblemished forests and the pure heart of
childhood. Even adults, stained by the world and victims of " what man has made of man," could find deep
spiritual inspiration among the mountains. Why then
should not a child absorb from scenery the same benign
influences with even less difficulty? The child, as the *Immortality Ode* asserts, has heaven lying about it in its
infancy. If then we do not snatch it away from the breast
of Mother Nature, it will continue to draw nourishment
from the infinite. The shades of the prison-house need
not close upon the growing boy unless he is put in prison.

When Nature says of Lucy that

> " . . . a lovelier flower
> On earth was never sown,"

she is using a conventional metaphor in a more than conventional sense. The flower, quietly soaking in sunlight and moisture and turning them into fragrance and beauty, is just what a child should be. Romantic literature is full of Lucies, and many of them are compared to flowers.

Thus Southey likens Emma, a Somersetshire maiden, to

> " . . . . . . a plant whose leaf
> And bud and blossom all are beautiful."

Her connection with the scenes from which she draws her beauty is so close that she seems almost a part of the landscape.

> " . . . 'Twas like a dream
> Of old romance to see her when she plied
> Her little skiff on Derwent's glassy lake;
> The roseate evening rising on the hills,
> . . . .
> Mountains and vales and waters, all imbued
> With beauty, and in quietness; and she
> Nymph-like, amid that glorious solitude
> A heavenly presence gliding in her joy."

In this poet the educative value of scenery is associated with the Noble Savage idea. Mooma, the Indian maid of the *Tale of Paraguay*, is plainly a child of nature. She and her brother grow up in the heart of the South American wilderness.

> " . . . The boy *in sun and shower*
> Rejoicing in his strength to youthhead *grew:*
> And Mooma, that beloved girl, a dower
> Of gentleness from bounteous nature drew,
> With all that should the heart of womankind imbue." [2]

[2] Italics, mine. *Cf. Three Years She Grew.*

Although Southey's return to nature was quite independent of Wordsworth's, his portrayals of natural children seem to derive from the greater poet.

The Paraguayan forest is a suitable place for the rearing
of a child because " never evil thing . . . had power to
enter there." Natural virtues are best preserved when
entirely segregated from corrupting influences. The one
tree with which the child of nature must not claim kinship
is the tree of the knowledge of good and evil.

> " Something of what in Eden might have been
> Was shadow'd there imperfectly, I ween,
> In this fair creature; safe from all offense,
> Expanding like a shelter'd plant serene,
> Evils that fret and stain being far from thence,
> Her heart in peace and joy retained its innocence."

This vegetable manner of growth, this vegetable kind of
goodness, are characteristic of the type. Mooma feeds
that mind of hers " in a wise passiveness," and the innocence of " a shelter'd plant serene " is her reward.

> " Her soul its native purity sincere
> Possess'd, by no example here defiled;
> From envious passions free, exempt from fear,
> Unknowing of all ill, amid the wild
> Beloving and beloved she grew, a happy child."

The romantic desire for freedom of the instincts is sometimes accomplished by a rather timid craving for moral
and intellectual insulation. It is well, as Coleridge says,
" to destroy the bad passions not by combating them, but by
keeping them in inaction " ; and they can of course be
kept inactive nowhere more easily than in the forest.
Except in moments of mystical confidence, romantic naturalism is suffused with this negative and pessimistic tinge.

That Southey's *Tale of Paraguay* owes much to Bowles'

Missionary has already been suggested. Southey's Yeruti and Mooma are closely patterned after Bowles' Lautaro and Olola. The latter is wildly and exotically picturesque:

> " Her ancles rung with shells, as unconfined
> She danced, and sung wild carols to the wind.
> With snow-white teeth, and laughter in her eye,
> So beautiful in youth she bounded by."

Olola's sylvan gaiety, however, implies no lack of the gentler virtues. Her possession of these is abundantly attested by her pleasant relations with the lower animals:

> " The tame alpaca stood and licked her hand;
> She brought him gathered moss, and loved to deck
> With flowery twine his tall and stately neck,
> Whilst he with silent gratitude replies,
> And bends to her caress his large blue eyes."

Sympathy with wild creatures is characteristic of the type. Southey's Kailyal, in the *Curse of Kehama*,

> " . . . . seemed a thing
> Of Heaven's prime, uncorrupted work, a child
> Of early nature undefiled,
> A daughter of the years of innocence."

This child of heaven, of nature and of the Golden Age is loved by all the denizens of the forest and the river.

> " . . . When she stood
> Beside the glassy pool, the fish, that flies
> Quick as an arrow from all other eyes,
> Hovered to gaze on her; the mother-bird,
> When Kailyal's step she heard,
> Sought not to tempt her from her secret nest,
> But, hastening to the dear retreat, would fly
> To meet and welcome her benignant eye."

Birds are not difficult to tame, but it is something to win
the affection of a fish. Fellow-feeling is the chief requisite for the feat. Thus Wordsworth's Westmoreland
Girl, being linked "with the inferior creatures" by
"scarcely less than sacred passions," makes

> "Anglers, bent on reckless pastime,
> Learn how she can feel alike
> Both for tiny harmless minnow
> And for fierce sharp-toothed pike."

One thinks also of Emily and her friendship with the
White Doe of Rylstone; of little Barbara Lewthwaite —
more clearly a child of nature — and her pet lamb. In the
fringe of associations which hover about this subject are
Peter Bell's ass, and Coleridge's. The former is the victim of a man who has resisted the influence of mountains;
the latter is invited to join the pantisocratic group by a poet
who then regarded himself as a child of nature. Lucy,
Ruth, the Westmoreland Girl, Emma, Mooma, Olola,
Kailyal, Emily and Barbara might well be greeted by
Cythna as kindred spirits at Shelley's feast of liberation.[3]
It is evident that humanitarian feeling toward animals,
based not so much on reflective pity as on a genuine kinship with all instinctive and irreflective beings, is often
associated with the type which we are examining.

But to return to the floral metaphor which has been our
guide. The hero of Godwin's *Fleetwood* says of the
woman who became his wife: " Her delight was in flowers;
and she seemed like one of the beauties of her own parterre, soft and smooth and brilliant and fragrant and unsullied." Byron contrasts Aurora Raby, the gem, with
Haidee, the flower. Of the latter he elsewhere says that
" like a lovely tree, she grew to womanhood."

[3] *Vide supra*, pp. 307–308.

John Mitford's *Miscellaneous Poems* are dedicated to the dead " A.B.," who seems to have had the same rearing as Lucy. Indeed, she is called a " Child of Nature,"

> " The mildest and the maidenliest creature born,
> So gentle, and so gracious — in serene
> And tender hope, the opening blossom grew."

And John Hamilton Reynolds, of all unlikely people, provides another flower maiden in " the youthful Margaret," who " lived beneath a mountain's brow," and seemed " the spirit of the place."

> " Though wild is life's tempestuous gale,
> May she escape the stormy hour;
> And, like the violet of the vale,
> Live an unbroken flower." [4]

It is of course not always necessary that the child of nature should be compared to a flower if only she is represented as unconsciously drawing goodness and beauty from her surroundings. Such is the portrayal of Theora, an Irish girl, by Humphry Davy.

> " . . . . . Amidst the groves
> And greens and nodding rocks that overhang
> The grey Killarney, passed her morning days,
> Bright with the beams of joy."

Theora's communion with natural objects fosters a number of essentially romantic qualities, chief of which is an exquisite sensitiveness.

> " Hence were her passions tuned to harmony,
> Her azure eye oft glistened with the tear
> Of sensibility, and her soft cheek
> Glow'd with the blush of rapture."

[4] *The Naiad, with Other Poems*, p. 42. *Cf.* Wordsworth, " A violet by a mossy stone."

Her woodland rambles have made her a republican and a feminist.

> " . . . . . . In her bosom glowed
> The sacred fire of freedom. Hence she scorn'd
> The narrow laws of custom that control
> Her feeble sex."

And since she is the creation of a physicist, her opinions are not restricted to social questions.

> " . . . . . . Great in her energies
> She roam'd the fields of Nature, scann'd the laws
> That move the ruling atoms." [5]

This poem is probably a by-product of Davy's association with Coleridge and Southey.

Campbell's Gertrude is certainly an example of the type.

> " It seemed as if those scenes sweet influence had
> On Gertrude's soul, and kindness like their own
> Inspired those eyes affectionate and glad,
> That seemed to love whate'er they looked upon."

The ascription of " kindness " to the woods of Wyoming shows how squarely Campbell, despite his conventionality, fits into the Wordsworthian tradition.   The poet is anxious to explain that nature has given Gertrude a more than physical beauty:

> " Nor guess I, was that Pennsylvanian home,
> With all its picturesque and balmy grace,
> And fields that were a luxury to roam,
> Lost on the soul that looked from such a face."

In every representation of a natural maiden is implied a contrast with an unnatural one, and sometimes this contrast is not merely implicit but explicit.   Thus Laman Blanchard

[5] *Annual Anthology*, Vol. I, p. 281.

tells of Mary and her sister, who pass their childhood on the moors. The sister is adopted by a wealthy woman, becomes vain and worldly, and forgets Mary. The lot of Mary, who remains in the wilds,

> " . . . . . . is happier far,
>   Far richer in all natural treasures,
>   Than theirs who scorn it often are;
>   Thou heir of Nature's purer pleasures,
>   Companion of the sun and star,
>   Fond dancer to aërial measures! "

The examples which have been presented differ in minor respects, but display several common characteristics. These children usually derive from nature great physical beauty; love of the scenes amid which they live; a sense of kinship with all living creatures; exquisite sensibilities; and a moral instinct independent of, and often hostile to, analytical reason.

Now that the traits of the female of the species have been illustrated we may glance at a few male specimens. The brothers of Mooma and Olola have already been mentioned. In Southey's *Thalaba* appear a similar pair, but the hero of the poem naturally outshines the girl Oneiza.

> " It was the wisdom and the will of Heaven,
>   That in a lonely tent had cast
>   The lot of Thalaba.
>   There might his soul develop best
>   Its strengthening energies;
>   There might he from the world
>   Keep his soul pure and uncontaminate,
>   Till at the written hour he should be found
>   Fit servant of the Lord, without a spot."

As in the case of Mooma, seclusion in the wilds is essential to the preservation of natural goodness.

Wordsworth's own Lucy is matched by the boy of Winander, into whose mind, when echo refused to answer his hootings, " the visible scene . . . would enter unawares." Over his grave the poet mused in much the same spirit as that in which young Coleridge bent over Lee Boo's tomb, with its inscription,

> " Stop, Reader, stop! Let Nature claim a Tear;
> A Prince of *Mine*, Lee Boo, lies buried here! "

The Danish Boy, beloved by sheep and mountain-ponies, has all the earmarks of the type.

But Godwin's Fleetwood is probably the best example of the male child of nature. The reader will remember how he grows up as " a wild roe among the mountains of Wales," where " a constant familiarity " with " mountains and precipices, . . . the roaring of the ocean and the dashing of waterfalls " makes him " the spoiled child of the great parent, Nature."

Fleetwood provides a logical transition to the autobiographical element in the child of nature conception. As we have already observed, both Wordsworth and Byron imagine their own boyhood to have been powerfully influenced by scenery. To themselves they appeared quite as much the children of nature as any of the poetical figures who have been mentioned in this chapter. Coleridge's son, Hartley, is apostrophized in *Frost at Midnight:*

> " But *thou*, my babe! shalt wander like a breeze
> By lakes, and sandy shore, amid the crags
> Of ancient mountains, and beneath the clouds."

The term " child of nature " has no absolutely fixed meaning. Hermsprong tells Miss Campinet that he learned his philosophy from " the sons of nature " — the Indians. Crèvecoeur says that the Indians " are much more closely connected with nature than we are; they are her immediate children, the inhabitants of the woods are her undefiled offspring." Neither Bage nor Crèvecoeur is a devotee of the cult of scenery. They are using " nature " in the broadly romantic sense of a standard of uncorrupted simplicity from which civilized man has foolishly departed. In that sense savages had been called " children of nature " since the time of Montaigne.

But to a large group of romanticists, of whom Wordsworth is the great example, scenery provided the best evidence of what the universe fundamentally is. Flowers and birds, mountains, grassy fields and streams, were felt to possess the untrammeled beauty, simplicity, spontaneity and unreflective goodness which find an echo in the heart of man whenever he casts off the perverting influences of civilization. Thus wild and semi-wild scenery became a body of symbols representing the romantic ideal of nature. And since the symbol often looms as large as the thing it symbolizes, " nature " was often, for practical purposes, taken as synonymous with " scenery " ; although just as great abstractions loom up behind religious images, so behind " natural objects " hovered the universal spirit which gave those objects their value. With Wordsworth, love of external nature sometimes causes the symbol to absorb the thing symbolized, so that trees and mountains seem to have a power of their own, an efficacy such as might be ascribed by a devout Catholic to a religious image. But in both cases the uninitiated may be deceived by a verbal code which the adept is using with full understanding. Just as the Catholic knows that the efficacy of a relic is derived from God, so Wordsworth knows that natural objects derive their " power to kindle or restrain " from the " wisdom and spirit of the universe."

At the height of Wordsworth's naturalistic enthusiasm,

however, nature as God and nature as scenery are almost inextricably mingled. When the dove descends to the Sangrael, what theology can distinguish the gift from the giver? This sublime confusion of the physical and the metaphysical is, indeed, the essence of romanticism. Coleridge, in his later years of transcendental Toryism, regarded this tendency in Wordsworth as a serious philosophical error. He is glancing at his old friend when he says, " The word Nature, from its extreme familiarity, and, in some instances, fitness, as well as from the want of a term, or *other* name, for God, has caused very much confusion in the thoughts and language of men. Hence a Nature-God, or God-Nature, not God *in* Nature." [6]

The Nature who takes Lucy unto herself is more, far more, than the " sun and shower " in which the child grew, but it is *through* the sun and shower that Nature's educative force will be exerted. Bearing this qualification in mind, we may say that with the rise of the Wordsworthian nature-cult, the savage, who had long been known as a child of nature, might become more specifically a child of scenery. Thus Byron's Albanians are the offspring of the mountains, and the same poet says of Daniel Boone's clan,

> " The free-born forest found and kept them free,
> And fresh as is a torrent or a tree."

Wordsworth believes that

> " .   .   .   the everlasting streams and woods,
> Stretched and still stretching far and wide, exalt
> The roving Indian, on his desert sands."

This belief was no doubt fostered by reports of the religion of savages, in which the personification of natural objects necessarily plays so important a part.

[6] Allsop, *Letters, Conversations and Recollections*, pp. 119–120.

Honesty compels the admission, however, that susceptibility to scenic influences is not often definitely ascribed to
actual savages. The romantic poets were more likely to
use indigenous types as examples of " the education of
nature," probably because such types represented more
closely their own personal experience. Nevertheless, it is
likely that belief in the plastic power of scenery strength-
ened the prevalent sympathy for the savage; and that,
conversely, the older cult of primitive man gave some encouragement to the cult of scenery.

The phrase " child of nature " was influenced by
changes not only in the meaning of " nature," but by
changes in the meaning of " child." To many romanticists, the child, as a purely intuitive being, is a " mighty
prophet, seer blest." This conception of childhood accords
perfectly with the virtues of the Noble Savage. Hawkesworth says of the Tahitians that " if we admit that they
are upon the whole happier than we, we must admit that
the child is happier than the man." The writer is here
thinking chiefly of the freedom from care enjoyed alike
by child and savage. The comparison may be based, however, on more mystical grounds. Both " the naked Indian
of the wild " and " the cradled child " are, as Wordsworth
tells us, swayed by " presentiments." Thus the Noble
Savage idea can easily be made to fit both the cult of
scenery and the cult of the child.

Boys and girls who grow up under the sway of nature
are, in romantic literature, often spoken of as savages.
Godwin makes Fleetwood say, " In Merionethshire I had
been a solitary savage." Wordsworth's boyhood was like
that of " a naked savage in the thunder-shower." Byron
yearns for the days when he " roved a young Highlander."
His comparison between the Albanians and the Scotch, and
his description of Torquil in *The Island,* show that to him,

as to Scott, a Highlander was something very like a Noble Savage. Moreover, Fleetwood, Wordsworth and Byron, on their first introduction to civilization, react in the true Noble Savage manner.[7]

Wordsworth's daughter, Dora, is gleefully described by Dorothy Wordsworth as being very wild. Of the little girl, Coleridge, playfully garbling a passage in *Ruth*, says, " The wild cat of the wilderness was not so fair as she." [8] One should not, of course, generalize too widely upon such a slender foundation; but the fact that when Dora was a month old Wordsworth penned a chain of reflections beginning " Hadst thou been of Indian birth " [9] perhaps adds some significance to Coleridge's jest.

Dorothy Wordsworth's enjoyment of nature was so intense, immediate and sensuous that it reminds her brother of his own boyish, or savage, delight in scenery.

> ".   .   .   Oh! yet a little while
> May I behold in thee what I was once,
> My dear, dear Sister! "

Although Dorothy adored her brother and his poetry she was too genuinely close to nature to share his philosophy, which was, as Shelley wickedly but acutely suggests, in part a substitute for a frank and intimate union with the earth-bride.[10] To William, Dorothy must always have seemed a little pagan, a little savage. No doubt he consoled himself with the reflection that God was with her when she knew it not.

This unconscious communion with nature is enjoyed by all children of nature, and Wordsworth may have re-

---

[7] *Vide supra*, pp. 152–153, 172, 230.

[8] *Letters of the Wordsworth Family*, Vol. I, p. 390. "Panther," not " wild cat," is the expression used in *Ruth*.

[9] *Vide supra*, p. 181.

[10] *Vide supra*, p. 304.

garded his sister as related in this respect to Lucy. De Quincey, writing on Dorothy, says: "A happier life [than marriage to Hazlitt or other suitors] was hers in youth, coming . . . near . . . to that which was promised to Ruth — the Ruth of her brother's creation." That the Wordsworth household should suggest the same poem to both Coleridge and De Quincey is certainly significant. They are thinking, no doubt, of Ruth's early life and of the roseate promises held out by her lover — not of the tragic sequel. Dorothy, De Quincey continues, was a fiery, elemental, "gypsy" spirit. "Her time fleeted away like some golden age, or like the life of primeval man." [11] The conclusion is almost Euclidean. Dorothy Wordsworth, because of her closeness to nature, is compared to Ruth, who is a child of nature. For the same reason she is compared to primitive man, who is, according to the ideas of the time, represented by the Noble Savage. Now since she is, on practically identical grounds, compared to two things, those two things — the child of nature and the Noble Savage — must have something in common.

But before we append a $Q.E.D.$, let us return to imaginative literature in order to examine a character who is at the same time a perfect child of nature and a perfect Noble Savage. This character is Immalee, whose story furnishes an idyllic interlude in Maturin's *Melmoth the Wanderer*. Maturin's book is, incidentally, the only novel of terror in which the Noble Savage idea plays an important part.

Immalee is reared on a deserted island in the mouth of the Ganges. " She lived like a flower amid sun and storm, blooming in the light, and bending to the shower, and drawing the elements of her sweet and wild existence from both. And both seemed to mingle their influence kindly for her, as if she were a thing that nature loved, even in

[11] De Quincey, *Reminiscences*, pp. 362–363.

her angry mood, and gave a commission to the storm to nurture her, and to the deluge to spare the ark of her innocence, as it floated over the waters. This existence of felicity, half physical, half imaginative, but neither intellectual nor impassioned, had continued to the seventeenth year of this beautiful and mild being." The paraphrase of Wordsworth's *Three Years She Grew* is probably deliberate.

Maturin elaborates with great ingenuity the popular comparison between the child of nature and vegetation. Immalee cannot distinguish herself from the trees and flowers which are her only playmates. When she met Melmoth, " she told him that she was the daughter of a palm-tree . . . but that her poor father had been long withered and dead — that she was very old, having seen many roses decay on their stalks."

Not unnaturally, the fiendish Melmoth sees in Immalee an easy prey. But he meets with a surprise. Immalee may think that her father was a palm-tree, but she has a native moral sense transcending worldly wisdom. " Her instinctive and unfailing *tact* in matters of right and wrong formed an array that discomfited and baffled the tempter more than if he had been compelled to encounter half the *wranglers* of the European academies of that day. In the logic of the schools, he was well versed, but in this logic of the heart and of nature, he was ignorance itself." The opposition of nature, heart and virtue to analytical intelligence which characterizes the child of nature is especially marked in Immalee.

Melmoth, craftily conjecturing that to make the maiden think will be to corrupt her virtue, decides to show her all the ills of civilized life. The instrument of disillusion, a telescope, has been employed before, though for a different purpose. In Rogers' *Voyage of Columbus,* Cora, a shy and lovely girl, is shown a mirror and a telescope. The latter especially delights her, since it enables her to see her lover in his canoe, far out to sea. Rogers' note on this passage reads: " For the effects of the telescope, and the mirror, on an uncultivated mind, see Wallis's Voyage Round the World."

One cannot tell whether Maturin derived the telescope idea from Rogers or directly from Wallis. Melmoth's telescope, of course, is a magical one which enables the gazer to behold from an island in the Ganges all the vices in the world. Immalee's reaction to what she sees, too, is quite different from Cora's. Her attitude is one of incredulous horror, and her replies to Melmoth's cynical explanations prove her a genuine Noble Savage.

Melmoth says of the inhabitants of the civilized world: " In order to make their thinking powers more gross, and their spirits more fiery, they devour animals, and torture from abused vegetables a drink that, without quenching thirst, has the power of extinguishing reason, inflaming passion, and shortening life." Immalee, the palm-tree's daughter, while no doubt distressed at the thought of abusing a vegetable, can hardly tell what these words mean. Nor can she understand how " four thousand of them will live together in a space smaller than the least and lightest colonnade of her young banyan-tree, in order, doubtless, to increase the effects of foetid air, artificial habits, and impracticable exercise."

" Another amusement of these people," Melmoth continues, " . . . is what they call law. They pretend to find in this security for their persons and their properties. . . . Of the security it gives to the latter, judge, Immalee, when I tell you, that you might spend your life in their courts, without being able to prove that those roses you have gathered and twined in your hair were your own." But

Immalee has no desire to prove a title to her roses. She has, indeed, so little sense of property that she cannot "comprehend how there could be an unequal division of the means of existence." "Why," she asks, "should some have more than they can eat, and others nothing to eat?"

Melmoth attempts to explain the reasons for which men go to war: "Some of them fight for ten inches of barren sand — some for the dominion of the salt wave — some for anything — and some for nothing — but all for pay and poverty, and occasional excitement, and the love of action, and the love of change, and the dread of home, and the consciousness of evil passions, and the hope of death, and the admiration of the showy dress in which they are to perish." Again the villain's words fail of their effect. The emotions connected with war mean nothing to this child of nature. "She could not," for example, "be conscious of fear, for nothing of that world in which she had lived had ever borne a hostile appearance to her." True to her type, she enjoys the vegetable happiness of seclusion and ignorance.

While such a creature would, as will later be made plain, seem to some romanticists the embodiment of genuine religion, she would obviously shrink in dismay from formal theology. In Immalee's reaction to Melmoth's account of creeds, schisms and inquisitions, opposition to rationalism appears very plainly. "*Religion!*" she exclaims at the first mention of the word; "what is that? Is it a new thought?" Under the instruction of Melmoth, she has grown suspicious of thoughts. It seems to her that "to think . . . is to suffer — and a world of thought must be a world of pain!"

As Melmoth continues his description of orthodox religion, Immalee's fears prove justified. "Hold!" she

cries, " too many thoughts will kill me." She cannot
understand how inhabitants of " the world that thinks "
— her own term for civilized society — can disagree in
matters of faith. " Surely they must know that a difference cannot be acceptable to Him who is One." She
receives a concrete illustration of the workings of theology
when she beholds, through her telescope, the car of Jug-
gernaut crushing the bodies of sacrificial infants. " The
world that thinks does not feel! " is her shocked comment.
" I never saw the rose kill the bud! " That appeal from
thought to emotion, and from men to plants, is highly
characteristic of romantic naturalism.

From the torrent of bitter words into which she has been
plunged Immalee emerges frightened, saddened and disgusted, but with her simple heart unscathed. " The acrid
and searing irony of his [Melmoth's] language had made
no impression on one with whom ' speech was truth,' and
who could have no idea why a circuitous mode of convey-
ing meaning could be adopted, when even a direct one was
often attended with difficulty to herself."

But I begin to wander from the purpose for which
Immalee has been introduced to the reader. This maiden,
reared among the influences which made Lucy beautiful
and good, is plainly a child of nature. As a figure of primitive simplicity and intuitive virtue meant to teach a lesson
to sophisticated society, she is plainly a Noble Savage.

My object in this chapter has been, not to prove that
Lucy and all her kin are Noble Savages, but to suggest
that the two conceptions are harmoniously related. Several of the children of nature whose virtues have been set
forth are savages. Conversely, the influence of scenery
sometimes operates upon the savage as it does upon the
child. Moreover, boys and girls who, in poetry or in actual
life, grow up among natural objects, are frequently

likened to little savages. To both types, simplicity, instinctive goodness and seclusion from evil influences are common. We may at least say, then, that the Noble Savage gives something to the child of nature, and that the child of nature gives something to the Noble Savage. It is not merely for the sake of rhyme that in Mrs. Hemans' " dream of all things free," the " happy forest child " should be followed by the " Indian 'midst the wild." [12]

[12] *Vide supra,* p. 285.

Chapter XI

ROMANTIC LOVE AND THE NOBLE SAVAGE

IN the foregoing discussion one important element which helps to compose the child of nature was intentionally omitted so that it might receive separate treatment. That element is the desire for fresh, sincere and unsophisticated love. Obviously the chances of man's receiving from woman a devotion at once ingenuous and passionate are greatly increased when the beloved is a child of nature. As Campbell sings:

> " O Love! in such a wilderness as this,
> Where transport and security entwine,
> Here is the empire of thy perfect bliss,
> And here thou art a god indeed divine."

Lucy herself grows into a woman fit for a poet's worship.

All three of the great Lakists associated their personal love-affairs with their admiration for nature. Wordsworth's wife is described in *Louisa* [1] as " nymph-like " in her fleetness and strength. The wildest weather cannot prevent her from roaming over the moors;

> " And, when against the wind she strains,
> Oh! might I kiss the mountain rains
> That sparkle on her cheek."

[1] Thomas Hutchinson believes that Louisa can only be Joanna, Mary Hutchinson's sister, arguing that all Wordsworth's pseudonyms are metrically equivalent to the real names which they disguise (*Oxford Edition*, p. 897). But *Louisa* is written with such warmth, and agrees so perfectly with *A Farewell*, that to identify Louisa with Mary is at least a permissible guess.

Such a girl is the ideal bride for Wordsworth. Her "vital feelings of delight" will furnish him with many reflections on the plastic influence of natural objects.

In *A Farewell*, therefore, he confidently addresses his "little nook of mountain-ground" :

> "We go for One to whom ye will be dear;
> And she will prize this Bower, this Indian shed,
> Our own contrivance, Building without peer!
> — A gentle Maid, whose heart is lowly bred,
> Whose pleasures are in wild fields gatherèd
>
> .   .   .   .
>
> Will come to you; to you herself will wed;
> And love the blessed life that we lead here."

Dove Cottage is here compared to a redman's abode. Ruth's lover invites her to a similar home:

> "Sweet Ruth! and could you go with me
> My helpmate in the woods to be,
> Our *shed* at night to rear;
> Or run, my own adopted bride,
> A sylvan huntress at my side,
> And drive the flying deer."

Perhaps not only Coleridge and De Quincey, but Wordsworth himself, thought of Dove Cottage in terms of *Ruth*.

While Wordsworth would be the last man to carry his sweetheart off to the American wilderness, Coleridge had precisely this intention. His more philosophical visions of pantisocracy were tinged by dreams of woodland rambles with Sara Fricker,

> "Far from folly, far from men,
> In the rude romantic glen."

And when both pantisocracy and Sara disappoint him, he finds solace in thoughts of a much lovelier child of nature — Dorothy Wordsworth,

" .   .   .   .   .   vowed and dedicate
    To something more than Nature in the grove."

The desire for a Lucy-bride is felt not only by the
Lakists but by the revolutionary group. Thomas Day
actually journeyed into Wales, " hoping, perhaps, to find
there that pastoral innocence which poets have depicted."
He describes in fervent verse the lovely lady of his mind.

> " Not such thy looks, not such thy air,
>   Not such thy unaffected grace
> As, mid the town's deceitful glare,
>   Marks the proud nymph's disdainful face." [3]

That he never found his nonpareil is not surprising. His
wife was to combine primeval innocence with the highest
mental cultivation. Besides being " simple as a mountain
girl in her dress, her diet, and manners, and fearless and
intrepid as the Spartan wives and Roman heroines," she
must possess " a taste for literature and science, for moral
and political philosophy."

But such a mate might be reared if she were caught
young enough. Day accordingly adopted two twelve-
year-old orphan girls, whom he named — perhaps to
appease the censorious — Sabrina and Lucretia. His intention was to educate them " according to his own ideas
and those of Rousseau," and to marry the one who succeeded the better in absorbing those ideas. This experiment was a failure. Day at last compromised with the
wicked world by marrying Miss Esther Milnes, but only
on condition that she " retire wholly from fashionable
society, and spend the remainder of her days in rural
seclusion." [4]

[2] *British Poets*, Vol. LVIII, p. 148.
[3] *Ibid.*, p. 185.
[4] *Ibid.*, pp. 150–153.

If Marguerite in *St. Leon* accurately represents the character of Mary Wollstonecraft, Godwin found the combination of moral simplicity and intellectual refinement for which Day sought in vain. It is interesting to see the Jacobin ideal of a rationalistic Arcadia applied to affairs of the heart. Thelwall, however, did not attempt to find a milkmaid who should also be a Roman matron. He married a country girl of fifteen,

> " Arrayed in rustic innocence, and gay
> With all the modest graces that adorn
> The unadulterate mind." [5]

The later romantic poets, also, felt that courtship was at its purest and best when conducted against a scenic background. *Caroline* clearly indicates that in Campbell's mind Nature and love are intimately related. He prepares a bridal bower to which he invites the South Wind to come

> " . . . from some enchanted isle
> Where Heaven and Love their Sabbath hold,
> Where pure and happy spirits smile,
> Of beauty's fairest, brightest mould:

> " From some green Eden of the deep,
> Where Pleasure's sigh alone is heaved,
> Where tears of rapture lovers weep,
> Endeared, undoubting, undeceived."

The South Wind is evidently supposed to bring with it a breath of the ideal passion of some such " green Eden " as Tahiti.

In 1822 Shelley abandons Platonizing and urges Jane to come with him

> " Away, away, from men and towns,
> To the wild wood and the downs —

[5] *Poems Chiefly Written in Retirement,* p. 121.

> To the silent wilderness
> Where the soul need not repress
> Its music lest it should not find
> An echo in another's mind,
> While the touch of Nature's art
> Harmonizes heart to heart."

Surely Wordsworth, a score of years earlier, might have written these lines to the prospective sharer of his " Indian shed." Shelley's friend, Thomas Love Peacock, though in most respects a hostile critic of romanticism, was truly romantic in his choice of a bride. In Merionethshire, " the land of all that is beautiful in nature, and all that is lovely in woman," [6] he found Jane Gryffydh — his " mountain Fair," his " milk-white Snowdonian antelope," as Shelley calls her. [7]

The evidence thus far presented suggests that the love of a child of nature entered not only into the poems but into the lives of several romantic writers. The Lucy-bride conception arises, of course, as a reaction against the sinister artificiality of the relations prevailing between the sexes in the early part of the eighteenth century. The return to human nature was inextricably combined with the return to nature in the sense of scenery. The man of feeling shrank from the town, and from the vices of the town; he fled to the fields, and to the virtues of the fields. The champions of nature would therefore find in urban woman's distaste for the country a cardinal sign of her degenerateness; and would, conversely, be ready to trace a causal connection between the innocence of the country girl and her rural environment. We prefer, says Young, the " depraved allurements" of " painted art" to the beauties of nature.

[6] Quoted by Brimley Johnson, *Poems of Thomas Love Peacock*, p. ix.   [7] *Letter to Maria Gisborne*.

" Such Fulvia's passion for the town; fresh air
(An odd effect!) gives vapours to the fair;
Green fields, and shady groves, and crystal springs,
And larks, and nightingales, are odious things;
But smoke, and dust, and noise, and crowds delight;
And to be pressed to death, transports her quite." [8]

We may be sure that Fulvia's character is as vicious as her tastes are artificial.

A new literary tendency gravitates toward some older tradition with which it has elements in common. The association of rusticity with maidenly innocence would obviously find support in the pastoral. Thomson's Celadon and Amelia are a pastoral couple to whom the early stirrings of romantic naturalism have given a touch of genuineness.

" They loved: but such their guileless passion was,
As in the dawn of time informed the heart
Of innocence and undissembling truth.
'Twas friendship heighten'd by the mutual wish,
Th' enchanting hope, and sympathetic glow,
Beamed from the mutual eye." [9]

The Florio-Julia episode in Rogers' *Pleasures of Memory* shows how this Arcadian spirit might be applied to a Lake Country tragedy. Its artificiality shows also, however, what a wide gap lies between the pastoral proper and the true romantic attitude toward rustic life. The older form could never be wholly purged of its pseudo-classical taint.

The lover of nature might, nevertheless, pierce through the elegancies of the pastoral to the fundamental idea of a Golden Age in which women had been modest, ingenuous and affectionate. The use of the Golden Age to reinforce the naturalistic ideal of womanhood is well illustrated by

[8] *Poetical Works*, Vol. II, pp. 102–103.
[9] *Summer*, ll. 177–182.

Hayley's *The Triumphs of Temper*. This poem is an expansion into six mortal cantos of the Cave of Spleen
episode in *The Rape of the Lock*. Serena, the heroine, is a
young woman

> " Whom Nature blest, forbidding modish Art
>   To cramp thy spirit, or contract thy heart."

She has, however, succumbed to the power of Spleen, the
malign spirit who is responsible for the fine airs and
vapours and spitefulness of fashionable ladies. Temper
— the word is used as a synonym for " sensibility " —
realizes Serena's fundamental goodness, and seeks to reform her. He begins by reminding her of the Arcadian
origin of her sex:

> " When lovely Woman, perfect at her birth,
>   Blest with her early charms the wond'ring earth,
>   Her soul, in sweet simplicity array'd,
>   Nor shar'd my guidance, nor requir'd my aid."

Woman, that is, did not need to cultivate sensibility, since
she possessed the quality as a natural gift.

> " Her tender frame, nor confident nor coy,
>   Had every fibre tun'd to gentle joy:
>   No vain caprices swelled her pouting lip;
>   No gold produc'd a mercenary trip;
>   Soft innocence inspired her willing kiss,
>   Her love was nature, and her life was bliss."

This idyllic state has been corrupted, Temper continues,
by the influence of Spleen. The innocent maiden's desire to please has given place to " fashion's pert tricks " ;
her simple tastes to artificial cravings; her health
to feigned maladies which become real through pretense.

> " Such, and a thousand still superior woes,
> From Spleen's new empire o'er the earth arose:
> Each simple dictate of the heart forgot,
> Then first was form'd the mercenary plot;
> And Beauty practis'd that pernicious art,
> The art of angling for an old man's heart.
>
> . . . .
>
> Courtship was traffic; and the married life
> But one loud jangle of incessant strife."

We have already noted how much encouragement was lent to the Arcadian tradition by the goodness and happiness of savages and rustics. A common observation of the traveler in wild lands, or of the reader of the traveler's account, is that the natives equal or excel the primitivistic visions of the poets and philosophers. Such, for example, is Montaigne's conclusion from what he has learned of the cannibals. Albrecht Haller assures the Noble Savages of the Alps:

> " Ihr Schüler der Natur, ihr kennt noch güldne Zeiten!
> Nicht zwar ein Dichterreich voll fabelhafter Pracht;
>
> . . . .
>
> Was Epictet gethan und Seneca geschrieben,
> Sieht man hier ungelehrt und ungezwungen lieben."

Unsophisticated love is one of the privileges of the Swiss,

> " Denn hier, wo die Natur allein Gesetze giebet,
> Umschliesst kein harter Zwang der Liebe holdes Reich.
>
> . . . .
>
> Die Liebe brennt hier frei und scheut kein Donnerwetter,
> Man liebt für sich selbst und nicht für seine Väter." [10]

Wilson's angling expedition with Wordsworth convinces him that the poets have been truthful in their tales of " simple shepherds in the age of gold." Although he

[10] *Die Alpen. Versuch Schweizerischer Gedichten*, pp. 4, 6.

admires the men who visit " the angler's tent," it is chiefly the beauty and innocent frankness of the Westmoreland girls that suggest legendary dales,

> " Where without guile swains woo'd their happy maids,
> And love was friendship with a gentler name."

Just as male rustics can support the ideal of natural man, so female rustics can support the ideal of natural woman.

Arcadian woman can of course be admired not merely because she is free from civilized vices, but because she is free from civilized conventions. When Rousseau exclaims, " Oh! how delightful were the days of love and innocence, when the women were affectionate and modest, the men simple and constant," [11] he is thinking of the Golden Age in terms of ingenuous morality; but when Joseph Warton writes in *The Enthusiast* of

> " . . . nymphs who fondly clasp'd their fav'rite youths,
> Unawed by shame, beneath the beechen shade,
> Nor wiles nor artificial coyness knew.
> Then doors and walls were not; the melting maid
> Nor frown of parents fear'd nor husband's threats,
> Nor had curs'd gold their tender hearts allured; "

what chiefly interests him in the Golden Age is the facility and freedom of Arcadian courtship.

These two views are less divergent than they appear. Romantic love has both a negative and a positive aspect. According to their temperaments, writers of the period may emphasize either the sheltered innocence of unsophisticated love-making, or its wild frankness. Nor is the gulf between the two very great. Even writers who do not share the " free love " doctrines of Blake, Godwin and Shelley admire the spontaneity of rustic and savage

---

[11] *New Heloise*, Letter CXLIII.

passion. This same spontaneity, when carried to an extreme, approaches the sexual anarchy which was part of Blake's message to an enslaved world.

The most delightful thing about the child of nature is that she shows her feelings. She has neither the cynical defensive wit of the lady of quality nor the clumsy bashfulness of the bourgeois prude. Through the bright eyes of Wordsworth's Highland Girl shine the kindliness of an innocence that has never been abused.

> " . . . Thou dost not need
> The embarrassed look of shy distress,
> And maidenly shamefacedness:
> Thou wear'st upon thy forehead clear
> The freedom of a Mountaineer."

As late as 1828, some warmth crept into Wordsworth's bones and made him write *The Triad*. All three of the fair maidens there celebrated are children of nature, but the second best exemplifies

> " . . . the charm that manners draw,
> Nature, from thy genuine law."

Should she in her sportiveness commit some tiny error, she

> " Sheds round the transient harm or vague mischance
> A light unknown to tutored elegance.
> Hers is not a cheek shame-stricken,
> But her blushes are joy-flushes."

The charms of ingenuousness are more than sufficient to excuse its faults.

Those Westmoreland girls who made Christopher North think of the Golden Age have this same spontaneity:

> " No thought had they to give or take offence;
> Glad were their bosoms, yet sedate and still,
> And fearless in the strength of innocence."

Immalee, whose artless goodness is familiar to us, falls deeply in love with Melmoth. Beneath his wild bitterness she has discerned the human heart. "Before I saw you," she says, "I only smiled, but since I saw you, I weep, and my tears are delicious." Be it said to Melmoth's credit that he refuses to let this Noble Savage share his fiend-driven life, and leaves her to the uninterrupted enjoyment of her tears.[12]

These citations illustrate the attitude of civilized man toward natural artlessness. In other cases the writer or his spokesman stands entirely out of the picture, the better to behold the love of two ingenuous beings. The perfect example of Paul and Virginia has numerous English analogues in which brother-and-sister affection grows into a passion pure and deep, as when Lamb's Rosamund Gray and Allan Clare gaze at each other over the pages of that mild substitute for the tale of Lancelot, *Julia de Roubigné*.

Oneiza calls Thalaba "brother," but Southey wonders whether it was "sister-love" that made her put silver rings on her ankles and arms, stain her fingernails and eyelids, and twine red flowers in her hair. These innocent arts are surely the spring buds of an affection more than sisterly.

Gertrude of Wyoming and Young Waldegrave are an ingenuous couple.

> "Three little moons, how short! amidst the grove
> And pastoral savannahs they consume!
> While she, beside her buskined youth to rove,
> Delights, in fancifully wild costume,
> Her lovely brow to shade with Indian plume."

[12] Of course Immalee later appears in Spain as Isidora, and is there married by Melmoth in spectre bridegroom style. But Immalee and Isidora are the same person only in the sense that the various ideal women of *Tales of Hoffmann* are the same.

The Juan-Haidee episode, if one disregards the cynical asides of the poet, perfectly represents the Paul and Virginia type of love. Juan and Haidee are likened to a pair of children, and to

> " .   .   . two beings from out a rill,
> A nymph and her beloved, all unseen
> To pass their lives in fountains and on flowers,
> And never know the weight of human hours."

Wilson's *Isle of Palms*, the story of which has previously been related, demands closer scrutiny in connection with its portrayal of romantic love. Mary, the heroine, is a sister of Lucy even down to the horticultural simile.

> " Far from the haunts of men she grew
> By the side of a lonesome tower;
> Like some solitary mountain-flower."

She was as familiar to the stream as its own ripplings, or as the moonbeams which played upon it. The caves of the hills echoed to her footsteps.

Fitz-Owen is also a child of nature:

> " To him, a mountain Youth, was known
> The wailing tempest's dreariest tone.
> He knew the shriek of wizard caves,
> And the trampling fierce of howling waves.
> The mystic voice of the lonely night
> He had often drunk with a strange delight."

From the woman nature has drawn forth sweetness and gentleness, and from the man a kind of noble fierceness. They are ideal mates, for each complements the other.

Cast upon a desert island, they are irresistibly drawn toward each other. " Pure were their souls, as infant's breath." The loveliness of their surroundings sanctifies their passion:

> " No place for human frailty this,
> Despondency or fears;
> Too beautiful the wild appears
> Almost for human bliss.
> Was love like theirs then given in vain?
> And must they, trembling, shrink from pure delight? "

On the contrary, they consult their own bosoms and attribute to God the answer which they themselves have placed there.

> " No fears felt they of guilt or sin,
> For sure they heard a voice within
> That set their hearts at rest;
> They pass'd the day in peaceful prayer
> And when beneath the evening air
> They sought again their arbour fair,
> A smiling angel met them there,
> And bade their couch be blest."

Across the years it is hard to understand why the not very startling occurrences related in Wilson's poem should require such elaborate justification. Were it not for the day of prayer and the smirking angel the actions of these young people would seem much less reprehensible. That ingenuous love should be argued for so ingeniously is an anomaly. Wilson defends with pious phrases that freedom in which Blake and Shelley boldly rejoice.

Byron's *The Island* represents a final step in the transition from ingenuousness to libertarianism. The mutiny of the *Bounty* is condoned as an incident in the eternal quest of man for " Nature and Nature's goddess — woman." The motives of the rebels have an almost religious justification, for

> " .　　.　　.　　all our dreams of better life above
> But close in one eternal gush of love."

Torquil and Neuha, " the half savage and the whole," are allowed to represent those who are thus anticipating the joys of immortality.

> " Both children of the isles, though distant far;
> Both born beneath a sea-presiding star;
> Both nourished amidst nature's native scenes,"

they remind one of Mary and Fitz-Owen. But no " smiling angel " is invoked to approve their marriage. " The love which maketh all things fond and fair " is its own excuse for being.

Byron feels that the union of Neuha and Torquil is a true and beautiful one.

> " Rapt in the fond forgetfulness of life,
> Neuha, the South Sea girl, was all a wife,
> With no distracting world to call her off
> From love; with no society to scoff
> At the new transient flame; no babbling crowd
> Of coxcombry in admiration loud,
> Or with adulterous whisper to alloy
> Her duty, and her glory, and her joy:
> With faith and feelings naked as her form,
> She stood as stands a rainbow in a storm."

Byron's young mutineer need hardly have journeyed to the South Seas for such a bride. He might have found in the Lake Country, in Wales, or in his own native highlands a maiden whose love would have been equally free from urban trammels. Neuha, of course, has certain exotic distinctions of color and costume; and her passions have a picturesque violence unknown to British children of nature. But fundamentally her virtues are those of the rustic girls who spring up in opposition to Millamant. Byron's Neuha and Wordsworth's Lucy are sisters under their skins. In *The Island* the potential identity of mild innocence and unbridled passion, and the close connection between romantic love and the Noble Savage idea, are clearly apparent.

If at this point we recall Captain Bligh's own narrative, together with the testimony of Cook and Hawkesworth, the wide discrepancy between the facts about South Seas love and Byron's interpretation of those facts will be striking. He has given a quite ordinary craving for sexual indulgence both Arcadian prettiness and anarchistic grandeur, and turned libertines into libertarians. In this transmutation, however, Hawkesworth to some extent anticipated the poet. It will be remembered that a particularly flagrant example of Tahitian bestiality makes Hawkesworth wonder " whether the shame attending certain actions, which are allowed on all sides to be in themselves innocent, is implanted in Nature, or superinduced by custom." [13] Surely where there is no shame there is no sin. The innocent Tahitians behave in a way that would have disturbed Wordsworth, but after all, they may be excused on much the same grounds as the merry girl in his *Triad:*

> " Hers is not a cheek shame-stricken,
> But her blushes are joy-flushes;
> And the fault (if fault it be)
> Only ministers to quicken
> Laughter-loving gaiety
> And kindly sportive wit."

Byron's interpretation of Tahitian manners accords with the tradition of ingenuous love.

This general sketch has drawn closer and closer to the Noble Savage, until at last with Byron we are well within the boundaries of our subject. Of all Noble Savages, the

[13] *Vide supra,* p. III.

South Sea Islander is most popular as a lover — " What Otaheité is, let Britain be! " To what has already been said on this point I need only add that Cook, in his later days, tried to alter those ideas of savage license which he, through Hawkesworth, had done so much to inculcate. The women of Tahiti, he assures the reader of his *Voyage Towards the South Pole*, are not so bad as they have been painted. Those who have brought discredit upon the whole community are merely prostitutes. Since Cook goes on to say, however, that prostitution is very lightly regarded in Tahiti, his revision of his earlier statements is not very sweeping. In any case, the legend had developed too far to be checked.

Not all Tahitian women in romantic poetry have the untamed wildness of Neuha. Avanna, the native wife of Fitzallan in Miss Mitford's *Christina*, is a much milder child of nature, comparable, in her gentleness, beauty and innocence, to an English rose.

> " Not purer that bright stainless flower, —
> Man had not told her of her power;
> On nature's beauties she would dwell,
> On floweret fair and brilliant shell,
> But never did that maiden guess
> Her own unrivall'd loveliness."

Thus in Tahiti may be found not merely the freedom, but the innocence, of romantic love.

Avanna's flowerlike character is inherited by her daughter, Christina. When Henry proposes marriage to the half-caste girl, she says that, being " unskill'd in courtly art," she cannot express her thanks in words. But she goes on to display a pretty, if somewhat conventional, grasp of metaphor. Henry, she says, is like a wanderer who desires to pluck a wild rose. But the flower, after a brief happiness on his breast, will soon wither.

> " No; blushing rose and island maid
> Rest safest in their native shade."

When Henry appeals to Fitzallan, Christina's guardian, he meets with the same attitude, made all the firmer by a knowledge of European vices.

> " And shall I send this lily fair
> To that wide world of strife and care?
>
> .   .   .   .
>
> No; sweetest bud of innocence,
> Kings shall not dare to snatch thee hence."

Quite evidently, the conception of the child of nature has tempered the license of South Seas manners.

Except for the satire on Omai's relations with English ladies, to which allusion has previously been made,[14] I find no treatment of love between a male South Sea Islander and a white woman. The reason is not far to seek. The literature of the age was produced either by men, or by man-dominated women. If Mary Wollstonecraft had turned her attention to the theme, there would be a different story to tell.

Nothing illustrates the enduring influence of Aphra Behn's *Oroonoko* better than the stamp it placed upon representations of the Negro's love. Perhaps the physical unattractiveness of the Negro necessitated the ascription to him of passions heroic rather than sentimental. In any case, the black lover is generally a Royal Slave, with certain alterations in the type due to the pressure of later and more specifically romantic tendencies. In Mrs. Behn's work, too, is probably to be sought an explanation of the fact that African chieftains are much commoner figures than African maidens.

[14] *Vide supra*, p. 73.

The Dying Negro of Day and Bicknell [15] is an enslaved prince who, as the reader will remember, has fallen in love with a white woman. Before killing himself rather than be separated from her, he compares the timid passion of Europeans with the fire that rages in his own breast:

> " No pangs like these my pallid tyrants know,
>   Not such their transports, and not such their woe.
>
> .   .   .   .
>
> Damp'd by base lucre, and repell'd by fear,
> Each nobler passion faintly blazes here.
> Not such the mortals burning Afric breeds,
> Mother of virtues, and heroic deeds;
>
> .   .   .   .
>
> Nature has there, unchilled by art, impress'd
> Her awful majesty on every breast.
> Where'er she leads, impatient of control,
> The dauntless Negro rushes to the goal;
> Firm in his love, resistless in his hate,
> His arm is conquest, and his frown is fate."

These rantings bear a strong resemblance to those of Oroonoko, which in turn are derived from heroic drama. They remind one of Dryden's comparison between Almanzor and the Noble Savage.

A gentler aspect of the negro's love appears in the lines:

> " Ne'er had my youth such winning beauties seen,
>   Where Afric's sable beauties dance the green,
>   When some sweet maid receives her lover's vow,
>   And binds the offer'd chaplet to her brow."

Here one seems to see the protagonist of an heroic drama laying aside his blood-stained sword to roar as gently as any sucking dove in pleading for the favor of his lady. And yet this is courtly love with a difference:

[15] *Vide supra,* p. 146.

> " O could I burst these fetters which restrain
>   My struggling limbs, and waft thee o'er the main
>
>   .   .   .   .
>
>   To some wild mountain's solitary shade,
>   Where never European faith betray'd;
>   How joyful could I, of thy love secure,
>   Meet every danger, every toil endure!
>
>   .   .   .   .
>
>   When scorching summer drinks the shrinking streams,
>   My care should screen thee from its sultry beams;
>   At noon I'd crown thee with the fairest flowers,
>   At eve I'd lead thee to the safest bowers."

These lines take us closer to romanticism, for they add to the old " love and valor " the new cult of nature. *The Dying Negro* is interesting, then, as showing how old themes merge with new tendencies. Here certain elements of earlier literature are in process of becoming romantic material.

An anonymous poem of the 1790's presents a dialogue between Ampanini, King of Madagascar, and Vainah, a beautiful black captive. Her lover, the king's rival for her hand, has been slain in battle. In response to her plea for liberty, Ampanini cries,

> " Go, lovely Vainah! where thou wilt,
>   Go, lovely Vainah, void of fears;
>   Perish the wretch, whose lips of guilt
>   Would snatch a kiss suffus'd with tears." [16]

Oroonoko would be capable of such chivalry. And yet the passage has a trace of eighteenth century sensibility — something that suggests the atmosphere of sentimental comedy and bourgeois tragedy, something that suggests Thomson's praise of the Lapps,

[16] *A Song of the Negroes in Madagascar. The Persecutor*, p. 109.

> "   .   .   .   whose spotless swains ne'er knew
>   Injurious deed, nor, blasted by the breath
>   Of faithless love, their blooming daughters woe." [17]

With William Roscoe, the Oroonoko tradition, which in the foregoing citations has begun to waver, definitely collapses. His portrayal of love in Africa is wholly naturalistic. The joys of love are not restricted " to polished life." In fact, these " primeval blessings " are generally thwarted by greed, pride and superstition;

> "   .   .   .   but where Nature reigns,
>   And universal freedom, love exults
>   As in his native clime; there aims secure
>   His brightest arrow, steeped in keen delights,
>   To cultured minds, and colder skies, unknown."

In this poem, entitled *The Wrongs of Africa*, the tender passion of the negro, which has hitherto been somewhat apart from the general primitivistic current, definitely unites with the prevalent reaction against urban civilization.

Negro maidens are, as has been stated, much less frequent participants in love affairs than negro youths. Except for Vainah, indeed, the only example that I have come upon is Imoinda herself. The beauty of the African princess captivates not only Oroonoko, but her white masters. Her constancy has a firmness so nearly Roman that when Oroonoko slays her we think of the Virginia story.

In his epilogue to Southern's *Oroonoko*, Congreve puts Imoinda's love to satirical use. He refers to her as an " Indian," though Southern, as we know, has transformed Mrs. Behn's negress into a white girl. " You happy London wives," he makes the speaker inform the audience, will hardly envy this uncivilized girl's faithfulness, for

[17] *Winter*, ll. 884–886.

you " love at large, each day, yet keep your lives." Her error arose from mere lack of " town breeding."

> " Forgive this *Indian's* fondness of her Spouse;
> Their Law no Christian liberty allows:
> Alas! they make a Conscience of their Vows!
> If Virtue in a Heathen be a fault;
> Then damn the Heathen School, where she was taught.
> She might have learn'd to Cuckold, Jilt, and Sham,
> Had *Covent-Garden* been in *Surinam*."

Congreve should be added to the list of those wits who, like Swift and Gay, did not seriously believe in the Noble Savage, but appreciated his usefulness. Imoinda shows that female savages as well as male are apt satirical instruments.

Did Coleridge, when he wrote the epilogue to *Remorse*, have Congreve's lines in mind? Teresa, the orphan heiress (the Maria of *Osorio*), remains true to Albert during his six-years absence. The epilogue, while admitting the improbability of such conduct, urges the audience to " think first of poor Teresa's education " before condemning her. We must place her among our children of nature, for she was reared

> " 'Mid mountains wild, near billow-beaten rocks,
> Where sea-gales play'd with her dishevel'd locks."

The unfortunate child attended no young ladies' academy, paid no morning calls, was never taught to waltz, read nothing but virtuous old romances

> " Instead of — novels founded upon facts!
> Which, decently immoral, have the art
> To spare the blush, and undersap the heart!
> Oh, think of these, and hundreds worse than these,
> Dear disimproving disadvantages,
> And grounds for pity, not for blame, you'll see,
> E'en in Teresa's six years constancy."

The — to me — evident indebtedness of Coleridge to Congreve supports the comparison I have already drawn between *Osorio* and the earlier heroic dramas in which the Noble Savage plays a part.[18] What applies to Imoinda applies also to Teresa, the Spanish child of nature. But an important difference should be noted. Coleridge's Teresa, unlike Congreve's Imoinda, owes her virtues in part at least not merely to the negative blessings of ignorance of sophisticated vices but to the positive blessings of contact with a wild and beautiful environment. She has grown " in sun and shower," and " vital feelings of delight " have made her a fit bride for Albert. Once again we observe the fusion of the cult of scenery with the Noble Savage idea.

Since nothing more is to be said of negro love, the foregoing digression may be pardoned. But what of the Indian, the original Noble Savage?

The sexual habits of American Indians, as compared to those of the Tahitians, receive little attention from the explorers, and are less often reflected in English literature. While in Tahiti a definite cult of love seems to have existed, the redman was not an adept in the gay science. He satisfied the demands of instinct, but without sufficient violence or picturesqueness to give his courtship much literary appeal. He combined physical appetite and emotional indifference in a way that might well have baffled the romantic imagination. According to Vespucci, the natives of Honduras " are not very jealous, and are immoderately libidinous." [19] Above the tropics, the evidence is slight. " Carver " reports that there is little sex jealousy among the Indians, although the women are amorous. Of the men he says nothing. And indeed this is what one would expect of savage men leading hardy and bellicose lives in a temperate climate.

[18] *Vide supra,* p. 221.
[19] *Letter Concerning the Isles Newly Discovered,* p. 10.

To eighteenth century Europeans who desired escape from the complexities of society, the Indian's indifference to the finer points of courtship had its admirable side. Rousseau argues that primitive man was free from the vices arising from love, because love as it is under European conditions depends upon ideas of beauty and merit which were unknown to him. Since one woman was then as good as another, sexual relations must have been free from sophisticated pangs.

Robert Bage holds the same opinion. When Hermsprong is asked if savages are not at a disadvantage as regards the pleasures of love, he replies that he left America too young to have personal experience of the matter, and has " not yet learned all the refinements which constitute its value in Europe. All I have observed is, that you are not satisfied with it in the simple way in which our American Indians possess it."

To a genuinely disillusioned spirit, sheerly animal love is particularly attractive. If it renounces tenderness and subtlety, it escapes all the penalties of the complex. Disgust at the vileness of courts lies behind Beaumont's lines:

> " Oh, that I had been nourished in these woods,
>
> .   .   .   .
>
> And then had taken me some mountain-girl,
> Beaten with winds, chaste as the hardened rocks
> Whereon she dwelt, that might have strewed my bed
> With leaves and reeds, and with the skin of beasts,
> Our neighbours, and have borne at her big breasts
> My large coarse issue! This had been a life
> Free from vexation." [20]

And in *Locksley Hall*, Tennyson, momentarily shrinking from the march of Victorian progress, voices in similar

[20] *Philaster*, Act IV, scene ii.

terms a desire to mate with "some native woman" in the South Seas. The source of the *Philaster* passage is the opening of Juvenal's sixth satire. Reaction against the complexity of the reigns of Augustus, of James I and of Victoria finds one expression in the desire for real, if brutal, love.

But we already know what the Romantic Movement did to the Elizabethan "mountain-girl." It was no more willing to accept the love of savages without idealization. Over the supposedly simple and free sexual life of the Indian it shed such charming colors that the redman's appetite was transformed into an idyllic passion. In France, *l'esprit Gaulois* could render animalism amusing: the hero of *Arlequin Sauvage* makes violent and jolly love in a way which the serving-maid Violette distinctly likes. Anglo-Saxon morals, however, demanded both more propriety and more sentiment. Hermsprong himself so far relaxes from his Scythian attitude as to say that although among the Indians love is "a simple lesson of nature," and that they "never experience its pains" or "refine upon its pleasures," yet "the modesty of their young women is uncommon. They have delicacy also; and respecting men, a timidity of which here I have seen not many examples." Here, as beneath a microscope, one may see the simplicity of the animal turning into the simplicity of the Golden Age.

The physical attractiveness of some Indian women provided an incentive to this kind of idealization. Columbus, Sir Walter Raleigh and other voyagers, as we already know, testified to the beauty of the aborigines. Southey and Rogers are thus following an old tradition when they pay tribute to the statuesque and unfettered grace of the Indian form. In the *Voyage of Columbus*, the beauty of Cora is great enough to make Alonso, a young Spaniard, forget his sweetheart at home. The combination of simplicity, freedom and beauty, in the light of the Golden Age and of the cult of scenery, proved difficult to resist.

In the days of Aphra Behn, unconventional love was embodied in two literary conventions: the heroic, and the pastoral; the stormy passion of Almanzor, and the melodious plaints of the silly shepherd. The former type is illustrated, as we already know, in the relations between Oroonoko and Imoinda. But in the introduction to her book Astraea says that she has seen " a handsome young Indian, dying for love of a beautiful young Indian Maid; but all his Courtship was, to fold his Arms, pursue her with his Eyes, and Sighs were all his language: Whilst she, as if no such lover were present, or rather as if she desired none such, carefully guarded her Eyes from beholding him, and never approached him, but she look'd down with all the blushing Modesty I have seen in the most Severe and Cautious of our World." Here the stolid reserve of the Indian is transformed half into the despairing worship of the *soupirant*, and half into the bucolic bashfulness of Strephon.

Cawwawkee, the young Indian chief in Gay's *Polly*, represents a later stage of development. As a lover, he is not a savage at all, but that stock figure of sentimental drama, the man of honor. He woos Polly, not by laying direct siege to her heart, but by arousing her admiration for his courage and virtue. Had he appeared later in the century, he would deserve to be called a Sir Charles Grandison in warpaint.

If Cawwawkee is a man of honor, Miss Williams' Ataliba is a man of feeling. His love is " all uncultur'd by the toils of Art." The poet's Muse droops in the attempt to **relate**

> " How dear the Joys Love's infant wishes sought,
> How mild his spirit, and how pure his thought,
> Ere Wealth in sullen pomp was seen to rise,
> And rend the bleeding bosom's fondest ties." [21]

The satire on Omai's popularity with English women is paralleled in cruder form by Howard's *New Humorous Song on the Cherokee Chiefs, Inscribed to the Ladies of Great Britain.*[22] While it would be wrong to take such squibs seriously, it is possible that Omai and the Cherokee Chiefs made a few hearts of quality beat faster. The right to express in literature the desire for natural love was restricted to men, for the day of *The Sheik* had not yet arrived; but dreams are for women as well as for men.

A glance may now be turned toward Indian maidens. When they love, it is generally with the mild simplicity of Dryden's Cydaria, with whom " love is nature." [23] Constancy, another characteristic of the type, is exemplified by Grainger's Pereene.[24] In Elliott's *Kerhonah,* Nidaniss risks her own life to save the missionary whom she loves. But the Indian girls *par excellence* — though Colman does not seem quite certain whether they are red or black — are Yarico and Wowski. The former is a serious, the latter a comic character; but at bottom they possess the same traits. They are beautiful (for Wowski is beautiful to Trudge), wild and tender. They fall in love without tedious formalities, and in love they stay despite the cruelty of Inkle and the clownishness of his servant. The part of Yarico, I imagine, was played as that of a savage Miranda. Her love is meant by Colman to exhibit the same open-hearted tenderness.

[21] *Peru*, pp. 8–9.
[22] *Vide supra*, p. 73.
[23] *Indian Emperour*, Act. II, scene ii.
[24] *Vide supra*, p. 69.

Finally, when in the twilight of romanticism Southey publishes his *Tale of Paraguay*, we find in the South American jungle a picture of wedded respectability. Behold Quiara and Monnema,

> " .   .   .   .   true helpmates they,
> In joy or grief, in weal or woe to share,
> In sickness or in health, through life's long day;
> And reassuming in their hearts her sway,
> Benignant Nature made the burthen light.
> It was the Woman's pleasure to obey,
> The Man's to ease her toil in all he might,
> So each in serving each obtain'd the best delight."

Thus the Noble Savage, after patiently following the footsteps of romantic love, is led at last to Milton and the prayer-book; for his Mother Nature, who once had seemed to offer infinite innocence in infinite liberty, can now only lighten the eternal burden of duty.

Except for the South Sea Islanders, whose status as romantic lovers is beyond question, the courtship of the Noble Savage cannot be regarded as having been a very popular theme. But considering the hard facts that had to be brushed aside before the Negro and the Indian could be made to appear in the necessary glow of illusion, it would be surprising if the list of examples were longer. That list, too, would be considerably increased by the inclusion of songs in which the Indian or the Negro is made to sing of his love; but these must be reserved for treatment in that often-promised chapter on *Natural Man and Natural Poetry* which is at last within sight. Perhaps the material here collected will be sufficient to support the theme of the present chapter. The love of the Noble Savage, though it varies at different times and in the hands of different writers, is admired for the simplicity and the freedom which go to make up the conception of romantic love.

CHAPTER XII

THE NOBLE SAVAGE AND THE RELIGION OF NATURE

RELIGION had never been more a perfunctory social convention and less a force to inspire and console the human heart than about the middle of the eighteenth century. The tendencies which soon after began to restore poetry to religion, though exceedingly complex, may roughly be grouped under two heads: an attack upon the outworn creed that was still, with more or less unconscious hypocrisy, professed by the great majority of men; and an attack upon the cold intellectualism which had deprived that creed of its imaginative appeal. This division, however, is no more clean-cut than the corresponding division of revolutionary thought into Jacobin rationalism and romantic emotionalism. The attempt of men like Paine and Godwin to expose the fallacies of faith was not fruitless, for it stimulated a hard and honest kind of thinking which to-day is not quite unknown But on the whole the assaults of logic against formal religion were much less influential than the assaults of feeling. The former were largely absorbed by the latter, and what then remained of revolutionary scepticism was regarded with horror by many of Godwin's old disciples. The anti-intellectual tendency is therefore by far the more vigorous and the more characteristic of romanticism.

The desire to restore the warmth and mystery of religion took several forms, of which the common element is a hostility to analytical reason. Logic had left its proper domain of science to invade the dim land ruled by intuition. The time for retaliation had come: faith must not only defend its own boundaries, but must wage aggressive warfare against the hair-splitting dialectic which dares to oppose the alliance of the natural with the supernatural.

In this campaign the vanguard was provided by a group of mystics, of which the chief figure is William Law. Law's earlier writings were evangelical rather than truly mystical in tone, and exerted a great influence over John Wesley. His later, mystical works attracted to him several disciples. One was John Byrom, who wrote poems in defense of his master's tenets. Another was Henry Brooke, the pseudo-Platonic novelist. His *Fool of Quality* was admired by Wesley, who prepared an expurgated version of it for the improvement of his flock. " Enthusiasm," indeed, forms a strong bond between the bold and sometimes blasphemous ideas of the mystics and what one might call the intoxicated puritanism of the evangelists.

Blake not only illustrates this connection, but embodies in his poetry the essence of romantic hostility to the analytical spirit. His religious beliefs passed through three phases. The first, that of *Songs of Innocence,* is marked by a fresh, simple, childlike faith in the all-embracing love of God. Orthodox creeds are not so much assailed as ignored. The Christian lamb is more like the comrade of little Barbara Lewthwaite than like the symbol of atonement.

In the second phase, exemplified chiefly by the prophetic books written at Lambeth, Blake pits the innocent incontinence of true religion against the cold chastity of orthodoxy. In his mythology, the God who rules over men is simply " Your Reason," though Blake thinly disguises the term under the name " Urizen." It is *your reason*, the cynical " Geist der stets verneint," and not

Satan, that fell from heaven. Yet though Urizen has fallen, this demon, thanks to the blind belief of mortals, is able to clothe his evil thoughts in a mantle of reality. He typifies denial, restraint, control. Being the very embodiment of negation, he can create nothing. He has, however, an agent called Los, who creates an enslaved world, bound in chains of time and space. Los it is who has given to men fixed systems of philosophy. " I care not," he cries,

> " whether a man is Good or Evil; all that I care
> Is whether he is a Wise man or a Fool. Go! put off Holiness
> And put on Intellect." [1]

This phase of Blake's development roughly coincides with the period when revolutionary feeling was most violent. For a time the poet was a member of the circle which included Paine, Godwin, Mary Wollstonecraft and Holcroft; and both his general philosophy and his application of that philosophy to contemporary problems were in a sense contributions to the Jacobin cause. But like all true romanticists, Blake gradually withdrew from Jacobinism. In his case, the reaction implied a return to the Christian faith. The complex changes in his ideas, and the influence of those changes on his poems, cannot be discussed here. It is sufficient to say that by 1803 he is a staunch believer, burning with the ambition to rear a new Jerusalem in the green fields of England.

Blake now attacks infidelity, as before he had attacked orthodoxy. But since the established church had become permeated with rationalism and even with scepticism, his new campaign is not very different from the old. God is now the true father of mankind, and his kingdom represents the true universe of love, light and joy. But the

[1] *Poetical Works*, p. 408.

spirit of Urizen and Los is still abroad in the land. In the form of sceptical philosophy, it has turned religion into an oppressive institution. Blake's earlier aim has been to free human nature from an utterly sinister religion; his task now is to set both human nature and Christianity, which are essentially one, free from the bonds of doubt-breeding rationalism. Urizen is no longer Jehovah; he is perhaps Newton or Voltaire. But Urizen, as typifying the Everlasting No, is still the great enemy to be overthrown.

Parallels to Blake's feeling on this point are so numerous that only a few typical examples can be brought forward. One thinks of the Persian scholar in Saint-Pierre's *Le Café de Surate* " who had written all his life on theology, and who no longer believed in God." Such learning, as Young observes, gives " light, but not heat " ; and heat is of course the great desideratum. After his recoil from Godwinian philosophy, Wordsworth often expresses his aversion to those who

> ".   .   .   .   .   throned
> The human Understanding paramount
> And made of that their God."

Coleridge condemns those " rationally educated " persons who possess " microscopic acuteness," but who, " when they looked at great things, . . . saw nothing, and denied (very illogically) that anything could be seen "; [2] like the character in Saint-Pierre who denied the existence of the sun after long staring at it in an attempt to understand it. To these Urizenic figures might be added those frigid old men with whose logic Shelley contrasts Cythna's childish intuitive wisdom,[3] and the equally frigid Apollonius, in

[2] *Letters,* Vol. I, p. 17.
[3] *Revolt of Islam,* Canto II, stanzas xxii–xxiv.

Keats' *Lamia*, whose glance symbolizes the disillusionment created by philosophy.

These ideas filtered down to less important writers.
Charles Lloyd longs to live in a cottage, where he can
enjoy "the ignorance of innocence."

> " There, if the systematic school
> No sophist laws for life enact
> To chain the free-born mind to rule —
> The native feelings teach to act." [4]

The romanticist desired ignorance for its own sake no
more than anyone else. His frequent opposition to intellect was due to his recognition of analytical reason as the
great obstacle to that mystical marriage of the natural and
the supernatural which he wished to celebrate. When the
mind is purged of " sophist laws," the " native feelings "
can operate unchecked by the logic of the senses, and the
desired conclusion can easily be reached. As Della Crusca
sings to his Anna Matilda,

> " Tho' small the circle we can trace
> In the abyss of time and space;
> Tho' learning has its limits got,
> The feelings of the soul have not.
> Their vast excursions find no end;
> And RAPTURE needs not comprehend! " [5]

Just as retreat to the woods may be a step toward perfectibility, so a relapse into " the ignorance of innocence "
may imply a rebound into super-rational wisdom. It is
perhaps unfair that we should feel inclined to smile at
such ideas when they are expressed by poets like Lloyd and

---

[4] *Poems on Various Subjects*, p. 48. *Cf.* Clare's *The Happiness of Ignorance*. *The Rural Muse*, pp. 140–141.

[5] *Ode to Anna Matilda*. *The British Album*, p. 74.

Merry, for after all these little men are merely echoing the ideas of greater figures.

The union of this opposition to logic with the scenery-cult gives what may be called the religion of nature. Flowers, forests and mountains provided a meeting-ground between the supernatural and man. Through them breathed the spirit of the universe, and by seeking them man could find that spirit. Nothing, therefore, could so stimulate that rapture which transcends comprehension as " nature."

The religion of nature is not a fixed concept. Often, especially in the earlier work of romantic poets, it contains traces of Christian deism, necessitarianism, or unitarianism. Sometimes scenery is a mere incitement to quite orthodox piety; while at the other extreme one finds a pantheistic absorption of the creator by the thing created. Through all these varieties, however, run two constant factors: a sense of the superiority of feeling to thinking, and a sense of the religious significance of natural objects.

Thus Young, in his attempt to convert Lorenzo, sends him not to books, but to nature.

> " Read Nature; Nature is a friend to truth;
> Nature is christian; preaches to mankind;
> And bids dead matter aid us in our creed."

And Bowles, in a less evangelical and more truly romantic vein, speaks of that " sense of quiet gladness " which in the summertime

> " .   .   .   .   . steals
> From lowly nooks, and feels itself expand
> Amid the works of Nature, to the Power
> That made them."

Just as the lover of scenery shuns the town, so the worshipper of God in nature shuns man-made churches. True religion, says Joseph Hucks, avoids " the grandeur of the Gothic pile " to roam through the woods and listen to the birds.

> " Wher'er she goes, what'er her eye surveys,
> In Nature's works she reads her Maker's praise." [6]

Religious liberalism often joined hands with political liberalism. James Montgomery's Swiss refugee, driven from his home by Napoleon's soldiers, turns his eyes toward the American forests,

> " Where a tyrant never trod,
> Where a slave was never known,
> But where Nature worships God
> In the wilderness alone." [7]

The God of nature, besides consoling victims of political oppression, could soothe the pangs of those who suffered from a vaguer melancholy. "A smile of moonlight," says Christopher North, has often changed despair into peace; but the smile of moonlight is the smile of God.

> " Low as we are, we blend our fate
> With things so beautifully great,
> And though opprest with heaviest grief,
> From Nature's bliss we draw relief,
> Assured that God's most gracious eye
> Beholds us in our misery." [8]

Godwin's Fleetwood, to whose noble savagery we have so often referred, is at first " the awestruck and ardent worshipper " of the " divinity that presides over the constellations, the meteors, and the ocean." His reformation

---

[6] *Annual Anthology*, Vol. II, pp. 50–51.
[7] *Vide supra*, p. 292.
[8] *The Isle of Palms and Other Poems*, p. 22.

is accomplished by a tour in the Alps, where his mind rises in successive planes of reverie from William Tell to the South Sea Islands, and from the South Sea Islands to paradise.[9]   In much the same way, Wordsworth shook off the corrupting artificialities of Cambridge.   In the Alps, he writes his sister, " My whole soul was turned to him who produced the terrible majesty before me."

Wordsworth's devotion to natural religion is too well known to require any addition to the remarks made in the last chapter but one.   *The Tables Turned* contrasts " the lore which Nature brings " with " our meddling intellect." The message of the following stanza, that " one impulse from a vernal wood " may carry more moral instruction than the teaching of all the sages, is a clear instance of the association of nature with intuition in the war against rationalism.

Though Coleridge's transcendentalism gradually turned him into a disapproving critic of Wordsworth's nature-worship, he was for a time himself an ardent devotee.   In 1798 — on the whole the most significant year in the history of natural religion — he expresses the wish that his child shall " wander like a breeze " among the lakes and mountains, to

> "   .   .   .   .   .   . see and hear
> The lovely shapes and sounds intelligible
> Of that eternal language, which thy God
> Utters, who from eternity doth teach
> Himself in all, and all things in himself." [10]

Surely the bond between God and nature is here as close as in all but a very few of Wordsworth's poems.

Our own Ralph Waldo Emerson's philosophy has

[9] *Vide supra*, p. 153.
[10] *Frost at Midnight.*

sometimes been hailed as distinctively American. **But**
American writer was never more imitative than in the lines

> " O, when I am safe in my sylvan home,
> I tread on the pride of Greece and Rome;
> And when I am stretched beneath the pines,
> Where the evening star so holy shines,
> I laugh at the lore and the pride of man,
> At the sophist schools, and the learned clan;
> For what are they all, in their high conceit,
> When man in the bush with God may meet? "

Goodbye, proud world! is of 1839. In those days the
importation of ideas was a slow process. But at last Con-
cord has received the religion of nature. Its destructive
side is represented by flings at the scholar and the analyst;
its constructive side appears in the idea that when the tradition of intellect is destroyed the infinite may be found in
the forest.

One might imagine, not altogether frivolously, that the
man who can most easily meet God in the bush is the bush-
man. Now that the main outlines of natural religion have
been sketched, it remains to trace the connection between
that religion and the Noble Savage idea.

The early explorers found a perplexing situation: the
Indians appeared to have Christian virtues without Christian faith. Their religion — leaving out of account the
advanced barbaric civilizations of Peru and Mexico — was
so simple that it seemed no religion at all. The missionaries insisted, perhaps not without professional bias, that
the natives could easily be converted.

Difficulties, however, were soon encountered. The doctrine of atonement was certainly essential, but how could
it be impressed upon savages who did not realize that they
were sinful? There was the rub: the Indians knew nothing
about the fall of Adam, and hesitated to shoulder the

faults of a chief who had died so long ago. Some could not even understand why they should drape their bodies in repentance for acts which seemed quite natural — eating fruit and indulging in sexual pleasure. These troublesome matters could be explained by analogies between Christian theology and savage superstition: the Indians were already familiar with tabu, and with the idea of propitiatory sacrifice. For obvious reasons, however, these comparisons were more likely to be made by the Indians themselves than by their instructors.

Père Claude, a Brazilian missionary of the early seventeenth century, sums up his difficulties in the words, " Ces pauvres gens, aussi coupables que nous, diffèrent de nous en ce qu'ils ne se rendent même pas compte de l'énormité de la faute commise par nos premiers pères." Yet this Capuchin monk, although he admires the Indians, is forced to regard them as damned souls. The mere fact that they have no conviction of sin cannot possibly absolve them from the curse of Adam.

This orthodox view was too rigid to remain unshaken. Strangely, the heathen Indians seemed in many respects superior to the devout Europeans. Las Casas, as we know, draws a bitter contrast between his charges and their white oppressors. Père Claude himself asserts that "la Nature n'est pas si vitiée, ny la jeunesse tant corrompue entre ces Barbares et Payens comme elle est entre les Chréstiens." [11] Another missionary, Père Du Tertre, whom Chinard calls a " predecessor of Bernardin de Saint-Pierre," and who receives a chapter of Chateaubriand's *Génie du Christianisme*, is even more emphatic. On the day of judgment, he declares, the Indians may well bring accusation against the Christians; " et ne condamneront-ils point avec justice leur Ambition, leur Avarice, leur

[11] Quoted by Chinard, *L'Amérique et le rêve exotique*, pp. 9–10.

Luxe, leurs dissolutions, leurs trahisons, leurs envies, et mille autres péchez qui ne sont pas même connus parmy eux." [12]

If Indian innocence could soften the heart of seventeenth century orthodoxy, how appealing it must have seemed to later and more liberal generations! A deist would smile at the thought of judging the Indians in terms of a Hebrew legend; and a romanticist would recognize in the combination of goodness and creedlessness his own ideal of religion.

This change in attitude toward the Indian would not, indeed, be a violent one, for even in orthodox Christianity there was much that gave support to the Noble Savage idea. Against the hard intellectual doctrine of sin and atonement stood that faith in untutored goodness, that hostility to worldliness, which are essential to the Christian emotion. Man's feeling that to be simple is to be good overpowered theological subtleties. As the intellectual element of Christianity gradually receded before the emotional, the savage's qualifications to enter the kingdom of heaven became less and less questionable.

It was difficult even for theologians to consign to hellfire creatures who were not only ignorant of Adam and Eve, but whose virtues strikingly recalled those which flourished in Eden before the fall. The story of man's first disobedience is primitivistic as well as primitive. If myths are to be interpreted in terms of their spiritual significance, Eden is equivalent to the Golden Age. "Innocence corrupted by the impious craving for knowledge" is the moral of each. Milton is both Christian and romantic when he speaks of "Knowledge of good bought dear by knowing ill" and cries out upon that "dishonest shame of nature's works" which has

[12] *Ibid.*, p. 51.

> "   .   .   banished from man's life his happiest life,
> Simplicity and spotless innocence."

If the nakedness of Adam and Eve is justified by the fact that " they thought no ill," why not the nakedness of savages? Since the fall of man was caused by the desire for knowledge, it would seem unfair to condemn the Indians for their possession of that very ignorance which had constituted the blessedness of Adam. Perhaps the savage was intended by God as a living reminder of the primal innocent state.

Without pursuing this complicated subject further we may conclude that despite certain theological objections the virtues of the Indians seemed from the very first to corroborate the fundamental emotions of Christianity. Those emotions were largely stifled by the formal and institutional spirit, but were liberated when the return to nature swept creeds aside.

The romanticists of course were not unaware that savages had their own religious customs, and that many of these were barbarous and revolting. They might often, however, be interpreted as gropings toward the light — " varieties of religious experience " none the less important for being primitive. One should beware of branding as debased a superstition of which one could find traces in one's own heart.

We have already noted an affinity between the missionary impulse and the Noble Savage idea. The desire to convert the heathen may often be accompanied by a sense that the heathen have the roots of true religion in their hearts. " Not vain," says Coleridge in *The Destiny of Nations,*

> " Nor yet without permitted power impressed,
> I deem those legends terrible, with which
> The polar ancient thrills his uncouth throng;
>
> .   .   .   .

.   .   .   Wild phantasies, yet wise,
On the victorious goodness of high God
Teaching reliance, and medicinal hope,
Till from Bethesda northward, heavenly Truth,
With gradual steps, winning her difficult way,
Transfer their rude Faith perfected and pure."

Though the piety of this seems conventional enough, we
know that in 1796, when these lines were written, Coleridge had begun to feel deep interest in primitive superstitions. If Bethesda is moving northward to Lapland,
Lapland is moving south to Bethesda.

To trace parallels between romantic religion and the
actual religion of savages would be tempting. Savage religion is essentially magic, and magic can exist only when
natural phenomena are regarded as motivated entirely by
supernatural agencies. Moreover, the savage finds it hard
to distinguish the animate from the inanimate. A bear is
as much a person as he himself is, and a tree is as much a
person as a bear. The savage eats rabbit that he may run
swiftly, and marries in springtime that crops may be
fruitful. In his life, natural forces and human forces are
completely confused. He needs no " renascence of wonder," for to him everything is mysterious.

Let me hasten to say that the mystery of the savage is
not the mystery of the romantic poet. But is there no
connection between the two? That thrill of pagan terror
at the conclusion of Wordsworth's *Nutting* is atavistic —
the panic of a savage who has angered a tree-spirit. The
boy who hurried home from skating beneath the watchful
eyes of the mountains never quite grew up, although he
learned to clothe his feelings in the pantheistic rapture of
Tintern Abbey. The savage has achieved that supernat-
uralizing of nature toward which the romanticist aspires.
He has achieved it on a much lower plane, but the fact that
he has achieved it at all often arouses a feeling of admira-

tion, almost of kinship, in the romantic heart. Intuition is
not instinct, but it constantly appeals to instinct for evidence of the validity of its visions. Savage religion had
enough in common with romantic religion to enable a lover
of nature to view the one in the light of the other. Spirit-
ually, as in other ways, the Noble Savage was a promise
of what man might become.

Let us turn now to a few definite instances in which
savages are used to illustrate the beauties of natural religion. The deists of the popular, "common-sense," Bol-
ingbrokian school could on occasion resort to primitivism
in their anti-theological campaign.

> " Lo, the poor Indian! whose untutored mind
>   Sees God in clouds, or hears him in the wind.
>   His soul proud science never taught to stray
>   Far as the solar walk or milky way;
>   Yet simple nature to his hope has giv'n,
>   Behind the cloud-topped hill, an humbler heav'n."

Pope's lines are an impressive illustration of the gradual
melting of eighteenth century hard-headedness into romantic soft-heartedness.

Glynn, in a Cambridge prize poem entitled *The Day of
Judgement*, attacks scepticism in the manner of Young
rather than of Pope, but uses Pope's very words. He demands of the infidel

> " Why, on the brink of Orellana's stream,
>   Where never science rear'd her sacred torch,
>   Th' untutored Indian dreams of happier worlds
>   Behind the cloud-topt hill? "

The savage and his simple heart are by 1757 — the date
of this poem — stock properties of the early romanticists.

In this study certain affinities between Noble Savages
and Noble Peasants have been pointed out. Henry
Kirke White furnishes one more illustration when he

applies the " Lo! the poor Indian " theme to the English rustic.

> " Lo! the unletter'd hind who never knew
> To raise his mind excursive, to the heights
> Of abstract contemplation."

The hind feels God in his breast because his gratitude has been stirred by the bounties of nature. He is especially thankful, however, for being snugger than a suspiciously Thomsonian traveler lost in a storm.

> " He [the hind, not the traveler] turns to bless,
> With honest warmth, his Maker and his God.
> And shall it e'er be said, that a poor hind,
> Nursed in the lap of Ignorance, and bred
> In want and labour, glows with nobler zeal "

than the sophisticated philosopher? And then the familiar sneer at learning:

> " What is the pomp of learning? The parade
> Of letters and of tongues? E'en as the mists
> .   .   .   .
> That pass away and perish." [18]

Both the poor Indian and the poor peasant, then, may be used as examples of natural religion.

When Pope said that the Indian " sees God in clouds, or hears him in the wind " he could have had little idea of how greatly the savage's ability to find God in nature would impress succeeding generations. What was merely an indication of primitive simplicity becomes a proof of primitive inspiration. Explorers of the late eighteenth century, whose observations were influenced by contemporary Arcadian notions, fostered this change in attitude toward savage religion. Jonathan Carver is much im-

[18] *Poetical Works*, pp. 360–361.

pressed by a young chief who prays aloud to a waterfall. "I doubt not," he writes, "but that his offerings and prayers were as acceptable to the universal Parent of mankind, as if they had been made with greater pomp, or in a consecrated place. . . . Whilst I beheld the artless, yet engaging manners of this unpolished savage, I could not help drawing a comparison between him and some of the more refined inhabitants of civilized countries, not much, I own, in favor of the latter." This Indian's "untutored mind," far from holding him down to deistic common-sense, bids fair to scale the topmost heights of religious ecstasy.

The complete accord between such reports and the feelings of romantic poets is shown by Southey, who knew his Carver thoroughly. When in *Madoc* the Welsh voyagers tell their redskin hosts of the Christian God, the Indians reply,

> "And we too . . . we know
> And worship the Great Spirit, who in clouds
> And storms, in mountain-caves and by the fall
> Of waters in the woodland solitudes,
> And in the night and silence of the sky,
> Doth make his being felt." [14]

Churches separate worshippers; nature unites them. Be they white or coppery, those who find God in the bush can laugh at creeds. They speak the same language of the heart; they have thrown off Urizen.

One may readily imagine that when Wordsworth speaks of the Indian as "exalted" by the "streams and woods" and swayed by "star-guided contemplations," [15] he has found his philosophy of nature supported by the account

---

[14] *Cf.* Elliott's *Kerhonah*, in which the persecuted chief and his daughter pray to a waterfall for vengeance against the English.

[15] *Vide supra*, pp. 179, 190.

of some traveler who knew the tastes of the reading public. Once the Noble Savage idea gets started, it travels in a circle — literature colors observation, and observation influences literature.

A further step is to endow the savage not only with romantic simplicity, but with romantic scorn of complexity. Carver contrasts his young chief with " some of the more refined inhabitants of civilized countries " ; a more artful writer would have made the Indian himself point an accusing finger at civilization. As a matter of fact, the Indians did ask the explorers and missionaries many amusing and some very shrewd questions. In this respect they are like children. When in a modern problem-play a beautiful golden-haired child is made audibly to wonder why everybody cannot love everybody else, an impression of sublimity is gained by the dramatist. A naiveté due to lack of worldly experience glows like a flash of superrational insight. Similarly, when Indians scornfully asked what money was for or marvelled that rational beings should disagree on matters of faith, they were sometimes felt to be above levels of thought and conduct to which they had not yet climbed.

Such situations of course provided excellent material for writers who wished to expose the faults of organized Christianity. The interview between Gulliver and the old Houyhnhnm has as its background many real instances in which the savage had embarrassed the too confident missionary. Robinson Crusoe's attempt to instruct Man Friday in the tenets of the established faith belongs to the same tradition. Characteristically, Defoe's satire is quiet and subtle. Friday, unlike most literary savages, is made to seem genuinely naive; and Crusoe, unlike most civilized men in such interviews, does not too laboriously betray the conventions of which he is the spokesman. The untutored mind of this poor Indian cannot grasp the Christian explanation of the problem of evil. "But," he demands, "if God much stronger, much might as the wicked devil, why God no kill the devil, so make him no more do wicked?" Crusoe is "strangely surprised at this question." After a few more such posers, the white man escapes by "rising up hastily as upon some sudden occasion of going out; then sending him for something a good way off, I seriously prayed to God that He would enable me to instruct savingly this poor savage." To determine just how much of this is ironic is not easy, but one suspects that the author of the *Shortest Way With the Dissenters* is up to his old tricks.

With Sa Ga Yean Qua Rash Tow's comments on St. Paul's as reported by Addison we are already familiar, as we are with Bage's amusing story of the debate between the proselytizing white woman and the urbanely sceptical Great Beaver.[16] In general, however, wit plays little part in primitivistic thrusts at orthodoxy. At least in England, a sense of humor provides an unfavorable atmosphere for the Noble Savage. The earliest serious use of the Indian in an attack on Christian hypocrisy is the torture of Montezuma in Dryden's *Indian Emperour*. Observe this theological argument between the Christian Priest and the suffering Aztec:

> "*Chr. Pr.* Since Age by erring Child-hood is mis-led,
>   Refer your self to our unerring Head.
>   *Mont.* Man, and not err? What Reason can you give?
> *Chr. Pr.* Renounce that Carnal Reason, and believe.
>   *Mont.* The Light of Nature should I thus betray,
>   'Twere to wink hard that I might see the day."

All this while, torture is providing a most powerful pragmatic argument for the will to believe in the Pope, but

[16] *Vide supra*, pp. 44, 169.

Montezuma will not renounce the Light of Nature. Dryden had not yet written *The Hind and the Panther*.

Mackenzie's *Man of the World* — to take a long leap — provides a splendid example of the censoriousness of the Noble Savage even on his deathbed. When the old chief lies dying, Annesley, the white man whom he has befriended, cannot restrain his tears; but the Indian reproves this show of feeling. His "composure . . . would have done honour to the firmest philosopher of antiquity " — Socrates, who chided his friends for lamenting the approach of the jailer and the cup. "In those tears . . . there is no wisdom," the old Indian says. Lovers of sensibility, we know, have a paradoxical admiration for savage stoicism, though they always find beneath the impassive exterior the feeling heart.

Having reproved the white man, the dying chief launches out into a diatribe against civilized religion: "The children of the French king call themselves after the same God that the English do; yet their discourses concerning him cannot be true, because they are opposite one another. Each says, that God shall burn the others with fire, which could not happen if both were his children. Besides, neither of them act as the sons of Truth, but as the sons of Deceit; they say their God heareth all things, yet do they break the promises which they have called upon him to hear; but we know that the spirit within us listeneth, and what we have said in its hearing, that we do! " No time is left even to acknowledge the debt of a cock to Asclepius. "With such sentiments," says Annesley, "the old man resigned his breath, and I blushed for the life of Christians, while I heard them." Dr. Johnson pays tribute to this tradition in his Indian's speech in the *Idler*.[17]

In the general discussion of Mackenzie's contribution to

[17] *Vide supra*, p. 336.

our subject, there was noted a similarity between the tribe's farewell address to Annesley and the famous "prayer of Socrates." [18] Mackenzie evidently feels, with Montaigne, Haller and others, that the savages are true embodiments of the philosophic spirit. Devotees of natural religion can either attack the man of reason for what he is, or absorb him by claiming him as an ally. One becomes hardened to the Noble Savage as a mouthpiece of naturalistic emotions, but when he dons the *chiton* of "the best, and the wisest, and the most just" of the mind's martyrs, one marvels at the inappropriateness of the disguise.

In this study the term "Noble Savage" has sometimes been applied not merely to red, brown, or black aborigines, but also to simple souls of any color who are viewed by romantic writers in accordance with the formula which was established at the outset. Noble Savages in this broader sense are especially appropriate embodiments of natural religion, for since they have almost no correspondence with reality their intuitive worship of Nature's God can be portrayed as free from any revoltingly primitive elements. Paul and Virginia, for example, are as ignorant as Mauritians, but being mere figments of Saint-Pierre's imagination they possess a kind of abstract simplicity which rises above the reports of any explorer. Untainted by superstition is that creedless faith which impels them to kneel down wherever they chance to be and raise their innocent hands to heaven. Similarly, while Immalee's religion is fundamentally that of a savage, the unreality of her character enables Maturin to disentangle from the bestiality of primitive cults those elements which harmonize with his ideals.

Between such imaginary figures and the actual savage stands the peasant. He also is a fit vehicle for natural re-

[18] *Vide supra*, p. 92.

ligion. His contact with scenery and his freedom from cerebration are indubitable; while his virtues, like the savage's, shame the artificialities of civilization. Although his comparative lack of exotic appeal places some obstacles in the way of romanticizing his character, his respectability demands forgetfulness of fewer unpleasant facts than in the case of the savage.

When Henry Kirke White, as we have seen, substitutes " Lo! the unlettered hind " for " Lo! the poor Indian " he is altering words only, and not ideas. The religion of the Indian and of the peasant may be admired on exactly the same grounds. Wordsworth, in *Descriptive Sketches,* " sees God in clouds, and hears him in the wind ":

> " He holds with God himself communion high,
> There where the peal of swelling torrents fills
> The sky-roofed temple of the eternal hills,
>
> . . . .
>
> Awe in his breast with holiest love unites,
> And the near heavens impart their own delights."

Would not these lines apply equally well to the young chief whom Carver shows us communing with God by the side of an American " swelling torrent " ? The rustics of Wordsworth's maturer poems do not cultivate these ecstatic moments. Nature influences them almost without their knowing it: they feel only a kind of "blind love" for the source of that light which glows in their simple hearts. This view is perhaps a compromise between Wordsworth's sense of fact and his devotion to nature. In religion, his rustics are Noble Savages whose inspiration has become " a wise passiveness."

Robert Southey will serve to gather up the straying threads of this subject. The anti-Godwinian reaction writes of a Swiss peasant who to all intents and purposes

which followed the collapse of pantisocracy found him a
champion of the heart and a lover of nature. Accordingly
on a Sunday morning of 1795 he addresses some imaginary
worldling in the lines:

> " Go, thou, and seek the House of Prayer!
> I to the woodlands bend my way,
> And meet Religion there!
> She needs not haunt the high-arched dome to pray,
> Where storied windows dim the doubtful day:
> At liberty she loves to rove,
> Wide o'er the heathy hill or cowslipt dale."

This negative shrinking from doctrinal formality combined with the positive desire to meet God in the bush is
partly imposed by Southey upon his Noble Savages, and
partly supported by his researches into the actual religion
of primitive peoples. As he grows more conventional in
his thinking his wide knowledge causes him to repudiate
his early illusions about savages, but as long as he himself
is a worshipper at nature's shrine he finds in the literature
of exploration only encouragement for his romantic hypothesis. *Madoc* has already been cited to show how well
Indian faith could be made to harmonize with natural
religion.

That the nature-worship of *Madoc* belongs quite as
much to Southey as to the Indians which he depicts is to be
inferred from the presence of the same feeling in *Thalaba*.
The poet cannot refrain from mixing with his great mass of
Oriental lore his own religion. Consider this picture of
Thalaba and Oneiza worshipping with their father in the
desert:

> "   .   .   .   Sinks the word
> With deeper influence from the Imam's voice,
> Where, in the day of congregation, crowds
> Perform the duty-task?

> Their Father is their Priest,
> The Stars of Heaven their point of prayer,
> And the blue firmament
> The glorious temple, where they feel
> The present Deity."

These imaginary Noble Savages, no less than American Indians, can cry with Saint-Pierre's pariah, " Ma pagode, c'est la nature! "

But Southey carries the religion of nature even further in his *Joan of Arc*. A simple peasant girl to whom the blessed saints spoke in the apple-orchard, an intuitive mystic, champion of the oppressed, a victim of kingcraft and priestcraft, the Maid of Orleans provided a tempting subject. In the first edition, Southey, out of deference to epic traditions, lets his heroine's actions be guided in part by the miraculous intercession of a Christian Olympus; but in the second edition, which appeared in the great naturalistic year of 1798, all this machinery is stripped away, and Joan appears as a true child of nature. She is akin to Lucy, for her faith is due to the benign influence of the forests in which she was reared. She is a Noble Savage, for she owes her spiritual power to her ignorance of those rationalistic subtleties which have corrupted religion.

She tells the hesitant Dauphin that for her to doubt the authenticity of her mission would be as easy as to doubt

> " Creating Wisdom; when in the evening gale
> I breathe the mingled odors of the spring."

But the Dauphin, ill-qualified to understand the force of scenic inspiration, wonders whether streams and groves have made Joan a good Catholic. He convenes an ecclesiastical court,

> " And from their palaces and monasteries
>   Swarm'd forth the Doctors, men acute and deep,
>   Grown grey in study; Priests and Bishops haste
>   To Chinon — Teachers wise and with high names,
>   Seraphic, Subtle or Irrefragable,
>   By their admiring pupils dignified."

Clearly, men who know so much cannot be truly religious. They have grown blind from staring at the sun. The forces of the head are mustering against this single champion of the heart. The Noble Savage stands at bay before the hounds of theology.

When the mitred bigots ask this pretender to supernatural powers whether she has been faithful to the observances of Mother Church, Joan astounds them by replying that churches have always roused in her a feeling of repugnance.

> " The forms of worship in mine earlier years
>   Waked my young mind to artificial awe,
>   And made me fear my God. Warm with the glow
>   Of health and exercise, whene'er I passed
>   The threshold of the house of prayer I felt
>   A cold damp chill me."

In childhood, then, she worshipped " a God of terrors," but gradually she cast off her " artificial awe," and associated " the glow of health and exercise " with the effulgence of the divine spirit.

> " I saw the eternal energy pervade
>   The boundless range of nature;
>
>   .   .   .   .
>
>   .   .   .   .   .   .   Then I felt
>   That He who formed this goodly frame of things
>   Must needs be good   .   .   .   .   .
>
>   .   .   .   .

Methinks it is not strange, then, that I fled
The house of prayer, and made the lonely grove
My temple."

The church inspires terror; the grove, love. " Ma pagode, c'est la nature."

But to Joan's inquisitors her preference is simply pagan; it smacks of witchcraft. People do strange and fearful things in the woods. On this point Southey quotes from " the notes to the English version of Le Grand's Fabliaux " as follows: " In the Journal of Paris, in the reigns of Charles VI and VII, it is asserted that the Maid of Orleans, in answer to an interrogatory of the doctors, whether she had ever assisted at the assemblies held at the Fountain of the Fairies, near Domprein, round which the evil spirits dance, confessed that she had often repaired to a beautiful fountain in the country of Lorraine, which she named the good Fountain of the Fairies of our Lord." This accusation may have been a mere guess on the part of Joan's persecutors. On the other hand this peasant girl may well have taken part in some of those half-pagan rites which, as anthropologists tell us, are even yet practiced by nominally Christian rustics in parts of France.

Whether the charge had any such foundation or not, it is interesting to see how the religion of nature is able to accept it and interpret it in lofty spiritual terms. " There is," Joan readily admits,

".   .   .   a fountain in the forest called
The Fountain of the Fairies."

The place, so people say, is visited at midnight by elves who leave their circles on the sward. As a child Joan heard these tales " with a delightful wonder." And as she grew older " the strange and fearful pleasure " which she took in visiting the place did not disappear, but

> " .   .   .   now it woke
> Deeper delight and more mysterious awe.
> A blessed spot! Oh, how my soul enjoyed
> Its holy quietness! with what delight,
> Escaping from mankind, I hastened there
> To solitude and freedom! "

Yet the fountain is more than a refuge from the trammels
of civilization and the terrors of the church. It provides
a means of mystic contact with the godhead.

> " .   .   .   On a rock I sat;
> The glory of the tempest filled my soul,
> And when the thunders pealed, and the long flash
> Hung durable in heaven, and on my sight
> Spread the gray forest, memory, thought were gone,
> All sense of self annihilate, I seemed
> Diffused into the scene."

In this manner does Southey relate the medieval legend
of the " Fountain of the Fairies " with that mood of self-
annihilation in which the soul of the mystic becomes lost
in the infinite soul of the universe. Witchcraft is, one
might say, the childhood of the religion of nature.

Baffled by their victim's answer, the ecclesiastics shift
their ground and ask Joan whether she feels a proper conviction of sin. The conviction of sin belongs to the
province of dogmatic theology. As a product of reflection,
it has no meaning to Joan. She does not *feel* sinful; therefore she is innocent. " Was it strange," she asks,

> " .   .   .   that when I felt
> How God had made my spirit quick to feel
> And love whate'er was beautiful and good,
> And from aught evil and deformed to shrink
> Even as with instinct — father! was it strange
> That in my heart I had no thought of sin,
> And did not need forgiveness? "

Her theological position is exactly that of the Indians whom the missionaries found so unwilling to shoulder the curse of Adam, but her arguments are those of a romantic poet. There could be no clearer instance of the fusion of natural religion and the Noble Savage idea than in this contrast between Joan, whose emotions find God in his beautiful world, and her inquisitors, over whose learned and analytical minds reigns the hard spirit of Urizen.

Let us, finally, take a fragment of savage religion and ourselves interpret it in naturalistic terms. According to Man Friday, the creator of the world is "one Benamuckee, who lives beyond all. . . . All things say O to him." This deity, however, cannot hear his priests unless they climb to the top of the mountain on which he dwells. The worship of Benamuckee, therefore, consists of ascending a mountain in order to say O.

Now is this not, to the romantic sensibilities which we have hypothetically assumed, an attractive notion? We must not take it in crass literalness.

> "One who would peep and botanize
> Upon his mother's grave"

might assert that the syllable " O " represents some barbaric chant or some inarticulate grunt. But may not this exclamation have a deeper significance? Does it not contain much of the spontaneously passionate quality possessed by all true religion? " O! " — no more than that. No cold-blooded dialectic, no carelessly muttered creed, but a cry of joyful awe wrung from the simple heart in this moment of mystic contemplation.

And then the mountain. Let the theologian and the sceptic, bound alike in the toils of rationalism, mock the crudity of the notion that Benamuckee can hear from the summit what he cannot hear from the plain! To us the idea is not without sublimity. It is a childish but infinitely precious adumbration of the great truth that God discloses himself to those who seek out the fairest manifestations of his spirit. The mountain-top is the temple of nature's God and the praise which best befits him is a murmur of reverent delight. Man Friday's faith, then, holds spiritual values from which the civilized world has fallen away, and to which we must return along the paths of simplicity, intuitiveness and love of nature.

This representation of the romantic attitude toward savage religion is perhaps an unfair burlesque. And yet Rousseau, speaking of the reverence which nature arouses in him, says: "I have somewhere read of a wise bishop who, in a visit to his diocese, found an old woman whose only prayer consisted in the single interjection 'Oh!' 'Good Mother,' said he to her, 'continue always to pray thus. Your prayer is better than ours.' This better prayer is mine also." [19] The old woman and Man Friday might worship side by side. And though Professor Babbitt himself would not assert that Rousseau's religion is the cult of Benamuckee, we must take Rousseau's word for it that he sympathized with Man Friday's simple faith. He interprets it, of course, in terms of his own infinitely deeper view of life, but he could not so interpret it did he not recognize a certain kinship with it. "This better prayer is mine also."

[19] *Confessions*, Vol. II, p. 383.

Chapter XIII

NATURAL MAN AND NATURAL POETRY

SOME apology is due the reader for the following treatment of a subject which has received more scholarly attention than other aspects of the Noble Savage tradition. Miss Whitney has already shown the intimate connection between the idealization of primitive poetry and the idealization of primitive man.[1] Professor Tinker, in *Nature's Simple Plan*,[2] has suggestively discussed the same subject from the viewpoint of his Johnsonian studies. Professor Farley's papers on *The Dying Indian* and *Three "Lapland Songs"*[3] are efficient analyses of specific problems. Chapter VI of Dr. Bissell's dissertation includes a discussion of the Indian as a poet. My precursors, however, have by no means exhausted the possibilities of the theme and I have not hesitated to add my own gleanings to the material which they have collected.

Pseudo-classicism in literature is but a specific form of that hard intellectual control to escape from which the romanticists returned to nature. Just as love and religion had been stifled by a mass of conventions and dogmas, so poetry itself had been stifled by the authority of Aristotle. Blake's statement that "it is the Classics, and not Goths or

---

[1] *English Primitivistic Theories of Epic Origins; Modern Philology*, Vol. XXI, pp. 337–378.

[2] Chapter III, "Ancient Bard and Gentle Savage."

[3] *The Dying Indian; Kittredge Anniversary Papers*, pp. 251–260. *Three "Lapland Songs"; Publications of the Modern Language Association of America*, Vol. XXI, pp. 1–39.

Monks, that desolate Europe with wars " is explained by his association of classic restraint and poise with the spirit of Urizen. "Unity and Morality," he says, — meaning by the latter term the "decorum" of critical theory — "are secondary considerations, and belong to Philosophy and not to Poetry." He finds his aesthetic ideal in Gothic exuberance: "Grecian is Mathematic Form: Gothic is Living Form. Mathematic Form is eternal in the Reasoning Memory: Living Form is Eternal Existence." [4] Not many of Blake's contemporaries possessed insight enough to express the relation between philosophical and literary revolt with such clarity, but the feeling that Aristotelianism stands in the path not only of poetic liberty but of emotional liberty in general appears very frequently.

In poetry the romanticists desired the same simplicity, freedom, subjectivity, mystery and passion that they felt should characterize the whole of existence. Since these qualities could not spring from the barren soil of the eighteenth century, the poets of the new era looked for inspiration and practical guidance to earlier forms of literature which possessed those qualities. They returned, that is, to what seemed to them the nature, the primal innocent state, of English poetry. Milton they loved because the music of his verse and the grandeur of his images gave them a sense of sublimity and infinitude, and because they discerned in his minor poems something of their own feeling for nature. Shakespeare was the archetype of fertility and boldness. Across the years he seemed both Gothic and sylvan — an early man of nature, warbling his native wood-notes wild. To escape from Pope's trim garden into the lush wilderness of Spenser was delightful; and Spenser's richly monstrous fables

[4] *Poetical Works*, p. 431.

pointed to the Middle Ages, where, in romance and ballad, nature was suffused with supernatural colors.

Anonymous medieval poems were especially appealing because they satisfied both the romantic poet's egoism and his belief in essential humanity. Those longer and more ambitious productions which unmistakably bespoke individual authorship must have been composed by some bard untutored, but gifted with a wild natural genius not unlike that of his modern admirer. On the other hand, the simple popular ballads supposedly risen from the social heart of a whole "singing and dancing throng," testified abundantly to the primitive democracy of imagination. Says Professor Haller: "The popular origin of the old ballads, thoroughly accepted though widely misunderstood, reënforced the faith of men like Southey and Wordsworth in the virtue of simple human nature when uncontaminated by society."[5] It would be equally true to say that the idea of "communal composition" could hardly have flourished as it did except for the encouragement lent it by the prevalent Arcadian illusion. Primitive poetry and primitive goodness go hand in hand, one supporting the other.

Savage poetry is important in that it carried the tradition of primitive literature on into modern times. If the virtues of the Indian or South Sea Islander encouraged belief in natural man, his flair for imaginative expression encouraged belief in natural poetry. We must not expect, however, to find much real knowledge of aboriginal art. Just enough information filtered in through the explorers to suggest to the romantic mind an analogy between contemporary savage poetry and early European popular poetry. As with love and religion, the romanticist interprets savage practices in terms of his own ideals: he can

[5] *Early Life of Robert Southey*, p. 221.

put almost anything vaguely simple, balladlike and emotional into the mouth of an Indian. In his imitations some realistic color is occasionally present, but on the whole the song of the Noble Savage bears little relation to the genuine primitive stuff. Generally the savage disguise adopted by the poet creates no truer illusion than the burnt cork of the " nigger minstrel." The dramatic lyric gives the author an opportunity for vicarious emotional experience, enabling him to express, through the lips of another, emotions which in his own person he might hesitate to unbosom. Thus the mild, middle-class, feverishly religious, over-studious and consumptive Henry Kirke White breaks out in such titles as *The Shipwreck'd Solitary's Song*, *Lines Supposed to be Spoken by a Lover at the Grave of his Mistress*, *The Lullaby of a Female Convict to her Child*, and *Sonnet, Supposed to have been addressed by a Female Lunatic to a Lady*. Many poets of the age pretended to be Indians just as White pretended to be a female lunatic, or as Wordsworth pretended to be an indignant and high-minded Spaniard.[6]

The notion that the savage is a natural poet is perhaps the most widespread and enduring aspect of the Noble Savage idea. It is held by some writers who are otherwise not markedly favorable to primitive man, and my impression is that it preserves its fashionableness longer than other aspects. Also, so far as English literature is concerned, it is the first to appear. In Sidney's *Defense of Poesie*, after a section on the esteem in which Irish bards were held, and before similar sections on British, Danish and Norman bards, we find: " Even among the most barbarous and simple Indians, where no writing is, yet have they their Poets who make and sing songs which they call Areitos, both of their Auncestors deeds, and praises of

[6] In the sonnet, *Indignation of a High-minded Spaniard.*

their Gods." [7]   Thus in the age of Hakluyt, Indian poets were regarded as comparable to earlier but less exotic makers.

About a century must elapse, however, before primitive poetry is explicitly associated with primitive virtue. Sir William Temple, who is regarded as a pioneer in the revival of interest in Old Norse literature, provides the clue. His essay *Of Heroic Virtue* is, of course with numerous differences, a precursor of Carlyle's *Heroes and Hero-Worship*. One division of Temple's essay deals with northern heroes. The "Gothic" belief in immortality reminds him of "that Song or Epicedium of *Regnor Ladbrog*," and he quotes from *Literatura Runica* two stanzas of Wormius' Latin translation of this Icelandic death-song. "I am deceived," he adds, "if in this Sonnet . . . there be not a vein truly Poetical, and in its kind Pindarick." The transition from heroic virtue to heroic poetry is an easy one.

Ragnar Lodbrok enjoyed considerable popularity during the eighteenth century. It appears in Percy's *Five Pieces of Runic Poetry*, in Mallet's *Introduction à l'Histoire de Dannemarck*, and of course in Percy's translation of that work. What is more important for us, the poem was freely rendered by Thomas Warton the Elder. Joseph Warton, who edited his father's poetry, emulated his sire by writing in rather similar style of a *Dying Indian*.[8] Ragnar Lodbrok perishes in the serpent-pit of King Aella, and the Indian dies from a poisoned arrow:

> "The dart of Izdabel prevails! 'twas dipt
> In double poison."

[7] "Areitos" are mentioned as early as 1555, in Richard Eden's translation of *Peter Martyr's Decades*. (Whitney, *English Primitivistic Theories of Epic Origins*, p. 376.)

[8] *English Poets*, Vol. XVIII, p. 170.

Like Lodbrok, the dying chief expects to go to a sort of Valhalla in which beauty and savagery are mingled,—

" .   .   .   where ananas bloom
Thrice in each moon; where rivers smoothly glide,
Nor thund'ring torrents whirl the light canoe
Down to the sea; where my forefathers feast
Daily on hearts of Spaniards."

Lodbrok, in the life to come, will drink from the skulls of his enemies. Both Viking and sachem lay injunctions upon their children, and both relate earlier deeds of valor and cruelty:

" .   .   .   .   .   O my son,
I feel the venom busy in my breast.
Approach, and bring my crown, deck'd with the teeth
Of that bold Christian who first dar'd deflow'r
The virgins of the Sun; and, dire to tell!
Robb'd Pachacamac's altar of its gems!
I marked the spot where they interr'd this traitor,
And once at midnight stole I to his tomb,
And tore his carcase from the earth, and left it
A prey to poisonous flies. Preserve this crown
With sacred secrecy: if e'er returns
Thy much-loved mother from the desert woods,
Where, as I hunted late, I hapless lost her,
Cherish her age."

But Warton, as a disciple of eighteenth century naturalism, cannot forbear to add two savage flings at Christian civilization. The first, a rather daring one, is probably derived from some explorer's report of Indian scepticism: the son must tell his mother that the dead chief has never worshipped " with those that eat their God." The second shows acquaintance with the custom of putting to death the old and sick:

> " .   .   .   .   And when disease
> Preys on her languid limbs, then kindly stab her
> With thine own hands, nor suffer her to linger,
> Like Christian cowards, in a life of pain."

Despite these variations, the similarities between the two poems are marked enough to suggest that Joseph Warton was trying to write the death of an Indian Lodbrok. The conclusions of the pieces are analogous. The Viking goes to Odin, and the Indian to " great Capac." Even if he did not have in mind the actual poem which his father had translated, Joseph Warton would be the first to admit that in courage, vengefulness, family loyalty and belief in a future life the two dying heroes are comparable.

That savage songs are regarded in much the same light as bardic odes or medieval ballads, and that they are related to the romantic conception of savage life, is indicated also by the following lines from Gray's *Progress of Poesy:*

> " In climes beyond the solar road,
> Where shaggy forms o'er ice-built mountains roam,
> The Muse has broke the twilight gloom
>   To cheer the shivering Native's dull abode.
> And oft, beneath the odorous shade
> Of Chili's boundless forests laid,
> She deigns to hear the savage youth repeat,
> In loose numbers wildly sweet,
> Their feather-cinctured Chiefs, and dusky Loves.
> Her track, where'er the Goddess roves,
> Glory pursue, and generous Shame,
> The unconquerable Mind, and Freedom's holy flame."

The author's gloss on this passage reads: " Extensive influence of poetic genius over the remotest and most uncivilized nations; its connection with liberty, and the virtues that naturally attend on it. (See the Erse, Norwegian and Welsh fragments, the Lapland and American songs.) " To this scholar-poet, all primitive song, Scandinavian, Celtic or Indian, exhibits freedom from technical bondage, wild sweetness, and the rugged nobility of natural man.

Indian myths and superstitions readily lent themselves to an inflated and grandiose treatment which recalls the Celticism of Gray's *Bard* and the Druidism of Mason's *Caractacus*. The influence of Gray is plainly seen in John Scott's *The Mexican Prophecy, an Ode*.[9] Here, after a narrative passage, an idol speaks, prophesying the fall of Mexico, but also the eventual fall of the Spaniards. In Bowles' *Missionary*, a Chilian wizard sings a " Song to the God of War " in which he urges the malignant spirits to support his tribe against the Europeans. The tone is laboriously " spooky." Rogers' *Voyages of Columbus* contains a very similar ode. One of the Zemi — gods who preside over the Caribbean islands — warns the gods of the mainland that Columbus' fleet is approaching. Moore's *Song of the Evil Spirit of the Woods* belongs to the same type.[10] These poems hardly even pretend to be primitive. Whereas Klopstock had really tried to restore early Germanic poetry, Gray had created a highly artificial mode by combining medieval material with classical form and adding a dash of romantic "enthusiasm." This Cambro-classicism is simply transferred from the Welsh bard to the Indian wizard or god. The medley of Celtic and Indian lore demanded by the plot of Southey's *Madoc* is therefore not incongruous. When Hoel, Madoc's young son, dies, the Aztecs sing a funeral hymn not very dif-

[9] *English Poets*, Vol. XVII, p. 487.
[10] *Vide supra*, pp. 252, 270. Moore's sojourn in America produced a much more genuinely primitive lyric in the *Canadian Boat Song*, a voyageur's chanty.

ferent from that which might have been intoned over his body had he perished in the shadow of Snowdon.[11]

Poets who feel the influence of the ballad revival often mingle savage songs with their other representations of unsophisticated poetry. Bowles dabbled weakly in the bardic vein. His *Hymn to Woden* is a Teutonic battle-piece in which the Valkyries are called " weird sisters." *The Harp of Hoel* is declared to be "a lyrical ballad . . . founded on a story connected with an old Welsh melody." It is Cymric material, but treated like a border ballad. In *Coombe-Ellen,* he interpolates a Welsh battle-song after the manner of Gray. Such efforts are allied in spirit to his imitations of savage poetry. The *Song of an American Indian* has earlier been mentioned as a conventional catalogue of woodland joys. In *The Missionary,* however, we come upon a song of victory which bears a touch of true Indian bloodthirstiness:

> " Shout, Chili, in triumph! The battle is won,
> And we dance round the heads that are black in the sun."

Although Campbell once shocked Southey by expressing contempt for old Scotch ballads,[12] he was by no means averse to imitating these forms. Besides the famous *Lord Ullin's Daughter, Lochiel's Warning* and *Glenara* are essays in Scottish minstrelsy. Irish lore forms the stuff of *O'Connor's Child* and *Reullura.* And Campbell, as we know, made the Indian speak poetry. In general, however, while Wordsworth wished to bring poetry

[11] *Poetical Works,* Vol. V, pp. 278 ff. The hymn, like the rest of the poem, is in blank verse; only the supernaturalism, the images, and the general bardic atmosphere of the piece suggest the Celtic tradition.

[12] *Life and Correspondence of Robert Southey.* To Coleridge, August 4, 1802.

back to native simplicity, Campbell would elevate primitive art to what he deemed a higher standard of dignity. The two songs of Outalissi in *Gertrude* are therefore conscious and polished. A rather wide knowledge of Indian customs and beliefs is only dimly visible through the glossy veneer.

Byron's espousal of the cause of Pope makes it surprising that he should admire savage poetry. As a youth, however, the "young Highlander" imitated Ossian in *The Death of Calmar and Orla*. Later, his translation of the *Romance Muy Doloroso del Sitio y Toma de Alhama* testifies to his interest in balladry. The *Stanzas to a Hindoo Air* and the *Translation of a Romaic Love Song* are essays in the exotic; and the *Hebrew Melodies* add a very weak dash of primitivism to a blend of the fashionable *Lalla Rookh* and Holy Land crazes. Much more significantly for us, Albania provides him with examples of natural song as well as of natural goodness. In the notes to *Childe Harold* II, Byron gives two Arnaout folksongs, with a translation. His memories of Suliote hospitality are mingled with wild music, for the kindly cutthroats who shelter him from the storm dance and sing about their night-fires.

The second canto of *The Island* opens with a song by the natives of Toobonai. Byron's comments on "this ditty of Tradition's days" are more important than the song itself, for they represent point by point the romantic attitude toward primitive poetry. First, white civilization kills native genius. The Toobonian lay represents

> ".   .   .   the harmony of times
> Before the winds blew Europe o'er these climes.
> True, they had vices — such are Nature's growth —
> But only the barbarian's — we have both."

Natural poetry is an essential part of the natural life. Second, a song such as this,

> " Which leaves no record to the sceptic's eye,
> But yields young history all to harmony,"

is a more attractive record than monuments, hieroglyphics, or learned tomes. Aristotle thought poetry more philosophical than history because it is more creative. Byron finds " one long-cherished ballad's simple stave " more interesting than history because it is more emotional, picturesque and pathetic. The records of mankind must be passionate.

Third, " rude rhymes " like these " inspired the Norseman's solitude." The savage minstrel suggests the scôp.

Finally, Byron reasserts the connection between unsophisticated freedom and savage art, and implies that Toobonian poetry is not excelled by European poetry in its power to arouse emotion. Traditional lays exist

> ".   .   .   .   wherever rise
> Lands which no foes destroy or civilize,

> "   .   .   and what can our accomplished art
> Of verse do more than reach the awakened heart? "

The unity of all unsophisticated poetry receives further support from Mrs. Hemans. Her *Lays of Many Lands* mingles three Indian poems with imitations of Moorish, Norse, Swiss, Welsh, Medieval English, Medieval German, Ancient Greek, Modern Greek and Suliote popular poetry. Most of the pieces bear notes referring to books of travel. The project was suggested to her, she says, by Herder's *Stimmen der Völker in Liedern;* but her poems, unlike those of Herder's collection, are original.

The three Indian songs are all based on superstitions related by travelers. In *The Messenger Bird*, a savage addresses the traditional messenger of the spirit world. What of the departed? We call them, but they answer not. " Say, do they love there still? " *The Stranger in Louisiana* makes use of the native custom of weeping at a stranger. When the Indian of this region first sees a stranger, he thinks that he beholds a dead friend returned to life, and weeps on discovering his mistake. A sort of Terrestrial Paradise forms the foundation of *The Isle of Founts*. There is a beauteous island in a swamp. It can be seen at a distance, but only a few can approach it closely. Those who do so are never thereafter content with the life of mortals.

The namby-pamby Thomas Haynes Bayly follows Mrs. Hemans' lead in a group called *Melodies of Various Nations*. The only Indian poem is a feeble love-song beginning:

> " You think I am unfeeling;
>   But ah! you do not mark the tear
> That o'er my cheek is stealing,
>   When no gay friends are near."

But the most interesting as well as the most complicated evidence of the connection between Indian poetry and the ballad revival in general is furnished by Southey's *Songs of the American Indians*. This group of dramatic lyrics has already been used to show Southey's attitude toward the Noble Savage.[13] Their outstanding feature is an unusual desire to find romance *in* the Indian instead of imposing romance *upon* him. The versification of these poems is, however, equally important, for in them appear for the first time those unrhymed and irregular though

[13] *Vide supra*, pp. 202–204.

highly rhythmical stanzas which later characterize *Thalaba*. For these forms Southey seems to have been indebted to Dr. Frank Sayers, who in turn drew them in part from English unrhymed odes and in part from German attempts to recapture the spirit of old Teutonic lays. In his *Early Life of Robert Southey*, Professor Haller has ably discussed the relations between Southey and Sayers, but since he does not mention in this connection the *Songs of the American Indians*, which are an important link between Sayers and Southey's later work, I may be pardoned for repeating his findings with certain additions of my own.[14]

The five songs were written at Westbury in 1799, and were first published over the pseudonym " Erthusyo " (R. Southey) in the 1800 volume of the *Annual Anthology*. In 1798, Southey had visited Norwich and had there met William Taylor and Dr. Frank Sayers. Of the two, Taylor's knowledge of things Teutonic was by far the greater. Sayers took German lessons of Taylor, but never acquired either real proficiency in the language, or much admiration for it.[15] His chief literary interest was in unrhymed poetry, of which he published a defense in 1793. In this dissertation the examples are drawn chiefly from English writers of the ode, especially Gray, Collins, and Mason. Three years earlier, Sayers had given creative expression to his theories in *Dramatic Sketches of Northern Mythology*. In Mason's work, as Professor Haller observes, the Norwich physician found " both the idea of writing upon ' Northern Mythology ' and of doing so in the form of the Greek drama." [16] While the choruses of

---

[14] The chief passages on Sayers in the *Early Life of Robert Southey* are pp. 45–46, 76–80, 83–88, 90–93.

[15] *Collective Works of the Late Dr. Sayers*, Vol. I, p. xxxviii (Taylor's Memoir).   [16] *Early Life of Robert Southey*, p. 83.

Mason's dramas, however, were odes in the manner of Gray, Sayers followed Klopstock and Stolberg in abandoning rhyme altogether. In matter and spirit, too, the work of Sayers is reminiscent of Klopstock. To this extent, then, Taylor's German lessons bore fruit.

In the preface to the first volume of his collected poems, Southey acknowledges his indebtedness to Sayers. Collins' *Ode to Evening* he admired, but until he opened the *Dramatic Sketches*, and heard Sayers speak out loud and bold, he had regarded all other experiments as failures. Their authors used either familiar metres which aroused too strong an expectation of rhyme, or cumbersome and monstrous pseudo-Pindaric arrangements. " Dr. Sayers went upon a different principle, and succeeded admirably." His poems convinced Southey "that the kind of verse in which his choruses were composed was not less applicable to narration than to lyrical poetry." Hence *Thalaba*. But Southey neglects to state that before applying Sayers' metre to narrative poetry he used it precisely as Sayers had done — in lyrics. The *Songs of the American Indians* are short dramatic lyrics strongly resembling the choruses of Sayers' *Sketches* in their lack of rhyme and their irregular metre.

The most marked rhythm of Klopstock's bardic choruses is an iambic-anapaestic surge:

> " Der Adler Heerzug schwebt voran;
>   Sie blicken herab auf die Legionen.
>   Wie schlägt ihr Fittig, wie tönt ihr Geschrey!
>   Laut fodert es Leichen von Wodan! " [17]

A similar movement appears in Sayers' *Moina:*

> " 'Tis Harold — undaunted in fight,
>   He smil'd at the shivering of spears,
>   He fell in the clashing of arms.

[17] *Hermanns Schlacht*, p. 19.

> Rise, Odin, rise,
> See, he enters thy shining abode,
> And terrible sits by thy side."

And in Southey's *Songs of the American Indians:*

> " He returned, in the glory of conquest returned:
> Before him his trophies were borne,
> These scalps that have hung till the sun and the rain
> Have rusted their raven locks."

The similarity is clear enough. In *Thalaba*, Southey attains much subtler rhythmic effects, but in his Indian songs he clings rather closely to his model.

Klopstock and Southey — to leave Sayers out of consideration — are akin in spirit as well as in form. Both are attempting to dignify primitive life through poetry supposed to be characteristic of that life. The *Bardengebrüll* of which Klopstock is the best example is recognized as an early symptom of German romanticism. Tacitus had not only regarded the Germani as Noble Savages, but had praised their poetry and their tribal bards along with their courage, chastity and Spartan high-mindedness. Hence the German romanticists could find in their own racial past an intimate union between natural man and natural poetry. Through Sayers, this cluster of associations is passed on to Southey, who feels no incongruity in making Indians the heirs of the Teutonic bards. It is merely a question of exchanging one Noble Savage for another.

During the Romantic Movement, enthusiasm for the primitive blurred the distinctions between different levels of antiquity. Modern scholarship has proved that Shakespeare's plays abound in medieval lore, and that medieval ballads in turn abound in situations and superstitions common to many savage races. Without the knowledge which we possess, the romanticists nevertheless sensed a common element of imaginative luxuriance in all old poetry; and being partisans of analogy and foes of analysis, they were prone to lump together all literature that was unhampered by pseudo-classic trammels. Even Hazlitt could mention in the same breath Homer, the Bible, Dante and Ossian as " four of the principal works of poetry in the world." [18] Wolf's " decomposition " of the *Iliad* and *Odyssey* played straight into the hands of the naturalists. His investigations seemed to prove that "Homer" was merely a collection of lays which had taken form long before the use of writing, and which had been passed down from mouth to mouth until finally they were polished and welded together by minds critical rather than creative. This theory made it easy to over-emphasize the popular and traditional aspect of the Homeric poems. What was the *Iliad*, after all, but a series of border ballads, and the *Odyssey* but a cluster of *märchen*? Thinking of Homer in this fashion by no means implied any deprecation of classic genius, for to a romanticist a ballad or a *märchen* could be a terribly solemn thing. The discovery merely gave a new and sublimer meaning to Pope's " Nature and Homer were, he found, the same."

When Homer is seen as primitive, the savage can be seen as Homeric. Thus Southey says of the *Iliad*, " The people to whom the poem relates seem to have been as nearly as possible in the same stage of barbarism or civilization (call it which you will) as the South Sea Islanders when the missionaries became acquainted with them." [19] Helen Maria Williams carries us a step further. In *Julia*, she calls the " southern isles " to attest

[18] *Works*, Vol. V, p. 15. Miss Whitney (*op. cit.*, pp. 361 ff.) shows that Ossian and Homer were frequently compared, and not always to the advantage of the latter.

[19] *Correspondence with Caroline Bowles*, p. 350.

> " How heav'n taught verse can melt your souls:
>   Say, when you hear the wand'ring bard,
> How thrill'd ye listen to his lay,
> By what kind arts ye court his stay,
>   All savage life affords, his sure reward."

And the next stanza compares the Tahitian bard's reception to that of a minstrel at an Homeric feast.

There can be no question, then, as to the unity of " natural " poetry. The savage maker stands on the same plane as bard, scôp, minstrel and rhapsode. But the association of primitive poetry with primitive virtue, though it has been given some incidental support in the foregoing pages, needs to be brought home.[20]

" In Eden," Cowper writes,

> " ere yet innocence of heart
> Had faded, poetry was not an art;
> Language, above all teaching, or, if taught,
> Only by gratitude and glowing thought,
> Elegant as simplicity and warm
> As ecstasy, unmanacled by form,
> Not prompted, as in our degen'rate days,
> By low ambition and the thirst of praise,
> Was natural as is the flowing stream,
> And yet magnificent — a God the theme! " [21]

The poetry of Eden was free, spontaneous, impassioned, natural and sublime; and these qualities are associated with that " innocence of heart " which " art," in literature as in life, has tarnished.

Since Eden and the Golden Age are interchangeable conceptions, it is no surprise to find Cowper's friend Hayley bemoaning the flight of that

[20] For additional evidence on this point, Miss Whitney's paper should be consulted.

[21] *Table Talk*, ll. 584–593. I believe no one has pointed out that this passage almost certainly finds a direct source in ll. 47–66 of Beattie's *Epistle to the Reverend Thomas Blacklock*. (*Works*, pp. 160 ff.)

> " blest poetic time
> When Fancy wrought the miracles of Rhyme;
>
> .   .   .   .
>
> Return, sweet season, grac'd with Fiction's flowers,
> Let not cold System cramp thy genial powers! "

Here is a plea for the overthrow of critical rules and the restoration, in all her Arcadian liberty, of fancy.

The longings of both Cowper and Hayley are sung in proper heroic couplets. The next generation tried to put into practice the theory of these earlier writers. Although Coleridge's triumphant sublimations of the medieval spirit are too familiar to require comment, we do not always recognize those works as an outgrowth of naturalistic philosophy. Yet the relation is not difficult to trace. Those lines *To a Young Lady* which tell of mourning over the tomb of Lee Boo conclude with the flourish,

> " No purple bloom the Child of Nature brings
> From Flattery's night-shade: as he feels he sings."

The Noble Savage cannot be deceitful, even in love-poetry. In 1799, five years later, Coleridge shrinks in disgust from the concert room,

> " where, to a gaudy throng,
> Heaves the proud harlot her distended breast
> In intricacies of laborious song."

To these corruptions he prefers old ballads sung by Anne, whose

> " voice remeasures
> Whatever tones and melancholy pleasures
> The things of Nature utter; birds or trees,
> Or moan of ocean-gale in windy caves." [22]

Ballads suggest the primal poetry of the earth-spirit.

[22] *Lines Composed in a Concert Room.*

Kubla Khan represents a loftier phase of the wish to attain the inspired fervor of the old, the exotic, and the natural. The familiar notion that this poem is incomprehensible must be due to the obscurity of the relation between its two parts; for neither part in itself is difficult, granted that "willing suspension of disbelief" which Coleridge always demands. But surely the second part — was it really written before or after the intrusion of the person from Porlock? — explains why the poet can never complete the magical palace.

> " A damsel with a dulcimer
> In a vision once I saw:
> It was an Abyssinian maid
> And on her dulcimer she played,
> Singing of Mount Abora.
> Could I revive within me
> Her symphony and song
> To such a deep delight 'twould win me,
> That with music loud and long,
> I would build that dome in air."

The Abyssinian maid, like Lewti, " is not kind." She will not permit her wild fervor to be recaptured by the modern poet.

Thalaba is to Southey what the Abyssinian maid is to Coleridge. We see the youth

> " Singing with agitated face,
> And eloquent arms, and sobs that reach the heart,
> A tale of love and woe."

The complete abandonment to the poetic passion is the ideal which has ousted the formal craft of pseudo-classicism. Thalaba has attained the goal aspired to by Burns, who placed on the title-page of his Kilmarnock poems the lines:

> " The Simple Bard, unbroke by rules of Art,
> He pours the wild effusions of the heart:
> And if inspir'd, 'tis Nature's pow'rs inspire;
> Hers all the melting thrill, and hers the kindling fire."

The *Solitary Reaper* also has a " symphony and song " of which Wordsworth longs to possess the secret. " Will no one tell me what she sings? " One may well doubt whether the *Lyrical Ballads* could have taken shape without the encouragement of the Noble Savage idea. Coleridge's attempt to lift the natural up to the supernatural, and Wordsworth's attempt to find infinite significance in common things, alike depend in large measure upon the belief that in primitive simplicity lie innocence, intuitive wisdom, and the true spirit of poetry.

The poet of nature, as Southey and Coleridge have shown us, can be a savage. Miss Williams has a Peruvian bard, Zamor, over whose " tuneful breast " the dews of inspiration are shed, for the Muse

> " . . . loves to breathe her hallow'd flame where Art
> Has never veil'd the soul, or warp'd the heart."

Zamor loves the Zephyr and the rill. Another child of fancy, " his wild warblings charm'd the festal hour."

> " The heart's responsive tones he well could move,
> Whose Song was Nature, and whose theme was Love."

Perhaps it is only fair to hear a minority report at this point. In *The Progress of Civil Society*, R. P. Knight has the courage to insist that the shepherd was the first true poet. He sang of nature and love, while in the case of the savage, though he had often

> " . . . howl'd his war-song through the echoing wood;
> And oft to measured sounds had learn'd to advance,
> In the rude mazes of the mimic dance;

> Yet no rich images, by fancy dress'd,
> Or pleasing sentiments, the song express'd:
> In strains of death alone its frenzy rose,
> And only breathed defiance to his foes."

Knight is evidently trying to dissociate the cult of the shepherd from the cult of the savage. Though he knows more about Indians than Miss Williams, however, his view is not the accepted one. For most people of the age, the Noble Savage was quite as much a poet as the Arcadian shepherd, and his poetic genius was closely linked with the other good gifts of nature.

We are now in a position to examine two common types of savage poetry — the death-song and the love-song. Professor Farley, in an interesting essay contributed to the *Kittredge Anniversary Papers,* has studied *The Dying Indian.* As he points out, tales of savage fortitude under torture were common, and " it was natural that these recitals, always shocking but often thrilling, should fire the imagination of some of the poets, for the victim was usually represented as chanting a death song in which he derided his enemies." Probably the best example of this type is the *Death Song of a Cherokee Indian.* The opening lines will give an idea of its nature:

> " The sun sets in night, and the stars shun the day,
> But glory remains, when their lights fade away.
> Begin, ye tormentors: your threats are in vain:
> For the son of Alknomock can never complain."

The authorship of this poem has been ascribed to Philip Freneau, to Royall Tyler and to Mrs. Anne Hunter. Most authorities, according to Professor Farley, regard the song as Freneau's, though " the evidence does not seem conclusive in the case of any one of the three candidates." Although the problem is not vitally important, it is perhaps worth solving. To my mind, there can be little doubt that Mrs. Hunter wrote the poem.

Professor Farley says that the *Death Song* appeared in the *Poems* of Mrs. Anne Hunter, 1806. The British Museum, however, possesses an 1802 edition of the *Poems*, on pp. 80-81 of which we find the *Death Song*. In her *Rosamond* (1821) Maria Edgeworth quotes it, ascribes it to Mrs. Hunter, and prints part of a note on the poem by Mrs. Hunter. The entire note does not seem to be familiar to Professor Farley, who uses only the portion quoted by Maria Edgeworth. I quote it from the 1802 edition of Mrs. Hunter's *Poems:* " The idea of this ballad was suggested several years ago by hearing a gentleman, who had resided several years in America amongst the tribe or nation called the Cherokees, sing a wild air, which he assured me it was customary for those people to chaunt with a barbarous jargon, implying contempt to their enemies in the moments of torture and death. I have endeavoured to give something of the characteristic spirit and sentiment of these brave savages. We look upon the fierce and stubborn courage of the dying indian with a mixture of respect, pity, and horror; and it is to those sensations excited in the mind of the reader, that the Death Song must owe its effect. It has already been published with the notes to which it was adapted." [23]

It is conceivable that a minor poet might let the effusion of another slip into her work; but to lie about the theft so elaborately would require a hardened criminal. There is no reason to suppose that Anne Hunter was a literary kleptomaniac. She came of a decidedly respectable family, and was the wife of Dr. John Hunter, the eminent anatomist. Among her friends she numbered Elizabeth Carter and Mrs. Delaney. Her social and literary parties

[23] *Poems,* p. 81.

were well attended. No less a man than Haydn set some of her songs to music. Of her, Walter Scott writes to Joanna Baillie: " I value her applause not a little, for my sense of it is proportioned to my estimation of her acknowledged merits."[24]

The "gentleman who had resided . . . amongst . . . the Cherokees " sounds a trifle dubious. But the fact is that there *was* such a gentleman in England toward the close of the eighteenth century. His name was William Augustus Bowles, and he called himself "Ambassador from the United Nations of Creeks and Cherokees to the Court of London."[25] Though Bowles may not have been Mrs. Hunter's informant, the existence of such a person shows that her story is not impossible.

What are the claims of Freneau? The *Death Song* is printed and attributed to him in the third edition, 1790, of Matthew Carey's *American Museum*. No author is given in the second edition, 1787. Professor Farley has not seen the first edition, also of 1787, nor have I. According to Professor Pattee, Freneau's editor, the poem does not appear in any of Freneau's own collected editions of his poems.[26] Professor Pattee includes the poem in his edition, but with this significant note: "The authenticity of a poem suspected to be Freneau's may always be gravely doubted if it is not found to be included in his collected works, for he hoarded his poetic product, especially in his earlier period, with miserly care."[27]

If Carey was wrong in ascribing the song to Freneau,

[24] *Familiar Letters*. To Joanna Baillie, June 10, 1810.

[25] *Authentic Memoirs of William Augustus Bowles* was published in London, 1791.

[26] These editions appeared in 1786, 1788, 1795, 1809 and 1815. I have myself examined all but the 1788 and 1815 editions.

[27] *Poems of Philip Freneau*, Vol. II, p. 313.

his error can easily be explained. For as Professor Farley observes, the American did write two poems of the " Dying Indian " type — *The Dying Indian* and *The Prophecy of King Tammany*. They appear, to my own knowledge, in the 1786, 1795 and 1809 editions, and are duly printed by Pattee. Though they resemble the poem in question only as belonging to the same general species, one can easily see how Carey might have confused the Cherokee song with one of the death songs of which Freneau was actually the writer.

Could Mrs. Hunter have written the *Death Song* as early as 1787? In 1802, she stated that it had already been published with its musical setting, but she does not give the date. In dedicating the 1802 volume to her soldier son, however, she says that since 1799 she has been too anxious about him to write poetry. The *Dictionary of National Biography* asserts that many of her poems were written some years before publication. In 1787 Mrs. Hunter was forty-five, and there is no reason to think it impossible that the poem may have been in circulation as a song by that time.

The *Death Song* also appears in Royall Tyler's *The Contrast,* which was first performed in 1787 and first printed in 1790. It is sung by one of the characters at the beginning of the second scene of the first act. Farley quotes McKee, who in 1887 edited the play for the Dunlap Society, as being convinced " that *Alknomook* is the offspring of Tyler's genius." One may, however, be permitted to guess that the poem was an adopted child. It is not used as a speech, but as a song, and the songs in a prose play are not necessarily the work of the author. Quite possibly Tyler never knew who wrote the song, which may have been published anonymously with its music, or may have reached Tyler in pirated form.

No support is furnished the theory of Tyler's authorship by the fact that our death-song, sung by a character named Alkmonoak, is found in an English opera entitled *New Spain; or, Love in Mexico*. This piece, which is attributed to John Scawen, was first produced in 1790.[28]

I conclude that the evidence for Mrs. Hunter is strong; the evidence for either Freneau or Tyler, very slight. Especially since the ascriptions to the two men can so readily be explained, there is no reason to set aside the lady's explicit statement that she is the author. Let us give the *Death Song* to Mrs. Hunter; she needs, poor soul, everything she can get.

For several other Indian death-songs, American as well as English, the reader must be referred to Professor Farley's paper, and to Chapter VI of Bissell's dissertation. Joseph Warton's *Dying Indian*, which Farley mentions, has already been discussed. Farley does not, however, seem to have noticed the interesting fact that Freneau himself translated part of Wormius' Latin version of *Ragnar Lodbrok*.[29] I may also add a reference to that dialogue of Lyttelton's which has furnished us with an example of the satirical Noble Savage. Says the Duellist, "I sung very agreeably." "Let me hear you sing your *Death Song* or the *War Whoop*," scornfully retorts the Indian.[30] Evidently this savage *genre* was familiar to Englishmen as early as 1760.

The Indian does not always perish at the stake, and he has other types of song for other types of dissolution. We have already noticed Mrs. Hemans' *The Aged Indian*, in which a decrepit chieftain begs to be put to death, and

[28] I owe this reference, which Farley seems to have missed, to Bissell, *op. cit.*, pp. 140–141.

[29] *Poems* (1795), p. 268.

[30] *Dialogues of the Dead*, No. VI.

Mrs. Opie's *The Lucayan's Song,* in which the sentiment is anything but Spartan. A more interesting variant is found in Wordsworth's *Complaint of a Forsaken Indian Woman,* a dramatic lyric based on the Canadian explorer, Hearne. The mother, unable to keep up with the rest of the tribe, has been robbed of her child and left behind to die in the snow. The poem has some realistic touches — the northern lights, the frozen ashes of the camp fire, the wolf that has stolen the woman's provisions. Poignant emotions are expressed in the simplest diction, and with a dignity and restraint not inappropriate to savage stoicism. The dying squaw, indeed, is as good a vehicle for Wordsworth's theory of poetry as most of his English rustics. During the time when he was engaged in reforming poetic diction, he could hardly have failed to think of Indian songs. The prolonged strawberry festival which Ruth's lover substitutes for a true account of life in the American wilderness is concluded by the maidens'

> " Returning with a choral song
> When daylight is gone down."

One cannot be certain, however, that the maidens are Indians. The "pleasant Indian town " may be merely situated among the Indians, or be *like* an Indian village.

In a footnote, Professor Farley observes that there are Dying Negroes as well as Dying Indians. Since we have never been particular about the color of our Noble Savages, we may examine a few illustrations of the truth of this remark. Day and Bicknell's *Dying Negro* has already proved useful in more than one connection; and Bowles, as we know, wrote a poem with the same title. Closer to the Indian type is Roscoe's *The African* — the death-song of Maraton before he jumps from the deck of a slave-ship. He hears his dead wife Adila calling him from the land where servitude is unknown. He will go to her.

> " Tomorrow, the white man in vain
>   Shall proudly account me his slave;
> My shackles I plunge in the main,
>   And rush to the realms of the brave."

But it is especially interesting to find that Dr. Frank Sayers, whose *Dramatic Sketches* stimulated Southey to write his *Songs of the American Indians,* composed *The Dying African.* The last stanza runs:

> " Ye ruffians, who tore me from all I held dear,
>   Who mock'd at my wailings, and smil'd at my tear,
> Now, now shall I 'scape — every torture shall end,
>   For the strong arm of death is the arm of a friend." [31]

The final line, used as a refrain throughout the poem, suggests Mrs. Hunter's " For the son of Alknomock can never complain," which is similarly repeated. The metre is also the same. And sure enough, beneath the title of Sayers' poem stands " Tune — Son of Alknomoack." Dr. Sayers' negro is to die to the same music as Mrs. Hunter's Indian.

The savage may also sing of the death of others. In our discussion of *Madoc* we found that Southey quotes from Carver's *Travels* a passage which describes the sorrow of an Indian mother at the death of her son and her husband. The incident convinced the explorer that the Stoic of the woods did not lack parental tenderness.[32] " I observed," continues Carver, " that she went almost every evening to the foot of the tree, on a branch of which the bodies of her husband and child were laid, and, after cutting off a lock of her hair and throwing it on the ground,

[31] *Collective Works*, p. 293.   [32] *Vide supra*, p. 207.

in a plaintive melancholy song bemoaned its fate. A re-
capitulation of the actions he might have performed, had
his life been spared, appeared to be her favorite theme;
and, whilst she foretold the fame that would have attended
an imitation of his father's virtues, her grief seemed to be
suspended."

This funereal-epideictic singing finds its way into ro-
mantic literature. Southey himself reflects its influence in
the Aztec funeral hymn in *Madoc*. Three of the five
Songs of the American Indians also belong to this type:
The Huron's Address to the Dead, *The Peruvian's Dirge
Over the Body of His Father*, and *Song of the Chikkasah
Widow*. The first in particular has a touch of genuinely
primitive quality:

> " Brother, thou wert strong in youth!
>   Brother, thou wert brave in war!
>   Unhappy man was he
>   For whom thou hadst sharpened the tomahawk's edge;
>   Unhappy man was he
>   On whom those angry eyes were fixed in fight;
>   And he who from thy hand
>   Received the calumet,
>   Blest Heaven, and slept in peace."

In Campbell's *Gertrude of Wyoming*, Outalissi's final
speech, though called " the death-song of an Indian
chief," refers not to his own death but to that of Gertrude
and Albert.[33] In *Edith* Mrs. Hemans' converted Indians
sing a dirge which Christianity has almost transformed
into a hymn.[34] This writer has a poem entitled *The Indian With His Dead Child*, which, while not properly a
dirge, may conveniently be mentioned here. It is based
on the following passage in Tudor's *Letters on the Eastern*

[33] *Vide supra*, p. 265.   [34] *Vide supra*, p. 287.

States of America: " An Indian, who had established himself in a township of Maine, feeling indignantly the want
of sympathy evinced towards him by the white inhabitants,
particularly on the death of his only child, gave up his
farm soon afterwards, dug up the body of his child, and
carried it with him two hundred miles through the forests
to join the Canadian Indians." The savage is made to
say:

> " I have raised thee from the grave-sod,
>   By the white man's path defiled;
> On to the ancestral wilderness,
>   I bear thy dust, my child."

The South Sea Islands also have their keening. In Miss
Mitford's *Christina*, after the massacre of the whites,
Christian's Tahitian wife, Iddeah, renders what is called
" The Widow's Dirge":

> " Fly, night of murder, woe and dread,
>   Fly, for thy work is done!
> The dawn will wake in blushes red,
> Will glance on every honor'd head;
>   But when shall rise our sun? "

Negroes stand mutely at the funeral pyre no more than
other savages. King Ampanini, whose chivalrous treatment of the captive Vainah we have already admired,[35]
later bewails the loss of his son. He is joined in the dirge
by choral groups of men and of women. No more will the
youth take part in fighting or love-making — the two
favorite pursuits of every descendant of Oroonoko.[36]

The mention of love-making brings us to the second
important type of savage poetry. As I said in dealing

---

[35] *Vide supra,* p. 404.

[36] *A Funeral Song of the Negroes in Madagascar. The Persecutor,*
pp. 110–111.

with the Noble Savage as a romantic lover, primitive love-songs are rather numerous. Besides the examples here to be described, the reader should examine those mentioned by Dr. Bissell in Chapter VI of his dissertation. What must be a very early specimen is William King's *Indian Ode*. I am unable to date the poem, but King died in 1712. The ode is a conventional love-duet between Darco and Zabra, who seem to be Arabs, but might be any sort of savage. The following lines are a fair sample:

> " In gloom of night, when Darco's eyes
> Are guides, what heart can stray?
> Whoever views his teeth, descries
> The bright and milky way." [37]

How closely the various strands of our subject are united! It is appropriate that Thomas Warton the Elder, the translator of *Ragnar Lodbrok*, should give us an *Indian Love Ode*. Here a maiden begs a " lovely, fearful snake " not to glide away, but to remain long enough for her to remember its beautiful colors, which she wishes to imitate in a woven chaplet for her lover. The sub-title, *From the Second Volume of Montaigne's Essays*, points straight back to the essay *Of the Caniballes*, where we read: " Besides what I have said of one of their warlike songs, I have another amorous canzonet, which beginneth in this sence: ' Adder stay, stay good adder, that my sister may by the patterne of thy partie-coloured coat drawe the fashion and worke of a rich lace, for me to give unto my love; so may thy beautie, thy nimbleness of disposition be ever preferred before all other serpents.' The first couplet is the burthen of the song. I am so conversant with Poesie, that I may judge, this invention hath no barbarisme at all in it, but is altogether Anacreontick " — as

[37] *English Poets*, Vol. IX, p. 302.

Anacreontic, we may add, as *Ragnar Lodbrok* in Temple's opinion was Pindaric. It is interesting to see that Montaigne influences this special phase of a subject in which he is so important a figure.

There is, however, just a shadow of doubt as to the authorship of the *Indian Love Ode*. It appears in *Poems on Several Occasions by the Reverend Mr. Thomas Warton*, London, 1747, edited by his more famous son Joseph; yet it has been ascribed to Joseph Warton himself. In 1801, George Huddesford prints it in *Salmagundi*, a group of pieces chiefly by other hands which he includes in his *Poems*. The title is *Address of an Indian Girl to an Adder*, and the sub-title, "Written in the Year 1740, by a Scholar of Winchester College." In the table of contents, the poem is said to be "by the late Dr. Warton." [38] This can only be Joseph Warton. Huddesford's ascription might at once be cast aside as erroneous were he not so circumstantial as to place and date. Yet it seems so unlikely that Joseph slipped one of his own pieces among his father's poems that we had best, though not without hesitation, accept the elder Thomas as the author.

Thomson, it will be remembered, sang the innocence of the Lapps. Among their talents, we learn from the *Spectator*, is the composition of tenderly erotic poetry. Steele writes: "The following verses are a translation of a Lapland love-song, which I met with in Scheffer's history of that country. I was agreeably surprised to find a spirit of tenderness and poetry in a region which I never suspected for delicacy. . . . I have ventured to bind it in stricter measures, as being more proper for our tongue, though perhaps wilder graces may better suit the genius of the Laponian language." The binding process has certainly purged these lines of their wild Laponian grace:

[38] *Poems of George Huddesford*, Vol. I, p. 116.

> " Thou rising sun, whose gladsome ray
> Invites my fair to rural play,
> Dispel the mist, and clear the skies,
> And bring my Orra to my eyes." [39]

Love is the chief theme of Chatterton's *African Eclogues*. These three poems are not only rather striking in poetic quality, but emerge from a complicated background of history and myth which the too ingenious poet may either have invented or found in the work of some explorer. In any case, their stately mournfulness, and their way of referring to mysterious places and persons as if they were familiar to the reader, hint of Ossianic influence. All three poems were written in 1770, and it may be a mere coincidence that two of them end in suicide.

Narva and Mored is the story of two star-crossed lovers.

> " Far from the burning sands of Calabar;
> Far from the lustre of the morning star;
> Far from the pleasure of the holy morn;
> Far from the blessedness of Chalma's horn:
> Now rest the souls of Narva and Mored,
> Laid in the dust, and number'd with the dead."

Narva was a priest of Chalma's temple. One day the maiden Mored came bearing sacrifice, and the two fell in love. Realizing the impossibility of marriage, they leapt into a river locked in each other's arms.

The Death of Nicou has as its hero a Homeric young warrior, son of the African god of war. A malicious deity, from hatred of Nicou's father, arouses jealousy between the youth and his Patroclus, Rorest. They go to war

---

[39] *Spectator*, No. 366. The paper is by Steele, but the song itself is ascribed to Ambrose Philips. For an account of this and of other specimens of Lapland love-poetry, *cf.* Farley, *Three " Lapland Songs*," *P.M.L.A.*, Vol. XXI, pp. 1–39.

about a beautiful maiden. Nicou slays Rorest, then kills himself:

Heccar and Gaira is a dialogue between two warriors. Gaira relates that on returning from a tiger-hunt, he has found that the whites have taken his wife and children.

> " In the deep valley and the mossy plain,
> I sought my Cawna, but I sought in vain.
> The pallid shadows of the azure waves
> Had made my Cawna and my children slaves."

Despite Heccar's attempts to restrain him, he means to follow the whites and be revenged or die.

The curious quality of these poems, of which short extracts can give no conception, is probably due to the fact that they are hybrids. They apply to an unreal but realistically rendered Africa Chatterton's interest in early poetry. But since the impulse to medievalize the Negro is checked by a feeling that he is like an Homeric hero, Ossianic mystery and sentiment are blended with a classical stateliness and calm. They are not great works of genius, but there is nothing quite like them.

Of all savage love-songs, however, Coleridge's *Lewti* is probably the most noteworthy. Professor Lowes, in *The Road to Xanadu*, gives so elaborate an account of it that I need only remind the reader that the poem was originally entitled *The Wild Indians* [*sic*] *Love Chaunt* and that " Tamaha's stream " is the Altamaha River of our own American Georgia. The shift from America to Circassia, which puzzles Professor Lowes, seems not wholly inexplicable. We may imagine that Coleridge, in revising his first draft, felt that his love-chant was too good for a red Indian. Some more vaguely and less savagely exotic singer would be more appropriate. Now there is another Georgia besides the state watered by " Tamaha's stream " :

Georgia is, and was in Coleridge's time, an alternative name for Circassia or Caucasia. Is it not possible that the poet's mind leapt, by an illogical but perfectly natural association, from one Georgia to the other? This change, once made, would have found encouragement in the traditional beauty of Circassian women and the traditional fervor of Turkish love-poetry.

The anti-slave trade movement, to turn to a different type, provides a small group of songs in which the black pleads his own cause. Negro dramatic lyrics are usually inspired more by humanitarianism than by interest in primitive poetry. Blake's *The Little Black Boy* is unusual in extracting some beauty from a situation which generally provides material for mere preaching. Very different is Leigh Hunt's juvenile production, *The Negro Boy:*

> " Cold blows the wind, and while the tear
> Bursts trembling from my swollen eyes,
> The rain's big drops quick meet it there,
> And on my naked bosom flies! [*sic*]
> O pity, all ye sons of Joy,
> The little wand'ring Negro-boy."

In one instance, a humanitarian poet makes the negro speak in dialect. Amelia Opie's *The Negro Boy's Tale* presents the character of Zambo, a Jamaican slave who addresses his kind young mistress in these strains:

> " Dey say me should to oders do
> Vat I vould have dem do to me;
> But, if dey preach and practice too,
> A negro slave me should not be.

> . . . .

> " Missa, dey say dat our black skin
> Be ugly, ugly to de sight;
> But surely if dey look vidin,
> Missa, de negro's heart be vite.

> " Ah missa! smiling in your tear
> I see you know vat I'd impart;
> De cocoa husk de skin I vear,
> De milk vidin be Zambo's heart."

" Columbia countless Zambos sees " is Mrs. Opie's message to humanity.

One can hardly believe that Zambo's impossible speech added pathos or force to his criticism of society, for in that day the associations of dialect were broadly comic or satirical. I have found hardly any instances in which the Noble Savage of any hue speaks broken English. To make him do so would be to dispel the illusion that surrounds him. Man Friday, though an Indian, talks like an eighteenth century literary negro. Colman's Wowski has a comical jargon for which again burlesques of negro speech are evident models. These cases, and a trace of dialect in the omitted article of " And so say I to little English boy " in Blake's *Little Black Boy*, constitute the only exceptions that I have observed.

The plaint of the negro boy, then, may be set apart as a type in which the interest in primitive poetry, though not wholly absent, is rather weak. Less deliberately humanitarian, and more genuinely related to popular poetry, is Burns' *The Slave's Lament*:

> " It was in sweet Senegal that my foes did me enthrall,
> For the lands of Virginia-ginia, O;
> Torn from that lovely shore, and must never see it more,
> And, alas! I am weary, weary, O! "

The older and clumsier ballad which Burns reworked might have grown from a real negro song of labor.

Since in actually primitive poetry lyrical utterance is inseparable from music, it often seemed appropriate to provide imitations of savage songs with a musical setting.

The *Death-Song of a Cherokee Indian*, if we are to believe Anne Hunter's account, was originally published with notes, and it was certainly sung in Tyler's *The Contrast* and in *New Spain*. The Duchess of Devonshire, too, wrote a highly popular negro song which will soon be examined. Eighteenth century drama, bowing to the influence of opera, often made the savage warble his native wood-notes wild.

These notes were heard, indeed, in the dawn of the Restoration, for we find Davenant's Peruvians singing to Drake:

" With Boughs and with Branches trim up our Bowres,
   And strew them with Flowers:
   To receive such a Guest
   As deserves for a Feast
 All that the Forrest, or the Field,
 Or deeper Lakes and Rivers yield.

" The Lord of the Sea is welcom to Land,
   And here shall command
   All our Wealth, and our Arms;
   For his Name more alarms
 The Spaniards, than Trumpets or Drums:
 Hark how they cry, *Drake* comes, *Drake* comes! " [40]

Remarkable poets of nature, who can in one stanza recall *The Passionate Shepherd*, and in the next predict *Alexander's Feast!*

The negro still preserves the remains of a great racial tradition of dance and song which helped to make him a picturesque figure in the eyes of the eighteenth century humanitarians. One might suppose that first-hand knowledge of plantation songs would have made it difficult to

[40] *Cruelty of the Spaniards in Peru*, p. 16. For an account of an actual Brazilian song to Drake, *vide supra*, p. 12.

ascribe to the negro all the powers of bardism, but again
the will to idealize overcame the sense of fact. Hawkesworth inserts in his version of Southern's *Oroonoko* a
chorus of West Indian slaves:

> " Come, let us be gay, to repine is in vain,
>   When our loss we forget, what we lose we retain;
>   Our toils with the day are all ended at last;
>   Let us drown in the present all thoughts of the past,
>   All the future commit to the Powers above;
>   Come, give us a smile as an earnest of love."

But the poor slaves are unable to live up to their own
rather advanced metaphysics, for they feel that bondage
stifles all pleasure. Love and joy

> " Must both be free, for both disdain
>   The sounding scourge and galling chain."

We are far indeed from Vachel Lindsay's *The Congo*. In
Nature's Simple Plan, Professor Tinker calls Hawkesworth's song " an addition of his own." [41] The expression
is somewhat misleading, for the plantation ditty, while
certainly Hawkesworth's, is not so much an addition as a
substitution for two excessively absurd songs in Southern's
original version, dealing with *Pastorella* and *Bright Cyn-
thia's Pow'r*. Hawkesworth is at least a shade more
realistic.

Gay's Cawwawkee sings several songs, including sentimental duets with Polly, but his chant of battle is the
only one that even slightly reflects the influence of primitive poetry:

> " We the sword of justice drawing,
>   Terror cast in guilty eyes;
>   In its beam false courage dies;

[41] *Nature's Simple Plan*, p. 74.

> 'Tis like lightning keen and awing.
>> Charge the foe,
>> Lay them low,
> On then and strike the blow.
> Hark, victory calls us. See, guilt is dismay'd:
> The villain is of his own conscience afraid.
> In our hands are your lives and your liberties held,
> The courage of virtue was never repell'd."

In this, as Sir William Temple said of *Ragnar Lodbrok*, there is " a vein truly Poetical, and in its kind Pindarick."

Henry Brooke's *Montezuma* contains three Aztec songs. The first deals tamely with " the power of Beauty's charm," and is thus a lyrical pendant to the author's *magnum opus, Universal Beauty*. The second is an incantation of the " Arise, arise, arise! " sort, delivered by Montezuma and his high priest. It makes some attempt to be wild and mysterious. The third is a " song of triumph and thanksgiving," of which the following lines are unfortunately representative:

> " Now, through every glen and glade,
> In the sunshine, in the shade,
> Vacant innocence shall stray,
> Fearing neither wile nor way!
> Sons shall laugh within the shed,
> By their sires and grandsires spread;
> Peace shall slumber, toil shall snore —
> War and terrours are no more."

Inkle and Yarico is so full of singing that Colman, as the reader will remember, calls the piece an opera. Yarico's not unpathetic song reminding Inkle of their love in the forest has already been quoted.[42] She also sings on her first appearance. We are to imagine her — almost certainly, like the Indian Queen of Nell Gwyn and Mrs.

[42] *Vide supra*, p. 82.

Bracegirdle, costumed in feathers — emerging from her pelt-covered hut, advancing to the apron, and confiding her savage dreams to the sophisticated audience. The first stanza will be all languor; in the second, there will be imitatively ferocious gestures, and the music will tinkle more wildly.

> " When the chace of day is done,
>   And the shaggy lion's skin,
>   Which for us our warriors win,
>   Decks our cell at set of sun,
>   Worn with toil, with sleep opprest,
>   I press my mossy bed, and sink to rest.

> " Then, once more, I see our train,
>   With all our chace renew'd again:
>   Once more 'tis day,
>   Once more our prey
>   Gnashes his angry teeth, and foams in vain.
>   Again, in sullen haste, he flies,
>   Ta'en in the toil, again he lies,
>   Again he roars, and in my slumbers dies."

There is a ripple of applause. Yarico bows and preens her feathers, and the action of the play is resumed. Surely Keats is wrong in saying that Indians cannot tell their dreams.

Wowski, though a comic character, is given her share of pathos. She addresses Trudge in the lines,

> " White man, never go away,
>   Tell me why need you?
>   Stay with your Wowski, stay,
>   Wowski will feed you."

But not all of Colman's songs are serious. Though the connection between the following duet and primitive poetry is exceedingly tenuous, I cannot forbear giving it in full:

"*Wowski:* Wampum, Swampum, Yanko, Lanko, Nanko, Pownatowski,
Black men — plenty — twenty — fight for me.
White man, woo you true?
Trudge: Who?
Wowski: You.
Trudge: Yes, pretty little Wowski.
Wowski: Then I leave all, and I follow thee.
Trudge: Oh then turn about, my little tawny tight one!
Don't you like me?
Wowski: Iss, you're like the snow!
If you slight one. —
Trudge: Never, not for my white one;
You are beautiful as any sloe.
Wowski: Wars, jars, scars, can't expose ye
In our grot —
Trudge: So snug and cosey!
Wowski: Flowers neatly
Picked, shall sweetly
Make your bed.
Trudge: Coying, toying
With a rosy,
Posey,
When I'm dozey,
Bear-skin night-caps too shall warm my head."

Colman could easily provide the "lyrics" for a modern musical comedy.

Up to the present point we have considered the relation of savage poetry to the ballad revival and to the general naturalistic illusion, and have briefly illustrated certain representative divisions of pseudo-primitive song. It may now be instructive to compare a few savage lays with their actual sources.

In one important instance, an Indian's song can be traced to the Swiss peasant. The whole story is worth recount-

ing.   Olola, the Indian child in Bowles' *Missionary,*
" sung wild carols to the wind."   This idea seemed to
Southey worthy of fuller treatment when in his *Tale of
Paraguay* he created the very similar character of Mooma,
whose natural innocence has already been described.   Remains now to add that her chief delight is, like Nedda in
Pagliacci, to imitate the songs of the birds.

> " For these had been her teachers, these alone;
>   And she, in many an emulous essay,
>   At length into a descant of her own
>   Had blended all their notes — a wild display
>   Of sounds in rich, irregular array."

We are given specific details as to her method of singing.
She has at her command diminuendo and crescendo.   In
bravura passages she sometimes finds it difficult to sus-
tain the pitch, but saves the performance by the introduction of a cadenza so moving that she herself is reduced to
tears.

> " In joy had she begun the ambitious song,
>   With rapid interchange of sink and swell;
>   And sometimes high the note was raised, and long
>   Produced, with shake and effort sensible,
>   As if the voice exulted there to dwell:
>   But, when she could no more that pitch sustain,
>   So thrillingly attuned the cadence fell,
>   That, with the music of its dying strain,
>   She moved herself to tears of pleasurable pain."

Such, prior to the sophisticating contagion of words, is the
poetry of natural man.   Medieval ballads are, after all, the
outcome of a long tradition of song.   Beneath their conventions must lie something literally primitive, an art of
rude onomatapoetic gurglings.   In Mooma this " cuck-
cuck, jug-jug, pu-we, to-witta-wo " is restored to poetry.

Yet Mooma's song is based either on contemporary Swiss yodling, or on something terribly like it. Southey explains that this passage originates in his memories of the Staubbach, where — he quotes from the journal of his tour — " while we were at the waterfall, some half-score peasants, chiefly women and girls, assembled just out of reach of the spray and set up . . . a song, not of articulate sounds, but in which the voice was used as a mere instrument of music, more flexible than any which art could produce." [43]

Southey also quotes a sonnet by Wordsworth [44] on this identical theme, for it appears that one could not visit the Staubbach without being entertained by the yodlers. There was probably an excellent echo. " The vocal powers of these musical beggars," says Wordsworth, " may seem to be exaggerated; but this wild and savage air was utterly unlike anything I had ever heard. The notes . . . seemed to belong in some way or other to the waterfall, and reminded me of religious services chanted to streams and fountains in Pagan times." They might also have recalled Carver's young Indian who prays to the cataract.

Wordsworth finds the music "shrill and wild," but pleasing. His enjoyment of the scene, however, is marred by his pity for the poverty of the yodlers. His sister Dorothy has no such social qualms, and keenly enjoys " the savage air " for what it is. " I was close to the women when they began," she says, " and hence probably it was that I perceived nothing of *sweetness* in their tones.

[43] *Works,* Vol. VII, pp. 125–126.
[44] *On approaching the Staub-bach, Lauterbrunnen.* (*Memorials of a Tour on the Continent*, No. XII.) The sonnet as quoted by Southey differs in several points from the poem as printed in the Oxford Edition. In his notes Wordsworth refers to Southey's description of the incident.

I cannot answer for the impression on the rest of the party
except my brother, who being behind, heard the carol
from a distance; and the description he gives of it is similar to Mr. Southey's in his Journal." [45] One likes Dorothy's ability to combine truthfulness with loyalty to her
brother; but perhaps the poet's desire to find beauty in
primitive song influenced his description no less than the
distance at which he listened.

Before we definitely trace Mooma's warblings to this
incident, however, we must consider a letter in which
Southey " honestly " tells Caroline Bowles " that the real
ground of that description is the pleasure that I have myself in pouring forth ' the voice which echo loves,' and
making a great noise indoors, out of doors, when I am at
liberty." [46] Is Mooma, the child of nature who moves
herself to tears by her emulation of the birds, Robert
Southey himself? There is a certain incongruity in the
thought.

As a poet, the South Sea Islander attracted less attention
than the Indian. Love, the preëminent distinction of
Tahiti, had not yet been associated with the Hawaiian
ukulele. In at least one instance, civilized man was disappointed with a specimen of Polynesian art. From
Fanny Burney's *Early Diary*, Professor Tinker draws an
amusing account of Omai's rendition of a native song.
She was disturbed at the jocular content of the ditty, and at
Omai's attempt to represent the scene by grimace and gesture. Tinker's own interpretation of Miss Burney's reaction is beyond praise: " Had Omai," he says, " sung in a

---

[45] *Journal of Dorothy Wordsworth*; Thursday, August 10, 1820.
When the Wordsworths visited the place, two women were the only
singers, as contrasted to the " half score peasants " heard by Southey in
1817.

[46] *Correspondence with Caroline Bowles*, p. 90.

minor key something vaguely sublime and wildly passionate — had he somehow or other happened to recall
Ossian to her mind — she would have been transported
with delight. But there was no hint of the heroic in what
he sang — no note of primitive passion. . . . His piece
was in no way like *The Bard* or the odes of Mason. It
was something quite different in kind from the poetry that
Miss Burney knew. . . . But the loose numbers, the
wild sweetness, the bursting heart, the rude eloquence of
Nature — these were not in it, for these things belong to
romanticism, and not to primitive poetry." [47]

Captain Wilson, we recall, was so alarmed by the singing of the Pelewans that at first he thought an attack was
in preparation. Later, all fright assuaged, the savages
and their English guests held a joint concert.[48] The description of the native method of balladry would be profoundly suggestive to a medievalist: " Raa Kook gave out
a line, or stave, which was taken up by another Rupack,
seated at a little distance, who sang a verse, accompanied
by the rest of the natives." When Lee Boo goes to England, he tries to entertain his white friends with a Pelewan
lay, but with no better luck than Omai. The white gentry
think his voice unmelodious.

It was perhaps fortunate for the writers of the age that
they had so little knowledge of genuine primitive poetry:
their illusions otherwise might not have sustained the
shock. A few such cold douches as those administered by
Omai and Lee Boo were not, however, sufficient to quench
their ardor. They were determined at all costs to find the
man of nature beneath the savage. Lee Boo's father, Abba

[47] *Nature's Simple Plan*, pp. 83–84. *Cf. Early Diary*, Vol. II. pp.
132–133.

[48] *Vide supra*, p. 113. For a similar international *musicale, cf.
Journal of Joseph Banks*, p. 99.

Thule, was no bard of Morven: witness his depraved fondness for the English sailor songs sung by young Cobbledick. But Bowles can put into his mouth such lines as

> " I linger on the desert rock alone,
> Heartless, and cry for thee, my son, my son."

Byron, in the Toobonian song to which reference has already been made, shows the same readiness to idealize the poetry of the South Seas. The passage in question opens the second canto of *The Island*. The natives lament the passing of the old days before the Fijians made war upon them, but decide to forget their sorrows in dancing and drinking. The song is taken, says Byron, " from an actual song of the Tonga Islanders, of which a prose translation is given in ' Mariner's Account of the Tonga Islands.' " Here is a portion of Mariner's translation: " But now the dance is over; let us remain here to-night, and feast and be cheerful, and to-morrow we will depart for the *Mooa*. How troublesome are the young men, begging for our wreaths of flowers, while they say in their flattery, ' See how charming these young girls look coming from *Licoo!* ' "

" I have altered and added," says Byron, "but have retained as much as possible of the original." This is the result:

> " But now the dance is o'er — yet stay awhile;
> Ah, pause! nor yet put out the social smile.
> To-morrow for the Mooa we depart,
> But not tonight — tonight is for the heart.
> Again bestow the wreaths we gently woo,
> Ye young enchantresses of gay Licoo! "

Not Campbell, not Rogers even, could do worse. And these are called " untaught melodies! "

In Albania, however, the hospitable Suliotes sing a song much truer to the spirit of the original. Their own daring is the theme:

> " Oh! who is more brave than a dark Suliote,
> With his snowy camese and his shaggy capote? "

One can fairly see them jumping about. The stanzas of this song " are partly taken," says Byron, " from different Albanese songs, as far as I was able to make out by the exposition of the Albanese in Romaic and Italian." Hobhouse, the poet's companion, describes the incident thus: " After eating and drinking, the greater part of them assembled round the largest of the fires, and . . . danced round the blaze to their own songs . . . with astonishing energy. All their songs were relations of some robbing exploits. One of them, which detained them more than an hour, began thus — ' When we set out from Parga there were sixty of us ' : then came the burden of the verse —

> ' Robbers all at Parga!
> Robbers all at Parga!' " [49]

Byron's version is neither so simple nor so monotonous, and his Suliotes do not call themselves robbers; but he embroiders much less than in his Toobonian lay. The general character of the scene is at least preserved.

In the work of Mungo Park, the most influential African explorer of the period, there is much that would enhance the Negro's poetic reputation. The Africans, he says, love both music and poetry. Negro bards belong to an official and highly respected class, and " are in a great measure exempted from that neglect and indigence, which in more polished countries commonly attend the votaries of the Muses." These " singing men," as they are called, per-

[49] *Travels in Albania*, Vol. I, pp. 166–167.

form the functions of medieval minstrels. They earn their living chiefly by extemporizing songs in honor of the tribal potentates. "But a nobler part of their office is to recite the historical events of their country: hence, in war, they accompany the soldiers to the field; in order, by reciting the great deeds of their ancestors, to awaken in them a spirit of glorious emulation." For what other purpose did the Teuton bards of Klopstock's fancy follow Hermann's army into battle?

In Africa the composition of historical poetry is not a dead art to be exhumed by the antiquary, but a living process which anyone may see in operation. When Park and the slave-train with which he is travelling entered a certain town, they went to the assembly-platform, "where the people gathered round us to hear our *dentegi* (history); this was related publicly by two of the singing men: they enumerated every little circumstance which had happened to the coffle [slave-train]; beginning with the events of the present day, and relating everything in a backward series, until they reached Kamalia."

Few writers of the age could fail to be attracted by Park's account. As a poet, the Negro seemed to combine the spontaneity of the savage and the dignity of the Teutonic bard. Thus the slave in Rogers' *Pleasures of Memory* believes that when he dies he will return to Congo's shore, and there

> "The oral tale of elder time rehearse,
> And chant the rude traditionary verse."

Following Rogers' lead, Montgomery, in *The West Indies*, describes the African as

> ". . .   most delighted, when, in rudest rhymes,
> The minstrel wakes the song of elder times,
> When men were heroes, slaves to Beauty's charms,
> And all the joys of life were love and arms."

Here, perhaps through the influence of *Oroonoko*, Dryden's formula for heroic drama merges with the ballad-cult and the Noble Savage idea.

With the Negro, as with other savages, poetic talent is allied to Arcadian virtues. After praising African hospitality, Montgomery introduces a specimen of negro poetry as an illustration of this trait:

> " The winds were roaring, and the White Man fled,
> The rains of night descended on his head;
> The poor White Man sat down beneath our tree,
> Weary and faint, and far from home was he:
> For him no mother fills with milk the bowl,
> No wife prepares the bread to cheer his soul;
> — Pity the poor White Man who sought our tree,
> No wife, no mother, and no home has he." [50]

This passage has a history quite as interesting as the yodling of Mooma. In Park's *Travels*, to which Montgomery refers us, we find that the explorer once rested beneath a tree where a few women were working. " They lightened their labor by songs, one of which was composed extempore; for I was myself the subject of it. It was sung by one of the young women, the rest joining in a sort of chorus." Here, then, is folk-song in the making. But the benevolent sentiments expressed by the song give it more than anthropological importance. " The air was sweet and plaintive, and the words, literally translated, were these. — ' The winds roared, and the rains fell. — The poor white man, faint and weary, came and sat under our tree. — He has no mother to bring him milk; no wife to grind his corn. *Chorus.* Let us pity the poor white man; no mother has he, etc., etc.' Trifling as this recital may appear to the reader," says Park, " to a person in my sit-

[50] *Poetical Works*, Vol. I, pp. 154–155.

uation, the circumstance was affecting in the highest degree. I was oppressed by such unexpected kindness; and sleep fled from my eyes." [51]

Enter now Georgiana Cavendish, Duchess of Devonshire, who " was pleased to think so highly of this simple and unpremeditated effusion, as to make a version of it with her own pen; and cause it to be set to music by an eminent Composer. With this elegant production, in both parts of which the plaintive simplicity of the original is preserved and improved, the Author thinks himself highly honoured in being permitted to adorn his book." [52]

One can imagine the tears dropping from those large Gainsborough eyes upon the words of Park. This is what the Duchess made of the affecting incident:

> " The loud wind roar'd, the rain fell fast;
> The White Man yielded to the blast:
> He sat him down, beneath our tree;
> For weary, sad, and faint was he;
> And ah, no wife, or mother's care,
> For him, the milk or corn prepare."

Chorus.

> " The White Man, shall our pity share;
> Alas, no wife or mother's care,
> For him, the milk or corn prepare."

Granting the exigencies of versification, Park is right in saying that " the plaintive simplicity of the original is preserved." The second line is extraneous decoration, and the actual song of the negro women was probably free from grammatical errors; but on the whole Georgiana faithfully versifies the words set down by the explorer.

[51] *Travels in Africa*, p. 198.
[52] Postscript to 1799 edition of Park's *Travels*, in which Georgiana's song is printed as an appendix.

In the second part, however, the " simplicity of the original " is " improved," as follows:

> " The storm is o'er; the tempest past;
>   And Mercy's voice has hush'd the blast.
>   The wind is heard in whispers low,
>   The White Man, far away must go; —
>   But ever in his heart will bear
>   Remembrance of the Negro's care.

Chorus.

> " Go, White Man, go; — but with thee bear
>   The Negro's wish, the Negro's prayer;
>   Remembrance of the Negro's care."

That is not in Park, nor was it in the minds of the women who befriended him. It is the thought of a highly civilized opponent of the slave trade.

Georgiana's words were set to pleasantly tinkling music by G. G. Ferrari, and included in the second — in reality the first complete — edition of Park's *Travels*. The song became popular; it was better suited to fashionable drawing-rooms than the recitals of Omai and Lee Boo. I have sung it to my own family circle, but with doubtful success. Its charms have faded.

Ten years after the work of the Piccadilly Beauty, this chant of pity is, as we have seen, used by James Montgomery. His version follows Park very closely, and he does not mention Georgiana, although he could hardly have been ignorant of her song. This provincial editor may have looked askance at his fashionable ally in the anti-slavery cause.

The story has a later development. In Bowles' *Missionary*, that same Olola who in childhood " danced and sung wild carols to the wind," leads a group of maidens who attempt to console a captive white woman in these familiar words:

> " Let us pity the poor white maid!
> She has no mother near!
> No friend to dry her tear!
> Upon the cold earth she is laid:
> Let us pity the poor white maid! " [53]

" From Mungo Park," reads the succinct footnote. Since the purpose of Montgomery's *West Indies* was to give the Negro dignity equal to that of the Indian, it seems hardly fair of Bowles to transfer this song from Africa to Chile.

The hospitality of the negro women was known also to Crabbe. His *Woman!* is headed by a passage from Mungo Park to the effect that the female members of almost every tribe treated him with kindness. Crabbe elaborates this theme, adding that the same is true of Lapland. There the women sing:

> " 'Tis good the fainting soul to cheer,
> To see the famish'd stranger fed;
> To milk for him the mother-deer,
> To smooth for him the furry bed."

This is not very close to the negro song, but the reference to Park is unmistakable evidence of what was in Crabbe's mind. Though he seems to relax from his habitual opposition to naturalism, he is after all praising not the Noble Savage, but woman. One paragraph in Park's *Travels*, then, provides material for Montgomery, the Duchess of Devonshire, Bowles and Crabbe.

Barring a few special students, we of to-day do not think of the Indian as a poet. We do, however, think of him as an orator. Words like " powwow," " council-fire " or " calumet " call up the image of some aged chieftain

[53] *Poetical Works*, Vol. I, p. 340.

who, after what seems an endless period of silent smoking, rises and addresses the assembly in words of Laconic brevity and point, but of more than Laconic picturesqueness. The romanticists were in possession of more real facts about Indian oratory than about Indian song, and one suspects that the rhetoric of the redman was more influential than his barbaric chants in establishing his poetic reputation.

The conception of the Indian as an orator goes back to Columbus himself. "The king," reports the discoverer, "is a man of remarkable presence, and with a certain self-contained manner that is a pleasure to see." Here are the traditional poise and reserve of the sachem. The chief Topiawari impresses Raleigh not only by the dignity of his manner but by his words, in which an unconscious poetry seems to lurk.[54] The Indian, having a very limited abstract vocabulary, is forced to convey most of his scanty abstract ideas in concrete terms. Hence he frequently appears to be consciously imaginative when he is merely groping for expression. The whites brought to America, also, a host of things which were utterly strange to him, and which he could comprehend only by comparing them to familiar objects. Thus he fabricated a number of quaint metaphors which seemed indicative of poetic fancy — "fire-water" is a stock example. In every language, too, much primitive poetry is embedded. Many of our commonest words were once bold figures of speech. Their poetry emerges anew if they are translated literally into another tongue. "Dark and Bloody Ground" gives us a much deeper thrill than "Kentucky" could have given the redman. Thus Indian efforts to speak English, and English efforts to translate Indian, no doubt added to the savage's reputation as a coiner of images.

[54] *Vide supra*, p. 14.

Logan's speech, as we already know, is the most famous specimen of Indian oratory, though it is possible to feel that its merits have been overrated. At least Thomas Jefferson goes too far when he writes, " I may challenge the whole orations of Demosthenes and Cicero, and of any more eminent orator, to produce a single passage, superior to the speech of Logan." [55] Just what the wronged chief said we shall never know. His address was no public harangue, but was privately delivered, in the Indian tongue, to one John Gibson, who translated it and brought it to Lord Dunmore.[56] Whether Gibson was an accurate translator, and whether he resisted the temptation to " touch up " the original, are questions for speculation.

Mackenzie's *Man of Feeling* and *Man of the World* show how the Indian was supposed to talk: " May the Great Spirit bear up the weight of your old age, and blunt the arrow that brings it rest! " " He only is worthy to lift the hatchet of the Cherokees, to whom shame is more intolerable than the stab of the knife, or the burning of the fire." " I have lived a thousand moons, without captivity and without disgrace; in my youth I did not fly in battle, and in age, the tribes listened when I spake."

These balanced, image-laden cadences remind one of Ossian; it seems that the Indian sings pseudo-Celtic songs, and speaks pseudo-Celtic prose. When Immalee — not an Indian, to be sure, but a true Noble Savage — is deserted by Melmoth, she breaks forth with: " Roar on, terrible ocean! thy waves, which I cannot count, can never wash his image from my soul — thou dashest a thousand waves against a rock, but the rock is unmoved — and so

[55] *Notes on the State of Virginia*, p. 86.
[56] *Ibid.*, pp. 323–324. Jefferson gives Gibson's affidavit to this effect.

would be my heart amid the calamities of the world with which he threatens me,— whose dangers I never would have known but for him, and whose dangers for him I will encounter." This is certainly pure Ossian, and yet its grandeur is not far above the powers of Mackenzie's sachems.

The Indian's habit of concrete, imaginative expression influences poets as well as novelists. Campbell, as we know, prints the Logan oration in the notes to *Gertrude*, though if he intended Outalissi to resemble Logan in his speech he has certainly departed widely from the model. In Bowles' *Missionary*, Attacapa's lament for his son is avowedly based on Logan's oration. The paraphrase, however, is so very poetic that the flavor of the original is lost. Bowles' own conception of an Indian orator is Caupolican, who is made to address an assembly in words patterned on those of Milton's Satan. One prefers savages who talk Ossian. The accents of Logan are heard, I think, in Kerhonah's address to the waterfall-god:

> " God of the Mohawks! everlasting Voice!
> Behold, in me, the son of Maspatake,
> The king of kings. When o'er the waters first
> The White Man came, he bade the strangers welcome,
> And gave them food and lands, and smoked with them
> The pipe of peace. Behold their gratitude!
> The son of Maspatake, a fugitive,
> Driv'n from his father's graves, hath now no home,
> No people, and no hope! except in thee,
> God of the Mohawks! hear me and avenge! " [57]

The influence of the tradition of Indian oratory upon Wordsworth is shown in his comparison of the Wanderer's " eloquent harangue " to an oration,

[57] *Poetical Works of Ebenezer Elliott*, p. 99.

> " Such as, remote, 'mid savage wilderness,
> An Indian chief discharges from his breast
> Into the hearing of assembled tribes." [58]

In what possible sense are the Wanderer's words like those of an Indian? Merely because they are "poured forth with fervor in continuous stream"? That the simile is based on a comparison of lung-power seems improbable. The leech-gatherer's words "came feebly, from a feeble chest"; and yet

> " . . . each in solemn order followed each,
> With something of a lofty utterance drest —
> Choice word and measured phrase, above the reach
> Of ordinary men."

The curious comparison seems suggested rather by the Wanderer's serene simplicity and patriarchal dignity.

There can be no doubt that images form the primary stuff of poetry, and that pseudo-classicism had departed much too far from this necessary sensuous foundation. It was a wholesome instinct that made the romanticists return to simplicity and concreteness. They were restoring the roots without which flowers cannot grow. They naturally tended, however, to reverse the error of the pseudo-classicists by exaggerating the importance of sense-impressions and by underestimating the importance of constructive brain-work. De Quincey feels impelled to attack the consequent fallacy "that the savage has more imagination than civilized man." "As to savages," he says, "their poetry and their eloquence are always of the most unimaginative order: when they are figurative, they are so by mere necessity; language being too poor amongst savage nations to express any but the rudest thoughts, so that

[58] *Vide supra*, p. 184.

such feelings as are not of hourly occurrence can be expressed only by figures." Figurative language is no indication of "imaginative power; it is one of the commonest expressions of the over-excitement of weakness. . . . In all the specimens of savage eloquence which have been reported to us there is ever the mark of an infantine understanding." [59]   Failure to realize that, as Santayana says, "what we call the innocence of the eye is often merely the imbecility of the mind" was one cause of the glorification of primitive poetry.   Another cause was the idea that the Noble Savage, being naturally good, must be naturally poetic.

There were other critics who objected on more general grounds to the primitivistic element in the romantic theory of poetry.   Peacock, who in *Melincourt* pokes fun at the craze for ballads, is more serious in his essay, *The Four Ages of Poetry*.   "A poet in our times," he declares, "is a semi-barbarian in a civilized community.   His ideas, thoughts, feelings, associations, are all with barbarous manners, obsolete customs, and exploded superstitions. . . .   While the historian and the philosopher are advancing in, and accelerating, the progress of knowledge, the poet is wallowing in the rubbish of departed ignorance, and raking up the ashes of dead savages to find gewgaws and rattles for the grown babies of the age." [60]

---

[59] *Works*, Vol. X, p. 443 (*False Distinctions*).

[60] *Four Ages of Poetry*, p. 16.   In this as in other respects, Peacock is a difficult man to pin down.   The British Museum possesses an unfinished manuscript *Essay on Fashionable Literature* by Peacock (Addit. 36,815, Vol. I, ff. 67–85).   Here he defends Coleridge against the *Edinburgh Review* by showing that *Christabel* is a praiseworthy attempt to revive the qualities of the medieval ballad.   This essay was written in the summer of 1818, two years before the publication of *Four Ages of Poetry*.   I am informed that it will be printed in Vol. VIII of the *Halliford Edition of the Works of Thomas Love Peacock*.

Hazlitt, though himself a lover of ballads, is moved by his dislike for the Lakists to say that they " took the same method in their new-fangled ' metre ballad-mongering' scheme, which Rousseau did in his prose paradoxes — of exciting attention by reversing the established standards of opinion and estimation in the world. They were for bringing poetry back to its primitive simplicity and state of nature, as he was for bringing society back to the savage state." [61] Beneath the personal spleen which animates this passage lies a sub-stratum of truth. Interest in primitive poetry, like other elements of romantic naturalism, is embodied in the Noble Savage, who sings because he is good and is good because he sings.

[61] *Works*, Vol. V, p. 163.

CHAPTER XIV

CONCLUSION

SINCE at several points in the preceding pages I have paused to gather up the loose threads of the discussion, no formal summary will here be necessary. We know more than we did about the popularity of the Noble Savage from 1730 to 1830. We have traced his relation to the chronological stages into which the period falls, to various forms of literature and groups of writers, and to individual authors. In the foregoing topical chapters, also, we have come to understand how the Noble Savage idea is interwoven with other strands that make up the thought-fabric of the Romantic Movement. Of those strands, the plastic influence of natural objects, ingenuous and passionate love, the religion of nature and the revival of primitive poetry have received special attention; but the historical treatment of the subject has shown that the Noble Savage is also related to sensibility, humanitarianism, and political radicalism, and to the cult of the peasant and the child. These facts, though they have always been perfectly evident to anyone with enough curiosity to read and compare, have not before been dug out and thrown together in such profusion.

It is perhaps unfortunate that one cannot be satisfied with these simple results. When one has collected so much material, however, one is tempted to use it in framing some sort of answer to the troublesome question of Southey's little Wilhelmine: "But what good came of it at last?" The Noble Savage is used by many romantic writers as a vehicle for many romantic ideas. The rise and fall of an author's romanticism is often paralleled by the rise and fall of his sympathy for the Noble Savage. Enemies of romanticism often accept this figure as a symbol of the tendencies which they oppose. One therefore feels drawn toward the conclusion that completely to understand the Noble Savage would be to clarify one's conception of romanticism.

This conclusion, however, should not be accepted without certain qualifications. It should now be evident that the Noble Savage played some part in romantic thought; but the importance of that part may be overestimated. Both the Romantic Movement in general and individual romantic writers rather early abandoned the cult of primitive man and adopted other means of delivering their message. Several important romanticists do not react favorably to the savage, and even of his partisans few are at any time ready to swallow him whole. In using the Noble Savage as a means of studying romanticism, one sees chiefly the earlier, cruder, and more extravagant aspects of the movement; and when great writers come within range of our chosen peep-hole, they are not likely to present to us their most admirable qualities. For this reason the present study is likely to be regarded as an addition to that chorus of invective which of late years has been raised against romanticism.

As recently as a score of years ago, it was fashionable to regard the Romantic Movement as a beneficent revolution against the tyranny of the eighteenth century, an awakening of spring after a long, hard winter. Though this view is still perhaps the most popular, it has recently been attacked by a group of critics who find in the Romantic Movement the source of much of that feebleness, eccentricity and disorganization which afflict contemporary thought. With these critics, I am at least in partial sympathy. Since one's sympathies are dictated largely by prejudice, I should explain at the outset what my prejudices are.

To me, unintellectual activities have a profound appeal. Nothing delights me more than the free play of instincts and of their sublimations in sentiment and emotion. Although literature and art seem to me at their finest when to the eye and heart of a child is added the creative intelligence of a rational man, I am not cold to the wild spontaneity of even the least classical genius. Mystery excites me, and I have often imposed strangeness upon things which were probably not strange at all. My return to nature takes place nearly every summer, when I go fishing in the Maine woods. There guides and farmers frequently convince me that the world has done terrible things to human nature; and there, like Pope's poor Indian, I have seen God in clouds, and heard him in the wind. My own child has furnished more than one corroborative footnote to the *Immortality Ode*. Both in their playful and solemn aspects, then, my emotions are in a normal state of activity.

Yet I deeply distrust that type of thought which claims to derive truth from some inspiration superior to logical reasoning. I cannot conceive of any other means of understanding the universe than accurate observation and cautious inference — in other words, scientific method. No hard-and-fast line, of course, can be drawn between thinking and feeling. The most rigidly scientific procedure is deeply interfused with passion and desire. We dream a world, then try to find in nature some corroboration of our vision. Hypotheses are often happy guesses dictated by what we hope to be true, and the most pretentious rationalistic structures have a foundation of instinct.

Especially in nonmaterial fields, where experiment is impossible, speculation is often a form of poetry — bold, free and imaginative. Yet though thinking and feeling constantly overlap, there is a real difference between the Will to Think and the Will to Believe. Both the Man of Reason and the Man of Feeling may instinctively be impelled to form the same hypothesis. The differentiating test comes when facts prove the hypothesis to be untenable. Then the Man of Reason, often with sorrow, discards his false vision; but the Man of Feeling preserves the illusion by appealing from the facts to what he calls a super-rational standard — faith, insight, inspiration. And his upward flight is generally accompanied by a scornful kick at the poor, honest logic-chopper who remains below in the darkness.

In the darkness with that logic-chopper I am content to remain, holding that to part with a false hypothesis is a braver and more beautiful act than to retain it on any terms, and that he who affects to scorn logic in behalf of some " higher truth" is really falling back upon those primitive impulses which represent the childhood of reason. This thin rationalism is just what might be expected of an immature, egotistic and academic person. Like the similar affliction of the young Jacobin, it is liable at any moment to collapse into the warmest emotionalism. Older and wiser men have assured me that as time goes on I shall appreciate the feebleness of human reason. I appreciate it already. The typical young rationalist supposes that reason can do a great deal; I recognize that reason can do hardly anything, but I know of nothing that can do more. Must we wilfully extinguish our sole candle because it flickers dimly, and will probably go out at the next blast of the gale? Since our tools are blunt, shall we throw them away and dig with our hands? If reason were a

hundred times weaker than it has proved itself to be, I
still should cling to it. I cherish it as a Platonic idea;
cherish it so warmly that every foolish effort of man to
think straight and keenly seems beautiful, and every
failure a tragedy. A passionate enmity toward all evasion
of the responsibilities imposed by scientific method is, then,
the prejudice for which the reader must make allowance.

These are uncomfortable days for a rationalist. Science
now deepens instead of clarifying the mystery of existence.
Matter, the resting-place of the lazy mind, has been
analyzed into positive and negative charges of electricity:
the world is one quiver of energy. This discovery—
supposing it to be valid, which it probably is, and final,
which it almost certainly is not—can surprise only those
who have entertained a crude conception of science. The
new physics, relativity and other strange marvels of the
age have confronted us with problems which are to be
solved, if at all, only by the same patient investigation, the
same honest thinking, that have brought us face to face
with those problems. But when we suddenly find ourselves ignorant, there is a grave temptation to justify
ignorance by calling it sublime.

On the distant borders of exact science lies psychology.
Here the most important discovery has been the fact that
our reason is largely a disguise for our passions. A large
portion of mental life lies below the level of controlled,
conscious, volitional thinking. Whether we call it the
psyche or the subconscious, it strongly influences our mental processes. The dreaming and the waking states are less
different than we have realized. Even that touch of discipline which waking man imposes on his disorderly
images is often harmful. " Rationalizing " is merely the
invention of excuses for our passions. There is a "real"
and an "apparent" reason for all our beliefs, and the

former is invariably absurd. If we stifle our subconscious desires, the psycho-analysts tell us, we may form ugly festers of perversion and madness.

Psychology has acquired its semi-scientific status partly at least by applying a technical jargon to familiar facts. Any college freshman who sees sheep huddling together can now speak of the gregarious instinct, quite unaware that he is defining in terms of the thing to be defined. Similarly, our talk about the subconscious is little more than a new way of expressing the sadly familiar truth that at bottom we are passionate beasts who have acquired a superficial skill in dialectic. The doctrine that the suppression of our animal impulses is necessarily unwholesome and dangerous is not held by legitimate psychologists. That such a suppression is often harmful has been known for centuries. The new psychology, in showing us that our minds are little flowers of intelligence struggling upward from a marsh of brute instinct, has not proved that those flowers should sink back into the mud. But these discoveries are tempting many to ask why, since we are fundamentally unreasonable, we should strive so hard to reason.

In the philosophy of the age, the most characteristic movement is pragmatism and its various offshoots. If we believe with William James that truth is not absolute, but relative and instrumental, we assume a greater obligation than ever before to think hard and straight. Instead of pointing the bowsprit of our craft toward one clear star, we must creep along in the fog and take soundings — and woe betide us if those soundings are inaccurate. But what a temptation to blunder along in the dark! If there is no one truth, why should we behave as if there were? Since things are what they are experienced as being, we can manufacture any truth that we desire by imagining the proper sort of experience. Though James himself would be the last man to approve of such madness, his doctrine of the Will to Believe has lent much encouragement to it. To many people, the Will to Believe means what Blake meant when he said, " A firm persuasion that a thing is so, makes it so." Thus pragmatism, originally scientific in spirit, places the stamp of "philosophy" upon the wildest vagaries of superstition.

This, then, is assuredly not the time for glib confidence in the power of reason. Never has there been such a mass of concrete facts with such impotence to put them together; never such an elaborate mechanism for investigating the universe with such nerveless hands to use it; never such huge institutions of learning with such scorn of everything that learning should mean. One can only say: " I know that I am a stupid animal living in a mysterious and hostile world. Yet must I try to understand. I know that in this task I shall be led astray by dreams and passions; that I shall find what I want to find only by inventing lies. But if I try hard to be honest, and listen as little as possible to the beast within me, I may still gather some bitter fruit from the tree of the knowledge of good and evil."

Not many people, however, say anything of the sort, for it is easier to create illusion out of disillusion. Those who hanker for a world of strangeness in which their instincts may happily gambol now think themselves free from Urizen's chains. We knew all along that the pretensions of reason are absurd. Since matter has been dissipated into thin air, why is not *naïveté* the truest wisdom? Einstein has given us four dimensions; why not six or seven? The senses are weak; throw them overboard. Logic is a disguise for passion; let us, therefore, be passionate and illogical. If madness comes from stifling instinct, true sanity lies in giving free rein to all our impulses. Since there is no such thing as absolute truth, we can believe what we please and it will be true. Everything is illusion; hence what we dream is as valid as what we see. This world is a figment of our thought; we can make it beautiful by pretending that it is beautiful. If we long to see spirits, spirits will appear. If we mutter the proper incantations, our diseases will be cured. What pedantic fool would hesitate to discard reason when the results of sympathetic magic are so simple and sure? In short, the discovery that intellect is feeble has led us to glorify those things which constitute the feebleness of intellect.

The picture may be overdrawn. Were it not overdrawn, it would not be a picture. But I would ask those teachers and scholars who will probably be the only persons to read this book whether they have not, in their attempts to bring reason to their classes, to fellow students, or to the public, generally met with sullen or scornful opposition. The world simply will not think. Has it ever wished to think? Perhaps not, but there has never been a time when the natural stupidity of the human animal was more powerfully supported by that higher kind of muddle-headed emotionalism which masquerades in the robes of philosophy.

Let us listen to Rabindranath Tagore. "I have been told by a scholar friend of mine," says he, " that by constant practise in logic he has weakened his natural instinct of faith. The reason is that faith is the spectator in us which finds the meaning of the drama from the unity of the performance, but logic lures us into the greenroom, where there is stagecraft, but no drama at all, and then this logic nods its head, and wearily talks about disillusionment. But the greenroom, dealing with the fragments, when questioned, either looks foolish or wears the sneering smile of Mephistopheles; for it does not have the secret of the unity, which is somewhere else. It is for faith to answer, 'Unity comes to us from the One, and the one in ourselves opens the door and receives it with joy.' " [1]

This attempt to throw logic overboard in order to be free to "dream true" is familiar to students of romanticism. We have seen it in Shelley's ideal mind, which will be "an ocean of clear emotion"; in Coleridge's recommendation of fairy tales as a means of training the child to grasp large conceptions; in Wordsworth's scorn for "that false secondary power by which we multiply distinctions"; in Blake's detestation of analysis. It would be difficult or impossible to prove that the present distrust of intellect is a direct heritage from the Romantic Movement. The fact probably is that the world is periodically inundated by waves of transcendental thought. But since the most recent and most powerful of such waves swept over Europe between 1780 and 1830, it is natural for loyal servants of Urizen to feel a certain animus against that period. Too bewildered to be quite sure of what we are fighting here and now, we look back a century and seem to recognize our enemy in more manageable form.

A person deficient in sympathy for romanticism will set much store by these words of Novalis: " The world must be romanticized. If we do this, we shall discover in it the meaning it had from the beginning. The lower self becomes, through this process, identified with its higher self. . . . By giving the common a noble meaning, the ordinary a mysterious aspect, the known the dignity of the unknown, the finite the appearance of the infinite, — I romanticize." [2] German romanticists, of course, went further in formulating a philosophy than their English brethren; but some such attempt to fuse that which is sup-

---

[1] *The Poet's Religion. Century Magazine*, June, 1921.
[2] Quoted by Wernaer, *Romanticism*, p. 34.

posedly above reason with that which is admittedly below reason is implicit in much English literature of the period.

In striving to soar above mere logical analysis, the English romanticists frequently brought forward, as illustrations of the truth of their creed, beings who are unable to analyze — the child, the peasant and the savage. How this fact is to be interpreted will depend upon the temperament of the interpreter. To some, it will merely imply that the romanticists championed a fresh and wholesome simplicity of mind against the stodgy pedantry of the eighteenth century. To others, it will imply that the romanticists, in seeking to rise above scientific method, fell below it. Though a distinction undoubtedly exists between instinct and intuition, my prejudices lead me to minimize that distinction. The least disciplined emotions of a man who is capable of reasoning are far above the instinctive reactions of the Hottentot. Yet when civilized man casts aside analytical thought in favor of something "higher," he becomes far more *like* the Hottentot than before he ceased to reason. He can never sink to the truly primitive level, but sink he does. In romantic praise of the Noble Savage, therefore, I am prone to see evidence in support of my belief that transcendentalism is a glorified form of superstition.

But I should be a sorry champion of rationalism were I unable to probe my own prejudices. What has hitherto been said in this chapter illustrates the very tendency which in past ages has caused rationalism to collapse into romanticism — the tendency to ignore experience in order to arrive at some preconceived opinion. As if I were writing a play, I have created a hero, Right Reason; a villain, Romanticism; and a villain's tool, the Noble Savage. These characters were meant to have some foundation in reality, but they are growing much larger and simpler

than life. I have checked myself upon the verge of becoming positively romantic in my attack upon romanticism.

The remedy for this extravagance is a quiet return to
the historical method. If the romanticists had revolted
against reason, they would indeed deserve condemnation.
As a matter of fact, however, they reacted against a sterile
and pretentious imitation of reason which had withered
man's emotions without widening his intellectual horizon.
Their protest took an extreme form, but have many revo-
lutionaries clung to the golden mean? The romantic feeling for nature is not at bottom false or unwholesome. As
a civilization develops, it piles up a mass of useless objects, formulas and conventions that bear no relation to
the real needs of man. When these parasitic growths
threaten the life of the tree, they must be torn away. It is
good for man's pride to know that the scenes which he has
influenced least are often the most beautiful, that riches
are not the proper goal of human effort, and that an intelligent peasant may be wiser than a stupid scholar. Those
who returned to nature, of course, instead of being content
with what they found there, insisted on seeing "heaven
in a wild flower," and scorned Peter Bell less for his indifference to actual primroses than for his refusal to regard
them as symbols of the infinite. In thus blurring the distinction between the real and the unreal, the romanticists
struck a blow at the perhaps narrow type of reason which
I prize so highly. Yet do we not all tend to shed over our
preferences a supernatural glamour? Does not the love
of anything imply that we regard that thing as better than
it is? Passion, not cool reason, impels us to contemplate
one essence rather than another; and that passion is stimulated by opposition. Instead of soberly using what few
grains of truth they possess, men shout absurdities at each
other. If eighteenth century pseudo-rationalism had not

gone so far in one direction, romanticism would not have gone so far in the other. When we substitute history for metaphysics, and human beings for abstract definitions, the romantic excesses are perfectly comprehensible.

If romanticism were inherently vicious, we should expect its fruits to be poisonous. But among those fruits were the dignity of the individual, sympathy for the weak and oppressed, political liberty, appreciation of nature, pure love, deeper insight into the heart of man, and great literature. In some hands, to be sure, these good gifts respectively became hysterical egotism, sentimentality toward social problems, anarchy, primrose-worship, sexual license, morbid introspection, and irresponsible rhapsody. But despite my prejudices I am ready to grant that the occasional corruption of these benefits was largely due to the human weakness of those who received them, and to the opposite faults of the preceding age. On the whole, few reactions have produced more desirable results. Thus it is quite possible to distrust romanticism in the abstract and yet to recognize that, regarded as a particular movement at a particular time, it satisfied a real need. And the scholar in this field, since his prime business is to concern himself with the real facts of literary development, had best regard past movements not in relation to his own philosophy, but in relation to historical evolution. If he works in this spirit, he will find himself so completely occupied in trying to understand romanticism that he will have no time to scold at it.

To this extent, what is true of romanticism is true of the Noble Savage. Abstractly regarded, it must seem regrettable that civilized man, shrinking from his upward march, should turn with admiration to the lower type from which he has laboriously struggled; even more regrettable, that he should confuse bestial content with true happiness, and mental incapacity with mystical inspiration. But if we compare the ideal savage with the ideal civilized man whom Chesterfield held before the eyes of Philip Stanhope, we observe not a conflict of truth and error, but one error striving to correct another. The Noble Savage came at a time when he was needed. His virtues, though grossly misunderstood and exaggerated, helped men to see the superficiality of those ideals of polish, worldly power, luxury, common sense and elegant learning which they had been holding before them.

The history of the human mind, though no less confused than other kinds of history, presents a series of efforts to think scientifically, each of which proves so unsuccessful that it is followed by a period in which feeling is held superior to logic. There is an irregular alternation between cool, responsible, objective thought, and warm, hasty, subjective emotion. Man's reason is so emotional, and his emotions so cerebral, that the slow revolutions of this cycle are difficult to trace. The transition is most evident in the eighteenth century, when the Enlightenment, corrupted by its own ambition, melts into romanticism. Within this cycle, and corresponding with it, runs a smaller cycle in which lower types of humanity periodically emerge to justify the romanticist's attack upon organized civilization and his campaign against analytical reason.

To protest against these tidal movements of intellect is probably as futile as to protest against the succession of day and night. Human reason being as weak as it is, we may be thankful that its repeated failures are soothed by periods of transcendental illusion until it is ready to make one more effort. A few spirits will always be suspicious of romanticism, and unable to feel, with the great majority of men, its power to make the world a place of beauty and hope. In condemning romanticism, however, such persons are likely to find themselves in the position of the recruit who asserted that he alone, of the whole marching company, was in step. It is a little foolish to quarrel with the slow, steady breathing of the universe. I should wish this book, then, to be regarded not as a storehouse of polemic ammunition, but as a groping attempt to interpret one aspect of a mystery before which at the last I willingly bow my head.

APPENDIX

This Appendix makes no attempt to present a bibliography of the Noble Savage, but is simply a list of sources drawn upon for this study.

Annual Anthology, The. Bristol, 1799–1800.

Anon. Caraboo. A Narrative of a Singular Imposition. London, 1817.

——, The Death of Capt. Cook. A Grand Serious Pantomimic Ballet. London, 1789.

——, An Heroic Epistle from Omiah to the Queen of Otaheite. London, 1775.

——, The Interesting and Affecting History of Prince Lee Boo. London, 1789.

——, Omiah's Farewell; Inscribed to the Ladies of London. London, 1776.

——, The Persecutor, with Other Poems. London, 1816.

——, The Story of Inkle and Yarico, . . . Attempted in Verse by the Right Hon. Countess of ——. An Epistle from Yarrico to Inkle. London, 1738.

Babbitt, Irving. Rousseau and Romanticism. Boston and New York, 1919.

Bacon, Francis. Works. ed. Spedding, J., Ellis, R. L., and Heath, D. D. London, 1857.

Bage, Robert. Man as He is Not; or, Hermsprong. London, 1809.

Banks, Joseph. Journal. ed. Hooker, Sir Joseph D. London and New York, 1896.

——, Supplément au Voyage de M. de Bougainville, ou Journal d'un Voyage autour du Monde, Fait par Mm. Banks et Solander. Traduit de l'Anglois par M. de Fréville. Paris, 1772.

Barton, Bernard. Poems and Letters. ed. Barton, Lucy. London, 1853.

Bayly, Thomas Haynes. Songs, Ballads, and Other Poems. London, 1844.

Beattie, James. Poetical Works. Aldine Edition. London, 1866.

Beers, Henry Augustin. A History of English Romanticism in the Eighteenth Century. London, 1899.

Behn, Aphra. Plays, Histories and Novels. London, 1871.

——, Works. ed. Summers, Montague. London, 1915.

Bernbaum, Ernest. Mrs. Behn's Oroonoko. Kittredge Anniversary Papers, pp. 419–434. Boston, 1913.

Bissell, Benjamin. The American Indian in English Literature of the Eighteenth Century. Yale Studies in English, LXVIII. New Haven, 1925.

Blake, William. Poetical Works. ed. Sampson, John. Oxford Edition. London, 1914.

Blamire, Susanna. Poetical Works. Edinburgh, 1842.

Blanchard, Laman. Poetical Works. London, 1876.

Boswell, James. Letters. ed. Tinker, Chauncey Brewster. Oxford, 1924.

——, Life of Johnson. ed. Morris, Mowbray. New York and Boston, n. d.

Bourne, E. G. The Travels of Jonathan Carver. American Historical Review, Vol. XI, pp. 287 ff.

Bowles, William Augustus. Authentic Memoirs. London, 1791.

Bowles, William Lisle. Poetical Works. ed. Gilfillan, George. Edinburgh, 1855.

——, Scenes and Shadows of Days Departed. London, 1837.

British Essayists, The. ed. Chalmers, Alexander. London, 1823, etc.

British Poets, The. Chiswick, 1822.

Brooke, Henry. Collection of the Pieces Formerly Published. London, 1778.

Brunton, Mary. Self-Control. London, 1832.

Burney, Frances. Early Diary. ed. Ellis, Annie Raine. Bohn's Popular Library. London, 1913.

Burns, Robert. Complete Poetical Works. ed. Douglas, W. S. Kilmarnock, 1876.

Byron, George Gordon, Lord. Works. ed. Coleridge, E. H., and Prothero, R. E. London, 1898.

Campbell, Thomas. Complete Poetical Works. ed. Robertson, J. Logie. Oxford Edition. London, 1907.

Carver, Jonathan. Travels Through the Interior Parts of North America. London, 1778.

Cestre, Charles. John Thelwall. New York, 1906.

Chatterton, Thomas. Complete Poetical Works. ed. Roberts, Henry D. The Muses' Library. London, 1906.

Chinard, Gilbert. L'Amérique et le rêve exotique dans la littérature française au XVIIe et au XVIIIe siècle. Paris, 1913.

——, L'Exotisme américain dans la littérature française au XVIe siècle. Paris, 1911.

Clare, John. The Rural Muse. London, 1835.

Coleridge, Samuel Taylor. Complete Poetical Works. ed. Coleridge, Ernest Hartley. Oxford, 1912.

——, The Friend. London, 1812.

——, Letters. ed. Coleridge, Ernest Hartley. Boston and New York, 1895.

——, Letters, Conversations and Recollections of S. T. Coleridge. ed. Allsop, T. New York, 1836.

Collins, William. Poetical Works. Aldine Poets. London, 1906.

Colman, George, the Younger. Inkle and Yarico. London, 1787.

Columbus, Christopher. Authentic Letters. ed. Curtis, W. E. Field Columbian Museum Publications. Chicago, 1895.

——, The Journal of Christopher Columbus, etc. Hakluyt Society. London, 1893.

Conder, Josiah. The Star in the East; with Other Poems. London, 1824.

Cook, James. Journal. ed. Wharton, W. J. L. London, 1893.

——, A Voyage to the Pacific Ocean. London, 1784. [Vol. III is by Capt. James King.]

——, A Voyage Towards the South Pole, and Round the World. London, 1777.

Cooper, Lane. Wordsworth's Sources. Athenæum, April 22, 1905.

——, A Glance at Wordsworth's Reading. Modern Language Notes, March, 1907, and April, 1907.

Cottle, Joseph. Malvern Hills, and Other Poems. London, 1802.

——, Reminiscences of Samuel Taylor Coleridge and Robert Southey. New York, 1847.

Cowper, William. Complete Poetical Works. Oxford Edition. London, 1913.

Crabbe, George. Poetical Works. ed. Carlyle, A. J., and Carlyle, R. M. London, 1908.

Crèvecoeur, J. Hector St. Jean de. Letters from an American Farmer. ed. Lewisohn, Ludwig. New York, 1904.

——, Voyage dans la Haute Pennsylvanie. Paris, 1801.

D., J. W. Inkle und Yariko; oder, Er war nicht ganz Barbar. Cassel, 1798.

Davenant, Sir William. The Cruelty of the Spaniards in Peru. London, 1658.

——, The History of Sir Francis Drake. The First Part. London, 1659.

Day, Thomas. The History of Sandford and Merton. London, 1812.

Defoe, Daniel. Robinson Crusoe. Globe Edition. London, 1868.

Dennis, John. Select Works. London, 1718.

De Quincey, Thomas. Collected Writings. ed. Masson, David. London, 1896.

——, Literary Reminiscences, from the Autobiography of an English Opium-Eater. Boston and New York, n. d.

Drayton, Michael. Minor Poems. ed. Brett, C. Oxford, 1907.

Drevetière, Delisle de la. Arlequin Sauvage. Receuil de Pièces de Théâtre. Dublin, 1749.

Dryden, John. Comedies, Tragedies, and Operas. London, 1701.

Elliott, Ebenezer. Poetical Works. Edinburgh, 1840.

Emerson, Ralph Waldo. Poems. ed. Milford, Humphrey. Oxford Edition. London, 1914.

English Poets from Chaucer to Cowper, Works of the. ed. Chalmers, Alexander. London, 1810.

Erasmus, Desiderius. The Praise of Folly. tr. Copner, J. London and Edinburgh, 1878.

Farley, Frank Edgar. The Dying Indian. Kittredge Anniversary Papers, pp. 251–260. Boston, 1913.

——, Three "Lapland Songs." Publications of the Modern Language Association of America, Vol. XXI, pp. 1–39.

Fauchet, Claude. A Discourse on the Liberty of France. tr. Harvest, William. London, 1790.

Fontenelle, Le Bovier de. Nouveaux Dialogues des Morts. Amsterdam, 1694.

Freneau, Philip. Poems. ed. Pattee, Fred Lewis. Princeton Historical Association. Princeton, New Jersey, 1902–1907.

——, Poems. Philadelphia, 1786.

——, Poems Written Between the Years 1768 and 1794. Monmouth, New Jersey, 1795.

——, Poems Written and Published During the American Revolutionary War. Philadelphia, 1809.

Garnett, Richard, and Gosse, Edmund. English Literature: An Illustrated Record. New York, 1903–1904.

Gay, John. Plays. London, 1772.

Glen, William. The Lonely Isle, a South-Sea Island Tale. Glasgow, 1816.

Godwin, William. The Enquirer. London, 1797.

——, Enquiry Concerning Political Justice. London, 1842.

——, Fleetwood; or, the New Man of Feeling. London, 1805.

——, St. Leon. London, 1799.

Goldsmith, Oliver. Works. Bohn's Libraries. London, 1910.

Gray, Thomas. Poetical Works. Aldine Poets. London, 1912.

Greg, W. W. Pastoral Poetry and Pastoral Drama. London, 1906.

Hakluyt, Richard. Principal Navigations, etc. Glasgow, 1905.

Haller, Albrecht von. Versuch Schweizerischer Gedichten. Bern, 1732.

Haller, William. The Early Life of Robert Southey. Columbia University Studies in English and Comparative Literature. New York, 1917.

Hawkesworth, John. A New Voyage Round the World. New York, 1774.

——, Oroonoko, a Tragedy by Thomas Southern. With alterations by John Hawkesworth, LL.D. London, 1775.

Hayley, William. Poetical Works. Dublin, 1785.

Hazlitt, William. Collected Works. ed. Waller, A. R., and Glover, Arnold. London, 1902.

Hemans, Felicia Dorothea. Poems by Felicia Dorothea Browne. London, 1808.

——, Poetical Works. London, 1914.

Hobbes, Thomas. Leviathan. Oxford, 1881.

——, Philosophical Rudiments Concerning Government and Society. London, 1651. [Hobbes's own tr. of De Cive.]

Hobhouse, John Cam, Lord Broughton. Travels in Albania. London, 1855.

Holcroft, Thomas. Adventures of Hugh Trevor. London, 1794.

——, Anna St. Ives. London, 1792.

Hone, William. The Every-Day Book and Table Book. London, 1841.

Howard, Henry. A New Humorous Song, on the Cherokee Chiefs. London, n. d.

Howard, Sir Robert. Five New Plays. London, 1692.

Huddesford, George. Poems. London, 1801.

Hunt, James Henry Leigh. Juvenilia. London, 1802.

Hunter, Anne. Poems, by Mrs. John Hunter. London, 1802.

Hunter, John D. Memoirs of a Captivity Among the Indians of North America. London, 1823.

Hurdis, James. Poems. Oxford, 1808.

Imlay, Gilbert. A Topographical Description of the Western Territory of North America. New York, 1793.

Jefferson, Thomas. Notes on the State of Virginia. Trenton, 1803.

Keate, George. An Account of the Pelew Islands. London, 1788.

Keats, John. Complete Poetical Works. ed. Forman, H. Buxton. Glasgow, 1900–1901.

——, Poetical Works and Other Writings. ed. Forman, H. Buxton. London, 1883.

Klopstock, Friedrich G. Hermanns Schlacht. Hamburg u. Bremen, 1769.

Knight, Richard Payne. The Progress of Civil Society. London, 1796.

Lahontan, Louis de. Dialogues de Monsieur le Baron de Lahontan et d'un Sauvage. Amsterdam, 1704.

Lamb, Charles. Works. London, 1855.

Landon, Letitia. Poetical Works. ed. Scott, William Bell. London, n. d.

Landor, Walter Savage. Poems. London, 1795.

——, Works. London, 1846.

Las Casas, Bartholomew. Tyrannies et Cruautez des Espagnolz, Commises es Indes Occidentales, etc. Rouën, 1630. [A French tr., anon., of the Breuisima relación de la destruyción de las Indias.]

Lennox, Charlotte. Euphemia. London, 1790.

——, The Life of Harriot Stuart. London, 1751.

Ligon, Richard. A True and Exact History of the Island of Barbadoes. London, 1657.

Lloyd, Charles. Poems on Various Subjects. Carlisle, 1795.

Lovejoy, A. O. The Supposed Primitivism of Rousseau's Discourse on Inequality. Modern Philology, Vol. XXI, pp. 165–186.

Lowes, John Livingston. The Road to Xanadu. Boston and New York, 1927.

Lyttelton, George. Dialogues of the Dead. London, 1760.

Mackenzie, Henry. The Man of Feeling. London, 1893.

——, The Man of the World. London, 1787.

Mallet, Paul-Henri. Northern Antiquities [Introduction à l'Histoire de Dannemarck.] tr. Percy, Thomas. London, 1770.

Mariner, William. An Account of the Natives of the Tonga Islands. London, 1818.

Maturin, Charles Robert. Melmoth the Wanderer. London, 1892.

Merry, Robert. The British Album, containing the Poems of Della Crusca, Anna Matilda, etc. Boston, 1793.

Mitford, John. Agnes, the Indian Captive. London, 1811.

——, Miscellaneous Poems. London, 1858.

Mitford, Mary Russell. Christina, the Maid of the South Seas. London, 1811.

Montaigne, Michel de. The Essayes of Michael Lord of Montaigne. tr. Florio, John. London, 1908.

Montgomery, James. Poetical Works. London, 1841.

Moore, Thomas. Poetical Works. ed. Godley, A. D. Oxford Edition. London, 1910.

More, Hannah. Works. London, 1818.

More, Paul Elmer. With the Wits. Shelburne Essays, Tenth Series. Boston and New York, 1919.

More, Sir Thomas. Utopia. tr. Robynson, Ralph. Arber's English Reprints. London, 1869.

Morley, John. Rousseau. London, 1886.

Murphy, Arthur. Alzuma, a Tragedy. London, 1773.

Opie, Amelia. Poems. London, 1802.

——, The Warrior's Return, and Other Poems. London, 1808.

Park, Mungo. Travels in the Interior Districts of Africa. London, 1799.

Parodies and Other Burlesque Pieces by George Canning, George Ellis and John Hookham Frere, with the whole Poetry of the Anti-Jacobin. ed. Morley, Henry. London, 1890.

Peacock, Thomas Love. Essay on Fashionable Literature. British Museum Add. Ms. 36815, Vol. I.

——, Peacock's Four Ages of Poetry; Shelley's Defence of Poetry; Browning's Essay on Shelley. ed. Brett-Smith, H. F. B. Percy Reprints, No. 3. Oxford, 1921.

——, Poems. ed. Johnson, Brimley. New Universal Library. London, 1906.

——, Works. New Universal Library. London, 1905–1906.

Pierce, Frederick E. Currents and Eddies in the English Romantic Generation. New Haven, 1918.

Pope, Alexander. Works. ed. Elwin, Whitwell, and Courthope, W. J. London, 1871–1879.

Reynolds, John Hamilton. The Naiad: A Tale. With Other Poems. London, 1816.

Rogers, Samuel. Poetical Works. Aldine Edition. London, 1892.

Roscoe, William. Poetical Works. Liverpool, 1853.

Rousseau, Jean-Jacques. Confessions. tr. Wilson, Edmund. London, 1924.

——, Eloisa. [La Nouvelle Héloïse.] London, 1795.

——, Émile, or Education. tr. Foxley, Barbara. London, 1911.

——, Œuvres Complètes. Paris, 1826.

——, The Social Contract. tr. Tozer, Henry J. London, 1905.

——, The Social Contract and Discourses. tr. Cole, G. D. H. Everyman's Library. London, 1913.

Saint-Pierre, Jacques Henri Bernardin de. Paul et Virginie, suivi de la Chaumière Indienne et du Café de Surate, etc. Paris, 1823.

Sayers, Frank. Collective Works. ed. Taylor, William. Norwich, 1823.

Scott, Sir Walter. Familiar Letters. ed. Douglas, David. Edinburgh, 1894.

——, Poetical Works. ed. Robertson, J. Logie. Oxford Complete Edition. London, 1904.

——, The Waverley Novels. Selected Edition. London, n. d.

Shelley, Percy Bysshe. Complete Poetical Works. ed. Hutchinson, Thomas. Oxford Edition. London, 1917.

Sheridan, Richard Brinsley. Pizarro; a Tragedy Taken from the German Drama of Kotzebue. London, 1799.

Sidney, Sir Philip. The Defence of Poesie. Cambridge, 1904.

Smith, Charlotte Turner. Elegiac Sonnets . . . and Other Poems. London, 1795.

——, The Old Manor House. London, 1793.

Smollett, Tobias. Works. ed. Saintsbury, George. New York, 19—.

Southern, Thomas, the Elder. Oroonoko: a Tragedy. London, 1696.

Southey, Robert. Correspondence with Caroline Bowles. ed. Dowden, Edward. Dublin, 1881.

——, Life and Correspondence. ed. Southey, Charles Cuthbert. New York, 1855.

——, Poetical Works. British Poets Series. Boston, 1880.

——, Wat Tyler, a Dramatic Poem. London, 1817.

Specimens of the Later English Poets. ed. Southey, Robert. London, 1807.

Stephen, Leslie. History of English Thought in the Eighteenth Century. New York, 1876.

Sterne, Lawrence. Works. ed. Saintsbury, George. London, 1894.

Swift, Jonathan. Prose Works. ed. Scott, Temple. London, 1897–1908.

Tacitus, Cornelius. The Description of Germanie. [Germania.] tr. Grenewey, Richard. London, 1640.

Tagore, Rabindranath. The Poet's Religion. Century Magazine, June, 1921.

Temple, Sir William. Works. London, 1720.

Thelwall, John. Poems Chiefly Written in Retirement. Hereford, 1801.

Thomson, James. Complete Poetical Works. Oxford, 1908.

Tinker, Chauncey Brewster. Nature's Simple Plan. Princeton and London, 1922.

Van Doren, Carl. The Life of Thomas Love Peacock. London, 1911.

Vespucci, Amerigo. Letter Concerning the Isles Newly Discovered in His Four Voyages. London, 1885.

Voltaire, François Marie Arouet de. L'Ingénu, histoire véritable. Utrecht, 1767.

Warton, Thomas, the Elder. Poems on Several Occasions. ed. Warton, Joseph. London, 1747.

Wernaer, R. M. Romanticism and the Romantic School in Germany. New York and London, 1910.

White, Henry Kirke. Poetical Works and Remains. ed. Southey, Robert. New York, 1869.

Whitney, Lois. English Primitivistic Theories of Epic Origins. Modern Philology, Vol. XXI, pp. 337–378.

Williams, Helen Maria. Julia. London, 1790.

——, Peru, a Poem. London, 1784.

Wilson, John. The Isle of Palms and Other Poems. New York, 1812.

Wolcot, John [Peter Pindar.] A Complimentary Epistle to James Bruce, Esq. London, 1790.

Wollstonecraft, Mary. An Historical and Moral View of the Origin and Progress of the French Revolution. London, 1794.

——, Letters to Imlay. ed. Paul, C. Kegan. London, 1879.

Wordsworth, Dorothy. Journals. ed. Knight, William. London, 1897.

Wordsworth, William. Letters of the Wordsworth Family. ed. Knight, William. Boston and London, 1907.

——, Poetical Works. ed. Hutchinson, Thomas. Oxford Edition. London, 1904.

——, Poetical Works. ed. Knight, William. London, 1896.

——, The Prelude. ed. Selincourt, Ernest de. Oxford, 1926.

Young, Edward. Poetical Works. Aldine Poets. London, 1852.

INDEX

This Index lists names and important topics relating to either or both of the terms "Noble Savage" and "Romantic Naturalism." These terms, and "American Indian," have not themselves been indexed, since for them the only possible directions would be, "See all the other items of this Index," or "the entire book, *passim*." The term "Nature" has been indexed, but occurrences of it have frequently not been noted when it appears on the same page with some more specific phrase which has been separately indexed, such as "Child of nature," or "State of nature."

COLUMBIA UNIVERSITY PRESS

COLUMBIA UNIVERSITY
NEW YORK

FOREIGN AGENT

OXFORD UNIVERSITY PRESS
HUMPHREY MILFORD
AMEN HOUSE, LONDON, E.C.